THE SPANISH
WORD FINDER

THE SPANISH WORD FINDER

SPANISH/ENGLISH
INGLÉS/ESPAÑOL

MIGUEL VIVES and JOAN PHILLIPS

HarperPerennial
A Division of HarperCollins *Publishers*

HarperCollins books may be purchased for educational, business, or sales
promotional use. For information, please write to: Special Markets Department, HarperCollins Publishers, Inc., 10 East 53rd Street, New York,
NY 10022.

Editorial services performed by ACCESS FOREIGN LANGUAGE TRANSLA-
TIONS SERVICES, Raul Cappuccio, M.B.A. and Brenda Cappuccio, Ph.D.

FIRST EDITION

Designed by Helene Berinsky

Library of Congress Cataloging-in-Publication Data

Vives, Miguel.
    Spanish word finder : Spanish/English, inglés/español / Miguel
Vives and Joan Phillips. — 1st ed.
      p. cm.
    ISBN 0-06-273226-9
    1. Spanish language—Dictionaries—English. 2. English language—
Dictionaries—Spanish. I. Phillips, Joan, 1942—   . II. Title.
PC4640.V57 1993
463'.21—dc20   93-19763

01 00 99 98 AC/RRD 10 9 8 7 6

Contents
✧
Índice de Materias

PREFACE

After many years spent living and working in Spain, England, Ireland, and the United States, we saw the need for a clear and simple English-Spanish word finder that would be a practical guide for anyone who is learning Spanish or is interested in improving their Spanish speaking and writing skills, whether they be students in a classroom setting, businesspeople traveling in Spain or Latin America, professionals who work with individuals for whom Spanish is their first language in the United States, or city dwellers wishing to communicate with their Spanish-speaking neighbors with precision.

The Spanish Word Finder is our response to this need. Probably the first thing you'll notice about it is that it is not a bilingual dictionary, but an easy-to-use alphabetically organized word list. While bilingual dictionaries have you sort through various usage directions, parts of speech abbreviations, and definitions to find the word you are looking for, *The Spanish Word Finder* goes straight to the translation you want.

Another useful feature of this book is the abundance of words you'll find from countries and regions where Spanish is spoken and written. You'll find commonly used Spanish words and their translations into English from Mexico, Guatemala, Ecuador, Costa Rica, Cuba, Argentina, Venezuela, and Bolivia, to name a few.

How many entries should such a quick-reference word list contain? What kind of words should it feature? It ought to be comprehensive in scope without becoming cumbersome. We therefore selected 15,000

English words and their 15,000 Spanish translations, a number a few times greater than the average individual's active vocabulary. Because we wanted a functional list of words that reflects today's industrial, service-oriented society, you'll find specific words related to everyday activities in the worlds of business and commerce, medicine and the law. You'll also discover useful computer and telecommunications terms as well. In sum, these 30,000 entries should more than suffice in handling daily situations in either language.

We hope you will enjoy *The Spanish Word Finder* and find it a useful companion when learning or honing your skills in Spanish.

Joan Phillips
Miguel Vives

PREFACIO

Después de haber pasado muchos años viviendo y trabajando en España, Inglaterra, Irlanda y los Estados Unidos, vimos que había la necesidad de un libro cuyo contenido fuera une extensa lista de palabras en inglés y español, que fuera claro y simple, que pudiera usarse como guía práctica para cualquier persona que estuviera estudiando inglés o estuviera interesada en mejorar sus conocimientos tanto hablados como escritos de dicho idioma, ya fuera un estudiante en el aula de enseñanza, gente de negocios que viaja por Estados Unidos o países anglo-parlantes, un profesional que trabaja con otras personas para las cuales el inglés es su primera lengua, o simplemente un ciudadano de habla hispana cuyo deseo es comunicarse con precisión con sus vecinos de habla inglesa.

The Spanish Word Finder es nuestra respuesta a esta necesidad. Probablemente la primera cosa que descubrirá es que no es un diccionario bilingüe clásico, sino una lista de palabras organizadas alfabéticamente para su fácil uso. Mientras que los diccionarios bilingües dan varias traducciones según su uso, abreviaciones según la clasificación de las palabras y definiciones para encontrar la palabra que se está buscando, *The Spanish Word Finder* va directamente a la traducción que se está buscando.

Otra característica muy práctica de este libro es la abundancia de palabras provenientes de países y regiones en donde se habla y escribe la lengua española. Encontrará palabras provenientes de Méjico,

Guatemala, Ecuador, Costa Rica, Cuba, Argentina, Venezuela y Bolivia, para mencionar algunas naciones.

¿Cuántas voces o entradas debe contener una lista de palabras con tales características? ¿Qué tipo de palabras debe tener dicha lista? La respuesta es simple: suficiente cantidad sin ser abrumante. Por consiguiente hemos seleccionado 30,000 palabras, 15,000 inglesas y el mismo número en español, que es un número varias veces superior al vocabulario activo de una persona normal y corriente.

Debido a que hemos querido hacer una lista funcional de palabras que reflejen las necesidades de una sociedad industrializada y con orientación a una economía de servicios, hemos incluido palabras específicamente relacionadas con actividades del mundo del comercio, de la medicina y del derecho. También se encuentran términos útiles relacionados con computadoras y telecomunicaciones. En suma, estas 30,000 voces deben ser más que suficientes para poder desenvolverse en situaciones normales en ambos lenguajes.

Esperamos que el *The Spanish Word Finder* sea de la máxima utilidad y ayuda para aquellas personas de habla hispana que están estudiando o mejorando sus conocimientos de inglés.

Joan Phillips
Miguel Vives

Abbreviations
✧
Abreviaturas

ABBREVIATIONS—ABREVIATURAS

America	**Amer.**	América
Argentina	**Arg.**	Argentina
Bolivia	**Bol.**	Bolivia
Central America	**C. Am.**	Centroamérica
Chile	**Chile**	Chile
Colombia	**Col.**	Colombia
coloquial	**coll.**	colloquial
Costa Rica	**C.R.**	Costa Rica
Ecuador	**Ecuad.**	Ecuador
Guatemala	**Guat.**	Guatemala
Honduras	**Hond.**	Honduras
Mexico	**Mex.**	México
Nicaragua	**Nic.**	Nicaragua
Panama	**Pan.**	Panamá
Peru	**Peru**	Perú
Puerto Rico	**P.R.**	Puerto Rico
El Salvador	**Salv.**	El Salvador
South America	**S. Am.**	Sudamérica
Spain	**Sp.**	España
Uruguay	**Uru.**	Uruguay
verb	**v.**	verbo
Venezuela	**Ven.**	Venezuela

Fundamentals of Spanish Grammar

GENDER OF NOUNS

In Spanish, as in English, nouns are words used to name persons, places, or things. Nouns in Spanish are either masculine, feminine or neuter. Generally, nouns ending in "o" are masculine, and nouns ending in "a" are feminine. In this book, nouns appear exclusively in the masculine form.

Converting a Masculine Noun to Feminine

To convert a masculine noun which names a person or animal and ends in "o" to feminine, replace the "o" with an "a," as shown in the examples below.

hermano (brother)	hermana (sister)
abuelo (grandfather)	abuela (grandmother)
niño (boy)	niña (girl)
perro (dog)	perra (bitch)
gato (cat)	gata (cat)
argentino (Argentinian)	argentina (Argentinian)
americano (American)	americana (American)
criado (servant)	criada (maid)

There are, however, exceptions to the above rule. For instance, some nouns appear the same in both the masculine and feminine form.

pájaro (bird)	pájaro (female bird)
médico (male doctor)	médico (female doctor)
hipopótamo (hippopotamus)	hipopótamo (hippopotamus)

Other nouns differ entirely between the two forms:

hombre (man)	mujer (woman)
marido (husband)	esposa, mujer (wife)
padre (father)	madre (mother)
actor (actor)	actriz (actress)
macho (male)	hembra (female)

Another set of nouns, those ending with the letters "l," "n," "r," "s," and "z," can be made feminine with the addition of the letter "a":

chaval (boy)	chavala (girl)
español (Spanish man)	española (Spanish woman)
león (lion)	leona (lioness)
pastor (shepherd)	pastora (shepherdess)
pintor (painter)	pintora (painter)
inglés (English man)	inglesa (English woman)
Luis (Louis)	Luisa (Louise)
rapaz (lad, kid)	rapaza (lass, girl)

However, nouns ending in "-sta" and "-nte" do not vary between the masculine and feminine form:

artista (artist)	artista (artist woman)
novelista (novelist)	novelista (novelist woman)
estudiante (student)	estudiante (student woman)
cantante (singer)	cantante (singer woman)

PLURALS OF NOUNS—PLURAL DE SUBSTANTIVOS

To form the plural of a Spanish noun, one generally adds the letter "-s" or the ending "-es" to the singular noun.

árbol (tree)	árboles (trees)
casa (house)	casas (houses)
coche (automobile)	coches (automobiles)
español (Spanish)	españoles (Spanish people)
hoja (leaf)	hojas (leaves)
pie (foot)	pies (feet)
pueblo (town)	pueblos (towns)
rey (king)	reyes (kings)
título (title)	títulos (titles)

ARTICLES—LOS ARTÍCULOS

An article is a word that precedes a noun or an adjective. The Spanish language has two types of articles: definite and indefinite.

The Definite Article—El Artículo Definido

The English word "the" is equivalent to "el" (masculine), "la" (feminine), "los" (masculine plural), "las" (feminine plural), and "lo" (neuter).

El hombre (the man)	Los hombres (the men)
El árbol (the tree)	Los árboles (the trees)
El animal (the animal)	Los animales (the animals)
La ventana (the window)	Las ventanas (the windows)
La flor (the flower)	Las flores (the flowers)
La mujer (the woman)	Las mujeres (the women)
Lo hermoso (the beautiful)	Lo humano (the human)

Sometimes, a contraction of two articles is preferable.

"al" is a contracted form of "a" + "el."
"del" is a contracted form of "de" + "el."

El niño se va al colegio (the child goes to (the) school)
El hombre del campo (the man of the country)

The Indefinite Article—El Artículo Indefinido

Before a masculine noun, the word "un" is used to express the equivalent of "a" or "an" in English. Before a feminine noun, "una" is used. "Unos" and "unas" are the plural forms of "un" and "una," respectively.

Un hombre (a man)   Unos hombres (some men)
Un árbol (a tree)   Unos árboles (some trees)
Una ventana (a window)   Unas ventanas (some windows)
Una flor (a flower)   Unas flores (some flowers)

THE SPANISH
WORD FINDER

Spanish–English
✧
Español–Inglés

A

a   at, in, to
a cuenta   on account
a cualquier hora   anytime
a diferencia de   unlike
a falta de   without
a favor de   on behalf of
a flote   afloat
a horas   hourly, part-time
a la deriva   adrift
a la moda   trendy
a la vista   on demand, on sight
a lo largo de   along
a medio camino   midway
a medio plazo   medium term
a menos que   unless
a menudo   often
a mitades   half-and-half
a pesar de   regardless, yet
a pie   afoot
a presión   pressurized
a propósito   incidentally
a prueba de golpes   shockproof
a saber   namely
a sabiendas   knowingly
a través de   across, through
a veces   sometimes, occasionally
a un lado   aside
abajo   below, beneath, downstairs, down

abajo firmante   undersigned
abandonar (v)   to abandon, forsake, give up, leave, maroon, relinquish
abandono   abandonment, dereliction, dropout
abaratar (v)   to cheapen
abastecedor   caterer, supplier
abastecer (v)   to stock, supply
abastecimiento   catering, supply
abatido   depressed, disheartened, Cuba, Col: slats, boards
abdomen   abdomen
abeja   bee
abertura   breach, opening, rift
abierto   clear, open, sincere, tolerant
ablandar (v)   to soften
abnegación   abnegation, self-sacrifice
abofetear (v)   to slap
abogacía   bar
abogado   advocate, attorney, lawyer, pleader, public attorney, solicitor
abogado de patentes   patent lawyer
abogado penalista   criminal lawyer

abolición abolition
abolladura dent, bruise
abonar (v) to credit
abono refund
abonos credits
aborción abortion
aborrecer (v) to loathe
abortar (v) to abort
aborticidio aborticide
aborto abortion, miscarriage
abrasador burning, blazing, scalding
abrasar (v) to burn, scorch
abrasarse (v) to swelter
abrasión abrasion
abrazadera brace, bracket, clamp, clasp
abrazo embrace, hug
abrazo amoroso cuddle
abrelatas can opener
abreviación abbreviation, abridgement
abreviar (v) to abbreviate, reduce, shorten
abreviarse (v) C.Am.: to hurry
abrigado sheltered, snug
abrigo coat, overcoat, shelter, protection, Arg.: blanket, quilt
abril April
abrochar (v) to button, buckle, fasten, Mex.: to catch, apprehend
abrogar (v) to repeal
abrupto abrupt, steep
absceso abscess
absentismo absenteeism
absolución absolution
absolver (v) to absolve, acquit, discharge
absorción absorption, takeover
abstenerse (v) to abstain, refrain
absurdo absurd, ludicrous, ridiculous
abuela grandmother

abuelo grandfather
abuelos grandparents
abundancia abundance, plenty, wealth
abundante plentiful, rife
aburrido boring, tedious
aburrimiento boredom
abusivo abusive, Am.: cruel, bullying
abuso abuse, misuse
acabado finished, complete, thorough
acabar (v) to complete, end, finish, terminate, S. Am., Col.: to disparage, slander; Arg., Uru., vulg.: to have an orgasm
acallar (v) to silence
acampador camper
acantilado cliff
acariciar (v) to caress, fondle, pet
ácaro mite, tick
acaudalado wealthy
acceso access, entry
acceso aleatorio random access
acceso directo direct access
acceso directo a la memoria direct memory access
acceso secuencial sequential access, serial access
accidentado rough, rugged, uneven
accidental accidental
accidente accident, casualty, crash, mishap
accidente múltiple pileup
acción action, act, share (capital), Peru: raffle ticket
acción criminal criminal action
acción líquida equity
acción ordinaria equity
acción penal penal action
acción recíproca interaction

acción transferible transferable
share

accionar (v) to drive, work,
power, Am.: to bring legal action
against

acciones equity capital, stock

acciones autorizadas authorized
stock

acciones convertibles convertible stock

acciones de primera clase blue
chip shares

acciones nominativas registered
shares

acciones ordinarias common
stock

acciones preferentes preferred
stock

accionista shareholder, stockholder

accionistas minoritarios minority stockholders

acéfalo acephalous

aceite oil

aceite de hígado de bacalao
cod liver oil

aceite de oliva olive oil

aceite de ricino castor oil

aceitoso oily

aceleración acceleration,
speedup

acelerador accelerator

acelerar (v) to expedite, hasten,
hurry, quicken, speed up

aceptación acceptance

aceptación bancaria bank acceptance

aceptación de pedido order acceptance

aceptación en blanco blank acceptance

aceptación sin reservas general
acceptance

aceptante accepting, acceptor

aceptar (v) to accept, acquiesce,
approve, honor

acerca de about, concerning

acercarse (v) to approach

acero steel

acero inoxidable stainless steel

acertijo riddle

acetona acetone

acidez acidity, heartburn, sourness

ácido acid

ácido ascórbico ascorbic acid

aclarar (v) to clear, clarify, rinse

acné acne

acolchar (v) to pad, quilt

acometer (v) to assail, attack,
rush upon, undertake

acomodado suitable, well-off,
well-to-do, Arg., Uru.: with an
easy job, having a special position because of personal influence rather than merit

acomodarse (v) to adjust, adapt,
fit in, nestle

acomodativo easy-going

acompañante escort

acompañar (v) to accompany,
escort

aconsejable advisable

aconsejar (v) to advise, exhort

acontecimiento event, happening, occurrence

acoplamiento coupling, hookup,
interface

acoplo cruzado cross coupling

acorazado battleship

acordar (v) to agree, decide, resolve

acorde chord

acorralado cornered

acortar (v) to shorten

acosamiento harassment

acosar (v) to badger, harass, pursue

acostumbrado customary, used to

acreditación accreditation

acreditado accredited, reputable

acreedor creditor

acreedores diversos sundry creditors

acrílico acrylic

acta affidavit, minutes, record

actas de la sociedad company deeds

actitud attitude, posture

activación activation

activador activator

activar (v) to energize

actividad activity, bustle

actividad febril hustle

activo active, asset

activo circulante working capital

activo corriente current assets

activo disponible quick assets

activo fijo capital assets

activo neto net worth

activo y pasivo assets and liabilities

activos assets

activos circulantes working assets

activos de producción plant assets

activos duraderos long-lived assets

activos fijos fixed assets

activos netos net assets

activos no corrientes non-current assets

activos nominales intangible assets

activos tangibles tangible assets

acto legal legal proceeding

actual current, present, topical

actualizado up-to-date

actualizar (v) to update

actualmente currently, presently

actuario actuary

actuario de seguros actuary

acuático aquatic

acuchillar (v) to slash, stab

acueducto aqueduct

acuerdo accord, agreement, pact, settlement

acumulación accumulation, collection, hoard

acumulación (de trabajo) backlog

acumulador accumulator

acumular (v) to accrue, amass, stockpile, Arg.: to attribute

acumulativo accumulative, cumulative

acuñación minting, coining

acuñación de moneda mint

acuñar (v) to mint, coin

acupuntura acupuncture

acusación accusation, charge, indictment

acusado accused, defendant

acusador accusor, accusing

acusar (v) to accuse, indict

acústico acoustic

adaptable adaptable

adaptación adaptation

adaptador adapter

adaptar (v) to adapt, fit, suit

adecuado adequate, appropriate, fit, fitting

adelante ahead, advance

adelantos recibidos de clientes advances from customers

además furthermore, moreover

adenoideo adenoid

adenoma adenoma

adeudado owing

adeudo debt, debit

adherir (v) to adhere, stick
adhesivo adhesive, glue
adición addendum, addition, insert, Am.: check (restaurant, etc.)
adicional extra
adicto addict
adiestrar (v) to train
adiós bye-bye, goodbye
adiposo adipose, fat
adivinanza guess
adivinar (v) to guess
adjetivo adjective
adjudicación award
adjuntar (v) to attach, annex
adjunto attached, enclosure
administración administration, paper work
administración judicial receivership
administrador administrator, executive, postmaster
administrador judicial receiver
administrador receptor receiver
administrar (v) to administer, direct
admirador admirer, fan
admirar (v) to admire
admisión admission, intake
admisión implícita implied admission
admisión judicial judicial admission
admitir (v) to admit
adolescencia adolescence
adopción adoption
adoptar (v) to adopt
adoración adoration, worship
adorar (v) to adore, worship
adornar (v) to adorn, embellish
adquirente acquiring, taker
adquirir (v) to acquire
adquisición acquisition, takeover

adquisición de datos data acquisition
adrenalina adrenalin
aduana customs, customshouse
adulación flattery
adular (v) to adulate, flatter
adulterar (v) to adulterate
adulterio adultery
adulto adult
adverbio adverb
adversario adversary, opponent
adverso adverse, opposite
advertencia caveat, warning
advertir (v) to notice, warn
aéreo aerial, airy
aeróbico aerobic
aerobio aerobe
aeropuerto airport
aerosol aerosol
aerotransportado airborne
afabilidad good nature, informality
afable, simpático amiable, smooth, sociable, suave
afagia aphagia
afasia aphasia
afectar (v) to affect
afecto affection, fondness, warmth
afectuosamente affectionately, fondly
afectuoso fond
afeitar (v) to shave
afianzar (v) to bail, strengthen
aficionado amateur, dabbler, enthusiastic, keen
afilado keen, sharp
afilar (v) to sharpen, Arg., Uru.: to court
afiliado affiliated
afín akin, related
afinador tuner
afinar (v) to refine, tune

afirmación affirmation, assertion

afirmante affirmant

afirmar (v) to affirm, assert, contend, state, Chile, Mex.: to hit, give blows

aflicción affliction, grief

afligido bereaved, grieving, sorrowing

afligir (v) to afflict, grieve

aflojar (v) to loosen, slacken, undo, Am., Col.: to pay up

afonía aphonia

afortunadamente fortunately

afortunado fortunate

África Africa

África del Sur South Africa

afrodisíaco aphrodisiac

afta thrush

agacharse (v) to stoop, crouch, squat

agarrar (v) to grasp, grip, cling

agencia agency, Chile: pawn shop

agencia de publicidad advertising agency

agencia mercantil mercantile agency

agente agent, broker, representative, factor

agente de aduanas customs broker

agente de Bolsa stockbroker

agente de cambio exchange broker

agente de cambio y bolsa stockbroker, stock exchange broker

agente de transportes forwarder

agente exclusivo sole trader

ágil agile, nimble, quick

agilidad agility

agitación stir, waving, shaking

agitar (v) to shake, rattle, churn, wave

aglutinación agglutination

agosto August

agotado exhausted, sold out, unobtainable, Am.: dead (battery, etc.)

agotador exhausting

agotamiento por calor heat exhaustion

agotar (v) to exhaust

agradable attractive, pleasant, pleasing

agradar (v) to please

agradecido grateful, thankful

agradecimiento gratitude

agravante aggravating, aggravation

agravar (v) to aggravate, make worse

agravio affront, grievance, tort

agravio a la propiedad property tort

agravio personal personal tort

agregado attaché, Arg., Par., Uru.: freeloader

agresor assailant, aggressor

agriar (v) to sour

agricultura agriculture, farming, husbandry

agrimensura surveying

agrio sour

agrupar (v) to bundle, group, gather

agua water

agua de lluvia rainwater

agua potable drinking water

aguanieve sleet

aguantar (v) to bear, endure, stand, suffer, hold up

aguas residuales sewage

aguas arriba upstream

agudeza sharpness, acuteness

agudo (enfermedad) acute

águila eagle, Chile: kite

aguja needle, pin, spire, Am.: stake

agujerear (v) to make holes, pierce, tap

agujero hole, leak

ahogamiento drowning

ahogar (v) to drown, smother, stifle, Peru: to stew

ahora now

ahorcar (v) to hang, Arg., Uru., Mex.: to lend money at usury rates

ahorrar (v) to save

ahorros savings

ahumar (v) to smoke

aire air

aire libre open air

aislado isolated, lonely

aislamiento isolation, insulation

aislar (v) to isolate, insulate

ajedrez chess

ajeno alien, foreign

ajo garlic

ajorca bangle

ajustar (v) to fit, adjust, regulate, square, Col.: to economize

ajuste adjustment, alignment, C. Am.: extra gratuity

ajustes a final del ejercicio year-end adjustments

ajustes en el nivel de precio price-level adjustments

al aire libre outdoors

al día siguiente overnight

al lado de beside

al pie de la letra verbatim

ala wing

alabanza praise, eulogy

alambre wire

alameda mall, shaded walk

alarido yell

alarma alarm

alarma de robo burglar alarm

alarmar (v) to alarm, startle

albacea executor

albacea universal general executor

albañil bricklayer, mason

albañilería masonry

alberca swimming pool

albinismo albinism

albino albino, Mex.: octoroon

albornoz robe, bathrobe

alborotador troublemaker

alboroto disturbance, brawl, racket, uproar, Mex.: joy; Am.: caramel corn

álbum album, picture book

albúmina albumin

alcachofa artichoke

alcahuete pimp

alcalde mayor

álcali alkali

alcalino alkaline

alcaloide alkaloid

alcalosis alkalosis

alcance reach, range, extent, scope

alcantarilla sewer, drain

alcantarillado sewer system

alcanzar (v) to attain, catch, overtake, reach, Am.: to pass, hand

alcoba bedroom

alcohol alcohol

alcohólico alcoholic

alcoholismo alcoholism

alcornoque cork tree

aleatorio accidental, random

alegación allegation, pleading

alegación especial special plea

alegar (v) to allege, plead

alegar falsamente (v) to misallege

alegato plea

alegato y defensa argument

alegrar (v)   to cheer, gladden, rejoice

alegre   cheerful, glad, happy, jolly, joyous, merry, perky, pleased

alegría   happiness, joy

alemán   German

Alemania   Germany

alentador   encouraging

alergia   allergy

alérgico   allergic

alerta   alert

alfabeto   alphabet

alfanumérico   alphanumeric

alfiler   pin, brooch

alfombra   carpet, rug, mat

álgebra   algebra

álgido   algid, icy, decisive

algo   something, somewhat

algodón   cotton

algoritmo   algorithm

alguacil   bailiff, court officer, marshal, Arg., Uru.: dragonfly

alguacil (policía)   sheriff

alguien   somebody, someone

algún día   someday

alguna cosa   something

alguna vez   sometime

alguno   some

aliado   allied, ally

alianza   alliance, Am.: wedding ring

aliar (v)   to ally

alias   alias

alicates   pliers, P.R.: accomplice, helper

aliento   breath

aligerar (v)   to lighten

alijo forzoso   jettison

alimentación   alimentation, food, feeding

alimentador   feeder

alimentador de papel   document feeder

alimentar (v)   to feed, nourish

alimenticio   nourishing

alimento   food, nourishment

alimentos   alimony

alinear (v)   to align, line, line up

alistar (v)   to list, enlist

aliviar (v)   to ease, relieve, lighten

alivio   comfort, relief, reprieve

almacén   depot, stockroom, store, warehouse

almacén de aduana   bonded warehouse

almacén de aduanas   custom warehouse

almacén de depósito aduanero   bonded warehouse

almacén de madera   lumberyard

almacén de ventas   outlet

almacenaje   storage

almacenar (v)   to store

almadía   raft

almeja   clam

almendra   almond, Cuba: excellent

almidón   starch

almohada   pillow, cushion

almohadilla   pad, small cushion, Chile, Peru: iron holder, Arg., Uru.: ink pad

almuerzo   lunch

alojamiento   housing, lodging

alquilar (v)   to rent, lease, charter, rent

alquiler   rent, lease, rental

alquimia   alchemy

alquitrán   tar

alquitranado   tarpaulin

alrededor   around, round, about

alrededores   outskirts, surroundings

alta fidelidad   hi-fi
alta frecuencia   high frequency
alta resolución   high resolution
altas finanzas   high finance
altavoz   speaker, loudspeaker
alteración (sistema)   change-over
alterar (v)   to alter, change, disturb
altercar (v)   to argue, bicker, quarrel
alternador   alternator
alternancia   alternation
alternativo   alternative, alternate, alternating
altitud   altitude, height
alto   high, tall, upper, lofty, stop, halt, Amer.: pile
alto nivel   high-level
altruísta   altruist
altura   height, altitude
alucinación   hallucination
alud   avalanche
alumbrado   lighting, Chile, Col.: tipsy
aluminio   aluminum
alumno   pupil
alvéolo   alveolus
alza   appreciation, rise, increase
alzada   appeal, height
alzamiento   uprising, lifting, rising
allá   there
allanamiento   housebreaking
allanar (v)   to level, flatten
allí   there
ama de casa   housewife
ama de llaves   housekeeper
amable   nice, kind, cordial, friendly, gentle, lovable
amado   sweetheart, dear, beloved
amalgama   amalgam

amalgamado   amalgamated
amanecer   daybreak, dawn
amar (v)   to love
amargo   bitter, Arg., Uru.: made without sugar
amarillento   yellowish
amarillo   yellow
amarrar (v)   to fasten, moor
amartillar (v)   to hammer, cock
amasar (v)   to knead, mass
ambicioso   ambitious, go-getter
ambidextro   ambidextrous
ambiental   environmental
ambigüedad   ambiguity
ambiguo   ambiguous, backhanded
ambivalente   ambivalent
ambos   both
ambulancia   ambulance
ambulatorio   ambulatory, walking, roving
amenaza   menace, threat
amenazante   threatening
amenazar (v)   to threaten, menace
América   America
América Central   Central America
América del Sur   South America
América Latina   Latin America
americano   American
ametralladora   machine gun
amianto   asbestos
amigo   friend, boyfriend, comrade
aminoácidos   amino acids
amistad   friendship
amistoso   friendly, amicable
amnesia   amnesia
amnesia temporal   fugue
amnistía   amnesty
amo   master
amoldarse (v)   to adapt oneself, mold

amoníaco ammonia
amontonar (v) to pile up, bank, lump, stack
amor love
amor propio self-respect
amoratado purple, livid, Amer.: black and blue
amorfo amorphous
amortiguar (v) to muffle, absorb
amortización amortization
amortizar (v) to amortize, redeem
amperio ampere
ampliación extension, enlargement, expansion
ampliar (v) to expand, enlarge
amplificador amplifier
amplio ample, broad
amplitud amplitude, breadth
ampolla bubble, blister
amputación amputation
analfabeto illiterate
analgésico analgesic
análisis analysis, breakdown, test
análisis de cuentas cronológico aging of accounts
análisis financiero financial analysis
analista analyst
analogía analogy
análogo analogous
anatomía anatomy
anatómico anatomical
ancla anchor
ancho wide, broad
anchura width, breadth
andamiaje scaffolding
andamio scaffold
andrajoso ragged, tattered
andrógeno androgen
androide android

anécdota anecdote
anegado waterlogged
anemia anemia
anerobio anaerobe
anestesia anesthesia
anestésico anesthetic
anestesista anesthetist
aneurisma aneurysm
anexar (v) to attach, annex
anexión annexation
anexo attached
anfetamina amphetamine
anfibio amphibian
anfitrión host
ángel angel
angina angina
angioma angioma
ángulo angle
ángulo recto right angle
angustia anguish, distress, anxiety
angustioso heartbreaking, distressed
anhelo aspiration, longing, eagerness
anilina aniline
anillo ring
anillo de boda wedding ring
animación (dibujos) animation
animado vivacious
animal animal
animal doméstico pet
animar (v) to enliven, encourage, vitalize
animarse (v) to brighten, become lively
ánimo encouragement, courage, spirit
animosidad animosity
animoso spirited
aniquilar (v) to annihilate, wipe out

aniversario anniversary, jubilee
ano anus
ánodo anode
anofeles Anopheles
anomalía anomaly
anónimo anonymous, nameless
anorexia anorexia
anormal abnormal, deficient
anotación annotation
ansiedad anxiety
ansioso anxious, avid, yearning
antagónico antagonistic
antagonismo antagonism
antagonista antagonist
antaño last year, yesteryear
antebrazo forearm
antecedente antecedent, previous
antecedentes penales criminal
record
antena antenna, aerial
antepasado ancestor, previous
anteproyecto blueprint, preliminary plan
anterior former, previous, prior
anteriormente formerly
antes before
antiácido antacid
antialérgico antiallergic
antianémico antianemic
antibiótico antibiotic
anticipado prospective
anticipar (v) to advance, anticipate, take place early
anticipo advance (payment), preview, retainer
anticoagulante anticoagulant
anticonceptivo contraceptive
anticonvulsivo anticonvulsant
anticuado old-fashioned, anti-
quated, out-of-date
anticuerpo antibody

antídoto antidote
antiespasmódico antispasmodic
antifebril antifebrile
antigüedad antique, antiquity,
age, seniority
antiguo old, ancient
antihistamina antihistamine
antiinflamatorio anti-
inflammatory
antimigraña antimigraine
antimonopolio antitrust
antioxidante antioxidant
antipatía antipathy
antiséptico antiseptic
antisocial antisocial
antología anthology
antónimo antonym
antorcha torch, lamp
ántrax anthrax
antropoide anthropoid
antropología anthropology
anual annual, yearly
anualidad annuity
anualidad ordinaria ordinary
annuity
anualidad pagadera annuity due
anualidades aplazadas deferred
annuities
anuario yearbook, directory
anulable voidable
anulación cancellation, annulment, abatement
anulado cancelled, annulled, discontinued
anular (v) to annul, cancel, defeat, overrule, nullify, set aside,
undo, void
anunciar (v) to announce, advertise, publicize
anuncio announcement, advertisement, bulletin
anzuelo hook, lure

añadir (v) to add

año year

año bisiesto leap year

año civil legal year

año fiscal fiscal year

añoranza hankering

aorta aorta

apaciguar (v) to appease, mollify

apagado dull, muted (sound), extinguished (fire)

apagar (v) to quench, dull, extinguish, put out

apagón blackout, Cuba, Mex.: cigar or coal that dies often

apaisado oblong

aparador dresser, sideboard, showcase, Arg., Mex., Uru.: display window

aparato apparatus, device, appliance, set

aparato de rayos X X-ray apparatus

aparecer (v) to appear, show up, loom

aparejar (v) to prepare, rig

aparejo gear, equipment, rig

aparentar (v) to look, pretend, feign

aparente apparent, evident, ostensible, seeming

aparentemente seemingly

apariencia appearance, aspect, semblance

apartado secluded, separated, isolated

apartamento apartment

apartamiento seclusion, separation

apartar (v) to separate, remove, alienate, avert

apartarse de (v) to diverge

aparte apart, aside

apasionado passionate

apatía apathy

apelación appeal

apelación limitada limited appeal

apellido name, family name, surname

apenado sorry

apendectomía appendectomy

apéndice appendix

apendicitis appendicitis

apetito appetite

ápice apex, top

apilar (v) to pile up, stack

apio celery

aplacar (v) to appease, placate

aplanadora bulldozer

aplastante overwhelming

aplastar (v) to flatten, crush, overwhelm, squash, Arg., Uru.: to tire

aplaudir (v) to applaud, cheer

aplauso applause

aplazamiento postponement, adjournment

aplazar (v) to postpone, adjourn, defer, shelve, Arg., Uru.: to flunk, fail an exam

aplicabilidad relevancy

aplicable applicable

apoderado proxy, authorized agent

apodo nickname

apogeo climax, apogee, heyday

apoplejía apoplexy, stroke

apostar (v) to bet, post

apóstol apostle

apóstrofe apostrophe

apoyar (v) to lean, rest, prop, recline, support, uphold

apoyo support, backup, favor, prop

apreciación appreciation

apreciar (v) to value, appreciate, prize

aprehensión apprehension

aprender (v) to learn

aprender de memoria (v) to memorize

aprendiz learner, apprentice

aprendiz profesional trainee

aprendizaje apprenticeship

apresurado hurried, hasty, precipitate

apresurar (v) to hurry, hustle, rush

apretado tight, dense

apretar (v) to tighten, grip, press, intensify, constrict, pinch, squeeze

apretón squeeze, hug, crush

apretón de manos handshake

aprieto difficulty, trouble

aprobación appropriations of retained earnings, approval, consent

aprobar (v) to pass, approve

aprobar una ley (v) to pass a law

apropiado appropriate, apt, becoming, proper

aprovechar (v) to avail, make use of, utilize

aprovisionamientos supplies

aproximado approximate

aproximar (v) to approximate, bring near

aptitud aptitude, competence, suitability, qualification

apto competent, suitable, fit, qualified

apuesta bet, wager

apuntador prompter (theater), pointing device

apuntar (v) to aim, level, prompt, record

apuñalar (v) to stab

apuro hardship, quandary, predicament, trouble

aquí here

aquiescencia consent

árabe Arab

Arabia Arabia

arado plow

arancel tariff, duty

aranceles customs duties

aranceles de importación import duties

araña spider

arar (v) to plow

arbitraje arbitration

arbitrario arbitrary

árbitro referee, umpire

árbol tree

árboles timber

arbusto bush, shrub

arcaico archaic

arcilla clay

arco arc, arch

arco iris rainbow

archipiélago archipelago

archivador file cabinet

archivo file

archivos records

arder (v) to burn, blaze

arder sin llama (v) to smoulder

ardid artifice, stratagem

ardiente ardent, burning, fiery, glowing

ardilla squirrel

arduo arduous

área area

arena arena, sand

arenoso sandy

aréola areola

Argentina Argentina

argentino Argentinian

argot slang

argumentar (v) to argue

árido arid, barren
aristocracia aristocracy
aristócrata aristocrat
aritmética binaria binary arithmetic
arma arm, gun, weapon
arma de fuego firearm
armadura armor
armamento arm
armario cabinet, closet, locker
armonía harmony, rapport, unison
armónico harmonic
aro hoop, ring, Amer.: wedding band
aroma scent, aroma
arpa harp
arquero archer
arquitecto architect
arquitectura architecture
arquitectura de red network architecture
arrancar (v) to extract, pull, wrench, start, set off, Amer.: to start an engine
arras earnest money, pledge, deposit
arrasamiento desolation
arrasar (v) to level, flatten
arrastramiento crawl
arrastrar (v) to drag, haul, lug, trail, creep
arrebatar (v) to grab, snatch, seize
arreglar (v) to cope, fix, rig
arreglo adjustment , arrangement, compromise, settlement
arremolinarse (v) to swirl
arrendador landlord, lessor
arrendamiento rent, rental, lease
arrendamientos en vigor operating leases

arrendar (v) to rent, lease
arrendatario tenant, lessee, leaseholder
arrepentirse (v) to regret, rue
arrestar de nuevo (v) to rearrest
arresto arrest
arresto domiciliario house arrest
arresto ilegal false arrest
arriba aloft, up, upstairs
arriendo rental
arriesgado risky
arriesgar (v) to imperil, risk, danger, venture
arrogancia arrogance
arrogante assuming, arrogant, cavalier, haughty
arrollar (v) to curl, roll up, Amer.: to rock a child
arroz rice
arruga crinkle, wrinkle
arrugar (v) to wrinkle, ruffle
arsenal arsenal, navy yard
arsénico arsenic
arte art
arte de vender salesmanship
arteria artery
arteriosclerosis arteriosclerosis
artesanía craft, craftmanship, handicraft
artesano artisan, craftsman
ártico arctic
articulación articulation
articulado articulate
artículo article, item
artículos de cristal glassware
artículos de tocador toiletries
artículos domésticos housewares
artículos monetarios monetary items

artículos no monetarios non-monetary items
artículos ocasionales non-recurring items
artificial artificial
artificialmente artificially
artificio artifice, art, craft
artillería artillery
artista artist
artístico artistic
artritis arthritis
artrosis arthrosis
arzobispo archbishop
as ace
asa grip, handle
asado broil, roast, roasted, Arg., Uru.: cookout, barbecue
asaltante assailant
asaltar (v) to attack, assail, storm, mug
asalto assault, attack, mugging
asamblea asembly, meeting, convention
asar (v) to roast
asbesto asbestos
asbestosis asbestosis
ascendente ascending, upward
ascender (v) to ascend, climb, rise
ascensión ascension
ascenso ascent
ascensor elevator
asco revulsion
asediar (v) to besiege
asegurado insured
asegurar (v) to insure, secure, promise, brace, underwrite
aseo bathroom
aseo público washroom
aséptico aseptic
aserradero sawmill
asesinar (v) to murder

asesinato murder
asesino assassin, murderer, killer
asesor consultant, advisor, counselor
asesor legal legal adviser
asfalto asphalt
asfixia asphyxia, suffocation
asfixiar (v) to suffocate
así so, thus
así así so-so
Asia Asia
asiático Asiatic
asiduo assiduous
asiento seat, chair, pew, bench, entry, Cuba: agricultural center
asiento de abono entry credit
asiento de cargo entry debit
asignación allotment, approval, allocation, assignment
asignación de beneficios no distribuidos appropriations of retained earnings
asignación de costes allocation of costs
asignar (v) to assign
asilo asylum, refuge
asimilación assimilation
asimilar (v) to assimilate
asir (v) to seize, hold, snatch, cling
asistencia attendance, welfare, Mex.: living room, Peru, Uru.: first aid clinic
asistente assistant, aide
asistir (v) to assist, attend
asma asthma
asociación association, partnership, society
asociado associate, associated
asociar (v) to associate
asolar (v) to raze, desolate

asombrar (v) to amaze, astonish, appall, stagger

asombro surprise, amazement

asombroso startling, staggering, amazing

aspa sail

aspecto aspect, side, complexion

aspecto notable highlight

aspereza roughness

áspero rough, rugged

aspiración aspiration

aspirador vacuum cleaner

aspirante candidate, aspirant

aspirar (v) to aspire, aspirate, breathe, inhale

aspirina aspirin

asqueroso revolting, sickening, sordid, disgusting

asterisco asterisk

astigmatismo astigmatism

astilla splinter

astringente astringent

astrología astrology

astronauta astronaut

astronomía astronomy

astronómico astronomical

astrónomo astronomer

astucia astuteness, trickery

astuto astute, clever, calculating, crafty, knowing, sly, tricky, wily

asunto affair, matter, subject, business, concern

asunto secreto cloak and dagger

asustar (v) to frighten, startle

atacante assailant

atacar (v) to attack, assail, contest, tackle

atacar de repente (v) to pounce

atado tied, inhibited, bundle

atadura fastening, tie

ataque attack, fit, raid, onslaught

ataque cardíaco heart attack

ataque de corazón heart attack

ataque violento onslaught

atar (v) to tie, bind, attach, bundle

atar con una cuerda (v) to rope

atareado busy

atascar (v) to stop, block, jam

atascarse (v) to get stuck, stall

ataúd coffin, casket

atavismo atavism

ateísmo atheism

atemorizado afraid

Atenas Athens

atención attention, attentiveness

ateniense Athenian

atentado attempt

atento polite, attentive, observant

aterrador terrifying

aterrorizar (v) to terrify, terrorize

atestado overcrowded

atestar (v) to cram, pack, attest

atestiguar (v) to testify to

ático attic, penthouse

atípico atypical

atlas atlas

atleta athlete, runner

atlético athletic

atmósfera atmosphere

atmosférico atmospheric

atolladero muddy place, quagmire

atómico atomic

átomo atom

atormentar (v) to torment

atornillar (v) to screw on

atracción attraction

atraco holdup, robbery

atractivo attractive, enticing, glamorous

atraer (v) to attract, lure

atragantamiento choking

atrapar (v) to catch, trap

atrasado slow, late, delayed, overdue, retarded, belated

atrasos arrears
atravesar (v) to cross, cross over
atrevido bold, daring, audacious
atrevimiento presumption, boldness, daring
atribución attribution
atribuir (v) to attribute, refer
atributo attribute
atrio atrium
atrocidad atrocity, outrage
atrofia atrophy
atroz atrocious, cruel, outrageous
atún tuna
aturdido dazed
aturdir (v) to stun, daze
audacia boldness
audaz audacious, bold
audible audible
audición hearing, audition
audiencia hearing, audience
audífono hearing aid
audiograma audiogram
audiómetro audiometer
auditivo auditory
auditor auditor
auditoría auditing
auditorio audience, auditorium
aullar (v) to howl, yell
aumentar (v) to increase, add to, amplify
aumento increase, gain, rise
aumento de salario wage increase
aún still, yet
aunque although, though
aura aura
aurícula auricle
auriculares earphones, headphones
auscultación auscultation
ausencia absence, lack, want
ausente absent

austeridad austerity
austero austere, stern
Australia Australia
australiano Australian
Austria Austria
austríaco Austrian
auténtico authentic, genuine
autismo autism
auto car, writ
auto-suficiente self-sufficient
autobiografía autobiography
autobús bus
autoclave autoclave
autócrata autocrat
autocrático autocratic
autodefensa self-defense
autodidacta self-educated
autodisciplina self-discipline
autodominio self-control
autoestopista hitchhiker
autógeno autogenous
autoinfección autoinfection
autointoxicación autointoxication
autómata robot
automático automatic
automatización automation
automóvil automobile
autónomo independent, autonomous
autopista highway
autopista de peaje tollway
autopsia autopsy
autor author, perpetrator
autoridad authority
autoridad completa full authority
autoritario authoritarian
autorización authorization, warrant
autorizado accredited, licensed
autorizar (v) to authorize
autoservicio self-service

autosugestión autosuggestion
auxiliar auxiliary, assistant, ancillary
auxilio help, aid, mayday
aval endorsement, collateral
avalador guarantor
avance advance, breakthrough
avanzar (v) to advance
avasallar (v) to subdue
avenida avenue
aventura adventure
aventura amorosa love affair
aventurero adventurer
avergonzado ashamed, embarrassed
avería breakdown, damage, fault
averiguar (v) to find out, trace, Mex., Hond: to argue
aversión aversion, distaste
aves poultry
aviación aviation
ávido avid, eager, acquisitive
avión airplane, aircraft, plane

avisador buzzer
avisar (v) to inform, advise, advertise, buzz
aviso notice
aviso judicial judicial notice
aviso público public notice
aviso rápido short notice
axioma axiom
axis axis
¡ay de mí! alas
ayer yesterday
ayuda aid, assistance, backing, help
ayuda médica medical help
ayudante helper, assistant, aide
ayudante (golf) caddie
ayudar (v) to help, assist
azafata stewardess
azotamiento whipping
azúcar sugar
azul blue
azul marino navy blue

B

babero bib
bacalao cod
bacilo bacillus, germ
bacteria bacteria, germ
bache hole, pothole
bahía bay
bailador dancer
bailar (v) to dance, prance
bailarín dancer
baile dance, dancing, ball
baile popular folk dance
baja de valores sell-off
bajar (v) to descend, lower, subside, stoop
bajo short, small, low, bass
bajo fianza under bond

bajo juramento under oath
bajón decline, bassoon
bala bullet, shot
balada ballad
balance balance (financial), Cuba, Col.: rocking chair
balance de comprobación trial balance
balance de comprobación ajustado adjusted trial balance
balance de cuentas balance
balance financiero financial statement
balancear (v) to swing, sway, balance
balanza scales

balcón balcony
baldosa tile
balístico ballistic
balneario spa
baloncesto basketball
balsa raft, balsa wood, Mex.: swamp
bálsamo balsam
baluarte bastion
ballet ballet
banalidades small talk
banca banking, bank, Arg., Uru.: banker (in games)
banca privada private bank
bancarrota bankruptcy
bancarrota inicial default
banco bank, bench, seat, Col.: plain; Arg., Col., Uru.: plateau
banco corresponsal correspondent bank
banco de depósito commercial bank, trust bank
banco de descuento discount bank
banco de inversión issuing house
banco hipotecario mortgage bank
banco nacional central bank
banco regional district bank
banco rural country bank
banda band, strip, side, gang
banda ancha wide band
banda de fluctuación fluctuation margins
banda sonora sound track
bandeja tray
bandeja de té tea tray
bandera banner, flag
banderola pennant
bandido bandit, outlaw
banjo banjo
banquero banker

banquete banquet
bañar (v) to bathe, wash, dip
bañera bath, bathtub
baño bath
baptista Baptist
bar bar, pub
barajar (v) to shuffle, Arg., Chile, Mex.: to stop, halt; Arg., Uru.: to intercept (something thrown)
barandilla rail
barato cheap, low-priced
barba beard
barbacoa barbecue
bárbaro barbarian
barbero barber, Mex.: flatterer
barbitúrico barbituric
barbudo bearded
barcaza barge
barco ship, vessel, boat
barco de vela sailboat
barco discrecional tramper
barítono baritone
barniz varnish
barómetro barometer
barón baron
baronesa baroness
barra ingot, bar, rail, rod, Arg., Col., Uru.: group of friends, gang
barra de labios lipstick
barranca ravine
barrer (v) to sweep, scavenge
barrera barrier
barrera del sonido sound barrier
barricada barricade, roadblock
barriga belly, stomach
barril barrel, cask
barrio suburb
barrio bajo slum
barro mud, Arg., Uru.: mistake
barroco baroque
basar (v) to base

báscula weighing platform, platform scales
báscula biestable flip-flop
base basis, base, bed, foundation
base de datos data base
base de datos relacionada relational data base
base de tiempo time frame
básico basic
bastante enough
bastardo bastard
bastón baton, stick, walking stick, cane
basura filth, garbage, rubbish, refuse, litter, trash
batería battery
batir (v) to beat, churn, Chile, Peru, Guat.: to rinse clothes
baúl trunk
bautizar (v) to baptize
bautizo baptism
bayoneta bayonet
bazar bazaar
bazo spleen
bebedor drinker
beber (v) to drink
bebida beverage, drink
bebida alcohólica booze
beca scholarship
beige beige
Belén Bethlehem
belga Belgian
Bélgica Belgium
beligerante belligerent
belleza beauty
benceno benzene
bendecir (v) to bless
bendición blessing
beneficencia welfare, charity, beneficence
beneficiario beneficiary, assignee
beneficiario del pago payee
beneficiar (v) to benefit, profit

beneficio advantage, benefit, profit, gain
beneficio anticipado anticipated profit
beneficio bruto gross profit
beneficio bruto (aumento sobre coste) mark-up
beneficio de la duda benefit of doubt
beneficios gains
beneficios acumulados accumulated earnings, earned surplus
beneficios antes de impuestos pretax earnings
beneficios de reembolsos redemption gains
beneficios netos net profits
beneficios no convertidos unrealized gains
beneficios no distribuidos retained earnings
beneficios remunerativos adicionales fringe benefits
benévolo benevolent
benigno benign
Berlín Berlin
beso kiss
bestia beast, animal, idiot, brute
Biblia Bible
bíblico Biblical
bibliografía bibliography
bibliógrafo bibliographer
biblioteca library
bibliotecario librarian
bíceps biceps
bicicleta bike, bicycle
bicho bug, insect, Amer.: penis
bichos vermin
bien well, good, right
bien conocido well-known
bien construido well-built
bien formado shapely
bien guardado well-kept

bien hecho well-made
bien informado well-informed
bien vestido well-dressed
bienal biennial
bienes estate, goods
bienes de equipo capital goods
bienes de lujo luxury goods
bienes disponibles assets in
hand
bienes dotales dower
bienes duraderos durable goods
bienes parafernales paraphernalia
bienes raíces realty, real estate
bienestar wellbeing, welfare,
comfort
bienhechor benefactor
bienvenido welcome
bifurcación fork, junction,
branch
bigamia bigamy
bigote mustache, whisker, Mex.:
croquette
bigotes whiskers
bikini bikini
bilateral bilateral
biliar biliary
bilingüe bilingual
bilis bile, gall
billete bill, note, ticket
billete de banco bank note, denomination
billete de vuelta return ticket
billetero billfold, wallet
billetes extranjeros foreign
notes
billón billion
bimensual bimonthly
binario binary
biografía biography
biología biology
biológico biological
biólogo biologist

biopsia biopsy
bioquímica biochemistry
birlar (v) to swindle out of,
sneak
bisabuela greatgrandmother
bisabuelo greatgrandfather
bisagra hinge
bisexual bisexual
bistec beefsteak
bit bit
bizco squinter, cross-eyed
biznieto greatgrandchild
bizquear (v) to squint
bizquera squint
blanco white, P.R.: application
blancura whiteness
blando soft
blandura softness
blanquear (v) to bleach, whiten
blanqueo bleach, whitening
blasfemia blasphemy
blindaje shield, armor
bloque block, group; Arg., C.
Am., Uru.: block of houses
bloquear (v) to tackle
bloqueo blockade
blusa blouse
bobina coil, spool
boca mouth
boca a boca mouth-to-mouth
bocadillo sandwich, snack; Cuba,
Hond.: potato dessert
boda wedding, marriage
bodega cellar, pantry, tavern,
bar, Amer.: grocery
bofetada slap, wallop
bogar (v) to row, sail
boicot boycott
boina beret
bola ball, Mex.: quarrel, uproar
bola de nieve snowball
bolígrafo ball-point pen
Bolivia Bolivia

boliviano Bolivian
bolsa bag, pouch, purse, market
Bolsa stock exchange
bolsa de compras shopping bag
bolsa de té tea bag
bolsa de valores stock exchange
bolsillo pocket
bolso handbag, bag, purse
bollo bun, bread roll, Col.: tamale; Sp., Uru.: fritter
bomba bomb, pump; Peru, Uru.: electric light bulb
bombardear (v) to bombard, bomb, shell
bombear (v) to pump; Arg.: to scout; Col.: to dismiss
bombero fireman
bombilla bulb; Arg., Par., Uru.: small tube
bombonería sweetshop
bondad goodness, kindness
bonificación allowance, increase
bono bond, coupon
bono amortizable anticipadamente callable bond
bono reembolsable callable bond
bonos al portador coupon bond
bonos municipales municipal bonds
bonos negociables negotiable bonds
bonos no garantizados unsecured bonds
bonos registrados registered bonds
borde brink, rim, edge, border, verge
borrable erasable
borrachera intoxication, drunkenness
borracho drunkard, drunk, intoxicated, Chile: overripe fruit

borrar (v) to erase, rub out, delete
borrón blot, smudge, slur
bosque forest
bosquejar (v) to sketch
bostezar (v) to yawn
bota boot
botánico botanic
bote de remos rowboat
bote salvavidas lifeboat
botella bottle, Cuba: soft job
botella de vino wine bottle
botín loot, Chile: sack
botón button, knob
botulismo botulism
bóveda vault, dome
boxeador boxer
boxeo boxing
boya buoy
boyante buoyant
bramido bellow, roar
Brasil Brazil
brasileño Brazilian
brazo arm
brebaje brew, potion, mixture
brecha breach, gap
breve brief, short, terse
brevemente briefly
brigada squad
brillante brilliant, bright
brillar (v) to shine, glitter, blaze
brillo shine, glitter, glare, luster, polish
brincar (v) to bounce, jump, leap
brinco hop, jump, leap
brindar (v) to toast
brindis toast
brioso dashing
brisa breeze
broche clip, clasp, Chile: paper clip; Ecuad.: cuff link
broma pesada practical joke

bromear (v) to joke, kid
bronceado tan
bronquitis bronchitis
brotar (v) to bud, sprout
brote bud, shoot
bruja witch
brujería witchcraft
brújula compass
brusco sudden, abrupt
Bruselas Brussels
brutal brute
bruto raw, brute, brutish
bucal oral
bueno good, fine
buena conducta good behavior
buena fe bona fide, good faith
buena salud fitness
buena voluntad willingness
bufanda scarf
bufete de abogado law office
bufido snort
bujía spark plug
bulto bundle, package, size, bulk, swelling; Col., Hond., Mex.: briefcase
bulla noise, crowd, fuss
buñuelo doughnut

buque boat, ship, vessel
buque petrolero oil tanker, tanker
burbuja bubble
burgués bourgeois, middle class
burlador sneering, mocking
burlar (v) to deceive, trick
burlas banter
burlón mocking
burocracia bureaucracy
burro ass, donkey, idiot, Mex.: step ladder; Col., P.R., Uru.: leapfrog
busca quest, search; Cuba, Mex.: fringe benefits
buscar (v) to search; Arg., Chile, Mex., Urug.: to provoke, annoy
buscar revolviendo (v) to rummage
busel (medida) bushel
búsqueda quest, search
búsqueda binaria binary search
búsqueda y reemplazo search and replace
busto bust
butaca easy chair, armchair
buzón mail box

C

caballería cavalry
caballero gentleman, knight
caballerosidad chivalry, gentlemanliness
caballo horse
caballo (potencia) horsepower
caballo de carreras racehorse
cabaña cabin, hut; Arg., Uru.: cattle breeding ranch
cabaret cabaret
cabecear (v) to nod
cabello hair

cabeza head
cabeza atómica warhead
cabeza de chorlito scatterbrain
cabeza de familia head of family
cabeza de la casa householder
cabeza de turco fall guy, scapegoat
cabeza descubierta bareheaded
cabina de teléfonos telephone booth
cabizbajo downcast, dejected
cable cable, rope, wire

cable coaxial coaxial cable
cablegrama cablegram
cabo cape, end, extremity, corporal
cacao cocoa
cacerola casserole, saucepan
cachemira cashmere
cachorro puppy, cub
cada every, each
cada día everyday
cada uno apiece
cadáver cadaver
cadena chain
cadena de tiendas chain store
cadena perpetua life imprisonment, life sentence
cadencia clock frequency
cadera hip
cadete cadet; Arg., Bol., Uru.: office boy
caer (v) to fall, drop, slip, tumble
caer a plomo (v) to plummet
café coffee, cafe; Amer.: reprimand; Mex.: irritation, annoyance
cafeína caffeine
cafetera coffee pot, percolator
cafetería snack bar, coffee shop
caída slip, fall, tumble
caída en desuso obsolescence
caja box, cashier, case, till
caja de ahorros savings bank
caja de cerillas matchbox
caja de conmutación switch box
caja pequeña petty cash
caja de seguridad safe deposit box, safe
caja de seguridad nocturna night safe
caja fuerte safe
caja de madera crate

cajero cashier's desk, teller
cajón till, drawer, chest
cajonero (mueble) drawer
cala inlet
calambre cramp
calamidad calamity, disaster
calavera skull, Mex.: tail light
calceta stocking
calcetín sock
calcio calcium
calculadora calculator
calculadora de bolsillo pocket calculator
calcular (v) to calculate, estimate, reckon
cálculo count, calculation
cálculo biliar gallstone
cálculo de intereses interest calculation
cálculo erróneo miscalculation
calderilla small change
caldo broth, soup, stock
caleidoscopio kaleidoscope
calendario calendar
calentador heater
calentar (v) to heat, warm up; Chile, Uru.: to annoy, irritate
calibre caliber, gauge
calidad quality
calidad tipográfica letter quality
caliente hot, warm
calificado qualified
calificar (v) to qualify, label
caligrafía calligraphy
calma calm, lull, unconcern
calma pasajera lull
calmante pain killer, sedative
calmar (v) to quiet, quell, lull
calor heat, warmth
calorías calories
calórico caloric
calumnia calumny, libel, slander

calumniador slanderer
calumniar (v) to malign, slander, libel
calvo bald
calzada causeway, driveway, roadway
calzar (v) to put shoes on, wedge
calzoncillos undershorts, underpants
callado quiet, reserved, secretive
calle street, road
callejuela alley, narrow street
callos tripe
cama bed, litter
camaleón chameleon
cámara chamber, vault
cámara acorazada safety vault
Cámara de Comercio Chamber of Commerce
cámara de compensación clearing house
camarada comrade
camarera waitress
camarero waiter
camarilla small room, ring
cambiante changing
cambiar (v) to change, vary, shift, alter
cambio change, shift, small change, exchange
cambio controlado controlled exchange
cambio fijo fixed rate
cambio de divisas foreign exchange, exchange
camello camel
camilla stretcher, litter
caminar despacio (v) to plod
caminata hike, long walk
camino lane, trail, way
camión truck

camionero truckdriver, teamster
camisa shirt
camiseta undershirt, vest, polo shirt
campamento camp
campana bell, Amer.: lookout
campaña campaign
campeón champ, champion
campeonato championship
campesino peasant
camping campground, camping
campo countryside, field
campo a través cross-country
campo de batalla battlefield
campo petrolífero oil field
camuflaje camouflage
Canadá Canada
canadiense Canadian
canal channel, canal
canal de datos data channel
canalón gutter, shovel
canalla rabble, mob, ruffian
canapé couch, sofa, canape
cancelación cancellation
cancelar (v) to cancel, annul
cáncer cancer
cancerígeno carcinogen
canción song
candado padlock
candidato candidate, aspirant
canela cinnamon
cangrejo crab
caníbal cannibal, man-eating
canino canine, dog
canon canon, royalty
cansadamente wearily
cansado tired, weary
cansancio tiredness, weariness
cansar (v) to tire
cantante singer, vocalist
cantar (v) to sing, crow, bawl
cantidad quantity, amount, sum

cantidad total lump sum
cantina canteen, snack bar, Amer.: bar, tavern
caña cane, reed, Amer.: sugar cane; Col., Ecuad., Ven.: hoax, rumor
caña de pescar fishing rod
cañón cannon, gun, tube, pipe, canyon
caos chaos
caótico chaotic
capa cape, cloak, layer, mantle, ply
capacidad capacity, capability, competence, calibre
capataz foreman
capaz competent, able, capable
capellán chaplain, priest
caperuza hood
capilar capillary
capilla chapel
capital capital
capital declarado stated capital
capital flotante hot money
capital legal legal capital
capital permanente permanent capital
capital propio equity capital
capital social capital, capital stock
capital suscrito outstanding stock
capitalización de interés capitalization of interest
capitalizar (v) to capitalize
capitán captain, skipper, chief
capitolio Capitol
capítulo chapter
capricho caprice, whim, crank, spleen
caprichoso moody, capricious, cranky

cápsula capsule
captura apprehension, capture
cara face, look
carabina carbine, rifle
carácter character, nature
caracteres gráficos graphic characters
característica characteristic, feature
carámbano icicle
carbón carbon
carbón vegetal charcoal
carbonizado charred
carbonizar (v) to char
carburador carburetor
cárcel jail, prison
cárcel del condado county jail
carcinógeno carcinogen
carcinoma carcinoma
cardenal cardinal
cardíaco cardiac
cardiografía cardiography
cardiógrafo cardiograph
cardiología cardiology
cardiopulmonar cardiopulmonary
cardiovascular cardiovascular
careo confrontation, comparison
careta mask
carga bulk, burden, cargo, load
cargado loaded
cargador mural wall charger
cargador rápido quick charger
cargar (v) to load, charge
cargo accusation, charge, count, debit
cargo en exceso overcharge
cargos aplazados deferred charges
cargos diferidos deferred charges
cargos por manipulación handling charges

cargos por operación handling charges
Caribe Caribbean
caricatura caricature
caricia caress, stroke
caridad charity
caries caries, cavities
cariño affection, fondness, love
carisma charisma
carmín rouge
carnal carnal, sensual
carnaval carnival
carne meat, flesh
carne de cerdo pork
carnicería meat market, blood bath, carnage, Ecuad.: slaughter-house
carnicero butcher
caro expensive
carótida carotid
carpeta folder
carpintero carpenter
carpo carpus
carrera career, race, run
carreta cart, wagon
carril track, lane, rail; Chile, Col.: train
carro cart, wagon
carta letter, card, charter
carta blanca carte blanche
carta comercial business letter
carta de autorización letter of authorization
carta de confirmación letter of confirmation
carta de crédito letter of credit
carta de crédito auxiliar ancillary letter of credit
carta de crédito comercial commercial letter of credit
carta de crédito documentario documentary letter of credit

carta de crédito irrevocable irrevocable letter of credit
carta de garantía letter of guarantee
carta de poderes power of attorney
carta de reclamación letter of complaint
carta perforada punched card
cartel cartel, poster
cartelera billboard
cartera briefcase, portfolio, wallet, discount and bills
cartera de efectos bill holdings
carterista pickpocket
cartero mailman
cartílago cartilage
cartografía cartography
cartón cardboard
cartucho cartridge
cartulina cardboard
casa house, home
Casa Blanca White House
casa de moneda mint
casa simple bungalow
casado married
casamiento wedding
casarse (v) to marry, wed, espouse
cascada cascade, waterfall
cáscara husk, rind
casco helmet, hull
casero homemade, domestic, landlord
caserón large house, barrack
casi almost, nearly
caso case, instance
caspa dandruff
casquillo socket; Peru, Ven.: horseshoe
cassette cassette
castañear (v) to snap
castaño rojizo auburn

castañuelas castanets
castellano Castilian
castigable punishable
castigar (v) to punish, castigate, victimize
castigo punishment
Castilla (región) Castile
castillo castle
casto chaste, pure
castración castration
casual accidental, casual
cataclismo upheaval, cataclysm
catalán Catalonian
catalán (lengua) Catalan
catalepsia trance, catalepsy
catálisis catalysis
catalizador catalyst
catalogar (v) to schedule
catálogo catalog
catálogos literature, catalogs
Cataluña Catalonia
catarata waterfall, cataract
catástrofe catastrophe
catedral cathedral
categoría category, quality, rank
categórico definite, categorical
catequismo catechism
católico Catholic
caución caution, bond, pledge
causa case, cause, reason, prosecution
causa determinante leading case
causa especial special case
causa indirecta remote cause
causa interpuesta intervening cause
causar (v) to cause, provoke
causar terror (v) to stampede
cauteloso wary, cautious
cauterización cautery
cautivar (v) to captivate, capture, charm

cautivo captive
caviar caviar
cavidad cavity, atrium
caza chase, hunt
caza de brujas witch hunt
cazador hunter
cazador furtivo poacher
cazar (v) to chase, hunt
cazar al acecho (v) to stalk
cazuela pan, casserole
cebada barley
cebo bait, lure
cebolla onion
cedazo sieve
ceder (v) to compromise, relinquish, give up
cedro cedar
cédula de identificación identity card
cefálico cephalic
ceguera blindness
ceja brow, eyebrow
celebración celebration
celebrar (v) to celebrate, praise
célebre famous, noted
celestial celestial
celibato celibacy
celofán cellophane
celoso jealous
célula cell
celulitis cellulitis
cementerio cemetery
cemento cement
cena dinner, supper
cenar (v) to dine, have supper
cenagal quagmire
cenicero ashtray
ceniza ash
censo census
censor auditor, censor
Censor jurado de cuentas Certified Public Accountant

censura reproach, censorship, censure

censurar (v) to censor, condemn, denounce

centavo cent, hundredth

centellear (v) to twinkle, spark

centelleo twinkle, sparkle

centeno rye

centésimo hundredth

céntimo cent

centinela sentry, sentinel

central depuradora waterworks

centralizar (v) to center, centralize

centrífugo centrifugal

centro center, core, downtown, hub

centro comercial shopping center

centro del blanco bull's eye

centro de la ciudad downtown

centro de conmutación switching center

centroamericano Central American

ceñir (v) to skirt, encircle, girdle

ceño scowl, frown

cepillar (v) to brush

cepillo brush, hairbrush

cepillo de dientes toothbrush

cera wax

cerámica pottery, ceramics

cerámico ceramic

cerca close by, near

cerca fence, near

cerca de close to

cercano handy, near, close

cercar (v) to surround, fence in

cerco siege, enclosure

cerdo hog, pig

cereal cereal

cerebelo cerebellum

cerebral cerebral

cerebro brain, cerebrum

cerebro anterior forebrain

ceremonia ceremony

cereza cherry

cerilla match

cero zero, nil

cerrado closed

cerradura lock, catch

cerrar (v) to close, lock, seal, shut, slam

cerro hill, ridge

cerrojo bolt, latch

certeza certainty

certificación certification

certificado certified, registered, certificate, warrant, testimonial

certificado de acciones stock certificates

certificado de adeudo certificate of indebtedness

certificado de avería certificate of damage

certificado de depósito certificate of deposit

certificado de descarga landing certificate

certificado de origen certificate of origin

certificado de recepción certificate of receipt

certificado de reintegro debenture

certificado de saldo de cuenta certificate of balance

certificado orden de pago debenture

certificados de constitución corporation certificates

cerveza beer

cerveza de barril draft beer

cesar (v) to stop, cease

cesárea caesarean

cesión assignment, cession, transfer, concession, surrender
cesión libre absolute conveyance
césped lawn, turf
cesta basket
ciática sciatica
ciático sciatic
cibernética cybernetics
cicatriz scar
cíclico cyclic
ciclista cyclist
ciclo cycle
ciclo de búsqueda search cycle
ciego blind
cielo heaven, sky
cien one hundred
ciencia science
ciencia del ordenador computer science
ciencia ficción science fiction
cieno slime
científico scientific, scientist
cierre fastener, closing
cierre patronal lockout
ciertamente certainly
cierto certain, sure
ciervo deer, stag
cifra number, cipher, digit, figure
cifrar (v) to code, scramble, summarize
cigarrillo cigarette
cigarro puro cigar
cilindro cylinder, roller
cima summit, spire, acme
cincel chisel
cinco five
cincuenta fifty
cine cinema
cínico cynical
cinta band, ribbon, tape
cinta magnética magnetic tape

cinta magnetofónica tape recorder
cintura waist
cinturón belt
cinturón de seguridad seat belt
ciprés cypress
circo circus
circuito circuit, trunk
circuito de servicio service circuit
circuito integrado integrated circuit
circulación circulation, traffic
circular circular
circular (v) to circulate
círculo circle
circuncisión circumcision
circunferencia circumference
circunflejo circumflex
circunstancial circumstantial, occasional
cirrosis cirrhosis
cirugía surgery
cirugía estética cosmetic surgery
cirujano surgeon
cisterna cistern
cistitis cystitis
cistotomía cystostomy
cita appointment, citation, rendezvous, quotation
citación call, citation, quotation, summons, subpoena
citar (v) to appoint, date, quote, cite, summon, make a date with
cítrico citric
ciudad city, town
ciudadanía citizenship
ciudadano citizen
cívico civic
civil civil, civilian
civilización civilization
civilizar (v) to civilize

clandestino clandestine, surreptitious, undercover
claraboya skylight
claramente defintely
claridad brightness, clarity
clarinete clarinet
claro bright, clear, definite, lucid
clase class, lecture, sort
clase alta high-class, upper-class
clase media middle-class
clásico classic
clasificación assortment, rating
clasificar (v) to grade, sort, classify
claustrofobia claustrophobia
cláusula article, clause
cláusula de revisión de precios escalator clause
cláusula derogatoria repealing clause
cláusula penal penal clause
clavar (v) to nail, tack
clavel carnation
clavícula clavicle, collar bone
clavo nail, tack
clemencia clemency, mercy
clemente clement, merciful, gracious
clero clergy
cliché cliché
cliente client, customer, patron
clima climate
clínica clinic
clítoris clitoris
cloaca sewer
cloro chlorine
cloruro de sodio sodium chloride
club nocturno night club
coacción coercion, duress
coaccionar (v) to coerce, compel
coactivo coactive

coacusado codefendant
coagular (v) to coagulate
coágulo clot
coalición coalition, alliance
coartada alibi
cobalto cobalt
cobraderos collectibles
cobrador collector, retriever
cobrar (v) to collect, receive, recover, retrieve, regain
cobro collection
cocaína cocaine, coke, crack
cocer (v) to stew
cocer (al horno) (v) to bake
cocer al vapor (v) to steam
cocer lentamente (v) to simmer
cocido stew, cooked
cocina cooker, kitchen, cuisine
cocinar (v) to cook; Arg., Col., Uru.: to bake
cocinero cook
coco coconut (palm)
cocodrilo crocodile
coche car, automobile
coche de bomberos fire engine
coche deportivo sports car
coche fúnebre hearse
codazo ligero nudge
codeína codeine
codicia greed
codicioso greedy, covetous, acquisitive
codificación coding
codificación automática automatic coding
codificar (v) to codify, encode
código code
código civil civil code
código de barras bar code
código de datos data code
código mnemónico mnemonic code

codo elbow
coeficiente coefficient, ratio
coeficiente de variación
coefficient of variation
coger (v) to catch, get, seize,
snatch, take, grasp, pick; Arg.,
Uru.: to have sex with
coger con trampas (v) to snare
cogirador co-drawer
cogote scruff, back of the neck
coheredero coheir
coherencia coherence
cohete rocket
coincidir (v) to coincide, agree
coito coitus
cojera limp, lameness
cojín cushion
cojinete de bolas ball bearing
cojo lame, crippled
cola cue, line, tail
colaborar (v) to collaborate
colador strainer, colander
colapso collapse
colateral collateral
colchón cushion, mattress
coleccionador collector
colega colleague
colegio school
colegio mayor college
cólera anger, rage, cholera
colérico irate
colesterol cholesterol
colgar (v) to hang, overhang
cólico colic
colina hill, knoll
colisionar (v) to collide
colitigante colitigant
colitis colitis
colmena hive, beehive
colmillo tusk, fang, canine tooth
colmo height, extreme, climax
colocar (v) to place, put, lay,
locate

colocar mal (v) to misplace
Colón Columbus
colón colon
color color, hue
colorar (v) to color
colorete rouge
columna column, pillar
columna vertebral vertebral column
collar collar, necklace
coma coma
comarca region
comatoso comatose
combate combat
combinación combination
combinado cocktail
combinar (v) to combine
combustible fuel, combustible
comedia comedy
comedor dining room
comentario comment
comenzar (v) to begin, start,
commence
comer (v) to eat, dine
comercial commercial
comercialización merchandising,
marketing
comerciante dealer, merchant,
trader, tradesman
comerciar (v) to trade
comercio commerce, marketing,
trade
comercio de exportación export
trade
comercio de trueque barter
comestible edible
comestibles grocery
cometer (v) to commit, perpetrate
cómico comedian, laughable
comida food, lunch, meal,
feed
comida campestre picnic

comienzo beginning, inception, start

comillas quotation marks

comisario quartermaster

comisión commission, committee, perpetration, Mex.: type of policeman

comisión fija flat commission

comisión oculta kickback

comisión por operación service charge

comisión sobre un préstamo procuration fee

comité committee

cómo how, what

comodidad comfort, convenience

cómodo comfortable, snug

compacto compact

compadecer (v) to pity, be sorry, sympathize

compañerismo fellowship

compañero buddy, companion, fellow

compañero de cuarto roommate

compañía company, enterprise, corporation

compañía afiliada affiliated company

compañía aseguradora underwriter

compañía asociada associated company

compañía de valores holding company

comparación comparison

comparar (v) to compare

compartimiento compartment

compartir (v) to share

compasión compassion

compasivo sympathetic

compatibilidad compatibility

compatible compatible, congenial

compendiar (v) to summarize, abridge, epitomize

compendio summary, abridgement

compensación compensation, clearing, offset, redress, setoff

compensar (v) to compensate, offset

compensatorio countervailing

competencia competition

competencia intensa cut-throat competition

competente capable, competent

competidor competitor

competir (v) to compete, race

compilador compiler

compinche pal

complacer (v) to please, gratify

complaciente complacent, willing, kind, obliging

complejidad complexity

complejo complex

complementario complimentary

complemento complement

completamente quite

completar (v) to complete, finalize

completo complete, full, outright, sheer, thorough, total, utter

complicado complicated, complex, elaborate

complicar (v) to complicate

cómplice accessory, accomplice

complicidad complicity

complot plot

componente component

componer (v) to compose, constitute, patch, repair, mend

comportamiento behavior

comportarse (v) to behave

composición composition

composición gráfica typesetting

compra purchase

compra a plazos installment purchase, hire purchase

compra de la parte de otro socio buy-out

comprador buyer, purchaser, shopper

comprar (v) to buy, shop, purchase

compras shopping

comprender (v) to see, comprehend, understand

comprensible intelligible, understandable

comprensión realization

comprensivo understanding

compresa compress

comprimir (v) to compress, squeeze

comprobación checkup , verification

comprobante voucher

comprobante de caja cash voucher, cash receipt

comprobar (v) to verify

comprometer (v) to implicate, risk, embarrass

compromiso commitment, engagement

compromisos existentes commitments outstanding

compuesto compound

computadora computer

computar (v) to compute

común common, joint, rife

comunicación communication

comunicación bidireccional both-way communication

comunicación bidireccional alterna either-way communication

comunicación de datos data communication

comunicación en doble sentido two-way communication

comunicación unidireccional one-way communication

comunicar (v) to communicate, contact, impart

comunidad community

comunidad bancaria banking community

comunismo communism

con with

con cuidado carefully, gently

con éxito successfully

con experiencia experienced

con poco personal understaffed

con talento talented

con todo yet

con traje de calle plain-clothes

concavidad concavity

concebible conceivable

concebir (v) to conceive

concedente licensor

conceder (v) to concede

concentrar (v) to concentrate

concepto concept

concernir (v) to concern

concesión allowance, award, concession, franchise, grant

concesionario franchiser, licensee

concierto concert

conciliación conciliation

conciliación bancaria bank reconciliation

conciliador peacemaker

conciliar (v) to adjust, conciliate, reconcile

conciso concise, terse

concluir (v) to conclude

conclusión conclusion

conclusivo conclusive

concluyente conclusive

concordar (v) to reconcile, assort

concordia rapport, concord, harmony

concreto concrete

concurrencia turnout

concurrir (v) to meet, gather, resort

concurso contest, trial, tournament, competition

concusión concussion

condado county, Chile: astute

condena conviction

condena grave heavy sentence

condena leve light sentence

condenar (v) to condone, condemn, damn, doom

condensación condensation

condescendiente acquiescent

condición condition, state, plight, status

condición precedente precondition

condicional conditional, contingent

condiciones terms

condiciones de entrega terms of delivery

condimento seasoning

condón condom

conducir (v) to conduct, drive, steer

conducta conduct

conducta ilegal malpractice

conducta profesional professional conduct

conducto chute

conductor conductor, driver, chauffeur

conectado connected

conectar (v) to connect

conector connector

conejo rabbit

conexión connection, link, relevance

conexión en cadena chain connection

conexo relevant

confeccionado ready-made

confederación confederation

conferencia conference

conferencia tripartita three-way conference

conferenciante lecturer, speaker

confesar (v) to confess, admit

confesión confession, deposition

confesión sin confirmación naked confession

confiabilidad reliability

confianza confidence, dependability, reliance, trust

confianza en sí mismo self-confidence

confiar (v) to confide, trust

confiar en (v) to rely on

confidencial confidential

confidente confidant

configuración configuration

confirmación acknowledgement, confirmation

confirmación de pedido order confirmation

confirmar (v) to confirm

confiscación confiscation, seizure

confiscar (v) to confiscate

confitura preserve

conflicto dispute, conflict

conforme agreeable

conformista conformist

confortable comfortable

confraternizar (v) to fraternize

confrontación confrontation

confundir (v) to confound, confuse, perplex

confusión confusion, disorder, jumble, mess, mix-up, turmoil

confuso confused, intricate, perplexing

congelación frostbite

congelar (v) to freeze, chill

congénito congenital

congestión congestion

conglomerado conglomerate

congregarse (v) to congregate

congreso congress

conjetura conjecture

conjetural conjectural

conjuntamente jointly

conjuntivitis conjunctivitis

conjunto assembly, kit

conjuración conspiracy

conmemorar (v) to commemorate

conmoción shock, stir

conmoción cerebral concussion

conmovedor poignant, touching, stirring

conmover (v) to touch, stir

conmutación switch

conmutar (v) to commute

connotación connotation

cono cone

conocer (v) to know, be acquainted with

conocido established, renowned, well known

conocimiento, trato knowledge, acquaintance, good sense

conocimiento aéreo airway bill

conocimiento de embarque bill of lading

conocimiento de embarque certificado certified bill of lading

conocimiento de embarque sin reservas clean bill of lading

conquistar (v) to conquer

consciente conscious, conscious (state)

consecuencia consequence, result, sequel

consecutivo serial, consecutive

conseguir (v) to get, obtain, achieve

consejero advisor, counselor

consejo advice, board, counsel

consejo de administración board of directors

consejo directivo board of directors

consenso consensus, accord

consentimiento assent

consentimiento implícito implied consent

consentimiento mutuo mutual consent

consentir (v) to consent, permit, acquiesce

conserje doorkeeper, janitor

conserva preserve

conservación conservation, preservation, upkeep

conservar (v) to conserve

conservativo conservative

considerable considerable , sizeable

consideración especial special consideration

considerando whereas

considerar (v) to consider

consigna consignment, baggage check, order, instruction

consignar (v) to consign, send, dispatch

consiguiente consequent, resultant

consistir (v) to consist

consola console

consolidación consolidation
consolidado consolidated
consolidar (v) to consolidate, strengthen
consonante consonant
consorcio consortium, pool, trust
consorcio bancario banking syndicate
conspiración conspiracy
constante chronic, constant, recurrent, steady
constelación constellation
consternación dismay, distress
consternar (v) to be dismayed, to appall
constitución constitution
constitucional constitutional
constituido en ley incorporated
construcción construction
constructivo constructive
constructor builder, maker
construir (v) to build, construct
cónsul consul
consulado consulate
consulta consultation, consulting room
consultar (v) to consult
consultivo advisory
consumidor consumer
consumir (v) to consume
consumo consumption
contabilidad accounting
contabilidad de costes cost accounting
contabilidad por acumulaciones accrual accounting
contable accountant, book-keeper
contactar (v) to contact, touch
contacto contact, touch
contador counter, meter, recorder

contagioso contagious, infectious
contaminación pollution
contaminar (v) contaminate, pollute
contar (v) to compute, relate, reckon, recount
contemplar (v) to contemplate
contemporáneo contemporary
contenedor container
contener (v) to contain, restrain
contestación reply
contestador automático answering machine
contestar (v) to answer, reply
contexto context
contienda strife, struggle
contiguo adjacent
contingencia contingency
contingente contingent
contingente de exportación export quota
contingente de mercancías goods quota
continuación follow-up
continuar (v) to continue, proceed, sustain, go on
continuidad continuity
continuo continuous, constant
contorno outline, contour
contorsión contortion
contra against, versus
contraalmirante rear admiral
contraapelación cross-appeal
contraataque counter-attack
contrabandista smuggler
contrabando contraband, smuggling
contracción contraction
contrachapado plywood
contractual contractual
contradecir (v) to controvert, contradict

contradeclaración counteraffidavit

contrademanda counterclaim

contraer (v) to contract, shrink

contraindicación contraindication

contraparte counterpart

contrapropuesta counterproposal

contraprueba counterproof

contraquerella cross action

contrario contrary, counter, converse, unwilling

contrarrestar (v) to counteract

contrasello counterseal

contraseña password

contraseña de acuñación hallmark

contraseña garantía hallmark

contrastar (v) to contrast

contraste contrast, fineness

contratante contracting

contratista contractor

contrato agreement, contract

contrato al contado spot contract

contrato cambio al contado spot contract

contrato de compraventa contract of sale

contrato de aceptación acceptance agreement

contrato llaves en mano turn key contract

contrato nulo void contract

contrato personal personal contract

contrato verbal parol contract

contratos de cumplimiento obligado executory contracts

contraventana shutter

contribución contribution

contribuir (v) to contribute, pay

contribuyente contributor, tax payer

control control, restraint, check

control a distancia remote control

control de calidad quality control

control de cambios exchange control

control de cuentas control accounts

control de error error control

control de ficheros file control

control de flujo flow control

control de natalidad birth control

control de proceso industrial industrial process control

control en línea on-line equipment

control numérico numerical control

control remoto radio control

controlador controller

controlar (v) to control

controversia controversy

contusión bruise, contusion

convalecencia aftercare

convalecer (v) to recover, convalesce

convención convention

conveniente convenient, suitable

convenio agreement, accord, covenant

convenio dependiente dependent covenant

convenio implícito implied covenant

convenir (v) to agree, suit, assort

convento convent

conversación conversation, talk

conversar (v) to talk

conversión conversion

conversión de datos data conversion

conversión de ficheros file conversion

convertibilidad total full convertibility

convertidor converter

convertidor de código code converter

convertidor de paralelo a serie parallel to serial converter

convertirse (v) to convert, transform

convidar (v) to invite, treat

convite invitation, treat, banquet

convocar (v) to call, convoke, summon

convocar de nuevo (v) to reconvene

convocatoria call, summons, edict

convulsiones convulsions

coñac brandy

cooperar (v) to cooperate

cooperativa co-op

coordinación coordination

coordinar (v) to combine, coordinate

copa cup

copartícipes partners

copia copy, replica, transcript

copia certificada exemplification

copia de carbón carbon copy

copiadora copier

copiar (v) to copy

copo de nieve snowflake

coque coke

coral coral

corazón heart

corbata tie

corchete clasp, hook and eye

corcho cork, float

cordial cordial, hearty

cordón de zapato shoelace

cordura sanity, prudence

Corea Korea

coreano Korean

coreógrafo choreographer

corista chorus girl

córnea cornea

corneta cornet

coro choir

corona crown, wreath

coronar (v) to cap, top, crown

coronario coronary

coronel colonel

corporación corporation

corporal carnal, bodily, corporal

corral de ganado stockyard

corrección amendment, propriety

correctamente properly

correcto all right, correct, right

corredor runner

correlacionar (v) to correlate

correo mail, post, courier

correo aéreo airmail

correo electrónico electronic mail

correr (v) to run, race, scurry, stream, Mex.: to throw someone out; Amer.: to fire someone from a job

correr rápido (v) to sprint

correspondencia correspondence

corresponder (v) to correspond, tally

correspondiente counterpart

corretaje brokerage

corrida de toros bullfight

corriente alterna alternating current

corriente sanguínea bloodstream

corriente, actual current

corriente current, customary, flow, regular, stream

corromper (v) to rot, spoil

corrompido corrupt

corrosión rust

corrosivo corrosive

corrupción corruption

cortacésped lawn mower

cortaduras cuts

cortante piercing, cutting, sharp

cortar (v) to chop, cut, pare, sever, slit, excise, hack

corte cut, cutting, chop, cut-off, incision, shape

corte de pelo haircut

cortejar (v) to court, woo

cortés polite, attentive

cortes cuts

cortesía courtesy, politeness

corteza crust, rind, skin

cortina curtain, screen

cortisona cortisone

corto short, brief

corto de vista short-sighted

corto plazo short-term

cortocircuito short-circuit

cosa thing

cosecha crop, harvest, yield

cosechar (v) to harvest, reap

coser (v) to sew, stitch

cosmético cosmetic

cósmico cosmic

costa coast, seashore

coste cost, value, cost insurance and freight

coste de bienes vendidos cost of goods sold

coste de capital cost of capital

coste de producción común joint cost

coste del producto product cost

coste incremental incremental cost

coste indirecto indirect cost

coste marginal marginal cost

coste original original cost

coste pertinente relevant cost

coste unitario unit cost

costes costs

costes acumulados accrued costs

costes comerciales cost of sales

costes de administración administration costs

costes de fabricación generales factory overhead costs

costes de mano de obra labor cost

costes de mantenimiento maintenance costs

costes de producción manufacturing costs

costes de reparación repair cost

costes de transporte transportation costs

costes de venta cost of sales

costes diferidos deferred costs

costes directos de fabricación direct manufacturing costs

costes fijos fixed costs

costes históricos historical costs

costes operacionales overhead costs

costes variables variable costs

costes vigentes unexpired costs

costilla rib

costo efectivo actual cost

costos de explotación operating costs

costra scab, crust

costumbre custom, habit, practice

costura needlework, sewing, seam

cotidiano day-to-day

cotización quotation

cotizar (v) to quote, price
cotizar más bajo (v) to underbid
coyuntura juncture
cráneo skull
crecer (v) to grow
crecer más que (v) to outgrow
creciente increasing, rising, crescent
crecimiento growth
credenciales credentials
credibilidad credibility
crédito credit, loan
crédito confirmado confirmed credit
crédito de exportación export credit
créditos diferidos deferred credits
crédito documentario documentary credit
crédito extranjero foreign credit
crédito renovable revolving credit
crédito revocable revocable credit
crédito simple clean credit
crédito subsidiario back to back credit
créditos credits
créditos hipotecarios mortgage credits
credo creed
creencia belief, creed
creer (v) to believe, trust
creíble believable, credible
crema de afeitar shaving cream
cremación incineration, cremation
crepúsculo twilight
cresta crest
cretinismo cretinism
creyente believer

cría breeding
criada maid
criado servant
criar (v) to breed, hatch
criatura infant, creature
criba sieve
cribar (v) to sift
crimen crime, felony
criminal criminal, felon
criminalista criminalist
criollo Creole, Amer.: domestic, native
crisantemo chrysanthemum
crisis crisis
cristal crystal
cristal a prueba de balas bulletproof glass
cristiano Christian
Cristo Christ
criterio criterion
criticar (v) to criticize
crítico critic, reviewer
cromo chrome
crónica chronicle, chronic
cronógrafo chronograph
cronología aging, chronology
cronológico chronological
cronómetro stopwatch, timer
cruce crossing, junction
crucero cruise
crucificar (v) to crucify
crucifijo crucifix
crucigrama crossword
crudeza rawness
crudo crude, raw, unripe, Mex.: hangover
cruel cruel, vicious
crueldad cruelty
crueldad mental mental cruelty
crujido crack
crujiente crisp
crujir (v) to crunch, creak
Cruz Roja Red Cross

cruzada crusade
cruzado cross
cruzar (v) to cross, span, intersect
cuadrado square
cuadrángulo quadrangle
cuadrante quadrant
cuadrar (v) to square
cuadriplegia quadriplegia
cuadro picture, painting, square, frame
cuadro de mandos switchboard
cuadrúpedo quadruped
cuádruple quadruple
cual which
cualidad atrribute
cualquier any, either, whichever
cuando when
cuantioso substantial
cuarenta forty
cuarentena quarantine
Cuaresma Lent
cuarta parte quarter
cuartel quarter, barrack
cuarteto quartet
cuarto fourth, quarter
cuarto oscuro dark room
cuatro four
cúbico cubic
cubierta cover, covering, deck
cubito de hielo ice cube
cubo cube, tub
cubrir (v) to cover, protect, drape, overlay
cuchara scoop
cuchara sopera soupspoon
cucharita teaspoon
cucharón tablespoon
cuchilla blade, chopper
cuchillo knife
cuchillo de tajar chopping knife
cuello collar, neck
cuello de botella bottleneck

cuenca basin
cuenta account, count, bill, reckoning, score, tally
cuenta abierta open account
cuenta al descubierto overdue account
cuenta atrás countdown
cuenta bancaria bank account
cuenta bloqueada blocked account
cuenta conjunta joint account
cuenta de balance consolidada consolidated balance sheet
cuenta de banco bank account
cuenta de caja cash account
cuenta de capital capital account
cuenta de compensación offset accounts
cuenta de créditos loan account
cuenta de depósito deposit account, escrow account
cuenta de ingresos totales all-inclusive income statement
cuenta de pérdidas y ganancias profit-loss statement
cuenta saldada closed account
cuenta patrimonial capital account
cuentas a cobrar receivables, accounts receivable
cuentas a pagar accounts payable
cuentas deudoras accounts receivable
cuentas pagaderas accounts payable
cuento story, tale
cuerda chord, cord, rope, string
cuerda floja (circo) tightrope
cuerdas vocales vocal cords
cuerdo sane
cuerno horn

cuero leather
cuero cabelludo scalp
cuerpo body, corps
cuesta abajo downhill
cuesta arriba uphill
cuestión issue
cuestión de derecho matter of law
cuestión de hecho matter of fact
cuestión especial special issue
cuestionable inconclusive
cuestionario questionnaire
cueva cave
cuidado attention, care
cuidados intensivos intensive care
culinario culinary
culo backside
culpar (v) to blame
culpa blame, guilt
culpabilidad guilt
culpable culpable, culprit, guilty
cultivable arable
cultivador grower
cultivar (v) to cultivate, farm
cultivo crop, farming
culto cult, well-educated
cultural cultural
cumbre acme, apex, summit, top
cumpleaños birthday
cumplido compliment, courtesy, Peru: reliable

cumplidor reliable
cumplimiento completion, fulfillment, performance
cumplir (v) to fulfill
cumplir una sentencia (v) to serve a sentence
cuna cradle
cuña wedge
cuñada sister-in-law
cuñado brother-in-law
cuota allocation, quota
cupo quota
cupón coupon
cupón de intereses interest coupon
cura priest
cura de urgencia first aid
curar (v) to heal
curativo healing, remedial
curiosear (v) to snoop
curiosidad curiosity
curioso curious, inquisitive, quaint, snoop
curriculum vitae resume
curry curry
cursor cursor
curva bend, curve
curvar (v) to bend, curve
custodia custody, ward
custodio custodian, custodial
cutáneo cutaneous

CH

chabola shack, Sp.: hut
chal shawl
chaleco salvavidas life jacket
chalet chalet
champiñón mushroom
champú shampoo
chamuscar (v) to scorch, sear

chantaje blackmail
chapa plate, sheet, veneer
chapear (v) to plate, cover with metal
chapucero clumsy, shoddy, crude
chaqueta coat, jacket

chaqueta de deporte blazer
chaquete (juego) backgammon
charco pool, puddle, pond
charla chat, talk
charla superficial small talk
charlar (v) to talk, chatter
chasis chassis, framework
chasquear (v) to disappoint, snap, Amer.: to chatter (teeth)
chasquido snap, click
chatarra scrap, scrap iron, junk
chauvinista chauvinist
cheque check
cheque a la orden order check
cheque abierto open check
cheque al portador check to bearer
cheque caducado stale check
cheque certificado certified check
cheque cruzado crossed check
cheque de banco banker's check
cheque de caja cashier's check
cheques de viajero traveler's checks
cheque en blanco blank check
cheque sin fondos uncovered check
chica girl
chicle bubble gum, chewing gum
chicle de mascar chewing gum

chico boy, kid
Chile Chile
chileno Chilean
chillar (v) to howl, scream, squeal, C. Amer.: to become ashamed
chillido scream, squeal
chimenea chimney
China China
chinche bedbug
chino Chinese
chip chip
chirrido squeak, shrill sound
chisme gossip, gadget, thing
chispa spark; Arg., Mex., Uru.: amusing
chiste joke, funny story
chistoso joker
chocar (v) to collide, crash, strike, shock
chocolate chocolate
chófer chauffeur
choque clash, impact, crash, shock, smash
choza shack, hut
chuchería trinket, snack
chulo pimp, vulgar, Amer.: good-looking
chupar (v) to suck, Amer.: to drink
chusma rabble, mob

D

dactiloscopia dactyloscopy
dado given
dados dice
daga dagger
damnificar (v) to damnify
daño damage, harm
daños directos direct damages

daños generales general damages
daños indirectos remote damages
daños punitivos exemplary damages, punitive damages
daños y perjuicios damages

dar (v) to donate, give
dar asco (v) to disgust, sicken
dar cama (v) to litter
dar crédito (v) to credit
dar cuerda (v) to rewind
dar derecho (v) to entitle
dar entrada (v) to admit
dar la bienvenida (v) to welcome
dar la mano (v) to hand
dar las gracias (v) to thank
dar órdenes a (v) to brief
dar patadas (v) to kick
dar pena (v) to grieve
dar poder (v) to empower
dar por terminado (v) to dismiss
dar propina (v) to tip
dar recibo (v) to receipt
dar sombra (v) to shade
dar un paso (v) to step
dar un puntapié (v) to boot
dar una conferencia (v) to lecture
dar vueltas (v) to rotate, revolve, spin
dar zancadas (v) to stride
dardo dart
darse cuenta (v) to realize
datar (v) to date
dátil date
datos data
datos alfanuméricos alphanumeric data
datos analógicos analog data
datos numéricos numerical data
de of, from
de al lado next door
de algún modo somehow
de aquí hence
de aquí en adelante henceforth
de avanzada edad elderly
de baja calidad shoddy

de clase obrera working class
de día daytime
de dos filos double-edged
de eso thereof
de este modo thus
de hecho de facto
de interés topical
de largo alcance far-reaching
de madera wooden
de mar adentro offshore
de moda fashionable
de nuevo anew
de oficina clerical
de otra manera otherwise
de pez fishy
de pie standing
de prueba experimental
de quién whose
de regimiento regimental
de secretario secretarial
de todas formas anyway
de todas maneras anyhow
de transición transitional
de verdad indeed
debajo under, underneath
debajo del pie underfoot
debate debate
debe debit
deber duty, task
deber (v) to owe, should, ought
deberes homework
debidamente jurado duly sworn
debido due
débil dim, infirm, puny, shaky, weak
debilidad weakness
debilitar (v) to impair, weaken
débito charge, debit
decadencia decay
decadente decadent
decaer (v) to wane
decano dean
decapitar (v) to behead

decencia propriety

decepción anticlimax, disappointment

decepcionar (v) to disappoint

decidir (v) to decide

decifrar (v) to decipher

decimal decimal

décimo tenth

decimosexto sixteenth

decimotercero thirteenth

decir (v) to say, speak, tell

decisión decision, finding, ruling

decisión del tribunal adjudication

decisión errónea invited error

decisivo crucial, final

decisorio decisory

declaración declaration, pronouncement, statement, tax return, deposition

declaración de aduana customs entry

declaración de culpabilidad plea of guilty

declaración de ingresos income statement

declaración jurada affidavit, sworn declaration

declarante deponent

declarar (v) to certify, declare, profess, state, testify

declararse (v) to declare oneself

declararse culpable (v) to plead guilty

declinar (v) to decline

declive slope

decomiso forfeit

decorar decorate

decorativo ornamental

decrépito decrepit

decretar (v) to enact

decreto decree, order

dedal thimble

dedicación implícita tacit dedication

dedicar (v) to dedicate, spend

dedo finger

dedo del pie toe

dedos fingers

dedos de los pies toes

deducción deduction

deducible deductible

deducir (v) to deduct, deduce, figure out

deductivo deductive

defecación defecation

defecto bug, defect, fault, failing, shortcoming

defectuoso crook, deficient, defective, faulty, unsound

defender (v) to defend, plead

defensa defense, plea

defensa especial special defense

defensa ficticia sham defense

defensa positiva positive defense

defensa propia self-defense

deferencia deference

deficiencia deficiency, defectiveness

déficit deficit

definir (v) to define

definitivo definitive

deflación deflation

deflector baffle

deformación warp

deformar (v) to deform

deforme shapeless

defraudador defrauder

defraudante deceptive

defraudar (v) to defraud

degeneración degeneration

degenerado degraded, degenerate

degradar (v) to degrade

dejación abandonment

dejar (v)   to forsake, leave
del trabajo y cuerpo   ergonomics
del norte   northern
del oeste   western
delantal   apron
delantero   forward, leading
delator   informer
delegación   delegation
delegado   delegate, deputy
delegar (v)   to delegate
deleite   delight
deletrear (v)   to spell
deletrear mal (v)   to misspell
delgadez   thinness
delgado   slim, slender, thin
deliberadamente   deliberately
deliberar (v)   to deliberate
delicado   dainty, delicate, squeamish, weakling
delicioso   delicious, luscious
delincuencia   delinquency
delincuente   delinquent, culprit, felon, offender
delirante   delirious
delirar (v)   to rave
delirio   delirium
delito   crime, felony, offense
delito menor   misdemeanor
delito penal   criminal offense
demagógico   demagogic
demanda   complaint, count, demand
demanda de reembolso   repetition
demandado   defendant, libelee
demandante   claimant, demandant, libelant, plaintiff, suitor
demandar (v)   to prosecute, sue
demasiado pesado   overweight
demencia   dementia
demente   crazy, insane
democracia   democracy

demócrata   democrat
demoler (v)   to demolish
demonio   demon
demostración   demonstration, show
demostrar (v)   to demonstrate, proof, prove
denegación   denial, refusal
denegar (v)   to deny, refuse
denotar (v)   to denote
densamente   densely
densidad doble   double density
denso   dense
dentado   jagged
dentadura   denture
dentadura postiza   false teeth
dental   dental
dentición   dentition, teething
dentista   dentist
dentro   inside, within
denunciación   denunciation
denunciante   denouncer
denunciar (v)   to denounce
departamento   department
departamento de contabilidad   accounting department
departamento de créditos   loan department
depender (v)   to depend
dependiente   dependent, subsidiary
deplorar (v)   to deplore
deportación   banishment, deportation
deporte   sport
deportista   sportsman
deportivo   sporting
depositante   depositor
depositario   bailee, depository, trustee
depósito   deposit, reservoir
depósito a plazo fijo   fixed period deposit

depósito aduanero bonded warehouse

depósito de aduana bonded warehouse

depósito de cadáveres morgue

depreciación depreciation

depreciación acelerada accelerated depreciation

depreciación acumulada accumulated depreciation

depreciar (v) to depreciate

depreciación depreciation

depresión depression, slump

deprimido depressed

depurar (v) to debug

derecha right

derecho law, upright, right, straight

derecho de recurso right of appeal

derecho de retracto right of redemption

derecho de sucesiones probate jurisdiction

derecho existente existing right

derecho hipotecario mortgage law

derecho patentario patent law

derecho político political law

derecho prendario right of lien

derecho privado private law

derecho público public law

derecho real real right

derecho usual customary law

derechos duty, rights, royalty

derechos aduaneros customs duties

derechos de aduana customs, customs duty

derechos de autor copyright

derechos de prioridad preemptive rights

derechos industriales royalties

derechos legales legal rights

derechos particulares private rights

derechos primarios primary rights

derechos singulares absolute rights

derivar (v) to derive

dermatitis dermatitis

dermatólogo dermatologist

dermatoma dermatome

dermis dermis

derogación abolition, derogation

derogatorio derogatory

derramar (v) to pour, spill

derrape skid

derretir (v) to thaw

derribar (v) to demolish, overthrow, topple

derrocar (v) to topple

derrochador wasteful

derrochar (v) to squander, waste

derroche waste

derrota rout

derrotar (v) to defeat, vanquish

derrumbarse (v) to collapse, Amer.: to fail

desabrochar (v) to unbutton

desactivación deactivation

desacuerdo disagreement

desafiador challenger

desafiar (v) to brave, challenge

desafío challenge

desagradable awkward, disagreeable, unpleasant

desagradar (v) to displease

desagradecido ungrateful

desagüe drainage

desahuciado broke

desahuciador ejector

desahuciar (v) to evict
desahucio eviction, ejectment, dispossession, ouster
desaire snub
desalentador discouraging
desalentar (v) to discourage
desalojar (v) to dislodge, oust
desamparado underprivileged
desaparecer (v) to disappear, to vanish
desaprobación disapproval
desaprobar (v) to disapprove, disallow
desarmado unarmed
desarmar (v) to disarm
desarme disarmament
desarraigar (v) to uproot
desarrollar (v) to evolve, develop
desarrollo development
desaseado unkempt
desastre disaster
desastroso disastrous
desatar (v) to loose, unfasten
desatender (v) to dishonor
desatento heedless
desatrancar (v) to unclog
desautorizado unauthorized
desautorizar (v) to disavow
desayuno breakfast
desayuno-almuerzo brunch
desbaratar (v) to thwart
desboque rampage
descalcificación decalcification
descalificado disqualified
descalzo barefoot
descansado restful
descansar (v) to relax, recline, repose, rest
descanso half-time, leisure, intermission, rest, recess, relaxation
descarado saucy

descarga shock
descarga eléctrica electrical shock
descargar (v) to discharge, roll out, unload
descargo discharge, release
descarrilamiento derailment
descartar (v) to discard, scrap
descendencia offspring
descender (v) to descend
descenso falling
descentralizar (v) to decentralize
descifrado decoding
descifrado de umbral threshold decoding
descifrador decoder
descolorido faded
descomponer (v) to decompose
desconcertante confusing
desconcierto embarrassment
desconectar (v) to disconnect
desconfianza mistrust
descongelar (v) to defrost
desconocido strange, unknown, unfamiliar
descontable bankable
descontar (v) to discount, rebate
descontrolado berserk
descortés uncivil
descosido disjointed
descrédito discredit
describir (v) to describe
descripción description
descripción de las mercancías description of goods
descriptivo descriptive
descubierto overdraft
descubrimiento discovery
descubrir (v) to discover, detect, uncover

descuento discount, deduction, rebate

descuento comercial trade discount

descuento comercial por pronto pago sales discount

descuento de compra purchase discount

descuento por pronto pago cash discount

descuidado careless, negligent, neglected, remiss, sloppy, thoughtless

descuidar (v) to neglect

descuido oversight

desde since

desdeñar (v) to despise

desdoblar (v) to unfold

desear (v) to fancy, wish

desechable disposable, throwaway

desechar (v) to scrap

desecho waste

desembalar (v) to unpack

desembarcar (v) to disembark, land

desembarco landing

desembolso outlay

desembolsos disbursements

desempleo unemployment

desencadenar (v) to trigger

desenmarañar (v) to untangle, unravel

desenterrar (v) to unearth

desenvolver to unwind, unwrap

desenvuelto informal

deseo wish, urge

desequilibrado unbalanced

desequilibrio imbalance

desertor runaway

desesperado desperate, hopeless

desesperación despair

desfalcador embezzler

desfalcar (v) to embezzle

desfalco embezzlement, peculation

desfavorable unfavorable

desfigurar (v) to deface

desfile parade, pageant, procession

desgana reluctance

desgarbado slovenly

desgarrar (v) to tear

desgaste attrition

desgracia accident, misadventure, misfortune

desgraciado unfortunate, unlucky

deshabitado unoccupied

deshacer (v) to undo

deshacerse (v) to crumple, crumple

deshacerse de una inversión (v) to divest

deshelar (v) to thaw

desheredar (v) to disinherit

deshidratación dehydration

deshidratar (v) to dehydrate

deshonestidad dishonesty

deshonesto crooked, dishonest

deshonor dishonor

desierto desert

desigual lumpy, patchy, unequal, uneven

desigualdad inequality, roughness

desilusionar (v) to disillusion

desinfectante disinfectant

desinfectar (v) to disinfect

desinflar (v) to deflate

desinteresado unselfish, uninterested

desleal disloyal

deslizar (v) to slide

deslucido dingy

deslumbrador glaring

deslumbrante dazzling
deslustrar (v) to tarnish
desmán rampage
desmayado unconscious
desmayarse to faint, faint
desmayo fainting
desmenuzar (v) to crumble
desmodulador scrambler
desmontar (v) to dismantle, strip
desmoralizado demoralized
desmoralizar (v) to demoralize
desnudar (v) to strip, undress
desnudo bare, nude
desobedecer (v) to disobey
desobediencia disobedience
desobediente disobedient
desocupado vacant
desocupar (v) to vacate
desodorante deodorant
desolladura excoriation
desorden chaos, clutter, muddle, turmoil
desordenar (v) to mess
desorganizar (v) to disorganize
despacho desk, study
despacho de aduana customs clearance
despacho de billetes ticket office
despacio slow
despectivo derogatory
despedida farewell
despedir (v) to dismiss
despegue takeoff
despejar (v) to clear
despensa pantry
desperdicios refuse
despertador alarm clock
despertar (v) to arouse, awake, rouse
despertar (el) awakening
despiadado ruthless

despilfarro extravagance
despiste mishap
desplazar (v) to displace
desplegar (v) to unfold
despojar (v) to divest
despojarse (v) to shed
desposeer (v) to divest
desposeimiento divestiture
déspota despot
despreciar (v) to despise
desprecio contempt, scorn, sneer
después after, thereafter
después de subsequently
destacado prominent
destacar (v) to highlight
destellar (v) flash
destello flash
destilar (v) to distil, exude
destinar (v) to destine
destinatario addressee, consignee, recipient
destino fate
destornillador screwdriver
destornillar (v) to unscrew
destreza prowess, skill
destrozado shattered, stricken
destrozador disruptive
destrozar (v) to maul, shatter
destrozo ravage
destrucción destruction
destruido wrecked
destruir (v) to blast, destroy, smash, vandalize, wipe out
desunir (v) to separate
desvalido underdog, helpless
desvalorar (v) to depreciate
desván attic, loft
desvanecerse to fade, fade
desvanecimiento dizziness
desvariar (v) to rave
desventaja disadvantage, handicap, drawback

desvergonzado shameless

desviar (v) to avert, deviate, reroute

desviar bruscamente to swerve, swerve

desviarse (v) to sheer, turn off, sheer

desvío bypass, detour

detallar (v) to detail, itemize

detalle (venta) retail

detalles particulars

detallista dealer, retailer

detallista al menor retailer

detectar (v) to detect

detective detective

detención arrest, roundup

detención preventiva preventive arrest

detener (v) to detain, stem, stop

detenerse (v) to rein, stop

detergente detergent

deteriorar (v) to deteriorate, perish, spoil

deteriorarse (v) to decay

determinar (v) to determine, define

detestable obnoxious, detestable

detestar (v) to detest

detonar (v) to detonate

detrás behind, rear

detrimento detriment

deuda debt

deuda a largo plazo long-term debt

deuda existente outstanding debt

deuda externa external debt

deudas a largo plazo long-term liabilities

deudas acumuladas accrued liabilities

deudas imprevistas contingent liabilities

deudor debtor

deudor sin garantía unsecured debtor

devaluación devaluation

devaluación de moneda currency devaluation

devanar (v) to wind, spin, reel

devastar (v) to devastate

devolución drawback, devolution, rejection, refund, return

devolución de impuestos investment tax credit, tax refund

devolución de inversiones investment tax credit

devolver (v) to return, send back, refund, repay

devorar (v) to devour, eat up, prey

día day

día de paga payday

día del juicio final doomsday

día laborable weekday

día laboral workday

diabetes diabetes

diabético diabetic

diablo devil

diadema tiara

diafonía cross talk

diafragma diaphragm

diagnosticar (v) to diagnose

diagnóstico diagnosis, diagnostic

diagonal bias, diagonal

diagrama diagram

diagrama de flujo flowchart

dialéctico dialect

diálogo dialog

diamante diamond

diámetro diameter

diapositivas slide projector

diario daily

diarrea diarrhea

días laborales working days

dibujo drawing

dibujo animado cartoon
diccionario dictionary
diciembre December
dictador dictator
dictar (v) to dictate, suggest
dicho said, saying
diecinueve nineteen
dieciocho eighteen
dieciséis sixteen
diecisiete seventeen
diente tooth
dientes teeth
diesel diesel
diestro dextrous, slick
dieta diet
diez ten
difamación defamation
difamador libeler, slanderer, defamer
difamante libelous
difamatorio defamatory
diferencia difference
diferencial differential
diferenciar (v) to differentiate
diferente different, dissimilar
diferir (v) to defer, postpone
difícil difficult
dificultad difficulty
difunto deceased
difusión spread, diffusion
digerir (v) to digest
digestión digestion
digital digital
dígito digit
dignarse (v) to condescend to
dignidad dignity
digno de confianza reliable
dilación delay
dilapidación dilapidation
dilapidar (v) to dilapidate, squander
dilatar (v) to expand, enlarge, delay, postpone

dilatorio dilatory
dilema dilemma, quandary
diligente diligent
diluvio flood, deluge
dimensión dimension
diminuto small, tiny, bantam
dimisión resignation
dimitir (v) to quit, relinquish, resign
dinámico dynamic
dinamita dynamite
dinero money
dinero falso counterfeit money
diodo diode
Dios God
dióxido dioxide
diploma diploma
diplomacia diplomacy
diplomático diplomat
diptongo diphthong
diputado congressman, representative
dique dam
dirección direction, management, steering
dirección (postal) address
dirección absoluta absolute address
dirección de base base address
dirección única one-way
directamente directly, firsthand
directivo managerial
directivos del banco bank officials
directo forthright, straight
director boss, director, executive, manager, warden
directorio directory
dirigido directed
dirigir (v) to aim, conduct, direct, run, steer, guide
dirigir la palabra (v) to address
disciplina discipline

discípulo disciple
disco disk, record
disco compacto ROM CD ROM
disco de una cara single-sided disk
disco duro hard drive
disco flexible floppy disk
disco magnético magnetic disk
discordia discord
discreción tact, discretion
discrepancia disagreement, discrepancy
discrepar (v) to differ, disagree
discretamente unobtrusive
discreto discrete
discriminación discrimination
discriminar (v) to discriminate
discriminatorio discriminatory
disculpa apology, excuse
disculpar (v) to excuse, forgive, apologize
discurso speech
discusión argument, debate, discussion
discutible controversial, questionable, debatable, arguable
discutir (v) to argue, discuss
disecar (v) to dissect
disentería dysentery
disentir (v) to disagree, dissent
diseñar (v) to design
diseño design
diseño funcional functional design
diseño por ordenador computer aided design
disfrazar (v) to disguise
disfrutar (v) to enjoy
disfrute enjoyment
disgustar (v) to annoy, upset, shock
disgusto chagrin

disidencia dissent
disidente dissident
disimulado concealed
disipar (v) to dispel
dislocación displacement, dislocation, sprain
dislocar (v) to dislocate
disminución del capital capital depletion, depletion
disminuido handicapped, impaired
disminuir (v) to decrease, diminish, lessen
disociar (v) to dissociate
disolución breakup, dissolution
disolver (v) to dissolve
disparar (v) to shoot, Mex.: to waste money
disparate nonsense; Arg., Uru.: exorbitant price
disparidad disparity
dispensar (v) to dispense
dispepsia dyspepsia
dispersar (v) to disperse, scatter
dispersión scattering, dispersion
disponer (v) to arrange, dispose
disponibilidad availability
disponibilidad monetaria monetary supply
disponibilidades en efectivo cash holdings
disponible available, vacancy
disposición disposition, arrangement
disposición de convocatoria call provision
dispositivo device
dispositivo de entrada y salida input-output device
dispositivos de entrada y salida I/O devices
dispuesto a prone

disputa argument, dispute, contest, quarrel
disputar to dispute, argue, bicker
distancia distance, mileage
distante remote
distensión strain
distinguir (v) to distinguish, single out
distinto different, distinct, separate
distorsión distortion
distorsión de retardo delay distortion
distraer (v) to distract, amuse
distribución distribution, handout
distribuidor distributor
distribuir (v) to distribute
distrito district, zone, constituency, precinct
distrito postal zip code
distrofia muscular muscular dystrophy
disturbio riot, disturbance
disuadir (v) to discourage, dissuade, deter
disuasión discouragement
diurético diuretic
divagar (v) to ramble, wander
divergencia divergence
diversificación diversification
diversificar (v) to diversify
diversión amusement, fun
diverso diverse, other, various
divertido amusing, funny
divertir (v) to amuse, divert, entertain
dividendo dividend
dividendo en acciones stock dividend
dividendos de capital capital dividends

dividido split
dividir (v) to divide, split, cut, share
divino divine
divisa foreign currency
divisar (v) to see, perceive, sight
divisas currency
división division, split
divorciada divorcee
divorcio divorce
divulgar (v) to spread, disclose, circulate
doblado bent, double, folded
doblaje dubbing (of film)
doblar (v) to double, fold, bend, dub (movies)
doble double, twofold, duplex
doce twelve
docena dozen
doctor doctor
doctor en derecho doctor of law
documentación documentation
documentación impresa hard copy
documental documentary
documentario documentary
documento document, note, record
documentos contra pago documents against payment
documentos de envío shipping documents
documentos de título muniments
documentos originarios source documents
documentos por pagar notes payable
dogma dogma
dogmático dogmatic
dólar dollar

dólar de compensación offset dollar

dólar USA buck

doler (v) to hurt, pain, ache, grieve, distress

dolor pain, ache, agony, sorrow

dolor de cabeza headache

dolor de dientes toothache

dolor de espalda backache

dolor de estómago stomachache

dolor de hambre hunger pain

dolor de oído earache

dolorido sore, tender

dolorosísimo excruciating

doloroso painful, sore

domar (v) to tame

domesticado tame

domesticar (v) to tame

doméstico domestic

domicilio home, domicile

dominante dominant, possessive

dominar (v) to dominate, subject

domingo Sunday, Sabbath

dominio reign, power, dominion

dominio absoluto freehold

dominó domino

donación donation

donante donor

donante de sangre blood donor

donar (v) to donate

donatario donee

donativo donation

donde where

dondequiera que wherever

dorado golden

dormido asleep, dormant

dormir (v) to sleep, Arg., Uru. coll.: to knock someone unconscious

dormitar (v) to doze, snooze, drowse

dormitorio bedroom

dos two

dos veces twice

dotación endowment, staff

dotar (v) to endow, provide

dote dowry, endowment

dragaminas minesweeper

drama drama

dramatizar (v) to dramatize

drenar (v) to drain

dril de algodón denim

droga drug, medicine

drogadicto junkie

drogar (v) to drug, dope

droguería drugstore

ducha shower

duchar (v) to shower

duda razonable reasonable doubt, rational doubt

dudar (v) to doubt, hesitate

dudar de (v) to question

dudoso doubtful, hesitant, questionable

dueño owner, landlord

dueño colindante abutter

dulce candy, cookie, sweet

dulzura sweetness

dumping (venta bajo coste) dumping

duodécimo twelfth

duodeno duodenum

duplicado duplicate

duplicar (v) to duplicate

durabilidad durability

duración duration

duradero durable, lasting

durante during

durar (v) to last

dureza hardness, toughness

duro hard, tough, stern

E

eccema eczema
echar (v) to throw
echar raíces (v) to root
eco echo
ecología ecology
ecológico ecological
economía economics, economy, thrift
económico inexpensive, saving, thrifty
economista economist
ecuación equation
ecuación contable accounting equation
Ecuador Ecuador, equator
ecuatorial equatorial
ecuatoriano Ecuadorian
eczema eczema
edad age
edema edema
edición edition
edicto edict, proclamation
edificio building
editar (v) to edit
editor editor, publisher
editor de textos text editor
editor personal desktop publishing
educación education
educado educated
educar (v) to educate
educativo instructive
efectivamente actually
efectivo actual, cash, cash in hand, effective, vested
efectivo en bancos cash in bank
efectivo en caja cash on hand

efecto a la vista sight draft
efecto bancario banker's draft, bank draft, bank bill
efecto comercial commercial draft
efecto documentario documentary bill
efecto impagado dishonored bill, dishonored draft
efecto secundario side effect
efectos pendientes de pago past due bills, overdue bills
efectos pignorados pawned bills
efectos sonoros sound effects
efectuado executed
efectuar (v) to effect
efectuar una audiencia (v) to hold a hearing
eficacia force
eficiente efficient
efímero short-lived
efusivamente warmly
egipcio Egyptian
Egipto Egypt
egocéntrico egocentric, self-centered
egoísmo selfishness
egoísta egoist, selfish
eje axis, axle
ejecución execution, levy, performance
ejecución de hipoteca foreclosure
ejecución de un pedido execution of an order
ejecución forzosa strict foreclosure

ejecutar (v) to execute

ejecutivo executive, official, officer

ejecutorio executory

ejemplo example, instance

ejercer (v) to exercise, practice

ejercicio exercise, fiscal year, practice

ejercicio acrobático stunt

ejercicios exercises

ejército army

el the

él he, him, it

el abajo firmante undersigned

el Cairo Cairo

el más alto uppermost

el más viejo eldest

el mayor greatest

él mismo himself

el yo ego

elaborar (v) to elaborate

elástico elastic, resilient

elección election

electricidad electricity

electricista electrician

eléctrico electirc

electrificar (v) to electrify

electrocardiógrafo electrocardiograph

electrodiálisis electrodialysis

electrodo electrode

electroencefalógrafo electroencephalograph

electrónica electronics

elefante elephant

elegancia elegance

elegante chic, elegant, posh, smart, tasteful, stylish

elegibilidad eligibility

elegible eligible

elegir (v) to choose, elect

elemental elemental

elemento element

elemento de arranque start element

elenco de estrellas all-star

elevado towering, elevated

elevar (v) to elevate, pump

eliminación elimination

eliminado stricken

eliminar (v) to eliminate, remove

élite elite

elocuencia eloquence

elocuente eloquent

elogiar (v) to eulogize, praise

eludir (v) to elude, shirk

ella she

ella misma herself

ello mismo itself

ellos they

ellos mismos themselves

emancipación emancipation

emancipado emancipated

embajada embassy

embajador ambassador

embalaje packaging, packing, package

embarazada pregnant

embarazo pregnancy

embarazoso embarrassing

embarcadero marina

embargado lienee

embargador lienor

embargar (v) to distrain, seize

embargo attachment, distraint, embargo, seizure

embargo preventivo lien

embarque shipment, shipping

embelesado spellbound

emblema emblem

embolia embolism

emboscada ambush

embotellamiento traffic jam

embriagado intoxicated

embriaguez intoxication

embrión embryo
embromar (v) to tease; Arg., Chile, P.R., Uru.: to harm, damage
emergencia emergency
emigración emigration
emigrante emigrant
emigrar (v) to emigrate, trek
eminente prominent
emisión emission, issue, release
emisión de acciones ordinarias issuance of common stock
emisión de acciones preferentes issuance of preferred stock
emisión de bonos bond issue
emisión issue, release
emisor emitter, sender
emisor perturbador jammer
emitir (v) to issue, release, to beam
emoción emotion, excitement, thrill
emocional emotional
emocionante thrilling
emocionar (v) to thrill
emolumento emolument
emolumentos perquisites
empalmar (v) to splice
empañar (v) to blur
empapado soggy
empapar (v) to saturate, soak
empaquetar (v) to pack, Amer.: to dress up
empaste filling
empatar (v) to tie
empate tie
empatía empathy
empeñar (v) to pawn, pledge
empeño pawn, pledge; Arg., Mex., Uru.: pawnshop
empeorar (v) to worsen
empezar (v) to begin, commence, start

empírico empirical
empleado clerk, employee
empleado de banco bank clerk
empleador employer
empleados de banca bank clerical staff
emplear (v) to employ, hire, use
empleo employment
empobrecer (v) to impoverish
emprendedor entrepreneur, enterprising
emprender (v) to undertake
empresa company, corporation, enterprise, firm, undertaking, venture
empresa dependiente subsidiary
empresa filial subsidiary
empresa matriz parent company
empresa no lucrativa non-profit organization
empresas filiales subsidiary companies
empréstito amortizable amortizable loan, reedemable loan
empréstito con garantía secured loan
empréstito de obligaciones convertible loan
empréstito internacional international loan
empréstito no amortizable non-amortizable loan
empréstito reembolsable al vencimiento straight loan
empujar (v) to barge, hustle, jog, poke, prod, push, roll, thrust
empuje push, thrust
empujón shove
emulación de terminal terminal emulation
en at, in, on, upon

en alguna parte someplace, somewhere
en alto aloft
en atención a in view of
en bastardilla italic
en blanco blank
en breve shortly
en buen estado operational
en conjunto overall
en conserva preserved
en cuanto a regarding
en depósito on consignment, escrow
en descubierto overdraft
en el caso de que supposing
en el futuro hereafter
en este respecto therein
en esto herein
en frente opposite
en garantía bonded
en los dieces teens
en medio in between
en ninguna parte nowhere
en otra parte elsewhere
en propio interés self-interest
en seguida forthwith, straight-away, hereupon
en su mayor parte mostly
en tierra ashore
en todas partes anywhere, everywhere
en total altogether
en vez instead
en vigor operative
en voz alta aloud, loudly
enajenable alienable
enajenación condemnation
enamorar locamente (v) to infatuate
enanismo dwarfism
enano midget
encabezamiento header, heading
encabezar (v) to head

encantador charming, ravishing
encantar (v) to captivate, charm, ravish
encanto charm, glamour, spell
encarcelación imprisonment
encarcelamiento incarceration, imprisonment
encarcelar (v) to imprison
encargar (v) to entrust
encargo commission
encarnar (v) to embody
encefalitis encephalitis
encendedor lighter
encender (v) to ignite, kindle, light
encerrar (v) to confine, encase, impound, shut
encía gum
encías gums
enciclopedia encylopedia
encierro confinement
encima over, upon
encoger (v) to contract, shrink
encogerse de miedo cower
encontrar (v) to find, meet, track
encuadernación binding
encubridor accessory
encubrimiento concealment
encuentro clash, find, meeting
encuesta poll
enchufar (v) to plug
enchufe jack, plug, socket
enchufe socket
enchufe de pared wall socket
enderezar (v) to straighten, unbend
endocardio endocardium
endocrina endocrine
endosado endorsee
endosador endorser
endosante endorser
endosar (v) to endorse

endoso endorsement
endoso condicional conditional endorsement
endulzar (v) to sweeten
endurecer to harden, stiffen, toughen
enema enema
enemigo enemy, foe
enemistad feud
enemistar to antagonize
enérgico energetic, strenuous
enésimo umpteenth
enfadado angry
enfadar (v) to upset
enfados tantrums
enfermedad disease, illness, sickness
enfermedad de Hodgkin Hodgkin's disease
enfermedad de Parkinson Parkinson's disease
enfermera nurse
enfermería sickroom
enfermero nurse
enfermizo sickly
enfermo diseased, ill, sick, unhealthy
enfermo interno inpatient
enfriar (v) to chill
enfurecer (v) to enrage, infuriate, madden
enfurecido infuriate
engañar (v) to bluff, beguile, cheat, delude, dupe, fool, mislead, trick
engancharse to hook
engaño cheating, deceit, double-cross, trick
engañoso fallacious, misleading
engatusar (v) to coax
engomar (v) to paste
engordar (v) to fatten
engorroso cumbersome

engrosar (v) to thicken
engullir (v) to swallow
enigmático puzzling
enjambre swarm
enjuagar (v) to rinse, wipe
enlace link, liaison, union, tie-up
enlazar (v) to link, tie
enmarañar (v) to tangle
enmienda amendment
ennegrecer (v) to blacken
enojado angry
enorme huge
enredar (v) to snarl, tangle
enredo mess up, tangle
enriquecer (v) to enrich
enriquecimiento enrichment
enrolar (v) to wind
ensalada salad
ensalada de col coleslaw
ensamblador assembler
ensanchar (v) to broaden
ensayar (v) to rehearse
ensayo rehearsal, test
enseñanza schooling, teaching, tuition
enseñar (v) to teach
ensuciar (v) to litter, soil
entablar (v) to board
entablar pleito (v) to bring a lawsuit
entender (v) to understand
entendido knowledgeable
enterado aware, Chile: arrogant
enteramente entirely
enteritis enteritis
entero complete, whole
enterrar (v) to bury
entidad entity
entidad contable accounting entity
entierro burial
entonces then

entrada admission, cue, entry, entrance, influx, input
entrada (en los libros) posting
entrar (v) to enter
entrar datos (v) to load
entrar sin derecho (v) to trespass
entre amid, among, between, midst
entre semana midweek
entreabierto ajar
entrega delivery
entrega de mercancías delivery of goods
entregar (v) to deliver, render
entrelazado interlace
entrenador coach, trainer
entrenar (v) to train
entrevista interview
entristecer (v) to sadden
entrometerse (v) to meddle
entusiasmo enthusiasm, zeal, ardor
entusiasta enthusiastic, wholehearted
enumerar (v) to enumerate
envase packaging, wrapping
envejecido aged
envenenamiento food poisoning, poisoning
envergadura scope
enviado envoy
enviar (v) to despatch, dispatch, remit, send, ship
enviar por correo (v) to mail
envidiable enviable
envidioso envious
envío remittance, shipment, shipping
envío al cobro collection remittance
envío por grupaje consolidated shipment

envío urgente special delivery
envoltura casing, wrapping
envoltura de texto word wrap
envolver (v) to wind, wrap
envuelto involved
enyesadura cast
enzimas enzymes
epidermis epidermis
epígrafe caption
epilepsia epilepsy
epiléptico epileptic
episodio episode
época season, time
equidad equity
equidad ordinaria equity
equilibrar (v) to poise
equilibrio poise
equipaje luggage
equipar (v) to equip
equipo team
equipo auxiliar ancillary equipment, equipment, outfit
equipo lógico software
equipos productivos equipment
equitación riding
equitativo equitable
equivalencia equivalence, par
equivalente equivalent, tantamount, worth
equivocación error, mistake
equivocado mistaken, wrong, misguided
equivocarse (v) to err
erección erection
erigir (v) to rear, erect
eritema erythema
erosión erosion
erótico erotic
errar (v) to err, miss
erróneo erroneous
error error, lapse, miss
error grande blunder
eructar (v) to belch

eructo belch
erudición scholarship
erudito erudite
erupción outbreak, rash
erupción dérmica pox
esbelto slim
esbozar (v) to sketch
escala scale
escaldadura scald
escalera ladder, stairway
escalfado poached
escalfar (v) to poach
escalo burglary, housebreaking
escalón stair
escalpelo scalpel
escandalizar (v) to scandalize
escándalo scandal, scene
escandaloso flagrant, scandalous, shocking
escapar (v) to escape
escapatoria loophole
escaramuza skirmish
escarlatina scarlatina
escarpado steep
escasez scarcity, shortage
escaso scanty, scarce, scant
escena scene
escenario stage
escéptico cynical
esclarecimiento clarification
esclavitud bondage, slavery
esclavo slave
esclerosis sclerosis
esclerosis múltiple multiple sclerosis
escoba broom
escocer (v) to sting
escoger to choose, select
escolar scholar
escolástico school, scholastic
escollo pitfall
escombros debris, rubble
esconder (v) to hide, secrete

escoria scum
escribir (v) to write
escribir con guión to hyphenate
escribir a máquina to type
escrito written
escrito (religioso) scripture
escritor writer
escritorio bureau, desk, writing desk
escritura deed, script, writ, writing, indenture
escritura a mano handwriting
escritura de compraventa deed of sale
escritura de constitución certificate of incorporation
escritura de garantía deed of covenant
escritura de traspaso deed of indenture
escritura de venta bill of sale
escroto scrotum
escrúpulo scruple
escrupuloso scrupulous
escrutinio scrutiny
escuadrón squadron
escuálido squalid
escuchar (v) to listen
escudo shield
escudriñar (v) to scrutinize
escuela school
escuela de conducir driving school
escuela de derecho law school
escuela primaria elementary school
escultor sculptor
escultura sculpture
escupida spit
escupir (v) to bark, spit
ese that
esencia nature

esencial essential, vital
esencialmente essentially
esfera sphere
esférico spherical
esforzarse (v) to endeavor, strive, struggle
esfuerzo effort, endeavor
esfuerzo strain
esguince sprain
eslinga sling
esmalte enamel
esófago esophagus, gullet
esos those
esotérico esoteric
espacio space
espacioso spacious
espada sword
espalda shoulder
España Spain
español Spaniard, Spanish
espantapájaros scarecrow
espantoso frightening
esparcir (v) to scatter
espárrago asparagus
espasmo spasm
espasmódico spastic
espátula spatula
especia spice
especial special, particular
especialidad speciality
especialista consultant, specialist
especialista médico practitioner
especializado skilled
especializarse (v) to major, specialize
especificación specification
especificaciones specifications
especificaciones técnicas data sheet
especificar (v) to specify, stipulate
específico specific

espectacular pageantry, spectacular
espectáculo show
espectador bystander, onlooker, spectator, viewer
espectro spectrum
espectroscopio spectroscope
especulación speculation
especular (v) to speculate
especulativo speculative
espejismo mirage
espejo mirror
espeluznante bloodcurdling
espera abeyance, respite, wait
esperado prospective
esperanza hope
esperanzado hopeful
esperar (v) to expect, hope, wait
esperma sperm
espermatozoide spermatozoid
espeso bushy, dense, thick
espesor thickness
espía spy
espiar (v) to spy
espina spine
espina de pez fishbone
espina dorsal backbone
espinaca spinach
espinal spinal
espinazo backbone, spine
espinilla shin bone, shin
espinoso thorny
espionaje espionage, spying
espiración expiration
espiral coil, spiral
espirar (v) to exhale
espíritu esprit, spirit
espiritual spiritual
esplendor splendor
esponja sponge
espontáneo spontaneous
espora spore

esporádico sporadic
esposa spouse, wife
esposas handcuffs
espuma foam, scum, surf
esputo sputum
esqueleto skeleton
esquema chart
esquí acuático water ski
esquiador skier
esquiar (v) to ski
esquilar (v) to shear
esquimal Eskimo
esquina coner
esquivar (v) to shun, sidestep, shirk
esquivo elusive
esquizofrenia schizophrenia
esquizofrénico schizophrenic
esta noche tonight
estabilidad steadiness, stability
estabilizador stabilizer
estabilizar (v) to stabilize
estable secure, stable
establecer (v) to establish, institute
establecerse (v) to naturalize
establecimiento establishment, premises
establo stall
estación season, station
estación de conmutación switching station
estacional seasonal
estacionamiento parking
estacionario stationary
estadio stadium
estadística statistic
estadísticas statistics
estado status, state
estado civil civil status
estado de ánimo morale
estado de cuenta statement, statement of account

estado financiero financial statement
estados financieros consolidados consolidated financial statements
estado legal legal status, status
Estados Unidos United States
estafa cheating, swindle
estafador crook, swindler
estafar (v) to bilk, defraud, twist
estallar (v) to pop
estallido blast, snap
estampado stamped
estampar (v) to stamp
estampida stampede
estancado stagnant
estancamiento stagnation
estancarse (v) to stagnate
estancia stay
estanque pond; Amer.: pillar (of a house)
estantc shelf, stack
estanterías shelving
estaño tin
estar a dieta (v) to diet
estar al revés (v) to be upside down
estar acorde a (v) to conform
estar de acuerdo (v) to agree, consent
estar dormido (v) to sleep
estar furioso (v) to rage
estar inmóvil (v) to hover
estar malhumorado (v) to sulk
estar situado (v) to stand, be located
estar sujeto a (v) to subject to
estático static
estatuario statutory
estatura stature
estatuto statute
estatutos bylaws
este this

estela trail
estereofónico stereo
estereotipo stereotype
estéril barren, infertile, sterile
esterilidad infertility, sterility
esterilización sterilization
esterilizador sterilizer
esterilizar (v) to sterilize
esternón sternum
esteroides steroids
estertor stertor
estilo style
estimar (v) to prize, rate
estimulante stimulating, stimulant
estimular (v) to stimulate
estímulo incentive, stimulus
estipulación stipulation
estipular (v) to stipulate
estirado tense
estirar (v) to stretch, to strain, to tug, tighten; Arg., Peru: to kill
estirón pull, tug
estómago stomach
estorbar (v) to curb, to hinder
estorbo curb, hindrance
estornudar (v) to sneeze
estornudo sneeze
estos these
estrabismo squint, strabismus
estrado stage
estrago havoc, ravage
estrangulación strangulation
estrangulador strangler
estrangular (v) to strangle, throttle
estrategia strategy
estratégico strategic
estrato stratum
estrechamente narrowly
estrechar (v) to constrict
estrecho narrow, strait
estrella star

estrellar (v) to crash
estremecerse (v) to quake
estremecimiento shudder
estreno inauguration, premiere
estreñimiento constipation
estrépito blare
estricto strict
estridente raucous, strident
estrofa stanza, verse
estrógeno estrogen
estrógenos estrogens
estropear (v) to spoil
estructura scaffold, structure
estructural structural
estruendo din
estrujar (v) to squeeze
estuche case, casket
estudiante learner, student
estudiar (v) to learn, study
estudio learning, survey, studio, study
estudio de mercado market survey, market research
estudio de viabilidad feasibility study
estudioso studious
estufa stove
estupefacto speechless
estupendo super
estupidez silliness
estúpido dumb, foolish, silly, stupid
etcétera etcetera
eternidad eternity
eterno everlasting, eternal, timeless
ética ethics
ética deportiva sportsmanship
ética profesional professional ethics
ético ethical
etimología etymology
etiqueta etiquette, label, tag

étnico ethnic
eufemismo euphemism
euforia exuberance
eufórico euphoric
eurodólar eurodollar
Europa Europe
europeo European
eutanasia euthanasia
evacuación evacuation
evacuar (v) to evacuate
evadir (v) to evade, dodge
evaluación evaluation
evaluar (v) to evaluate, price
evangelio gospel
evangelista evangelist, Mex.:
  public clerk
evaporación evaporation
evaporar (v) to evaporate
evasión evasion
evasor evader
evento event
eventual contingent
eventualidades contingencies
evidencia evidence
evidencia legal legal evidence
evidencia negativa negative evidence
evidencia por referencia
  hearsay evidence
evidencia real real evidence
evidencia verbal oral evidence
evidente noticeable, obvious
evitación avoidance
evitar (v) to avoid, to shun
evitar contacto (v) to bypass
evolución evolution
exacción levy
exacerbar (v) to exacerbate
exactamente exactly
exactitud accuracy, exactitude,
  reliability
exacto accurate, exact, precise,
  reliable

exageración exaggeration
exagerado exaggerated
exagerar (v) to exaggerate
examen examination, quiz
examinador examiner
examinar (v) to examine,
  search, review, scan
exasperante infuriating
exasperar (v) to exasperate
excavar (v) to excavate
excedente surplus
exceder (v) to exceed, outdo,
  outnumber, surpass
excelencia excellence
excelente excellent
excéntrico eccentric
excepción exception
excepcional exceptional, outstanding
excepto except, save
excesivo exceeding, excessive
exceso excess, redundancy
exceso de capacidad overflow
exceso de velocidad speeding
excitable temperamental
excitar (v) to excite, rouse
exclamación exclamation
exclamar (v) to ejaculate, exclaim
excluir (v) to bar, exclude, preclude
excluir de la abogacía (v) to
  disbar
exclusión exclusion, foreclosure
exclusiones exclusions
exclusivo exclusive, sole
excreción excretion
excremento excrement
excrementos feces
exculpar (v) to exonerate
excursión jaunt, ramble, sightseeing, spree, tour, trip
excusa excuse

exención exemption
exención personal personal exemption
exento exempt
exhibición display, fair
exhibicionismo exhibitionism
exhibir (v) to exhibit
exhortación exhortation
exigente exigent, demanding
exigible demandable, exigible, leviable
exigir (v) to want
exiliar (v) to exile
existencias inventory, supply, stock
existencias iniciales beginning inventory
éxito success, triumph
éxodo exodus
exonerar (v) to exonerate
expansible expandable
expansionista expansionist
expatriado expatriate
expectación expectation
expedidor shipper
expediente file, record
experiencia experience, knowhow
experimentar (v) to undergo
experimento experiment
experto adept, connoisseur, expert
expirar (v) to expire
explicación explanation
explicar (v) to explain
explicativo explanatory
explícito explicit
exploración exploration
explorador scanner, scout
explorar (v) to explore, prospect
explosión bang, blow-up, burst, explosion, outburst
explotar (v) to bang, explode
exponente exponent

exponer (v) to expose
exportación export, exporting
exportador exporter
exposición exposition, exhibit, exhibition
expósito foundling
expositor exhibitor
expresar (v) to word
expresión expression
expresivo expressive
expreso express
expropiación expropriation
expropiar (v) to expropriate
expuesto exposed
expulsar (v) to eject
expulsión ejection, expulsion, removal
éxtasis ecstasy, rapture
extender (v) to extend, spread, stretch
extendido extended, widespread
extensamente broadly
extensible expanding
extensión extension, range, reach, spread, stretch
extenso comprehensive, extensive, wide
exterior external, outer, outward
exterminar (v) to exterminate
extinción extinction
extinguir (v) to extinguish
extintor fire extinguisher
extirpación por raspadura erasion
extorsión extortion, racketeering, racket
extorsionador racketeer
extorsionar (v) to extort
extracto excerpt, extract
extractos de cuenta extracts of account, bank statement
extradición extradition
extrajurídico extralegal

extranjero alien, foreign, overseas
extraño alien, bizarre, weird
extraoficial unofficial
extraordinario extraordinary
extravagante extravagant
extraviado stray

extraviar (v) to mislay
extraviarse (v) to stray
extremidad extremity, tip
extremidades extremities
extremista extremist
extremo extreme
extrovertido extrovert

F

fábrica factory, mill
fábrica de cerveza brewery
fabricación manufacture
fabricación en serie mass production
fabricante manufacturer
fabricar (v) to manufacture
fabricar a la medida (v) to customize
fabuloso fabulous
facción faction
facial facial
fácil easy
fácil de usar user-friendly
facilidad ease
facsímil facsimile, fax machine
factible achieveable, feasible,
practicable
factor factor
factoring factoring
factura bill, invoice
factura comercial commercial
invoice
factura consular consular invoice
factura de venta sale invoice
factura pro-forma pro-forma
invoice
facturación billing
facturar (v) to bill, charge
facultad faculty
faena chore, Guat.: overtime

Fahrenheit Fahrenheit
faja sash
fajo de billetes wad
falanges phalanges
falda lap, skirt
faldilla flap
fallar (v) to bumble
fallecimiento decease
fallo award, verdict, dictum,
finding, failure, Chile: weak, faint
fallo concesión award
fallo definitivo peremptory rule
falsedad falsehood, treachery
falsificación counterfeit, forgery,
falsification
falsificado counterfeit
falsificador counterfeiter
falsificar (v) to falsify, forge,
tamper
falso bogus, dishonest, false,
phony, sham, two-faced, treacherous, untrue, fake
falta absence, default, want,
fault
falta de evidencia lack of evidence
falta de respeto disrespect
fama fame, reputation, renown
familia family
familiar familiar, kin, relative
famoso famous, famed, renowned

fanático bigot, fanatic
fanfarria fanfare
fanfarrón boaster
fangoso muddy
fantasía fancy, fantasy
fantasma ghost, phantom
fantástico fantastic
fardo bundle
faringe pharynx
farmacéutico dispenser, pharmaceutical, pharmacist
farmacia drugstore, pharmacy
farmacopea prescription book
faro beacon, lighthouse
faro delantero headlight
farol lamp post
fascinante fascinating
fascinar (v) to entrance
fase phase
fastidiar (v) to irk
fastidioso troublesome
fatal fatal
fatalidad doom, fatality
fatiga fatigue
fatigar (v) to tire
fauna wildlife
favor favor
favorable auspicious, favorable
favorecer (v) to befriend, favor,
  prosper
favorecido favored
favorito favorite
fe faith
fealdad ugliness
febrero February
febril feverish, hectic
fecha date
fecha atrasada backdate
fecha de cierre closing date
fecha de emisión date of issue
fecha de entrega delivery date
fecha de vencimiento date of
  maturity, due date, maturity date

fecha tope deadline
fecundidad fecundity
federal federal
felicidad bliss, happiness
felicitación Christmas card
felicitaciones congratulations
felicitar (v) to congratulate
feligrés parishioner
felino feline
feliz happy, merry
felpa plush
femenino feminine, womanly
feminismo feminism
feminista feminist
fémur femur
fenomenal phenomenal
fenómeno phenomenon
feo ugly
feria fair; C.R., Salv.: tip; Mex.:
  change
feria de muestras fair trade
fermentar (v) to ferment
fermento ferment
feroz ferocious, savage, fierce
ferretería hardware
ferrocarril railway, railroad
fértil fertile
fertilidad fertility
fertilizante fertilizer
fervor fervor
festival festival
feto fetus
feudal feudal
feudo feud, fief
fez stool
fiabilidad reliability
fiador guarantor
fiambre cold cuts
fianza bail, bond, surety
fianza de embargo attachment
  bond
fianza especial special bail
fianza ordinaria common bail

fianza sin valor   straw bail
fiarse de (v)   to confide
fiasco   fiasco
fibra de vidrio   fiberglass
fibra   fiber, thread
fibras ópticas   fiber optics
fibrosis   fibrosis
fíbula   fibula
ficción   fiction
ficticio   fictitious
ficha   card, token
fichero   card, file
fichero de cintas   magnetic tape
   file
fichero de datos   data file
fideicomisario   trust, trustee
fidelidad   fidelity
fiduciario   fiduciary
fiebre   fever
fiebre amarilla   yellow fever
fiebre de Malta   Malta fever
fiebre del heno   hay fever
fiebre remitente   remittent fever
fiebre tifoidea   typhoid fever
fiel   trusty
fiesta   holiday, party
**FIFO (primero-dentro/primero-
   fuera)**   first-in, first-out (FIFO)
figura   figure
figurar (v)   to figure
figurilla   statue
fijación   fixation
fijado   vested
fijamente   steadily
fijar (v)   to fix, set
fijar fecha de juicio (v)   to set
   for trial
fijarse en (v)   to mind
fijo   fixed, steady
fila   rank, row, tier
filamento   filament
filantrópico   philanthropic
filatélico   philatelic

filatelista   stamp collector
filete   steak
filial   affiliated
filmar (v)   to film
filo   edge
filosofía   philosophy
filósofo   philosopher
filtración   seepage
filtrar (v)   to percolate
filtro   strainer
fimosis   phimosis
fin   end
fin de semana   weekend
final   bottom, eventual, finish, final, terminal, ultimate
finalizar (v)   to exit
finalmente   eventually, finally
financiación   financing
financiar (v)   to finance
financiero   financial, financier
finanzas   finance
finca   estate
fingido   assumed
fingir (v)   to pretend
finiquito   quittance
fino   dainty, fine, genteel, subtle
finura   finesse, nicety
firma   firm, signature
firma de registro   specimen signature
firma y sello   hand and seal
firmante   signer
firmar (v)   to sign
firme   adamant, firm, sound, stable, steadfast, single-minded,
   steady
firmemente   steadily
firmeza   firmness, steadiness
fiscal   fiscal, prosecutor; Bol.,
   Peru: church warden
fiscal general   attorney general
fiscal público   district attorney
fisgón   snoop

físico physical
fisiológico physiological
fisioterapia physiotherapy
fisura fissure
flagrante blatant, flagrant
flatulencia flatulence
flebitis phlebitis
flecha arrow
flete freight
flete marítimo ocean freight
flexibilidad flexibility
flexible flexible, pliable, soft, supple
flip-flop flip-flop
flirt flirt
flirtear (v) to flirt
flirteo flirtation
flojo lax, slack, weak
flor bloom, flower
floración bloom
florecer (v) to flourish
florero vase
florista florist
floristería flower shop
flota mercante merchant fleet
flotar (v) to float
fluctuación float, fluctuation
fluidez fluency
fluido fluent, flowing
fluir (v) to flow, stream
fluorescente fluorescent
fluoruro fluoride
fobia phobia
foca seal
foco focus, spotlight
follaje foliage
folleto brochure, booklet, leaflet, pamphlet, tract
fomentar (v) to promote
fondo bottom, depth, fund
fondo de amortización sinking fund
fondo de comercio goodwill

fondo de inversión en bienes raíces real estate investment trust
fondo de pensiones pension fund
fondo estabilizador buffer pool
fondos disponibles ready money
fondos en plica escrow funds
fonética phonetics, phonetic
forastero outsider, stranger
forense forensic
forjar (v) to forge
forma form, shape
forma de pago terms of payment
formal formal, staid, trustworthy
formalidades formalities
formar (v) to compose, shape
formato format
formato de instrucción instruction format
fórmula formula
formular (v) to formulate
formulario form
fornicación fornication
fornido brawny, strapping
forro lining
fortaleza stronghold
fortuito accidental, casual, fortuitous, haphazard, incidental, random
fortuna fortune
forzado forced
forzar (v) to coerce, force, tamper
foso trench
foto photo
foto instantánea snapshot
fotocopia photocopy
fotocopiadora photocopier
fotografía photography
fotografiar (v) to photograph
fotográfico photographic

fotógrafo photographer
fracasado unsuccessful
fracasar (v) to fail
fracaso failure
fracción fraction
fractura fracture
fracturar (v) to fracture
fragancia aroma, fragrance
fragante fragrant
frágil frail, fragile
fragmento fragment
francamente candidly
francés French
Francia France
franco candid, exempt, frank, outspoken, straightforward
franco al costado del buque free alongside vessel
franco fábrica ex mill, ex factory
francotirador sniper
franela flannel
franqueo postage
franqueza candor
franquicia franchise
frase phrase
fraseología wording
fraternal fraternal
fraternidad brotherhood
fratricidio fratricide
fraude cheat, deceit, fraud, fraudulence
fraude flagrante positive fraud
fraudulencia fraudulence
fraudulento fraudulent
frecuencia clock speed
fregadero sink
fregar (v) to scour, scrub
fregasuelos mop
freír (v) to fry
frenético frantic
freno brake, curb, restraint
frente brow, forehead, front
fresa strawberry

fresco airy, fresh, saucy
fricción friction
frigorífico refrigerator
frío chill, cold, wintry
frito fried
frivolizar (v) to trifle
frívolo frivolous
frondoso lush
frontera border
frotamiento rub
frotar (v) to chafe, rub
fructuoso fruitful
frugal thrifty
frugalidad thrift
frustrar (v) to foil, frustrate
fruta fruit
fuego fire
fuego cruzado crossfire
fuegos artificiales fireworks
fuente fountain, source, well
fuente de alimentación power supply
fuera off, outside, out
fuera de borda outboard
fuero charter
fuerte hardy, loud, mighty, strong, sturdy, tough
fuerza constraint, force, might
fuerza muscular brawn
fuga getaway
fugitivo fugitive, runaway
fumar (v) to smoke
funámbulo tightrope walker
función function
función de la tarde matinee
funcionamiento operation
funcionar (v) to work
fundación foundation
fundador founder
fundamental basic
fundamento basis
fundar (v) to base
fundente melting

fundir (v) to melt, Amer., coll.: to go bankrupt
funeral funeral
funicular cablecar
furia fury
furiosamente wildly
furioso furious, raging
furor rage
furriel quartermaster

furúnculo furuncle
fusible fuse
fusil rifle
fusión merger
fusión de empresas merger
fusionar (v) to merge
fútbol football, soccer
futuro future, succeeding

G

gafas spectacles
gafas de nadar goggles
gafas de sol sunglasses
galaxia galaxy
galería arcade, gallery, mall
galleta cookie, wafer
galleta crujiente cracker
gallina hen
gallinero coop
gallo cock, rooster, Amer.: brave man
gama de precios price range
ganadero cattleman
ganado stock
ganado vacuno cattle
ganador winner
ganancias earnings, gains
ganancias de capital capital gains
ganancias inmediatas instant earnings
ganancias netas net earnings
ganancias por retiro retirement gains
gandul truant
ganga bargain
ganglio ganglion
ganglios ganglia
gangrena gangrene
gángster gangster

garabatos scribble, scrawl
garaje garage
garantía assurance, collateral, guaranty, surety, warranty
garantía de ejecución performance bond
garantía de licitación bid bond
garantía de título full covenant
garantía general general covenant
garantizado warranted
garantizar (v) to assure, vouch
garganta throat
gárgaras gargle
garra claw, talon, Col.: leather bag
garrapata tick
gas gas
gas lacrimógeno tear gas
gasa tissue
gasa esterilizada sterile gauze
gasolina gas, petrol
gastado corny, shabby, worn out
gastar (v) to expend, spend
gasto charge, expenditure, expense, spending
gastos acumulados accrued expenses
gastos anticipados prepaid expenses

gastos bancarios bank charges
gastos de correo postage
gastos de envío forwarding charges
gastos de impagados bad debt expense
gastos de manipulación handling charges
gastos de operación handling charges
gastos de pagas de vacaciones vacation pay expenses
gastos de personal payroll expenses
gastos definidos defined expenses
gastos en efectivo cash disbursements
gastos fijos fixed charges
gastos menores petty cash
gastos operativos outlays
gastritis gastritis
gastroenteritis gastroenteritis
gastrointestinal gastrointestinal
gastrónomo gourmet
gatillo trigger
gatito kiitten
gato cat
gaviota sea gull
gelatina jelly
gemelo twin
gemelos binoculars
gemido moan
gemir (v) to groan
gen gene
genealogía pedigree
generación generation
generador generator
general comprehensive, general
generalmente generally
género gender
género humano humankind
generoso generous

genes genes
genio genius, temper, wizard
genocidio genocide
gente people
genuino bona fide, genuine
geología geology
geometría geometry
gerencia management
geriatría geriatrics
gestión bancaria banking management
gestión de base de datos data base management
gesto gesture
gigante giant
gigantesco gigantic, mammoth
gigantismo gigantism
gimnasio gym, gymnasium
gimnasta gymnast
ginebra gin
ginecología gynecology
ginecólogo gynecologist
giradiscos turntable
girador drawer
girar (v) to draft, revolve, spin, turn
girasol sunflower
giro bill, draft, twist, twirl, whirl
giro bancario money order
giro en descubierto overdraft
giro de fondos remittance
gitano gypsy
glacial wintry
glándula gland
glandular glandular
glaucoma glaucoma
globo balloon, globe
globo del ojo eyeball
gloria glory
glorificar (v) to glorify
glucosa glucose
gobernador governor
gobernante ruler

gobernar (v) to govern, rule
gobierno government
gol goal
golf golf
golfo gulf
golondrina swallow
golpazo thump
golpe blow, beat, bash, chop, concussion, coup, knock, stroke, Mex.: sledge hammer
golpe aplastante knockout
golpear (v) to blow, beat, bat, bang, hit, knock, rap, slam, strike
golpecito rap, tap
golpetear (v) to patter
goma rubber
goma de borrar eraser
gonorrea gonorrhea
gordinflón chubby
gordo fat
gorra cap
gota drop
gota de agua raindrop
gotas drops
gotear (v) to drip, leak, trickle
gotera leak
gótico Gothic
gozar (v) to enjoy
grabación recording
grabado engraving, recorded
grabar (v) to engrave, print
grabar en cinta (v) to tape
grabar información (v) to write
gracia grace, wit
gracias thanks
gracioso graceful
grada tier
grado grade, degree
grado de servicio grade of service
graduado graduate

gradual gradual
gráfica graph
gráfica automatizada computer graphics
gráfico pictorial
gráficos graphics
gramática grammar
gramo gram
Gran Bretaña Britain, Great Britain
grande big, great, large
granero barn
granizo hailstone
granja farm
granjero farmer
grano corn, grain, pimple, spot
grapa clip, cramp, staple; Arg., Par., Uru.: brandy of inferior quality
grapadora stapler
grasa fat, grease
grasiento greasy
gratis free
gratitud thankfulness
grava gravel
gravable dutiable
gravable de impuestos taxable
gravamen encumbrance, lien
gravamen de abogado charging lien
gravamen de vendedor vendor's lien
gravamen específico particular lien
gravamen general general lien
gravamen posesorio possessory lien
grave demure, serious
gravedad gravity, severity
graznido squawk
Grecia Greece
griego Greek

grieta   chink, crack, rift
grifo   faucet, tap
grillo   cricket
gripe   flu, influenza
gritar (v)   to bawl, bellow, cheer, cry, scream, squeal, shout
grito   cheer, cry, outcry, scream, squeal, shout
grosero   rude
grosería   rudeness
grúa   crane
grueso   thick
grumo   clot
gruñido   snarl
grupo   batch, group
grupo de acción   task force
grupo sanguíneo   blood group
guante   glove
guapo   handsome, pretty, Sp.: ladies' man
guarda   constable
guarda-apariencia   face-saving
guardabarros   fender

guardaespaldas   bodyguard
guardapolvo   overalls
guardar (v)   to guard, keep, store
guardería infantil   nursery
guardia   sentry
guardián   custodian, guardian, keeper, watchman, warden
guardián de niños   babysitter
guasas   teasing
guerra   warfare, war
guerrero   warrior
guía   directory, guide
guiar (v)   to guide, lead
guía telefónica   telephone book
guija   pebble
guión   dash, hyphen, script
guirnalda   wreath
guisar (v)   to stew
guita   twine
guitarra   guitar
gusano   caterpillar
gustar (v)   to like
gusto   flavor, savor, zest

H

haber   credit
haberes   holdings
hábil   proficient, skilled, slick
habilidad   expertise, proficiency, prowess, skill
habilitar (v)   to enable, qualify
habitación   room
habitar (v)   to inhabit
habitat   habitat
habitual   habitual, usual
hablador   talkative
hablar (v)   to speak, talk
hablar bajo (v)   to whisper
hace tiempo   ago
hacer (v)   to build, do, make

hacer caer (v)   to trip
hacer contrabando (v)   to smuggle
hacer cosquillas (v)   to tickle
hacer demasiado (v)   to overdo
hacer erupción (v)   to erupt
hacer frente (v)   to confront
hacer garabatos (v)   to doodle
hacer índices (v)   to index
hacer lazo (v)   to loop
hacer malabrismos (v)   to juggle
hacer misterio (v)   to mystify
hacer observaciones (v)   to remark

hacer palmas (v)   to clap
hacer punto (textil) (v)   to knit
hacer racional (v)   to rationalize
hacer señales (v)   to signal
hacer señas (v)   to wave
hacer trucos (v)   to trick
hacer voto (v)   to vow
hacia   to, toward
hacia abajo   down
hacia arriba   up
hacia atrás   backward
hacia el norte   northbound
hacia la tierra   onshore
hacienda   estate, ranch; Arg.,
   Chile: livestock, cattle
hágalo Ud. mismo   do-it-yourself
Haití   Haiti
haitiano   Haitian
halagüeño   flattering
hallazgo   finding
hamaca   hammock
hambre   famine, hunger, starvation
hambriento   hungry
hamburguesa   hamburger
hangar   hangar
haragán   truant
haranganear (v)   to lounge
harapiento   ragged
harina   flour
harto   fed up
hasta   to, until
hasta ahora   hitherto
hasta el presente   all-time
haz de circuitos   trunk group
hazaña   exploit
hebilla   buckle
hebreo   Hebrew
heces   feces
hechicero   wizard
hechizo   spell
hecho   act, deed, event, fact,
   made, ready-made

hecho a mano   handmade
hecho a medida   custom made
hecho consumado   fait
   accompli
hecho por sí mismo   self-made
hecho relativo   relative fact
hectárea   hectare
hedor   stench, stink
helado   freezing, icy, iced, ice
   cream
hélice   propeller
helicóptero   chopper, helicopter
hembra   female
hemiplejía   hemiplegy
hemisferio   hemisphere
hemofilia   hemophilia
hemofílico   hemophiliac
hemoglobina   hemoglobin
hemorragia   hemorrhage
hemorragia nasal   nosebleed
hemorroides   hemorrhoids, piles
heno   hay
hepatitis   hepatitis
herbáceo   herbal
herbicida   weedkiller
heredar (v)   to inherit
heredera   heiress
heredero   inheritor, heir
heredero legal   legal heir
heredero natural   natural heir
heredero único   sole heir
hereditable   inheritable
hereditario   hereditary
herencia   inheritance, heredity,
   heritage
herencia conjunta   parcenary
herida   injury, hurt
herida abierta   open wound
herida de arma de fuego   gunshot wound
heridas   injuries, wounds
heridas internas   internal injuries

herir (v) to injure, hurt, spite, wound
hermana sister
hermanastro stepbrother
hermandad fraternity
hermano brother
hermano carnal full brother
hermético hermetic, watertight
hermoso fair, handsome, lovely
hernia hernia
héroe hero
heroico heroic
heroína heroin
herpes herpes, shingles
herradura horseshoe
herramienta implement, tool
hervir (v) to boil, seethe
heterodoxo unorthodox
hexadecimal hexadecimal
híbrido hybrid
hidrante hydrant
hidrato de carbono carbohydrate
hidráulico hydraulic
hidrocarburo hydrocarbon
hidrógeno hydrogen
hidroplano hydroplane
hiedra ivy
hielo ice
hierba grass, herb
hierro iron
hierro fundido cast-iron
hígado liver
higiene hygiene, sanitation
higiénico hygienic
hija daughter
hijastra stepdaughter
hijastro stepson
hijo son
hilado woven
hilo thread, twine, yarn
himno anthem, hymn
hinchado bloated

hinchar (v) to swell
hinchazón swelling
hiperactividad hyperactivity
hipérbole hyperbole
hipertensión hypertension
hipnosis hypnosis
hipnótico hypnotic
hipocondría hypochondria
hipocondríaco hypochondriac
hipócrita hypocrite
hipoteca mortgage
hipótesis hypothesis
hipotético hypothetical
hispánico Hispanic
histamina histamine
histerectomía hysterectomy
histeria hysteria
histérico hysterical
histerismo hysteria
historia history, story, tale
histórico historical, historic
hogar hearth
hoguera bonfire
hoja blade, foil, leaf
hoja de afeitar razor blade
hoja de balance balance sheet
hoja de cálculo spreadsheet
hoja de pedido order form
hoja de solicitud application form
hoja informativa newsletter
hojas sueltas loose-leaf
hola hello
Holanda Holland
holandés Dutch
hombre man
hombre de negocios businessman
hombres men
hombro shoulder
homenaje homage
homicidio homicide, manslaughter

homicidio no premeditado
manslaughter
homogéneo homogenous
homónimo homonym
homosexual homosexual
homosexualidad homosexuality
honestidad honesty
honesto honest
honor honor
honorario fee, honorary
honorarios de abogados legal
fees
honradamente honestly
honradez honesty, integrity
honrado honest, straightforward,
trustworthy
hora hour
hora de comer lunchtime
hora punta rush hour
horario schedule, timetable
horas suplementarias de trabajo
overtime
horda horde
horizonte horizon, skyline
hormigón concrete
hormona hormone
horno furnace, oven
horóscopo horoscope
horrendo dire
horrible horrible, shocking
horror horror, terror
horrorizado aghast
horrorizar (v) to horrify
horticultura horticulture
hospedaje lodging
hospedar (v) to house,
lodge
hospicio hospice
hospital hospital, infirmary
hospital geriátrico nursing
home
hospitalidad hospitality

hostal lodge
hostil hostile
hostilidad hostility
hotel hotel
hoy today
hoyuelo dimple
hueco cavity, hollow
huelga strike
huelguista striker
huella footprint, trace
huella digital fingerprint
huérfano orphan
huerto orchard
huesecillo del oído anvil
hueso bone
hueso occipital occipital
bone
hueso roto broken bone
hueso
temporal temporal bone
huésped host, lodger
huevo egg
huir (v) to flee
humanidad humanity
humanitario humanitarian
humano human
humeante smoky
humedad damp
humedecedor humidifier
humedecer (v) to dampen,
wet
húmedo humid, moist, wet
húmero humerus
humero Col.: dense smoke
humilde humble
humillación humiliation
humillante humiliating
humillar (v) to humiliate
humo smoke
humor humor, mood, temper
hundir (v) to sink
hundirse (v) to subside

húngaro Hungarian
Hungría Hungary
huracán hurricane
hurtar (v) to purloin, pilfer

hurto abstraction, burglary, larceny, theft
hurto menor petty larceny
husmear (v) to sniff

I

Iberia Iberia
icono icon
iconoclasta iconoclast
idea idea, thought
idea esencial root
ideal ideal
idealizar (v) to idealize
idear (v) to design
idéntico alike, identical
identidad identity
identificación identification
identificar (v) to identify
idílico idyllic
idioma idiom
idiota idiot
idiotez idiocy
idolatría idolatry
ídolo idol
iglesia church
ignición ignition
ignorancia ignorance
ignorante ignorant, uneducated
ignorar (v) to ignore
igual even, equal, peer, same
igualar (v) to equalize, match
igualdad parity
ilegal illegal, lawless, unlawful
ilegalidad illegality
ilegible illegible
ilegítimo bastard, illegitimate
ileso unhurt, unharmed
ilícito illicit, unlawful
ilimitado unconfined, unlimited
ilógico illogical

iluminación illumination
iluminar (v) to illuminate, lighten
ilusión illusion
ilusorio unreal, unrealistic
ilustración illustration
ilustrado enlightened
ilustrar (v) to exemplify, illustrate
imagen image
imaginación imagination
imaginar (v) to envision, imagine
imaginarse (v) to suppose
imaginativo imaginative
imán magnet
imbatido undefeated
imbécil asshole, imbecile, moron
imberbe beardless
imitación imitation
imitador copycat
imitar (v) to copy, impersonate, mimic
impaciente eager, impatient
impacto impact
impagado unpaid
impar odd
imparcial impartial, unbiased
impasible unemotional
impasivo impassive
impávido undaunted
impecable flawless
impedir (v) to preclude, prevent, thwart

impenetrable impenetrable
imperar (v) to reign
imperdible safety pin
imperdonable irremissible, unforgivable
imperecedero undying
imperfección flaw, imperfection
imperfecto imperfect
imperial imperial
imperialismo imperialism
imperio empire
impermeable raincoat, waterproof
impersonal impersonal
impertinencia impertinence
impertinente impertinent, pert
ímpetu impetus, momentum, rush
impetuoso impetuous
implacable relentless
implantar (v) to implant
implicar (v) to implicate, imply, involve
implícito implicit, implied
implorar (v) to implore
imponente depositor
imponer (v) to compel, levy, intrude
imponible taxable
impopular unpopular
importación import
importación temporal temporary import
importancia importance, prominence, value
importante important, material
importar (v) to import, matter
importe amount
importe neto net amount
imposible impossible
imposición imposition
impostor deceiver, impostor
impotencia impotence

impotente powerless
impregnar (v) to impregnate
imprenta printing
imprescindible imperative, indispensable, requisite
impresión impression, print, printout
impresionante impressive
impreso printed
impresora printer
impresora de matriz de puntos dot matrix printer
impresora de rueda de margarita daisy wheel printer
impresora láser laser printer
impresora rápida line printer
imprevisible unpredictable
imprevisto unforeseen
imprevistos contingencies
imprimir (v) to print, imprint, stamp
improbable improbable, unlikely
improcedente irrelevant
impropio improper, wrong
improvisación improvisation
improvisado impromptu
improvisar (v) to improvise
imprudencia recklessness
imprudente imprudent, reckless, unwise
impuesto duty, tax
impuesto adicional surtax
impuesto compensatorio compensatory duty
impuesto de "antidumping" anti-dumping duty
impuesto de consumo sales tax
impuesto de venta sales tax
impuesto directo direct tax
impuesto personal income tax
impuesto sobre capital capital levy

impuesto sobre consumo excise tax

impuesto sobre el capital capital tax

impuesto sobre el valor añadido value added tax

impuesto sobre ingresos personales income tax

impuesto sobre la propiedad property taxes

impuestos taxation, taxes

impuestos de aduanas customs duties

impuestos derechos aduaneros customs duties

impuestos locales local taxes

impuestos de servicios tax services

impugnación impeachment

impugnar (v) to contest, impeach, impugn

impulsar (v) to impel, operate, propel

impulso impulse, urge

impunidad impunity

in fraganti red handed

inacabable interminable

inacabado unfinished

inaccesible inaccessible

inaceptable inadmissible, unacceptable

inactivo inactive, static, sluggish

inadecuado inadequate

inadmisible inadmissible

inadvertido undetected, unnoticed

inaguantable horrid, unbearable, unendurable

inalienable inalienable

inapelable unappealable

inapropiado unsuitable

inasistencia nonattendance

inaudito unheard

inaugurar (v) to inaugurate

incalculable incalculable

incandescente incandescent

incapacidad disability, incapacity, inability

incapacidad mental mental incapacity

incapacitado disabled

incapacitar (v) to disqualify

incapaz inefficient, incapable, unfit, unable

incautación attachment, seizure

incautar (v) to confiscate, impound, seize

incendiar (v) to burn

incendiario arsonist, incendiary

incendio intencionado arson

incentivo incentive, inducement

incertidumbre suspense

incesante incessant

incesto incest

incestuoso incestuous

incidencia incidence

incidental incidental

incidente incident

incienso incense

incierto uncertain

incinerar (v) to cremate, incinerate

incitador instigator

incitar (v) to incite

incivilizado uncivilized

inclinación bias, inclination, slant, stoop, tilt

inclinación (cabeza) nod

inclinado leaning

inclinar (v) to incline, slope, stoop, tilt, tip

inclinarse (v) to bow

inclinarse a (v) to tend

incluir (v) to enclose, include

incluso including

incobrable noncollectible

incoherente incoherent
incomodidad discomfort
incómodo uncomfortable
incomparable incomparable, peerless
incomparecencia nonappearance
incompatible incompatible
incompetencia incompetence, malpractice
incompetente incompetent, unqualified
incompleto incomplete, sketchy
incomprensivo incomprehensive
incomunicado incommunicado
inconcluyente inconclusive
incondicional unconditional
incongruente incongruent
inconsciente oblivious, unconscious
inconsecuente inconsequent
inconsistente inconsistent
incontestado unchallenged
incontinencia incontinence
inconveniente inconvenient
incorporación incorporation
incorporar (v) to incorporate
incorrecto inaccurate, incorrect, inexact
increíble incredible, unbelievable
incriminar (v) to incriminate
inculto brash
incumbencia incumbency
incumplido unfulfilled
incumplimiento default, nonfulfillment, noncompliance
incumplimiento de contrato breach of contract
incumplimiento inicial default
incurrir (v) to incur
incursión raid
incursor raider

indebidamente improperly, unduly
indebido undue
indecente bawdy, indecent
indecible unspeakable
indeciso indecisive, undecided
indefectible unfailing
indefendible indefensible
indefenso unguarded
indefinido indefinite
indemne unharmed, undamaged
indemnización indemnity
indemnizar (v) to indemnify
independencia independence
independiente freelance, independent, self-employed, self-contained
indeseable undesirable
indexación indexing
India India
indicación de llamada en espera call waiting
indicador indicator, sign
indicar (v) to bespeak, denote, indicate, point
indicativo indicative
índice index, ratio, clue
índice de actividad activity ratio
índice de crédito lending rate
indiferencia apathy, disregard, indifference
indiferente apathetic, indifferent, insensitive, listless
indigestión indigestion
indignante indignant
indigno unworthy
indio Indian
indirecto indirect
indiscreción indiscretion
indiscutible unquestionable
indisposición malaise
indistinto vague
individual individual

indivisible indivisible
inducir (v) to induce
inductor inductor
indudablemente undoubtedly
indulgencia leniency
indultar (v) to reprieve
indulto pardon
industria industry, trade
industrial industrial
industrioso industrious
ineducado uneducated
inepto inept
inequívoco unequivocal
inercia inertia
inerte inert, slack
inesperado unexpected
inestable shaky, unsteady
inestimable invaluable
inevitable inevitable, unavoidable
inexacto imprecise
inexorable adamant
inexplorado uncharted
infalible infallible
infame infamous, vile
infamia infamy
infancia babyhood, childhood, infancy
infantería infantry
infanticida infanticide
infantil babyish, infantile
infatigable tireless
infección infection, taint
infección en el ojo eye infection
infección fungosa fungus infection
infectado infected
infectar (v) to infect
infeliz unhappy
inferencia inference
inferior inferior
inferior al normal substandard

inferioridad inferiority
inferir (v) to infer
infernal hellish, infernal
infidelidad infidelity
infiel unfaithful
infierno hell
infiltrarse (v) to infiltrate
infinito infinite
inflación inflation
inflamable inflammable
inflamación inflammation, soreness
inflamado sore
inflamar (v) to inflame
inflar (v) to inflate, swell
inflexible stiff, unbending
inflexión inflection
infligir (v) to inflict
influencia influence, leverage
influencial influential
influir en (v) to bias
información information
informal unreliable
informante informant
informar (v) to acquaint, enlighten, inform, report, tell
informática information
informática de gestión business data processing
informativo informative
informe report, record
informe anual annual report
informe de solvencia credit report
infracción infringement, infraction
infracción de la ley lawbreaking
infractor infringer, transgressor
infractor de la ley lawbreaker
infraestructura infrastructure
infringir (v) to infringe
infundado unfounded

infusión infusion
ingeniero engineer
ingenio wit
ingenioso ingenious, witty
ingenuidad naivety
ingenuo ingenuous, naive
Inglaterra England
inglés British, English
ingrediente ingredient
ingreso deposit, earning, income, revenue
ingresos diferidos deferred revenue
ingresos netos net income
ingresos residuales residual income
inhabilitado disqualified
inhalador inhaler
inherente inherent
inhibición inhibition
inhibir (v) to inhibit
inhumanidad inhumanity
inhumano inhuman
iniciación initiation
inicial initial
iniciales initials
iniciar (v) to initiate
inicio de juego kickoff
injuria abuse
injusticia injustice, inequity, unfairness
injustificable inexcusable
injustificado unjustified
injusto iniquitous, unfair, unjust, wrongful
inmaculado immaculate, undefiled
inmaduro immature
inmaterial immaterial
inmediatamente immediately
inmediato immediate, instant
inmenso immense, vast
inmersión immersion, plunge

inmigración immigration
inmigrante immigrant
inminente impending
inmoral immoral, promiscuous
inmortal immortal
inmóvil immovable, still
inmovilizar (v) to immobilize
inmune immune
inmunidad immunity
inmunización immunization
innecesario needless, unnecessary
innegable undeniable
inocencia innocence
inocente blameless, innocent
inocular (v) to innoculate
inofensivo harmless
inoportuno inappropriate, illtimed, inopportune
inorgánico inorganic
inquietar (v) to trouble
inquieto anxious, restless, restive, unsettled
inquietud anxiety, uneasiness, worry
inquilino occupant, tenant, tenancy
inquisición inquisition
insaciable insatiable
insania rage
insano morbid
insatisfacción dissatisfaction
inscribir (v) to enroll, register
inscribirse (v) to enroll
inscripción enrollment, inscription, registration
insecto insect
inseguridad insecurity
inseguro insecure, unsteady, unsafe, uneasy, wobbly
inseminación artificial artificial insemination
insensible numb, unfeeling

inserción dent, insertion
insertar (v) to insert
inservible unfit, useless
insignia badge
insignificante banal, petty, trifling
insinuación hint, implication
insinuar (v) to hint, insinuate
insípido tasteless
insistencia insistence
insistente insistent
insistir (v) to insist
insolación heat stroke, sunstroke
insolencia insolence
insólito unusual
insolvencia bankruptcy, default, insolvency
insolvente insolvent
insomnio insomnia
insonorizado soundproof
insostenible untenable
inspección inspection, survey
inspeccionar (v) to inspect
inspector controller, inspector, surveyor
inspiración inspiration
inspirar (v) to inspire
instalación installation
instalar (v) to install
instancia instance
instancia del demandado interplea
instancia perentoria peremptory plea
instantáneamente instantly
instantáneo instantaneous
instante tick
instigación abetment
instigador instigator
instintivo instinctive
instinto flair, instinct
institución institution
instituto institute

instrucción command, instruction
instrucción absoluta absolute instruction
instrucción de máquina machine instruction
instructor instructor
instruido well-educated
instruir (v) to instruct
instrumento instrument
insubordinado insubordinate
insuficiencia inadequacy, shortage
insuficiente inadequate, insufficient
insulina insulin
insultante taunting
insulto affront, insult; Mex., Nic.: indigestion
intachable unimpeachable
intacto intact, undamaged
integración a gran escala large scale integration
integrar (v) to integrate
integridad integrity
íntegro unabridged
intelecto intellect
intelectual intellectual
inteligencia intelligence, wit
inteligencia artificial artificial intelligence
inteligente brainy, intelligent, smart
intención intention, meaning, purpose
intencionadamente intentionally
intencionado calculated, deliberate
intencional intentional
intensidad intensity
intensificación escalation
intensificar (v) to intensify
intensivo intensive

intenso intense, vivid
intentar (v) to attempt, try
intento intent
intercalar (v) to sandwich
intercambiable interchangeable
intercambiar (v) to reciprocate
intercambio interchange, swap, trade in
intercambio de divisas swap
interceder (v) to intercede, plead
interceptar (v) to intercept
interdicto injunction
interés concern, interest
interés compuesto compound interest
interés minoritario minority interest
interesante interesting
interesar (v) to concern, interest
intereses a pagar interest payable
intereses acumulados accrued interest
intereses atrasados arrears of interest
intereses en retrasos interest in arrears
intereses hasta la fecha interest to date
intereses vencidos outstanding interest
interestatal interstate
interferencia interference
interior domestic, inner, indoor, inland, inward
interjección interjection
interlocutorio interlocutory
intermediario intermediary, middleman
intermedio intermediate, interim
interminable endless

intermitente intermittent
internacional international
internado (escuela) boarding school
internista internist
interno internal
interpelación interpellation
interpretar (v) to interpret, read
intérprete interpreter
interrogador questioner
interrogar (v) to debrief, interrogate
interrumpir (v) to discontinue, interrupt, suspend
interrupción interrupt, stoppage
interruptor switch
intersección crossing, intersection
intervalo gap, interval, interlude
intervención intervention
intervenir (v) to intervene, interfere, mediate
interventor auditor
intestinal intestinal
intestino bowel, intestine
intestino grueso large intestine
intimidad intimacy, privacy
íntimo intimate
intolerante intolerant
intoxicación intoxication
intoxicación de comida food poisoning
intranquilo restless
intransigente uncompromising
intrépido fearless, intrepid
intriga intrigue
intrínseco intrinsic
introducir datos (v) to download
introductorio introductory

introvertido introverted

intrusión intrusion, trespass

intruso intruder, squatter, trespasser

intuición intuition, insight

inundación flood

inundar (v) to flood, inundate, submerge

inútil futile, helpless, pointless, vain, worthless, useless

inutilizado disabled

inutilizar (v) to disable

invadir (v) to invade

invalidar (v) to cripple, override, quash, supercede, void

inválido cripple, invalid, void

invariable invariable

invasión invasion

invasor invader, raider

invencible invincible

invención invention

invendible unmarketable

inventar (v) to devise, fabricate

inventario inventory

inventario físico physical inventory

inventiva ingenuity

inventor inventor

invernar (v) to hibernate; Arg., Uru.: to pasture in winter pastures

inversión inversion, investment, reversal

inversiones a largo plazo long-term investments

inversiones temporales temporary investments

inversionista investor

inverso converse, reverse

inversor investor, inverter

invertido reverse

invertir (v) to invest, reverse

investigación inquisition, investigation, inquest, inquiry, research

investigación y desarrollo research and development

investigador investigator, researcher

investigar (v) to research

invierno winter

inviolable inviolable

invisible invisible

invitación invitation

invitado guest

invitar (v) to invite, treat

invocar (v) to invoke

involuntario involuntary

inyección injection, shot

inyectar (v) to inject

ir (v) to go

ir a la deriva (v) to drift

ir de excursión (v) to hike

ir deprisa (v) to scurry

Irak Iraq

Irán Iran

iris iris

Irlanda Ireland

irlandés Irish

ironía irony

irónicamente wryly

irónico ironic

irracional irrational

irrazonable unreasonable

irreal unreal

irreconciliable irreconcilable

irreflexivo impulsive

irrefutable irrefutable

irregular erratic, irregular

irresistible irresistible

irresoluto wavering

irresponsabilidad irresponsibility

irresponsable irresponsible

irrevocable irrevocable

irrigar (v) to irrigate
irritación aggravation
irritar (v) to aggravate
irrompible unbreakable
isla island
Islandia Iceland

Italia Italy
italiano Italian
itinerario itinerary
izquierda left
izquierdista leftist

J

jabón soap
jabón en polvo soap powder
jabonera soapdish
jabonoso soapy
jactarse (v) to boast
jamón ham
jaqueca migraine
jarabe syrup
jardín garden
jardín de infancia kindergarten,
  nursery school
jardinería gardening
jardinero gardener
jarro jug
jazz jazz
jeep jeep
jefe boss, leader, manager, principal; Peru, Uru.: officer (when
  speaking to a policeman)
jefe de cocina chef
jerga jargon, patter
jeringa syringe
jersey pullover
Jesucristo Christ
Jesús Jesus
jinete rider
jolgorio revelry
joroba hump
jorobado humpbacked, hunchback
joven junior, young
joven diezañero teenager
jovial jovial

joya gem, jewel
joyero jeweller, Amer.: goldsmith
juanete bunion
jubilación superannuation
jubilado retired
jubilar (v) to retire; Cuba, Mex.:
  to become expert at
jubiloso exultant, jubilant
judía bean
judicial judicial
judío Jewish, Jew
judo judo
juego gamble, gambling, game,
  set (in tennis)
juego de damas checkers
juerga spree
jueves Thursday
juez judge, trier
jugada move
jugador gambler, player
jugar (v) to gamble, play
juglar minstrel
jugo gástrico gastric juice
jugoso pithy, juicy
juguete toy
juguetería toy shop
juicio judgment, sense, trial
juicio de divorcio divorce suit
juicio de indagación inquest
juicio hipotecario foreclosure
juicio imparcial fair trial
juicio nulo mistrial
juicio penal penal suit

juicio secundario ancillary suit
junco junk
jungla jungle
junio (mes) June
junta board
junta de administración board of directors
junta de directiva board meeting
junta directiva board of directors
juntamente together
juntar (v) to couple, splice
junto a alongside, together
jurado juror
jurado de juicio petty jury
jurado especial special jury
jurado ordinario common jury
jurado procesal trial jury
jurado suplente talesman
jurados adicionales tales
juramento juration, oath
juramento condicional limited oath
juramento promisorio promissory oath
jurar (v) to swear, vow
juratorio juratory

jurídico juridical, jural, juristic
jurisdicción jurisdiction
jurisdiccional jurisdictional
jurisprudencia jurisprudence
jurista jurist
justamente fairly
justicia justice
justificable justifiable
justificante voucher
justificar (v) to justify
justo just, fair
juvenil boyhood, juvenile
juventud youth
juzgado court, court of law
juzgado criminal criminal court
juzgado de aduanas customs court
juzgado de guardia police court
juzgado de instrucción trial court
juzgado de noche night court
juzgado mayor higher court
juzgado menor lower court
juzgado municipal municipal court
juzgar (v) to judge

K

kilo (medida) kilo
kilogramo kilogram

kilómetro kilometer

L

La Haya Hague, The
laberinto maze
labio lip
labor toil
labor de equipo teamwork
laboratorio laboratory

laborioso painstaking
labrador tiller
lacre sealing wax
lactancia lactation
ladera hillside
lado side

ladrar (v) to bark
ladrido yap
ladrillo brick
ladrón burglar, crook, robber, thief
ladrón de tiendas shoplifter
lago lake
lágrima tear
laguna lagoon
lamentable lamentable, regrettable, sad
lamentación mourning
lamentar (v) to deplore, regret
lamento wail
lamer (v) to lick
lámina sheet
lámpara lamp, light
lana wool, C.Am.: rabble
lancha motora motorboat
langosta lobster
languidecer (v) to languish
lanoso woolly, fluffy
lanza lance
lanzadera shuttle
lanzamiento blast-off, pitch
lanzar (v) to pitch
lanzarse (v) to rush
lápiz pencil
lápiz de pastel crayon
lapso lapse
larga distancia long-distance
largo length, lengthy, long
largo alcance long-range
largo plazo long-term
laringe larynx
lástima de sí mismo self-pity
lastre ballast
lata can, tin can
lateral lateral
lateralmente sidelong
latido beat, heartbeat, throb
latido del corazón heartbeat

látigo whip; Ecuad., Hond.: whiplash
latino Latin
latinoamericano Latin-American
latitud latitude
latón brass; Bol., Col.: sword
latrocinio larceny
laurel bay leaf
lavable washable
lavabo bathroom, lavatory
lavadero laundry
lavado de cerebro brainwash
lavado de coche car wash
lavandería launderette
lavaplatos dishwasher
lavar (v) to wash, launder
lavativa enema
laxante laxative
lazo loop, snare, tie
leal loyal, trusty
lealtad loyalty
lealtad a la marca brand loyalty
lealtad natural implied allegiance, natural allegiance
lección lecture, lesson
lectura reading
lectura cuidadosa perusal
leche milk, Amer.: luck, good luck
lechuga lettuce
leer (v) to read
leer con atención (v) to peruse
legado bequest, devisal, legacy
legado remanente residuary legacy
legal legal, lawful, statutory
legalidad legality
legalista legalistic
legalístico legalistic
legalizado executed
legalizar (v) to legalize
legalmente legally
legar (v) to devise

legatario devisee
legendario legendary
legible legible
legión legion
legislación legislation, lawmaking
legislador legislator, lawmaker
legislar (v) to enact, legislate
legislativo legislative
legislatura legislature
legitimar (v) to legitimate
legitimidad legitimacy
legítimo legitimate, rightful
lego layman
lejano faraway
Lejano Oriente Far East
lejos away, far
lengua tongue
lenguaje language
lenguaje artificial artificial language
lenguaje de alto nivel high level language
lenguaje de computadora computer language
lenguaje de ensamblaje assembly language
lenguaje de mandatos command language
lenguaje de máquina machine language
lenguaje de programación programming language
lenguaje fuente source language
lenguaje resultante object language, target language
lente lens, magnifying glass
lenteja lentil
lento slow, sluggish
león lion, Amer.: puma
lepra leprosy
lesión injury, lesion, trauma
lesión mortal fatal injury

letal lethal
letárgico lethargic
letra bill, writing
letra a plazo corto short-term bill
letra bancaria bank bill
letra de cambio bill of exchange, draft
letra domiciliada domiciled bill
letra manuscrita handwriting
letra menuda small print
letras a cobrar notes receivable
letras a pagar notes payable
letras avaladas guaranteed bills
letrero placard
leucemia leukemia
levadura yeast
levantamiento lift
levantar (v) to arise, adjourn, lift, rear
leve light, slight
ley law, statute
ley civil civil law
ley común common law
ley marcial martial law
ley militar military law
ley moral moral law
ley orgánica organic law
ley permanente perpetual statute
ley real real law
leyenda legend
leyes antimonopolistas antitrust laws
leyes laborales labor laws
leyes penales penal laws
liar (v) to bind
libelo libel
liberación release
liberal liberal, open-minded
liberarse (v) to rid
libertad freedom, liberty

libertad condicional parole, probation

libertad provisional freedom on bail

libertar (v) to liberate, release

libertinaje promiscuity

libertino promiscuous

libra pound

librado drawee

librador drawer

librarse (v) to rid

libre free, exempt, unconstrained, vacant

libre a bordo free on board

librecambio free trade

libre de impuestos tax free, duty free

librería bookshop, bookseller

libreta bank book

libreta bancaria deposit passbook

libreta de ahorros savings passbook

libro book

libro de apuntes notebook

libro de bolsillo paperback

libro de caja cash book

libro de cocina cookbook

libro de cuentas account book

libro de texto textbook

libro de ventas sales journal

libro diario journal

libro mayor general ledger, ledger

licencia license

licencia de exportación export licence

licenciado licentiate

licenciar (v) to licence

licitación bidding, licitation

licor liquor

liderazgo leadership

LIFO (último-dentro/primero-fuera) last-in, first-out (LIFO)

liga league

liga elástica rubber band

ligamento ligament

ligeramente slightly

ligero light, thin

lima file, lime

limitación limitation, restriction

limitación de propiedad tail

limitado limited, restricted

limitar (v) to limit, restrict

límite boundary, deadline, limit

límite de crédito lending limit

límite de velocidad speed limit

limón lemon

limonada lemonade

limpiar (v) to clean, wipe; Mex.: to punish, beat; Chile, Uru.: to weed

limpiaventanas window cleaner

limpieza tidiness

limpieza de la casa housecleaning

limpio clean, neat, tidy

limusina (coche) limousine

linaje ancestry, lineage

linchar (v) to lynch

linde boundary

lindero boundary

lindes abuttals

lindo cute

línea line

línea conmutada switched line

línea de crédito line of credit

línea de flujo flow line

línea de montaje assembly line

línea fronteriza borderline

línea principal main line

línea secundaria sideline

lineal linear

líneas generales (de actuación) guidelines

linfa lymph

lingote de oro gold bullion, ingot of gold
lingüista linguist
lino linen
linterna flashlight, lantern, torch
liquidación clearance, sale
liquidador receiver
liquidar (v) to liquidate
liquidez liquidity
líquido fluid
líquido circulante cash flow
lírico lyric
Lisboa Lisbon
lisiado cripple
liso even
lista list, menu, register, roll, schedule
lista de bajas casualty list
lista de clientes mailing list
lista de contenido packing list
lista de espera waiting list
lista de precios price list
lista de precios actual current price list
lista de precios al detalle retail price list
lista de vino wine list
lista negra blacklist
listar (v) to list
listo clever, ready, sharp
litera bunk, litter
literatura literature
litigante litigator, litigant
litigar (v) to litigate
litigio cause, litigation, lawsuit
litigioso litigious
litoral coast, seashore
litro liter; Chile: coarse wool
liturgia liturgy
lo mismo ditto
lo que whatever
local local
local por alquilar space for rent

localidad locality
localizar (v) to localize, locate
localmente locally
loción lotion
loco crazy, insane, lunatic, mad
locomotor locomotive
locura craze, dementia, insanity, madness
logaritmo logarithm
lógica del programa program flowchart
lógico logic, rational, sensible
logística logistics
lograr (v) to accomplish, achieve, attain
logro attainment, accomplishment, achievement
lombriz intestinal hookworm
lomo ridge
lona canvas
Londres London
longevidad longevity
longitud longitude
longitud de onda wavelength
longitudinal longitudinal
los them
lote tally
lote de mercancías lot
lotería lottery
lubina bass fish
lubricante lubricant
lubricar (v) to lubricate
lucha fight, struggle, strife, tussle
luchar (v) to struggle, wrestle
lucrativo lucrative
lugar place, spot; Chile: toilet
lugar de nacimiento birthplace
lugar de pago place of payment
lugarteniente lieutenant
lujo luxury
lujoso plushy
lujuria lust
lumbago lumbago

lumbar lumbar
luminoso luminous
luna moon
luna de miel honeymoon
lunares de la piel moles
lunes Monday

lustre gloss, sheen, shine
luto mourning
luz glow
luz de la luna moonlight
luz de sol sunshine, sunlight
luz del día daylight

LL

llama flame
llamada call, recall, summons
llamada revertida toll free
llamada telefónica telephone call
llamado so-called
llamamiento appeal
llamar (v) to beckon, knock, page, recall, summon
llamar a (v) to hail
llamarada blaze, flare
llamativo eye-catching
llano level
llave key
llave de contacto ignition key

llegada arrival
llegar (v) to arrive, come
llegar a reach (v)
llegar a ser (v) to become
llenar (v) to stuff
lleno full
llevar (v) to convey, wear
llorar (v) to cry, mourn, weep
lloriquear (v) to snivel
lloroso tearful
llover (v) to rain, shower
llovizna drizzle
lluvia rain
lluvioso rainy

M

macabro macabre
macarrones macaroni
macedonia fruit salad
macizo solid
macroprogramación macroprogramming
machacar (v) to pound
macho male; C.R.: foreigner, Anglo
madera lumber, timber, wood
madrastra stepmother
madre mother
madrina godmother
madurar (v) to ripen

maduro mature, ripe
maestro teacher
mágico magical
magistrado magistrate
magistral magisterial
magnánimo magnanimous
magnate tycoon
magnético magnetic
magnetismo magnetism
magníficamente royally
magnífico grand, magnificent, superb
magnitud magnitude
mago magician

maíz corn
majestuoso stately
mal mischief, wicked
mal aconsejado ill-advised
mal ajustado misfit
mal entendido misunderstood
mal genio bad-tempered
mal olor stink
mal pagado underpaid
mala calidad shoddiness
mala conducta disorderly conduct, misbehavior, misconduct
mala hierba weed
maldición curse
maldito damn
malentendido misunderstanding
malestar unrest
maleta suitcase
malgastar (v) to squander; Arg., Uru.: knapsack
malhecho misdeed
malhechor malefactor
malhumorado ill-humored, petulant, surly
malicia malice, spleen
malicia premeditada preconceived malice
malicioso malicious
maligno malignant
malo bad, evil, wrong, villain
malparto miscarriage
malsano unhealthy
malvado villain
malversación malversation, malfeasance, misappropriation
malversador embezzler
Mancomunidad Commonwealth
mancha blur, stain, smudge, slur, smear
mancha pequeña speck
manchado spotty
manchar (v) to blemish, smear, stain, spot

manda bequest
mandar (v) to command, control, rule; Chile: to start (a race); Amer.: to hit, to omit
mandarina tangerine
mandatario mandatory; Amer.: leader
mandato mandate, writ
mandíbula jaw, mandible, maxilla
mando control
manejable manageable
manejar (v) to operate, ply, wield; Amer.: to drive a car
manera manner, way
manga sleeve; Amer.: crowd; Arg., Chile, Uru., Mex.: loading platform; Hond.: heavy cloak; Mex.: poncho
mangas de camisa shirt sleeves
mango grip; Mex. sl.: good-looking woman
manía fad, mania
maniático maniac
manicura manicure
manifestante rioter
manifestar (v) to say
manifiesto manifest
maniobra maneuver
maniobrar (v) to maneuver
manipulación handling
manipular (v) to manipulate
manivela crank
mano hand; Amer.: bunch, cluster
mano de obra manpower
manojo bunch; Amer.: hand of tobacco
manómetro pressure gauge
manotada slap
manta blanket; Col.: dance (folk); Arg.: poncho; Mex.: cotton cloth
mantel tablecloth

mantener (v) to maintain
mantenimiento maintenance
mantenimiento de ficheros file maintenance
mantequilla butter
manto robe
manual handbook, manual
manualmente manually
manuscrito longhand, manuscript
manzana apple; Amer.: Adam's apple
maña knack
mañana morning, tomorrow
mapa map
maquillaje make-up
máquina machine
máquina automática vending machine
máquina contable accounting machine
máquina de dictar dictating machine
máquina de escribir typewriter
máquina de escribir eléctrica electric typewriter
máquina de lavar washing machine
máquina de picar mincer
máquina fotográfica camera
máquina tragaperras slot machine
maquinaria machinery
mar sea
Mar Negro Black Sea
maratón marathon
maravilla marvel, wonder
maravilloso marvelous, stunning, wonderful
marca brand, mark, print, stamp
marca registrada registered trademark, trademark
marcado marked

marcador scorer
marcador de pasos pacemaker
marcador digital digital gauge
marcar (v) to dial, mark, score, sign
marcial martial
marco frame
marco (ventana) sash
marco de cuadro picture frame
marcha march
marcharse (v) to leave
marchitar (v) to wilt, wither
marea tide
mareado dizzy, seasick
marfil ivory
margarina margarine
margarita daisy
margen margin, verge
margen bruto gross margin
margen de beneficio profit margin
marginal marginal
marido husband
marina de guerra navy
marinero sailor, seaman; Chile, Ecuad., Peru: folk dance
marino marine, sailor
marioneta puppet
mariposa butterfly; Cuba: butterfly jasmine (Cuban national flower)
mariscal marshal
marítimo maritime
martes Tuesday
martillo gun cock, hammer
mártir martyr
martirio martyrdom
marxismo Marxism
marzo (mes) March
más most, more, plus
más adentro innermost
más alto upper
más allá beyond, farther

más bajo lower
más bien rather
más lejos further
más o menos roughly
más pequeño least
más tarde later
más vendido bestseller
masa bulk, lump, mass
masacre massacre
masaje massage
mascar (v) to chew, munch
máscara mask
mascarada masquerade
masculino masculine
masivo massive
masoquismo masochism
masoquista masochist
mastitis mastitis
masturbarse (v) to masturbate
matanza killing, slaughter
matar (v) to kill, slaughter
matasellos postmark
mate mate, checkmate
matemáticas mathematics
materia matter, stuff
materia prima raw materials
material material
materialista materialist
maternal maternal
maternidad motherhood, maternity
matiz tone
matón ruffian
matricidio matricide
matrimonial matrimonial, marital
matrimonio matrimony, marriage, wedlock
matrimonio inválido void marriage
matriz array, matrix, womb
matriz del talonario stub, check stub

matriz lógica programable programmable logic array
máximo maximum
mayo (mes) May
mayonesa mayonnaise
mayor greater, major, senior, utmost
mayordomo butler; Chile: foreman
mayoría majority
mayorista wholesaler
maza mace; Cuba: roller (in a sugar mill); Chile: hub (of a wheel)
mecánico mechanic
mecanismo gear, mechanism
mecanógrafa typist
mecanografía typing
mecanógrafo typist
medalla medal
medallón medallion, pendant
media stocking
media docena half dozen
media hora half hour
mediación mediation
mediador mediator
medianoche midnight
medias hosiery, hose
medicamento drug
medicamentos medicaments
medicina medicine
medicina forense forensic medicine
medicina preventiva preventive medicine
médico doctor, medical, physician
medida gauge, step, size
medida del tiempo timing
medieval medieval
medio half, mid, medium, middle, mean
medio ambiente environment

mediocre mediocre
mediodía noon, midday
mediooeste Midwest
medios leverage, resources
medios de vida livelihood
medios informativos media
medir (v) to measure, span
meditar (v) to muse, meditate, to deliberate
Mediterráneo Mediterranean
médula marrow
megáfono megaphone
mejillón mussel
mejor better, best
mejora betterment, improvement
mejorar (v) to ameliorate, better, improve, mend
mejoría amelioration, betterment
melancólico melancholic
melanoma melanoma
melodía melody, tune
melodrama melodrama
melón melon
membrana membrane
memorable memorable
memorándum memorandum
memoria memory, remembrance, storage
memoria asociativa associative storage
memoria auxiliar auxiliary memory
memoria de acceso direct access storage
memoria de acceso aleatorio random access memory
memoria de acceso directo random access storage
memoria central main storage
memoria de discos disk storage
memoria de discos magnéticos magnetic disk storage

memoria dinámica dynamic memory
memoria directa on-line storage
memoria externa external memory
memoria inalterable read only memory
memoria interna internal storage
memoria magnética magnetic storage
memoria permanente permanent storage
memoria secuencial serial storage
mención mention
mendigo beggar, pauper
menguar (v) to wane
meningitis meningitis
menisco meniscus
menopausia menopause
menor infant, least, minor
menos but, fewer, less
menospreciar (v) to underrate
mensaje message
mensajero messenger
menstruación menstruation
menstrual menstrual
mensual monthly
menta (hierba) mint
mental mental
mente mind
mentir (v) to lie
mentira lie, fallacy
mentón chin
menú menu
mercader merchant
mercado market, mart
mercado a la baja bear market
mercado alcista bull market
mercado de descuento de efectos discount market

mercado de futuros futures market

mercado en alza bullish

mercado financiero money market

mercado libre open market

mercado negro black market

mercados de capitales capital markets

mercados extranjeros foreign markets

mercancía merchandise, goods, wares

mercancías en tránsito goods in transit

mercancías generales commodities

mercancías usadas second-hand goods

mercantil commercial, mercantile

mercenario mercenary

mercurio mercury, quicksilver

merecer (v) to deserve, merit

merecido deserved, deserving

meridiano meridian

meridional southern

mérito credit, merit

merma shrinkage, waste

mermelada jam

mero mere

mes month

mesa board, desk, table

mesa de conferencias conference table

meta aim

metabólico metabolic

metabolismo metabolism

metacarpo metacarpus

metáfora metaphor

metal metal

metálico metallic

metalúrgico metallurgic

metamorfosis metamorphosis

metatarso metatarsus

meteoro meteor

meteorología meteorology

meteorólogo meteorologist

meter (v) to stow, put

meticuloso meticulous

metódico businesslike

metodista Methodist

método method, tactic

método contable de doble entrada double-entry accounting method

método de acceso access method

método de compra purchase method

método de coste medio average cost method

método de depreciación directa direct write-off method

método de inventario al detalle retail inventory method

método de inventario perpetuo perpetual inventory method

método de promedio ponderado weighted average method

método de vencimiento programado aging schedule method

métrico metric

metro meter

metro subterráneo subway

metrópoli metropolis

metropolitano metropolitan

mexicano Mexican

México Mexico

mezcla amalgam, mix, mixture, blend, compound

mezcla de lana tweed

mezclar (v) to blend, mix, mingle, shuffle

mi my
micosis mycosis
microbio microbe
microbios bacteria, germs
microcircuito microcircuit
microcirugía microsurgery
microdisco flexible microfloppy disk
microonda microwave
microordenador microcomputer
microorganismo microorganism
microprocesador microprocessor
microscopio microscope
miedo fear
miel honey
miembro limb, member
mientras while
mientras que whereas
miércoles Wednesday
miga crumb
migaja crumb
migaja de pan bread crumb
migraña migraine
migratorio migrant
mil one thousand, thousand
milagro miracle
milagroso miraculous
milenio millennium
miligramo milligram
militante militant
militar military, serviceman
milla mile
millón million
millonario millionaire
mimar (v) to pamper
mina mine
minar (v) to undermine
mineral mineral
miniatura miniature
minimizar (v) to minimize
mínimo minimum
miniordenador minicomputer

ministerio ministry
ministro minister
minoría minority
minuciosidad thoroughness
minuto minute
mío mine
miope short-sighted
miopía myopia
mirada look, peep, sight, stare
mirar (v) to look at, behold, glance, watch
mirar furtivamente (v) to peep
mirar fijamente (v) to stare
misa mass
miserable paltry
miseria misery, pittance, squalor
misericordia mercy
misericordioso merciful
misión mission
misionero missionary
mismo self
misterio mystery, mystique
misterioso uncanny
místico mystic
mitad de camino halfway
mitad de precio half price
mitigar (v) to mitigate
mobiliario paraphernalia
moción motion
moda craze, fashion
modalidad de acceso access mode
modelar (v) to format
modelo model, pattern, standard
modelo matemático mathematical model
módem modem
módem anulador null modem
moderadamente moderately
moderado moderate
modernizar (v) to modernize
moderno modern
modestia modesty

modesto modest
modificación alteration
modificador modifier
modificar (v) to modify
modo manner, mode
modo local local mode
modulación modulation
modulación lineal linear modulation
modular (v) to modulate
módulo module
módulo de programa program module
módulo de programación programming module
mofarse (v) to scoff, taunt
mofletes cheeks
moho mildew, mold
mojado damp, moist, wet
mojar (v) to dampen, moisten, soak
molares molar teeth
molde mold
molestar (v) to annoy, bother, pester
molestia nuisance
molesto annoying, irksome, unhappy, troublesome
molino mill
momentáneamente momentarily
momento moment
monarca monarch
monarquía monarchy
moneda coin, currency
moneda de depósito deposit currency
moneda de metal small change
moneda del país domestic currency
moneda en efectivo hard currency
moneda extranjera foreign currency

monetario pecuniary
mongolismo mongolism
monitor monitor
monja nun
monje monk
mono ape, monkey, cute
monopolio cartel, monopoly, trust; Ecuad., Peru: chamberpot; Chile: fruit/vegetable pile (in a market)
monopolizar (v) to monopolize
monótono humdrum, monotonous
monstruo monster
montaje assemblage, assembly
montaje mural wall mount
montaña mountain
montaña rusa roller coaster
montañoso hilly
montar (v) to assemble, ride
monto amount
montón heap, pile, stack
monumental monumental
monumento monument
monzón monsoon
morado bruise, purple; Arg.: cowardly
moral moral
moralidad ethics
moratoria moratorium
mordaz scathing
mordedura bite
mordedura de animal animal bite
morder (v) to bite
mordisco nibble
moreno brown, brunette, swarthy; Cuba: black person
morfina morphine
morfología morphology
moribundo dying
morir (v) to die
morir de hambre (v) to starve

moroso   delinquent
mortal   mortal
mortalidad   death rate, mortality
mortero   mortar
mortificar (v)   to mortify, spite
mortuorio   mortuary
mosaico   mosaic
mosca   fly
Moscú   Moscow
mosquito   mosquito
mostaza   mustard
mostrador   counter
mostrador de cambio de
   moneda   foreign exchange
   counter
mostrador de información   information counter
mostrador de servicios   service
   counter
mostrar (v)   to manifest, show
mote   nickname; Amer.: corn
   (stewed); Chile: error
motel   motel
motín   mutiny
motivación   motivation
motivo   motive, reason
motocicleta   motorbike, motorcycle
motor   engine, motor
motor de arranque   starter
motorista   motorist
mover (v)   to move, budge
móvil   moveable, mobile
movilidad   mobility
movimiento   bustle, movement,
   motion
mucoso   mucous
muchísimos   umpteen
mucho   much
muchos   many
mudo   dumb, mute, speechless
mueble   furniture
mueca de dolor   wince

muelas   molar teeth
muelle   dock, wharf
muermo   glanders
muerte   death
muerte accidental   accidental
   death
muerte civil   civil death
muerto   dead
muesca   nick, notch
muestra   sample, specimen, token
muestreo   sampling
mujer   wife, woman
mujer homosexual   lesbian
mujer soltera   spinster
muleta   crutch
mulo   mule
multa   fine, penalty
multicolor   multicolored, mottled
múltiple   multiple, manifold
multiplexación   multiplexing
multiplexor de datos   data multiplexer
multiplicar (v)   to multiply, proliferate
multitarea   multitasking
multitud   mob, multitude, throng
mundano   mundane
mundial   global, world-wide
mundo   world
munición   ammunition
municipal   civic, municipal
muñeca   doll, wrist
muñeco de nieve   snowman
mural   mural
murciélago   bat
murmullo   babble, murmur, mutter
murmurar (v)   to gossip
musculatura   musculature
músculo   muscle
musculoso   brawny
muselina   muslin
museo   museum

musgo moss
música music
música popular country music
musical musical
músico musician; C. Am.: poor
  horserider; Col.: drinker; Mex.:
  hypocrite
muslo thigh
musulmán Muslim
mutación mutation
mutante mutant
mutilación mutilation

mutilación criminal mayhem
mutilar (v) to cripple, deface,
  mutilate
mutualidad mutuality
mutuo mutual
mutuo acuerdo mutual consent
muy too, very
muy alto towering
muy conocido notorious
muy frío algid
muy sangriento bloody
muy trabajador hard worker

N

nacido born
nacido muerto stillborn
nacimiento birth
nación nation
nacional domestic, national
nacionalidad nationality
Naciones Unidas United Nations
nada nothing
nada cohibido uninhibited
nada prometedor bleak
nadador swimmer
nadar (v) to swim
nadie nobody, none
naipe card
nalgas buttocks
naranja orange; Mex.: grapefruit
narcisista narcissist
narciso daffodil
narcótico narcotic
nariz nose
narración relation
narrador narrator, teller
narrar (v) to narrate, to recite
narrativo narrative
nasal nasal
nata cream
natación swimming

nativo native
natural native, natural
naturaleza character, nature
naturalista naturalist
naufragar (v) to wreck
naufragio shipwreck, wreckage,
  wreck
náusea nausea
náutico nautical
navaja razor
naval naval
navegable navigable
navegación navigation, sailing
navegante navigator
navegar (v) to cruise, navigate,
  sail
Navidad Christmas
Navidades Christmas
nebuloso foggy, hazy
necesario necessary
necesidad necessity, need
necesitado needy
necesitar (v) to need, necessitate, require
necrológicas obituary
nefasto unlucky
nefritis nephritis

negable deniable

negación específica specific denial

negar (v) to deny

negativa denial, refusal

negativo negative

negligencia culpa, negligence

negligencia ilegal malpractice

negligencia indirecta prior negligence

negligencia profesional malpractice

negligente negligent

negociable negotiable

negociación negotiation

negociador negotiator

negociante poco escrupuloso wheeler dealer

negociar (v) to negotiate

negocio business; Arg., Uru., Chile: shop

negocio conjunto joint venture

negrilla (letra) boldface

negro black

neoyorquino New Yorker

nepotismo nepotism

nervio nerve, stamina

nervioso nervous

neumático tire

neumonía pneumonia

neuralgia neuralgia

neurastenia neurasthenia

neurocirugía neurosurgery

neurología neurology

neurólogo neurologist

neurona neurone

neurosis neurosis

neurótico neurotic

neutral neutral

neutralidad neutrality

neutralizar (v) to neutralize

neutro neuter

nevada snowfall

nevar (v) to snow

nevera freezer, refrigerator

ni nor

nicotina nicotine

nicho niche

nido nest

niebla fog, mist

nieto grandchild

nieve snow

nilón nylon

ninguno neither, none

niño, niña child, infant

niño listo whiz kid

nitrógeno nitrogen

nivel level, standard

nivel de solvencia credit rating

nivel de vida standard of living

no not

no (voto negativo) nay

no aceptación nonacceptance

no autorizado unauthorized

no caucionable nonbailable

no conveniente ill-suited

no cualificado unskilled

no culpable not guilty

no deseado unwanted

no disputado uncontested

no especificado unspecified

no gravable nonleviable

no gustar (v) to dislike

no jurídico nonlegal

no obstante nonetheless, notwithstanding

no pagado unpaid

no probado untested

no residente nonresident

no responsable nonliable

noble noble

noción notion

noche evening, night

nogal walnut

nómada nomad
nombramiento appointment, nomination
nombrar (v) to appoint, designate, nominate
nombre name, noun
nombre supuesto alias
nómina payroll
nómina de personal payroll
nominal nominal
nominativo nominative
nordeste northeast
norma norm, rule, standard
normal normal
normas de contabilidad accounting standards
noroeste northwest
norte north
nosotros we
nosotros mismos ourselves
nostalgia nostalgia
nostálgico homesick, nostalgic
nota memo, memorandum, note
nota de crédito credit note
nota de deuda promissory note
nota de pago promissory note
notable notable, remarkable, striking
notablemente notably
notación notation
notar (v) to notice
notarial notarial
notario notary
notario público notary public
notas de sociedad gossip column
noticia reassurance
noticias news
notificación advice, notification
notificación legal legal notice
notificar (v) to notify
notoriedad notoriety

novedoso innovative
novela romance, thriller
noveno ninth
noventa ninety
novia bride
noviembre November
nube cloud
nublar (v) to cloud
nuca scruff
nuclear nuclear
núcleo core, nucleus
nudillo knuckle
nudista nudist
nudo knot, snag, tangle
nuera daughter-in-law
nuestro our
nueva adaptación rearrangement
nueva audiencia rehearing
Nueva York New York
nueve nine
nuevo brand new, fresh, new, original
nuevo juicio new trial
nuez walnut
nuez de la garganta Adam's apple
nulidad nullity
nulo invalid, null, void
numeral numeral
numeral binario binary numeral
numérico numerical
número number
número de fabricación serial number
número decimal decimal numeral
numeroso numerous
nunca never
nunca más anymore, nevermore
nutrición nutrition, nurture

O

o or
obedecer (v) to comply, obey
obediencia obedience
obediente obedient
obesidad obesity
obeso obese
obispo bishop
objeción challenge, objection
objetivo aim, factual, objective, target
objeto object, thing
oblea wafer
oblicuo cross, oblique
obligación debenture, enforcement, must, obligation
obligación de reintegro debenture
obligación legal legal obligation
obligaciones liabilities
obligado bound, indebted
obligar (v) to compel, commit, constrain
obligatorio binding, compulsory, mandatory
obra hecha a mano handiwork
obra maestra masterpiece
obrero working man
obscenidad obscenity
obsceno bawdy, obscene
obscurecer (v) to overcast
observación observation, remark, surveillance
observador observant
observar (v) to observe, spot
observatorio look-out, observatory
obsesión hang-up, obsession
obsesionar (v) to obsess

obsolescencia física physical obsolescence
obsoleto obsolete
obstáculo clog, hurdle, impediment, obstacle, snag
obstetricia obstetrics
obstétrico obstetrician
obstinación obstinacy
obstinado obstinate
obstrucción obstruction
obstructivo obstructive
obstruir (v) to block, choke, obstruct
obtener (v) to acquire, obtain, procure
obtuso obtuse
obvio obvious
océano ocean
Océano Atlántico Atlantic Ocean
Océano Pacífico Pacific Ocean
ocioso idle
octágano octagon
octagonal octagonal
octavo eighth
octeto byte
octubre October
ocular ocular
oculista oculist
ocultar (v) to conceal, cover, screen
oculto concealed, lurking, occult
ocupación occupation
ocupado busy, engaged
ocupante inmate
ocupar (v) to engage
ocurrir (v) to occur
ochenta eighty
ocho eight

odiar (v) to hate
odio hate, hatred
odioso odious, obnoxious
odontología dentistry, odontology
oeste west
ofender (v) to offend
ofenderse por (v) to resent
ofendido resentful
ofensa misdemeanor, offense, transgression
ofensiva offensive, push
ofensivo insulting, offensive
ofensor offender
oferente offerer
oferta bid, estimate, offer, quotation, supply
oferta en firme firm offer
oferta especial special offer
oferta temporal temporary offer
oferta y demanda supply and demand
oficial, ejecutivo official, officer
oficina bureau, office
oficina central head office, headquarters
oficina de abogados law office
oficina de cambio exchange office
oficina de correos post office
oficina meteorológica weather bureau
oficio craft
ofrecer (v) to bid, offer, propose
ofrecerse voluntario (v) to volunteer
ofrecimiento offering
oftalmología ophthalmology
oftalmólogo opthalmologist
oído ear, hearing
oir (v) to hear
ojo eye
ojo de cerradura keyhole

ola wave
olas surf
oleaje surge
oler (v) to smell
olfatear (v) to sniff, smell
olfato smell
oliva olive
ológrafo holograph
olor odor, scent, smell
olvidar (v) to forget
olvido oblivion
olla pot
ombligo navel
omisión nonfeasance, omission
omitir (v) to omit, skip
omnipotente almighty, omnipotent
omnipresente ubiquitous
omoplato shoulder blade
once eleven
oncología oncology
ondulado corrugated
ondular (v) to undulate
oneroso onerous
opaco opaque
opción choice, option
opcional optional
ópera opera
operable operable
operación a plazo forward transaction
operación al contado cash transaction
operación de cobertura hedging
operación de consolidación funding
operaciones bancarias bank operations
operador operator
opinión opinion
opio opium
oponente opposer
oponerse (v) to counter

oponerse a (v) to oppose, object

oportunidad occasion, opportunity

oportunista opportunist

oportuno opportune, timely, well-timed

oposición opposition, objection

opresión hardship, oppression

opresor oppressor

oprimir (v) to depress, oppress

optar por (v) to opt

optativo optional

óptico optician, optic

optimismo optimism

optimista optimistic, optimist

optimización optimization

óptimo optimum

optometría optometry

opuesto opposed, rival

opulencia opulence

oración prayer, sentence

orador speaker

oral oral

órbita orbit

orden array, command, sequence, writ, orderly

orden de pago debenture, payment order

orden de registro search warrant

orden de reintegro debenture

orden del día agenda, docket

ordenado tidy

ordenador computer

ordenador analógico analog computer

ordenador central host computer

ordenador comercial workstation

ordenador de bolsillo laptop computer

ordenador de uso general general purpose computer

ordenador digital digital computer

ordenador híbrido hybrid computer

ordenador personal personal computer

ordenador industrial industrial computer

ordenador personal de sobremesa desktop computer

ordenador portátil portable computer

ordenamiento marshaling

ordenanza ordinance

ordenanza municipal municipal ordinance

ordenar (v) to command, order, ordain

ordenar sectores (v) to format

ordinal (número) ordinal

ordinario ordinary, regular, vulgar

oreja ear

orgánico organic

organigrama flowchart

organigrama de programación programming flowchart

organismo organism

organización de ficheros file organization

organización organization

organizador organizer

organizar (v) to arrange, organize, regiment, stage

órgano organ

órganos genitales genital organs

orgasmo orgasm

orgía orgy

orgullo pride

orgulloso proud

orientación orientation

oriental   oriental
orientar (v)   to orientate
orificio   orifice
origen   origin, source
original   original, unconventional
orilla   bank, shore
orina   piss, urine
orinar (v)   to urinate
ornamento   ornament
oro   gold
oro en barra   bullion
oro en barras   bar gold
oro fino   fine gold
oropel   tinsel
orquesta   band, orchestra
orquestar (v)   to orchestrate
roscar (v)   to screw
ortodoxia   orthodoxy
ortodoxo   orthodox
ortografía   spelling
ortopedia   orthopedics
ortopédico   orthopedic
orzuelo   sty
orzuelos   sties
oscilar   to oscillate, vacillate, waver
oscurecer (v)   to cloud, obscure

oscuridad   blackness, darkness
oscuro   dark, murky, obscure, shadowy
ósmosis   osmosis
oso   bear
oso de felpa   teddy bear
ostentoso   swanky
ostracismo   ostracism
otitis   otitis
otoño   autumn
otorgamiento   award
otorgamiento de fallo   award
otorgar (v)   to grant
otra vez   again
otras cosas   alia
otro   another, other
ovación   ovation
ovalado   oval
ovario   ovary
oveja   sheep
ovulación   ovulation
oxidado   rusty
óxido   rust
óxido de calcio   quicklime
oxígeno   oxygen
oyente   listener

P

pabellón   canopy, pavilion
pacer (v)   to browse, pasture, graze
paciencia   patience
paciente   patient
paciente externo   outpatient
pacificar (v)   to pacify
pacífico   peaceful, pacific
pacifista   pacifist
pacto   deal, covenant, pact
pacto de obligación mutua   mutual covenant

pacto sin causa   nude contract
padrastro   stepfather
padre   father, parent
padrino   godfather
paga   pay
paga extraordinaria   bonus
pagadero   due, payable
pagadero a la vista   payable on demand
pagadero al portador   payable to bearer

pagadero con cheque pay by check
pagado paid
pagado con antelación prepaid
pagador payer
pagar (v) to pay, compensate
pagar daños (v) pay damages
pagaré bill to order, note, promissory note
pagaré de pago promissory note
pagarés libres de intereses interest-free notes
página page
paginación pagination
pago payment
pago a cuenta down payment
pago al contado payment in cash
pago adelantado retainer
pago anticipado advance payment, prepayment
pago bajo mano kickback
pago complementario extra payment
pago contra entrega de documentos cash against documents
pago contra presentación de documentos cash against documents
pago contra reembolso cash on delivery
pago final final payment
pago global lump-sum payment
pago ilegal kickback
pago por anticipado payment in advance
pago por transferencia payment by transfer
pago vencido due payment
pagos disbursements
pagos a plazos time payments
pagos atrasados arrears

país country
País Vasco Basque Country
paisaje scenery
paisano civilian
Países Bajos Netherlands
paja straw
pájaro bird
paje page
pala scoop, shovel
palabra word
palacio mansion, palace
palacio de justicia courthouse
paladar palate
paladear (v) to relish
palanca lever
palanca de control joystick
palangana basin, washbasin; Amer.: braggart; C. Amer., Col.: platter
palestino Palestinian
paleta paddle, trowel
pálido faint, pale, wan
palillo toothpick
palillos chinos chopsticks
palma palm
palma (de mano) palm
palmada clap
palmera palm
palo mast, pole, stick; P.R.: cocktail
paloma dove
palpación palpations
palpitación palpitation
palpitaciones palpitations
paludismo malaria
pan bread; Arg., Chile: liver (of an animal); Chile: courage
pana corduroy
panadería bakery
panadero baker
Panamá Panama
páncreas pancreas
pandearse (v) to bulge

pandeo bulge
pandereta tambourine
panecillo bun
panel panel
panel de jurados jury panel
paneles paneling
panorama panorama
pantalones pants, slacks, trousers
pantalla display, lampshade, monitor, screen
pantalla de color RGB monitor
pantalla de humo smoke screen
pantalla monocroma monochrome monitor
pantalla sensorizada touchscreen
pantano marsh, swamp
pantanoso swampy
pantomima mime, pantomime
pantorrillas calves
panza paunch
pañal diaper
pañuelo handkerchief
papá dad
Papa pope
papaíto daddy
papel paper
papel (personaje) role
papel de calco tracing paper
papel de envolver wrapping paper
papel de escribir writing paper
papel de estaño tinfoil
papel de lija sandpaper
papel de seda tissue paper
papel moneda fiduciary money
papel pintado wallpaper
papeleo red tape
papelería stationery, stationery store
papeleta de voto ballot paper
paperas mumps

paquete packet, package, parcel; Amer.: incompetent person; Cuba, coll.: frame-up
paquete postal parcel post
par couple, pair
para abonar called up
para qué why
para siempre forever
paracaídas parachute
parachoques bumper
parada stand, standstill, stoppage, stop; Peru: market
parada de autobús bus stop
parado unemployed; Amer.: erect
paradoja paradox
paraguas umbrella
paraíso paradise
paralelo parallel
parálisis paralysis, palsy
paralítico paralytic
paralización stagnation
paralizado stagnant
paralizar (v) to paralyze
parámetro parameter
parámetro de incumplimiento default
parámetro inicial default
paranoia paranoia
paranoico paranoid
parar (v) to stop; Amer.: to begin to listen closely
pararse (v) to rest, stick
parásito parasite
parcial partial, prejudiced
parcialidad bias, prejudice
parchar (v) to patch
parecer (v) to seem
parecerse (v) to resemble
parecido like, similar
pared wall
pareja couple
paréntesis parenthesis
paria outcast

paridad parity
parlamento parliament
paro unemployment
parodia parody, travesty
paroxismo paroxysm
parpadeo blink, flicker
párpado eyelid, lid
parque park
parquímetro parking meter
parra vine
párrafo paragraph
parricida patricide
parrilla grill
parroquia parish
parroquial parochial
parte party, part, share, side
parte alta top
partición partition
participación participation, share
participante participant
participar (v) to participate
partícipe participant, sharer
participio participle
partícula particle
partida de nacimiento birth certificate
partida doble double entry
partidario backer, partisan, retainer, supporter
partido match, party
partir (v) to depart, split
partir por el medio (v) to halve
parto birth
pasado bygone, past, stale
pasado de moda unfashionable
pasajero passenger, transient
pasamano handrail
pasamanos banister
pasaporte passport
pasar (v) to happen, pass
pasatiempo hobby, pastime
pasear (v) to ramble, ride, walk

paseo esplanade, outing, promenade, ramble, stroll
pasillo corridor; S. Am.: dance (folk)
pasión passion
pasivo liability, passive
pasivo corriente current liabilities
pasivo limitado limited liability
pasivos no corrientes non-current liabilities
pasmado thunderstruck
pasmoso stunning, appalling
paso path, pace, pass, step, tread
paso largo stride
pasta batter, pastry, pulp
pasta de dientes toothpaste
pasta de harina pasta
pastel cake, pastel
pastelero confectioner
pasteurizar (v) to pasteurize
pastilla chip, tablet, pill
pasto pasture
pata paw
patada kick
patata potato
patente overt, patent
patente básica pioneer patent
paternal paternal
paternidad fatherhood, paternity, parenthood
patético pathetic
patín skate
patín de ruedas roller skate
patinaje skating
patinaje sobre hielo ice skating
patinar (v) to skate
patinazo skid
patinete scooter
patio patio
patio de recreo playground
pato duck; Amer.: homosexual
patólogo pathologist

patrimonial patrimonial
patrimonio patrimony, proprietorship
patriota patriot
patriótico patriotic
patriotismo patriotism
patrocinador sponsor
patrocinar (v) to patronize, sponsor
patrocinio sponsorship
patrón skipper
patrulla patrol
patrullar (v) to patrol
pausa pause, wait
pavimento pavement
pavo turkey; Chile, Pan., Peru: stowaway
payasada slapstick
payaso clown
paz peace
peaje toll
peatón pedestrian
pecado sin
pecador sinful, sinner
pecas freckles
pecera fishbowl
peculiar peculiar
peculiaridad quirk
pecho bust, breast, bosom, chest
pedal pedal
pedal de freno brake pedal
pedazo piece, chunk, patch, scrap, wedge
pedestal pedestal
pediatría pediatrics
pedicuro chiropodist
pedido purchase order
pedido de prueba sample order
pedir prestado (v) to borrow, beg, request
pedo fart
pedrisco hail
pegadizo catchy

pegajoso sticky
pegar (v) to affix, glue, slap, slug
pegarse (v) to adhere
peine comb
Pekín Peking, Beijing
pelar (v) to peel; Amer.: to slander
peldaño stair
pelea quarrel, scuffle, squabble
pelear (v) to fight, squabble
película film, movie
peligro danger, jeopardy, peril, risk
peligrosamente dangerously
peligroso dangerous, hazardous, perilous, unsafe
pelirrojo redhaired
pelo hair
pelota ball; Cuba, Mex.: passion
pelotón squad
peluca wig
peludo hairy; Arg., Uru.: armadillo
peluquero barber, hairdresser
pelvis pelvis
pellejo pelt
pellizcar (v) to nip
pellizcho pinch
pena penalty
pena acumulativa cumulative penalty
pena de muerte death penalty
pena máxima maximum penalty
penal penal
penalizar (v) to penalize
pendencia pendency
pendenciero quarrelsome, rowdy
pendiente earring, pending, slope
péndulo pendulum
pene penis
penetración penetration

penetrar (v) to permeate, penetrate, pierce
penicilina penicillin
península peninsula
penitencia penance
penitenciaría penitentiary
penitente penitent
pensamiento thought
pensar (v) to think, consider, reflect
pensativo pensive, thoughtful
pensión alimony, pension
pensionista pensioner
pentágono pentagon
penuria shortage
peón pawn
peor worse, worst
pepino cucumber
pepita de oro gold nugget
pequeñito tiny, toddler
pequeño baby, small
percepción perception
perceptible perceivable, perceptible
percibir (v) to apprehend, discern, perceive
percusión percussion
percha hanger, roost
perdedor loser
perder (v) to lose
perder la calma (v) to panic
perdición ruin, undoing
pérdida casualty, forfeit, loss
pérdida de peso loss in weight
pérdida directa direct loss
pérdida por devaluación de moneda exchange devaluation
pérdida total write-off
pérdidas de capital capital losses
perdido lost, damn, missing, stray
perdiguero retriever

perdón pardon, sorry
perdonar (v) to forgive
perecedero perishable
peregrinación pilgrimage
peregrino pilgrim
perenne perennial
perentorio peremptory
pereza indolence, laziness
perezoso lazy
perfección perfection
perfeccionar (v) to perfect, streamline
perfeccionista perfectionist
perfecto perfect
perfidia perfidy
perfil profile
perforación drilling, perforation, puncture
perforadora keypunch
perforar (v) to drill, punch
perfume perfume
pericardio pericardium
pericia proficiency
periferia periphery
periférico peripheral
perímetro perimeter
periódico newspaper, periodical, journal, periodic
periodismo journalism
periodista journalist, reporter
período period
período contable accounting cycle
período de gracia grace period
período de indisponibilidad downtime
periscopio periscope
perito proficient
peritonitis peritonitis
perjudicial damaging, harmful, prejudicial
perjuicio damage, detriment, nuisance, prejudice

perjuicio intencional wanton injury
perjurar (v) to perjure
perjurio damnification, false oath, perjury
perjuro perjurer
perla pearl
permanecer (v) to linger, stay
permanencia stay
permanente permanent
permeable permeable
permisible permissible
permisivo permissive
permiso license, leave, permit, permission
permiso de conducir driving license
permitir (v) to allow, enable, let, permit
pernicioso pernicious
pero but
perpendicular perpendicular
perpetrador perpetrator
perpetuidad perpetuity
perpetuo perpetual
perplejo confused, perplexed
perra bitch
perrera kennel
perro dog, hound
perro guardián watchdog
persecución chase
perseguidor pursuer; Cuba: patrol car; Peru: hangover
perseguimiento pursuit
perseguir (v) to chase, persecute
perseverancia perseverance
perseverar (v) to persevere
persistencia persistence
persistente persistent
persistir (v) to persist
persona person
personal personal, personnel, staff

personal (del jurado) array
personalidad personality
personalmente personally
personificación personification
personificar (v) to personify
perspectiva perspective, outlook, prospect, view
perspicaz discerning, discriminating, perceptive
persuadir (v) to persuade
persuasión persuasion
persuasivo persuasive
pertenecer (v) to belong
pertenecer a (v) to pertain
pertenencias appurtenances, belongings
pertinente pertinent, relevant
perturbación disturbance
perturbación accidental accidental jamming
perturbación del orden riot
perturbador rioter
perturbar (v) to perturb
Perú Peru
perverso depraved, perverse, wicked
pervertido pervert
pervertir (v) to pervert
pesadilla nightmare
pesado cumbersome, hefty, heavy, tiresome
pesar sorrow
pesar (v) to weigh; Col.: to sell meat
pesar más (v) to outweigh
pesca catch, fishing
pescado (de mar) seafood
pescador fisherman
pesebre crib
pesimismo pessimism
pesimista pessimistic, pessimist
peso weight, burden
peso bruto gross weight

peso neto net weight
peso pesado heavyweight
pestaña eyelash
peste plague
pesticida pesticide
pétalo petal
petición petition, prayer, request
petición admitida motion granted
peticionar (v) to move
peticionario petitioner
petrificar (v) to petrify
petróleo petroleum
petrolero tanker
pez fish
pezón nipple
pianista pianist
piano piano
picadura sting
picadura de avispa hornet sting
picadura de insecto insect bite
picante spicy, pungent
picapleitos pettifogger
picar (v) to bite, itch, mince, peck, pique, pick, sting
pícaro naughty, rascal, rogue
picazón itch
pico beak, pick
picotazo peck
pídola leapfrog
pie foot; Chile: down payment
piedad piety, pity
piedra rock, stone
piedra miliaria milestone
piel fur, leather, peel, skin
piel de cerdo pigskin
pierna leg
pieza component
pigmento pigment
pignoración pignoration
pijama pajamas
pila battery, cell, stack; Amer.: fountain; Cuba: faucet

pila plana cell flat battery
pila seca dry cell
pilar mainstay, pillar, pier
píldora pill
pilotar (v) to pilot
piloto pilot
pillaje plunder
pillo rascal, rogue
pimentón cayenne pepper
pimienta pepper
pinchazo blow-out, jab, puncture
pintar (v) to paint
pintoresco scenic
pintura paint
pinza peg
pinzas tweezers
piojo louse
piojos lice
piojoso lousy, scruffy
pionero pioneer
piquete picket
pirámide pyramid
pirata pirate
piratería piracy
pirómano arson, arsonist
pisada footstep, tread
pisar (v) to tread, trample
piscina pool, swimming pool
piso apartment, deck, story; Cuba: pasturing fee; Chile, Peru: place mat
piso de abajo downstairs
pisotear (v) to tread
pista clue, track
pista de aterrizaje runway
pistola pistol
pistolero gunman
pistón piston
pivote pivot
pizarra blackboard
placa plaque
placenta placenta

placer delight, pleasure; Cuba: plot (of vacant land)
plaga pest, plague
plagiar (v) to plagiarize, pirate
plagiario plagiarist
plan arrangement, plan, scheme; Arg., Chile, Guat., Mex., Ven.: plateau, plain
plan de pagos aplazados installment plan
planchar (v) to iron
planeta planet
plano flat, plan
planta facility, plant
planta baja ground floor
plantación plantation
plantar (v) to plant
plantilla stencil, template
plasma plasma
plástico plastic
plata silver
plataforma platform
plátano banana
platillo saucer
plato dish, plate
plato sopero soup plate
playa beach, shore
plaza square
plazo installment
plazo corto short term
plazo de validez expiration date
plazo limitado time limit
plazo límite deadline
plazo tope deadline
plebiscito plebiscite
plegado folding
plegar (v) to tuck
pleito dispute, lawsuit, suit
plena dedicación full time
plenario plenary
plenipotenciario plenipotentiary
pleno del tribunal full court
pleno verano midsummer

pleura pleura
plica escrow
plomo lead
pluma feather; C. Amer.: hoax; Col., Cuba, P.R.: faucet
plural plural
plusvalía goodwill
población population, town
poblar (v) to populate
pobre poor, needy, pauper
pobreza poverty
poco little
poco a poco piecemeal
poco amable unkind
poco amistoso unfriendly
poco aparente inconspicuous
poco común rare, uncommon, unusual
poco dispuesto reluctant
poco elegante dowdy
poco entusiasta unenthusiastic
poco frecuente infrequent
poco práctico impractical
poco profundo shallow
poco seguro unsure
poco severo lenient
pocos few
podar (v) to prune
poder might, letter of attorney, proxy, power
poder (v) to be able, can, may
poder con (v) to cope
poder judicial judiciary
poder legal power of attorney
poderes power of attorney
poderoso powerful
podiatría podiatry
podrido putrid
poesía poetry
poético poetic
polar polar
polea pulley
polen pollen

policía cop, policeman, police
poliéster polyester
poligamia poligamy
polio polio
poliomielitis poliomyelitis
pólipo polyp
politécnico polytechnic
política policy, politics
política bancaria banking policy
política monetaria monetary policy
político political, politician
póliza policy, scrip, warrant
póliza de seguro insurance policy
pólizas de depósito warrants
polo polo, pole
Polonia Poland
polvo dust, powder
pólvora gunpowder, powder
polvos de talco talc powder
pollo chicken
pomada ointment
pompa pomp
pomposo pompous
pómulo cheekbone
ponderar (v) to ponder, weigh
poner (v) to place, put, set, stow
poner en libertad (v) to free
poner en peligro (v) to endanger, jeopardize
popa stern
popular popular
popularidad popularity
popularizar (v) to popularize
póquer poker
poquito dash
por for, per, via
por ahí thereabouts
por casualidad casually
por ciento per cent
por cobrar collectibles

por consiguiente accordingly, therefore
por correo aéreo by airmail
por debajo below
por día per diem
por favor please
por ferrocarril by rail
por la noche overnight
por la presente hereby
por lo alto overhead
por lo general usually
por lo visto apparently
por mar by sea, by ship
por qué why
por referencias word of mouth
por tierra by land, overland
por todas partes throughout
por último ultimately
por vía de via
por vía marítima by ship
porcentaje percentage, percent
porción allotment, lot, portion
pornografía pornography
pornográfico pornographic
poro pore
poroso porous
porque because
portador bearer, carrier, courier, payee
portador del pago payee
portátil portable
portavoz spokesman
portazo slam
portero doorman, doorkeeper, goalkeeper, porter, usher
portes pagados freight prepaid
pórtico porch
Portugal Portugal
portugués Portuguese
posada inn; Cuba: hideaway; Hond., Mex.: Christmas party
posar (v) to pose
posarse (v) to perch

poseedor holder
poseer (v) to hold, possess
posesión possession, tenure
posesión efectiva seizing in
  deed
posesivo possessive
posesorio possessory
posfechado postdated
posibilidad chance, possibility
posible potential, possible
posible cliente prospect
posición position, stand, standing
posición de bit bit position
positivo positive
posponer (v) to postpone
postal postal
postcompilador postprocessor
postdata postdate, postscript
poste post
poste indicador signpost
posteridad posterity
posterior latter, posterior
posterioridad posterity
postnatal postpartum
postor bidder
postración prostration
postrar (v) to prostrate
postre dessert
postura pose
potencia power
potencial potential
potentado magnate
potente potent
potro colt
pozo well; Col., Chile: puddle;
  Ecuad.: stream, spring
pozo de petróleo oil well
práctica practice
práctica restrictiva restrictive
  practice
practicantes paramedics
practicar (v) to practice

prácticas comerciales legítimas
  fair price
práctico workable
pradera prairie
pragmático pragmatic
preámbulo preamble
precalentamiento warm-up
precario precarious
precaución caution, precaution
precedente foregoing, precedent
preceder (v) to precede
precepto precept
preceptor tutor
precio price
precio a la baja falling price
precio actual current price
precio de compra purchase
  price
precio de coste cost price
precio de etiqueta sticker price
precio de mercado market price
precio de reventa resale price
precio de ruina giveaway
precio de venta selling price
precio F.A.S. F.A.S. price
precio límite price ceiling
precio medio average price
precio neto net price
precio puesto en destino
  landed price
precio rebajado cut price
precio reducido cut-price
precio unitario unit price
precioso pretty, precious
precipicio precipice
precipitación precipitation, rainfall
preciso accurate, precise, strict
precompilador preprocessor
precontractual precontractual
precoz precocious
precursor precursor
predator predator

predecesor predecessor
predecir (v) to predict
predestinar (v) to predestine
predicado predicate
predicador preacher
predicar (v) to preach, predicate
predicción prediction
predisponer (v) to prejudice
predominante ascendant, prevalent, prevailing
predominio predominance
prefacio foreword
preferencia liking, preference
preferente preferential
preferido preferred
preferir (v) to prefer
prefijo prefix
pregunta question, inquiry, query
preguntar (v) to ask, inquire, question
prehistórico prehistoric
prejuicio prejudgment
prejuzgar (v) to prejudge
preliminar preliminary
preludio prelude
prematuro premature
premeditación premeditation
premeditado premeditated, willful
premeditar (v) to premeditate
premenstrual premenstrual
premiar (v) to award
premio bonus, award, purse, premium, prize
premio gordo jackpot
premisa premise
prenda garmet, pawn
prendar (v) to pledge
prender el alfiler (v) to pin
prensa press
prensa de billetes note printing press
preocupación preoccupation

preocupado concerned, preoccupied, troubled, worried
preocupar (v) to trouble
preparación preparation
preparado ready
preparar (v) to prepare, process
preparatorio preparatory
preposición preposition
prepucio foreskin
prerrogativa prerogative
presa barrage, dam, prey, reservoir
presagio omen, portent
prescribir (v) to prescribe
prescripción prescription
prescriptivo prescriptive
presencia presence
presenciar (v) to witness
presentable presentable
presentación introduction, presentation
presentar (v) to present, appeal, introduce, produce
presente present
presentimiento hunch, premonition
preservativo condom, contraceptive, preservative
presidencia presidency
presidencial presidential
presidenta del jurado forewoman
presidente president, chairman
presidente del consejo de administración chairman
presidente del jurado foreman of the jury
presidiario convict
presidir (v) to preside
presión crush, press, pressure, stress
presión sanguínea blood pressure

presionar (v) to depress, push
presionar en grupo (v) to lobby
prestador lender
préstamo loan
préstamo a bajo interés low-interest loan
préstamo a plazo fijo time loan
prestar (v) to lend, loan
prestatario borrower
prestigio prestige
presumido smug
presumir (v) to presume
presunción assumption, presumption
presuntivo presumptive
presuntuoso presumptuous
presupuestario budgetary
presupuesto budget, estimate
presupuesto de gastos expense budget
pretensión pretence
pretexto pretext, plea
prevalecer (v) to prevail
prevención anticipation, prevention
prevención contra fallos fail safe
preventivo preventive
prever (v) to foresee
previamente previously
previo previous, prior
previsible foreseeable
previsión foresight
previsor provident
prima bonus, premium
primario primary
primer pago down payment
primer plano close-up
primera clase first-class
primeramente initially
primero foremost, first, prime, premier
primeros auxilios first aid

primitivo primitive
princesa princess
principal main, prime, primary, principal
principalmente chiefly
príncipe prince
principiante beginner, novice
principio beginning, opening, outset, principle, start, tenet
principios de consolidación principles of consolidation
principio legal legal principle
prioridad precedence, preemption, priority
prioridad de paso right-of-way
prisa hurry, haste, rush
prisión prison
prisionero prisoner
privación starvation
privado private
privar (v) to deprive
privativo privative
privilegiado privileged
privilegio privilege, concession
proa prow
probabilidad likelihood, odds, probability
probable likely, probable
probablemente probably
probar (v) to attempt, chance, prove, test, taste, try
problema problem
problemático problematic
proceder (v) to proceed
procedimiento procedure, proceeding
procesable indictable
procesado defendant, indictee
procesador processor
procesador central central processor, mainframe
procesador de textos word processor

procesador matriz array processor

procesal processal, procedural

procesamiento indictment, prosecution

procesamiento a tiempo real real time processing

procesamiento de imagen image processing

procesamiento de información information processing

procesamiento en paralelo parallel processing

procesamiento por lotes batch processing

procesamiento secuencial sequential processing

procesar (v) to indict, prosecute, process

proceso proceeding, process, prosecution, trial

proceso aleatorio random process

proceso criminal criminal process

proceso de datos data processing

proceso de restablecimiento recovery procedure

proceso ejecutivo executory process

proceso en serie serial processing

proceso inicial original process

proclamación proclamation

proclamar (v) to proclaim

procreación procreation

procurador procurator, proctor

prodigio prodigy, profuse

prodigioso prodigious

producción output, production, yield

producir (v) to make, originate, provoke, produce, yield

productividad productivity

productivo productive

producto product

producto corriente commodity

producto de granja produce

producto nacional bruto gross national product

producto que no se fabrica más discontinued

productor producer

productos manufacturados manufactured goods

profanidad profanity

profano profane

profecía prophecy

profesar (v) to profess

profesión profession

profesional professional, practitioner

profesor professor, tutor

profundamente profoundly

profundidad depth

profundo profound

profusión profusion

profuso profuse

programa program, prospectus, schedule

programa auxiliar utility program

programa de aplicación application program

programa de base source program

programa de conexión driver

programa de ensamblaje assembly program

programa de prueba test program

programa resultante object program, target program

programa standard standard program

programación programming

programación lineal linear programming

programación no lineal nonlinear programming

programador programmer

programar (v) to computerize

programas software

programas fijos firmware

progresar (v) to progress

progresión progression

progresivo onward, progressive

progreso headway, progress

prohibición ban, embargo, interdiction, prohibition

prohibido forbidden

prohibir (v) to ban, forbid, interdict, prohibit, restrain

proletario proletarian

proliferación proliferation

prolífico prolific

prolijo wordy, meticulous

prólogo preface, prologue

prolongación extension, prolongation

prolongar (v) to prolong

promedio average

promesa assurance, commitment, pledge, promise, vow

promesa sin causa naked promise

prometedor promisor, promising, rosy

prometer (v) to assure, pledge, promise

promisorio promissory

promoción promotion

promoción de exportaciones export promotion

promoción de ventas sales promotion

promover (v) to further, promote

pronombre pronoun

pronosticable predictable

pronóstico del tiempo weather forecast

pronto prompt, soon

pronto pago prompt payment

pronunciación pronunciation

pronunciamiento pronouncement

pronunciar (v) to pronounce, enunciate

propaganda propaganda

propaganda postal junk mail

propagar (v) to propagate

propicio auspicious

propiedad estate, domain, holding, ownership, property

propiedad de una sola persona sole proprietorship

propiedad lindante abutting property

propietario proprietary, proprietor, owner

propina tip, gratuity

propio own, proper

proponente proponent

proponer (v) to propose, submit

proponerse (v) to intend

proporción proportion, ratio, rate

proporción de fallos failure rate

proporcional proportional

proporcionar (v) to afford, provide

proposición proposition

propósito purpose

propuesta proposal

propulsión propulsion

prorrateo apportionment

prórroga respite

prorrogar (v) to prorogue

prosa prose
proscribir (v) to outlaw, proscribe
proscripción proscription
proscrito outlawed, outlaw
prosperar (v) to fare, prosper, thrive
prosperidad prosperity
próspero flourishing, prosperous, thriving
próstata prostate
prostitución prostitution
prostituta call girl, prostitute
protagonista protagonist
protección patronage, protection, safeguard
protección de copia copy-protected
protección de datos data protection
protección de grabado write protect
protectivo protective
protector patronizing, protective
protector de línea data line protector, surge protector
proteger (v) to shield, shade, protect
protegido protégé
proteína protein
protesta protest
protestado protestee
protestador protester
protestante Protestant
protestar (v) to protest
protocolo protocol
prototipo prototype
provecho benefit, profit
provechoso profitable, useful
proveedor supplier
proveer (v) to cater, furnish, stock
proverbial proverbial

proverbio proverb
providencia providence
providencial providential
provincia province
provincial provincial
provisión provision
provisional makeshift, provisional, tentative, temporary, transitory
provocación provocation
provocar (v) to instigate, tantalize, trigger
provocativo defiant, provocative
proximidad proximity
próximo forthcoming, next
Próximo Oriente Near East
proyección projection
proyectar (v) to project, schedule
proyectil missile, projectile
proyecto project
proyecto de factura bill
proyecto de ley bill
proyector projector, spotlight
prudencia prudence, caution
prudente cautious, prudent, wise
prueba evidence, proof, test, trial, tryout; Amer. pl: sleight of hand
prueba admisible proper evidence
prueba falsificada framed evidence
prueba negativa negative proof
psicoanalista psychoanalyst
psicología psychology
psicólogo psychologist
psicópata psychopath
psicopatía psychopathy
psicosis psychosis
psiquiatría psychiatry
psoriasis psoriasis
pubertad puberty
púbico pubic
pubis pubis

publicación issue, publication, publishing
publicar (v) to publish, publicize
publicidad advertisement, advertising, publicity
público open, overt, public
pudín pudding
pudrir (v) to rot
pueblecito village
pueblo folk, people, village
pueblo natal home town
puente bridge, dental bridge
puente aéreo airlift
pueril childish, puerile
puerta door
puerto harbor, port
puerto de destino port of destination
puesta a cero reset
puesta de sol sunset
puesto booth, job, stall, station
puesto que inasmuch
pulcro sleek
pulga flea
pulgada inch
pulgar thumb
pulmonar pulmonary
pulmones lungs
pulmonía pneumonia
pulpa pulp
púlpito pulpit
pulsación pulsation
pulsar (v) to pulsate
pulsera bracelet
pulso pulse; Cuba: bracelet
pulverizar (v) to pulverize, powder, spray

punitivo punitive
punta peak, tip; Amer.: crowd
puntada stitch; Amer.: stitch or sharp pain in one's side
puntiagudo pointed
punto dot, point, spot, stitch
punto de control checkpoint
punto de interrupción breaking point
punto de reunión resort
punto de venta point of sale
punto de vista standpoint, viewpoint
punto destacado landmark
punto muerto deadlock
punto y coma semicolon
puntos de compresión pressure points
puntuación punctuation
puntual punctual
puntualidad punctuality
puntuar (v) to punctuate
punzada twinge
puñado fistful
puñal dagger
puñetazo punch
puño cuff, fist
pupila (del ojo) pupil
pureza purity
purga purge
purgar (v) to purge, vent
purgatorio purgatory
purificar (v) to purify, refine
puro pure, sheer, undefiled
pus pus
puta whore

Q

que than, which, what
qué what

que ahorra tiempo time-saving
que coopera responsive

que está en deuda indebted
que huele mal smelly
que recuerda reminiscent
que se acerca oncoming
que tiene éxito successful
quedar (v) to remain, stay
quedarse (v) to tarry
quedarse dormido (v) to oversleep
queja complaint
quejarse (v) to complain
quejido whimper
quemado charred
quemado de sol sunburned
quemador burner
quemadura burn
quemadura de sol sunburn
quemadura química chemical
burn
quemar (v) to burn, fire
querella complaint
querellante plaintiff
querer (v) to cherish, love,
would, will, want
querido beloved, darling

queso cheese
quiebra bankruptcy, failure
quien who, which
quienquiera whoever
quieto quiet, still
quilate carat
química chemistry
químico chemical
quimioterapia chemotherapy
quince fifteen
quinina quinine
quinteto quintet
quinto fifth; Chile, Mex.: coin
worth five centavos
quiosco kiosk, newsstand
quirófano operating theater
quiropráctico chiropractor
quirúrgico surgical
quiste cyst
quitamanchas stain remover
quitar (v) to deprive, remove
quitar valor (v) to detract
quitarse (v) to shed
quizás maybe
quórum quorum

R

rabia rabies, rage
rabiar (v) to storm
rabieta tantrum
rabino rabbi
rabioso raging, rabid
rabo tail
ración allotment, ration
racional reasoning, rational
racha puff
radar radar
radiación radiation, radiance
radiador radiator
radial radial
radiante radiant

radiar (v) to radio, radiate
radical radical
radio radius, radio, spoke, wireless
radioactividad radioactivity
radioactivo radioactive
radiodifundido broadcast
radiodifusión broadcasting
radiografía radiography
radiología radiology
radiólogo radiologist
raer (v) to scrape
raíz root
raja slit

ramera hooker
ramita twig
ramo bunch, bouquet
rampa ramp
rancio stale
rancho ranch
ranura slot
rápidamente quickly
rapidez rapidity, speed, swiftness
rápido rapid, quick, swift
rápidos rapids
rapto abduction, ravish, rape, rapture, trance
raptor abductor
raqueta racket
rara vez seldom
rareza oddity
raro odd, rare, singular, strange, weird
rascacielos skyscraper
rasgar (v) to scratch, slash, tear
rasguño scrape, scratch
raso satin
raspado curettage
raspadura abrasion, scrape
raspar (v) to chafe, scrape
rastrear (v) to track
rastro trail, trace
rasurar (v) to shave
rata rat
ratero pilferer
ratificar (v) to ratify
rato while
ratón mouse
ratonera mousetrap
ratones mice
raya scratch, stripe, streak
rayar (v) to scratch, Mex.: to pay workers, to collect wages
rayo lightning, ray, spoke, thunderbolt
rayo de sol sunbeam
rayón rayon

rayos X X-ray
raza breed, race
raza humana manhood
razón reason
razón fundamental rationale
razonable reasonable
razonar (v) to argue
razonar que (v) to reason
reabastecer (v) to refuel
reabrir una causa (v) to reopen a case
reacción reaction, response
reacción en cadena chain reaction
reaccionar (v) to react, respond
reaccionario reactionary
reacio unwilling
reactor reactor
readjudicar (v) to relet
reafirmar (v) to reaffirm
reajustar (v) to readjust
reajuste readjustment
real actual, real, royal
realeza royalty
realidad reality, truth
realimentación feedback
realista realist
realizable attainable, realizable
realización achievement, accomplishment
realizado accomplished
realizar (v) to materialize, implement, perform
realquilar (v) to sublet
realzar (v) to emboss, enhance
reanimar (v) to perk
reanudación resumption
reanudar (v) to resume
reaparecer (v) to reappear
reapertura reopening
reavalúo reappraisal
rebaja discount, rebate, reduction

rebajar (v) to discount, reduce, rebate

rebajar precios (v) to undercut

rebanada de pan loaf, slice of bread

rebaño herd

rebatir (v) to refute

rebelde rebellious, nonconformist

rebeldía contumacy

rebelión rebellion, revolt

rebobinado rewinding

rebobinar (v) to rewind

reborde ledge

rebosar (v) to overflow

rebotar (v) to bounce, rebound

rebote rebound

recaer (v) to relapse

recaída relapse

recambiar (v) to refill

recambio refill

recambios spare parts

recapitulación recap

recargador recharger

recargar (v) to recharge

recargo surcharge

recaudación collection

recelar (v) to suspect

recelo apprehension

receloso apprehensive

recepción reception

recepcionista receptionist

receptáculo receptacle

receptivo receptive

receptor receiver

recesión downturn, recession

receso recess

receta prescription, recipe

rechoncho plump

recibir (v) to receive

recibo receipt

recibo de almacén warehouse receipt

recién llegado newcomer

recién nacido newborn

reciente brand new, recent

recientemente lately

recinto precinct

recinto universitario campus

reciprocidad reciprocity

recíproco reciprocal

recital recital

reclamación claim, complaint, reclamation

reclamación fraudulenta false claim

reclamar (v) to complain, reclaim

reclinarse (v) to lean

recluta recruit

reclutamiento recruitment

reclutar (v) to recruit; Arg.: to round up cattle

recobrar (v) to recapture, repossess, regain, recoup

recobro recapture

recolección pickup

recomendación recommendation

recomendar (v) to entrust, recommend

recompensa recompense, reward

recompensar (v) to recompense, reward

reconciliar (v) to reconcile, reunite

reconocer (v) to acknowledge, confess, recognize

reconocible recognizable

reconocimiento authentication, acknowledgement, avowal, examination, recognition

reconocimiento de caracteres character recognition

reconocimiento de deuda promissory note

reconocimiento de pago promissory note

reconocimiento (médico) checkup

reconsiderar (v) to reconsider

reconstrucción reconstruction

reconstruir (v) to rebuild, reconstruct

reconvención countercharge

recopilación digest

recopilar (v) to compile

recordar (v) to recollect, remember, remind

recordatorio reminder

recorrer (v) to scour

recreación recreation

recriminación recrimination

recriminar (v) to recriminate

rectangular oblong, rectangular

rectángulo rectangle

rectificación amendment

rectificar (v) to rectify, redress

recto rectum

recubrimiento overlay

recubrir (v) to recap

recuerdo reminiscence, remembrance, recollection, souvenir

recuperable recoverable

recuperación recovery, recuperation, salvage, retrieval

recuperación de datos file recovery

recuperación de información information retrieval

recuperar (v) to recover, recuperate, recoup, salvage

recurso remedy, resource, recourse

recurso adicional cumulative remedy

recurso exclusivo exclusive remedy

recurso legal judicial remedy

recursos legales legal remedies

recursos naturales natural resources

recusable recusable

recusación challenge, recusation

recusar (v) to recuse

rechazable refusable

rechazar (v) to disown, repudiate, rebuff, repel, reject, refuse

rechazo repudiation, rejection, refusal

red network, net

red de conexión switching network

red de ordenadores computer network

red de ordenadores locales local area network

redactar (v) to word

redada roundup

redención redemption

redescuento rediscount

redimir (v) to redeem

rédito yield

redondo round

reducción abatement, cutback, reduction

reducción progresiva scaledown

reducir (v) to compress, reduce, slow; Amer.: to handle stolen goods

reembolsar (v) to reimburse, repay, refund

reembolso repayment, redemption, refund, reimbursement

reemplazar (v) to replace, supersede

reemplazo displacement

reencarcelar (v) to remand

reencarnar (v) to reincarnate

reexaminación re-examination

reexpedir (v) to redirect

referencia reference

referencia recíproca cross-reference

referéndum referendum

referir (v) to recount, refer, recite

refinamiento refinement

refinar (v) to refine

refinería refinery

reflejar (v) to reflect

reflejo reflex, shimmer

reflexión reflection, reflexive

reforma reform

reformación reformation

reformado reformed

reformar (v) to reform

reforzar (v) to reinforce, strengthen

refractar (v) to refract

refrán saying, proverb

refrenar (v) to curb, deter, stem

refrescante refreshing

refrescar (v) to refresh

refresco refresher, refreshment, soda

refriega fray

refuerzo reinforcement

refugiado refugee

refugiarse (v) to shelter

refugio haven, refuge, retreat, shelter

refutable refutable

refutación refutation, rebuttal

regalo gift, present, treat

regañar (v) to nag

regar (v) to water

regatear (v) to bargain

regeneración regeneration

regenerador regenerator

regente regent

régimen regime

regimiento regiment

regio regal, royal

región region, tract, vicinity

regional regional

registrado registered

registrador registrar

registrar (v) to log, register, record, ransack

registro examination, recording, record, registration, recorder, register, search

registro de desplazamiento shift register

registro de títulos register of deeds

registro de vuelo black box

regla rule, ruler

regla de cálculo slide ruler

regla especial special rule

reglamentación de la banca banking regulations

reglamento regulation, rule

reglamentos bylaws, regulations

reglamentos de la sociedad articles of incorporation

regocijarse (v) to exult, rejoice

regresión regression

regreso a casa homecoming

regulador regulatory

regular average, regular, so-so

regular (v) to regulate

regularidad regularity

rehabilitación rehabilitation

rehén hostage

rehipotecar (v) to repledge

rehusar (v) to refuse

reimpresión reprint

reimprimir (v) to reprint

reina queen

reinado reign

reinar (v) to reign

reincorporar (v) to roll in

reino kingdom, realm

Reino Unido United Kingdom

reintegrar (v) to reinstate

reintegro refunding, reinstatement

reinvertir (v) to reinvest

reír (v) to laugh

reiterativo repetitive

reivindicación replevy

relación relation, relationship, relevance, reference, ratio

relación contable accounting note

relacionado allied, related

relacionar (v) to relate

relajación relaxation

relajante relaxant

relajarse (v) to relax

relámpago lightning

relatar (v) to report

relativo relative

relato narration, report

religión religion

religioso religious

reliquia familiar heirloom

reloj clock, watch

reloj de arena timer

relojero watchmaker

relucir (v) to shine

rellenar (v) to cram, refill, replenish, stuff

relleno padding, replenishment

remache rivet

remanente remnant, residuary

remar (v) to paddle, row

rematar (v) to cap, top

remedio redress, remedy

remesa consignment, remittance

remesa documentaria documentary draft

remesa simple clean draft

remiendo mend

remisión remission

remitente payer

remitir (v) to refer, remit, send

remo oar

remolcar (v) to tow

remolino swirl

remolque trailer

remontarse (v) to soar

remordimiento remorse, regret

remoto remote

remover (v) to stir

remuneración remuneration

remunerar (v) to remunerate

renal renal

rencor rancor, spite

rencoroso vindictive

rendición surrender

rendimiento yield

rendimiento de la inversión return on investment

rendirse (v) to surrender

renegado renegade

renegociación renegotiation

renombre renown

renovación renewal

renovar (v) to renew, renovate

renta revenue

renuncia disclaimer, renunciation, resignation, reluctance, surrender, waiver

renuncia de derechos waiver of rights

renuncia implícita implied waiver

renunciar (v) to disclaim, forgo, renounce, relinquish, resign, revoke, waive

reñir (v) to feud, quarrel, squabble

reo culprit

reorganización reorganization

reorganizar (v) to reorganize

reparación redress, reparation, repair

reparación positiva affirmative relief

reparador remedial

reparar (v) to repair; Guat., Mex.: to rear (a horse)
repartir (v) to apportion, deliver
reparto allotment, delivery
repasar (v) to overhaul, review
repatriado repatriate
repentino sudden
repercusión repercussion
repertorio repertoire
repetición repetition, rehearsal, recurrence
repetido recurrent
repetidor repeater
repetir (v) to repeat
repetirse (v) to recur
repique peal
repisa de chimenea mantel
réplica answer, comeback, rejoinder, retort
replicante repliant
replicar (v) to answer, rejoin
réplicas cross talk
reposición rerun
reposo repose
represalia reprisal
represalias retaliation
representación representation
representación gráfica graphical display
representante agent, representative, rep
representar (v) to represent, stage
represión reprimand, repression
represivo repressive
reprimenda rebuke, reprimand
reprimir (v) to quell, repress
reproche reproof, reproach, reflection
reproducción replica, rendering, reproduction
reproducir (v) to reproduce
reptil reptile

república republic
República Dominicana Dominican Republic
republicano republican
repudiar (v) to disclaim
repuesto refill, spare
repuestos spare parts
repugnancia revulsion
repugnante distasteful, repellent, repugnant, sickening
repugnar (v) to disgust, sicken
repulsa rebuff, snub
repulsión repulsion
reputación reputation
reputar (v) to repute
requerir (v) to require
requiem requiem
requisito requirement
requisitorio requisitory
resaca hangover
resaltar (v) to project
resbaladizo slippery
resbalar (v) to slip, slide
resbalón slip
rescatable redeemable
rescatar (v) to rescue, reclaim; Mex.: to resell
rescate redemption, rescue, ransom
rescate de bonos redemption of bonds
rescindir (v) to rescind
rescisión rescission
rescisión tácita implied rescission
rescisorio rescissory
resentido resentful
resentimiento resentment
reserva reserve, buffer pool, constraint, qualification, reservation, stockpile
reserva de oro gold reserve
reservado aloof, private, re-

served, secretive, undemonstrative, withdrawn

reservar (v) to reserve, book

reservas reserves

reservas bancarias bank reserves

reservas obligatorias compulsory reserves

reservas para depreciación allowance for depreciation

reservas para devoluciones de ventas allowance for sales returns

reservas para impagados allowance for uncollectibles

reservas para morosos allowance for bad debts

resguardo collateral, slip

resguardo al portador bearer certificate

resguardo de acciones al portador bearer share certificate

resguardo de ingreso deposit slip

resguardo provisional binder

residencia residence

residencial residential

residente resident, commorant

residir (v) to reside

residual residual

residuo remainder, residue

resignado uncomplaining

resistencia resistance, endurance, resistor, resilience, stamina, strength

resistente resilient, resistant

resistir (v) to resist, stick, withstand

resolución resolution, resolve, ruling

resolución judicial judicial decision

resolutivo resolutive

resolver (v) to decide, solve

resonancia resonance, reverberation

resonante resonant

resonar (v) to blare, resound, reverberate

respectivo respective

respecto respect, regard

respetable respectable

respetar (v) to respect

respeto deference

respetuoso respectful

respiración breathing, respiration

respirador respirator

respirar (v) to breathe

respiro respite, reprieve

responder (v) to respond, reply

responsabilidad liability, responsibility

responsabilidad definida direct liability

responsabilidad directa primary liability

responsabilidad legal legal liability

responsabilidad personal personal liability

responsable accountable, liable, responsible

responsable legalmente legally liable

respuesta answer, response

resquicio slit

resta subtraction

restablecer (v) to reinstate

restablecimiento rehabilitation, revival

restante remainder

restar (v) to deduct, subtract

restauración restoration

restaurante restaurant

restaurar (v) to restore

restitución restitution
restituir (v) to pay back
resto balance, residue, rest, remnant, remainder
restos remains
restregar (v) to scrub
restricción restriction
restrictivo restrictive
restringido restricted
restringir (v) to restrict
resucitación resuscitation
resucitar (v) to resurrect, revive
resuelto resolute, single-minded, steadfast
resuelto de carácter strong-minded
resuellos pantings
resultado outcome, result, upshot
resultado final payoff
resumen abstract, digest, rundown, summary
resumir (v) to summarize
resurgimiento resurgence
resurrección resurrection
retaguardia rearguard
retardar (v) to retard, slow
retardo delay
retención retention, withholding
retener (v) to retain, withhold
reticencia reticence
reticente reticent
retina retina
retirada pullout, withdrawal
retirado retired, secluded
retirar (v) to disengage, recall, withdraw
retirarse (v) to retire
retiro retirement, retreat, seclusion
retiro (de fondos) fund withdrawal

retiro de moneda calling in of currency
retorcerse to squirm, writhe
retorno comeback, return
retractar (v) to recant, retract
retransmitir (v) to relay
retrasado mental moron
retrasar (v) to postpone
retraso delay, lag, postponement, slowdown
retratar (v) to depict, portray
retrato portrait, portrayal
retroactividad retroactivity
retroactivo retroactive
retroceder (v) to recede, recoil
retroceso backlash, recoil, recession, slump
retrógrado retrograde
retrospectivamente in retrospect
retrospectivo retrospective
retrovisor rear-view
retumbar (v) to resound
retumbo reverberation
reumático rheumatic
reumatismo rheumatism
reunión assembly, briefing, meeting, get-together, reunion, sitting
reunir (v) to collect, concentrate, gather, reunite
revaluación revaluation
revelación revelation, disclosure
revelador developer, revealing, telltale
revelar (v) to disclose, reveal
revender (v) to resell
reventa resale
reventar (v) to pop
reverencia reverence
reverenciar (v) to revere
reversible reversible
reversión reversion
reversión al estado escheat

revertir (v) to revert
revisar (v) to revise, review
revisión audit, revision, retrial
revista magazine, revue
revivir (v) to revive
revocable revocable
revocación repeal, cassation, reversal
revocar (v) to repeal, revoke, take back
revolcarse (v) to wallow
revolución revolution, rev, turn
revolucionar (v) to revolutionize
revolucionario revolutionary
revólver revolver
revolver (v) to scramble
rey king
reyerta brawl
ribera riverside
rico affluent, rich, wealthy
ridiculizar (v) to mock
ridículo ridicule, ridiculous
riego irrigation
rienda rein
riesgo danger, exposure, hazard, risk
riesgo evidente obvious risk
rifa raffle
rifar (v) to raffle
rifle rifle
rigidez rigidity, stiffness
rígido rigid, stiff
rigor rigor
riguroso rigorous
rima rhyme
rimbombante flamboyant
rimel (pestañas) mascara
rinitis rhinitis
riña bickering, squabble
riñón kidney
río river, stream
riqueza riches, richness, wealth

risa laugh, laughter
risilla giggle
risita chuckle
rítmico rhythmic
ritmo rhythm
rito rite
ritual ritual
rival rival
rivalidad rivalry
rizar (v) to curl
rizo curl
robado stolen
robar (v) to poach, rob, sneak, steal
robo burglary, heist, larceny, robbery, stealing, theft
robo de mercancías pilferage
robo de tiendas shoplifting
robot robot, android
robustez sturdiness
robusto robust, sturdy, strapping, stout
roca rock
rociar (v) to sprinkle, spray
rocío dew
rodada rut
rodaja slice
rodar (v) to roll; Hond.: to knock down
rodear (v) to encircle, skirt, surround, wreathe
rodilla knee
roedor rodent
rogar (v) to beg, pray, request
rogatorio rogatory
rojo red
rollo coil, roll
rollo de escritura scroll
Roma Rome
romano Roman
romántico romantic
rompecabezas jigsaw, puzzle
rompehielos icebreaker

romper (v) to break, disrupt, shatter
romperse (v) to crack
ron rum
roncar (v) to snore
ronco husky
ronda prowl
rondador prowler
rondar (v) to prowl
ronquido snore
ronquidos snoring
ronronear (v) to purr
roña scab
ropa cloth
ropa de cama bedding
ropa interior underclothes, underwear
ropa íntima lingerie
rosa rose
rosado rosy, rose
rosaleda rose garden
rosario bead, rosary
rosca screw
roscar (v) to screw
roseola roseola
rotación de stock inventory turnover
roto broken, ragged
rotura breach, breakage, break, rent
rozar (v) to rub

rubéola German measles, rubeola, rubella
rubio blond
rubor blush
rúbrica paraph, heading
rudimentario rudimentary
rudimento rudiment
rudo rude, rough
rueda wheel
rugido roar
rugir (v) to roar
ruido noise, clatter, rumble, sound
ruido sordo thud
ruidoso noisy, rowdy, vociferous
ruina ruin, undoing
ruinoso ruinous
ruleta roulette
rumbo route; Col.: humming bird; Guat.: spree
rumor rumble, rumor
rumores hearsay
ruptura break, rupture, split
rural rural
Rusia Russia
ruso Russian
rústico rustic
ruta route
ruta alternativa alternate routing
rutina routine

S

sábado Saturday
sábana sheet
sabandijas vermin
sabañón chilblain
sabedor conscious
sabiduría wisdom
sabio sage, wise
sable saber

sabor relish, savor, taste
saborear (v) to relish, taste
sabotaje sabotage
saboteador saboteur
sabroso palatable, savory, rich, spicy, tasty
sacacorchos corkscrew
sacapuntas pencil sharpener

sacar (v) to take out, withdraw
sacar afuera (v) to protrude
sacarina saccharin
sacarosa saccharose
sacerdocio priesthood
sacerdote priest
saco sack; Amer.: sports coat
saco de arena sandbag
saco de dormir sleeping bag
sacramento sacrament
sacrificio sacrifice
sacrilegio sacrilege
sacro sacrum
sacudida jolt, lurch, shake, toss
sacudir (v) to jerk, lurch, shake, rock, toss
sádico sadistic
sadismo sadism
saeta dart
sagaz sagacious
sagrado holy, sacred
sal salt; C. Amer., Cuba: bad luck
sala chamber, parlor, room
sala de arte picture gallery
sala de espera waiting room
sala de estar living room, sitting room
sala de juntas board room
sala del tribunal courtroom
sala principal main hall
salado salty
salario salary, wage
salchicha sausage
saldo acreedor credit balance
saldo inicial opening balance
saldos clearance sale
salida depart, exit, output, outlet, reset
salida de sol sunrise
saliente outgoing, protruding, rising
salino saline
salir (v) to leave, depart, rise

salir a chorros (v) to squirt
saliva saliva, spit
salmo psalm
salmonela salmonella
salobre salty
salón lounge, salon, saloon
salón de ventas showroom
salpicadura splash
salpicar (v) to splash
salsa sauce, seasoning; Chile: beating
salsa de tomate catsup, ketchup
saltar (v) to jump, leap, prance, skip, spring
salto dive, hop, jump, leap, pounce
salto mortal leapfrog
salud health
salud mental mental health
saludable wholesome
saludar (v) to greet, salute
saludo compliment, greeting, salute
salvación salvation
salvador rescuer, savior
salvaje savage, wild
salvamento rescue, salvage
salvaplatos tablemat
salvar (v) to rescue, save, salvage
salvia sage
salvo save
sanatorio sanatorium
sanción sanction
sanciones penalties
sanciones económicas economic sanctions
sandalia sandal
sandía watermelon
sangrar (v) to bleed
sangre blood
sangría bleeding
sanidad sanitation

sanitario sanitary
sano healthy, sane, sound, wholesome
santificar (v) to sanctify
santo saint
santuario sanctuary
sapo toad; Chile, Mex.: scoundrel
saqueador plunderer
saquear (v) to rifle
saqueo looting, pillage
sarampión measles, rubeola
sarcasmo sarcasm
sarcoma sarcoma
sargento sergeant
sarro dental tartar
sartén frying pan
sartorio sartorius
sastre tailor
Satanás Satan
satánico satanic
satélite satellite
sátira satire
satisfacción satisfaction, indulgence
satisfacer (v) to indulge, satisfy, suffice
satisfactorio satisfactory
saturar (v) to saturate
sauna sauna
saxofón saxophone
sebáceo sebaceous
seborrea seborrhea
secador dryer
secar (v) to dry, wither
sección section
secreción secretion
secretario secretary
secretario del juzgado court clerk
secreto secrecy, secret, undercover
secreto absoluto top-secret

sectario sectarian
sector sector
secuencia sequence
secuestrador abductor, kidnapper
secuestrar (v) to kidnap, sequester
secuestro abduction, kidnap, kidnapping, sequestration
secular secular
secundario secondary
sed thirst
seda silk
sedante sedative
sedición sedition
sediento thirsty
sediento de sangre bloodthirsty
sedimento sediment
sedoso silky
seducción seduction
seducir (v) to seduce, tempt
seductor seductive
seglar layman
segmento partition, section, segment
segregación segregation
segregar (v) to segregate
seguido consecutive
seguidor follower
seguir (v) to continue, follow, pursue, trace
según pursuant to
según cabe suponer supposedly
según parece allegedly
segunda clase second class
segundas nupcias remarriage
segundo second
seguramente surely
seguridad collateral, safety, security
seguridad de los datos data security

seguridad social social security

seguro certain, insurance, safe, secure, sure

seguro contra incendio fire insurance

seguro de mercancías insurance of goods

seguro de sí mismo self-confident

seguros insurance

seis six

selección choice, selection

seleccionar (v) to select

selectivo selective

sellado sealed, stamped

sellar (v) to seal

sello seal, stamp

sello de acuñación hallmark

sello de correos stamp

sello de garantía hallmark

sello de goma rubber stamp

sello particular private seal

semáforos traffic lights

semana week

semanal weekly

semántico semantic

sembrar (v) to seed

semejanza resemblance

semen semen

semicircular semicircular

semicírculo semicircle

semiconductor semiconductor

semifinal semifinal

semilla seed

seminario seminar

senado senate

senador senator

sencillamente simply

sencillez simplicity

sencillo plain, simple

senda path

sendero trail

senil senile

seno breast, antrum, bosom, sinus

sensación feeling, sensation, thrill

sensacional lurid, sensational

sensatez sanity

sensato sensible

sensible sensitive

sensor sensor

sensual sensual

sentar (v) to sit

sentarse (v) to sit down

sentencia sentence, verdict

sentencia de muerte death sentence

sentido feeling, sense

sentido de humor sense of humor

sentimental sentimental

sentimiento sentiment

sentir (v) to feel, regret

señal signal, sign, token

señal de comienzo start signal

señal de tráfico traffic sign

señal digital digital signal

señalar (v) to designate

señor lord, sir

señora lady, madam

señorita miss

señuelo decoy

separable unattached

separación removal, separation

separación con guión hyphenation

separación social apartheid

separado separate

separador separator

separar (v) to detach, separate, part

septicemia septicemia

séptico septic
septiembre September
séptimo seventh
sepultura grave
sequía drought
ser being
ser (v) to be
ser bizco (v) to squint
ser digno (v) to deserve
ser distinto (v) to differ
ser igual a (v) to be equal
serenata serenade
serenidad serenity
sereno serene
serie series, serial, run, succession
seriedad formality, reliability, thoughtfulness
serio businesslike, formal, reliable, serious, staid, sober
sermón sermon
seroso serous
serpiente snake, serpent
serrín sawdust
servicio service
servicio de reparto delivery service
servicio de zona ampliada extended area service
servicio militar conscription
servicio post-venta after sale service
servicio público public service, utility
servicios asesores de dirección management advisory services
servicios legales legal services
servidumbre easement
servilleta napkin
servir (v) to serve
sesenta sixty
sesión session
setenta seventy

seudónimo pseudonym
severo harsh, rigid, stern
sexo sex
sexto sixth
sexual sexual
sexualidad sexuality
si if, whether
sí yes
si bien though
SIDA AIDS
sidra cider
siega reaping
siempre always, ever
siempre joven ageless
siempre que provided, whenever
sien temple
sierra saw
siesta nap, snooze
siete seven
sífilis syphilis
siglo century
sigmoidoscopio sigmoidoscope
significación significance
significado purport
significante significant
significar (v) to mean, signify
significativo meaningful
siguiente following
sílaba syllable
silbar (v) to whistle
silbido hiss
silenciador muffler, silencer
silenciar (v) to silence
silencio silence, hush, quietness
silencioso silent
sílice silicon
silicosis silicosis
silueta silhouette
silvestre wild
silla chair
silla de ruedas wheelchair
sillón easy chair
sima chasm

simbiosis symbiosis
simbólico symbolic
simbolizar (v) to symbolize
símbolo symbol
símbolo abstracto abstract symbol
simetría symmetry
simétrico symmetrical
simiente seed
similar similar
simpático amiable, likeable, nice
simple simple, single
simplificar (v) to simplify
simulación make-believe, simulation
simulación en tiempo real real time simulation
simulado sham
simulador simulator
simular (v) to simulate
simultáneo simultaneous
sin without
sin acompañamiento unaccompanied
sin alterar unchanged
sin atractivo unattractive
sin ayuda unaided
sin casa homeless
sin cocer uncooked
sin cortar uncut
sin defensa undefended
sin día fijo sine die
sin dolor painless
sin dueño unclaimed
sin embargo however, nevertheless
sin empleo unemployed
sin escrúpulos unscrupulous
sin fondo bottomless
sin imaginación unimaginative
sin importancia immaterial, irrelevant, unimportant
sin información unaware

sin interés uninteresting
sin manchas spotless
sin muebles unfurnished
sin parada non-stop
sin querer unintentionally
sin salida impasse
sin sentido meaningless, senseless
sin temor fearless
sin usar unused
sin valor worthless
sinagoga synagogue
sinceridad sincerity
sincero sincere, hearty
sincopar (v) to syncopate
síncope syncope
sincronización synchronization
sindicato syndicate, trade union, union
síndrome syndrome
sinfonía symphony
sinfónico symphonic
singular remarkable, singular
siniestro casualty, damage, ominous, sinister
sinónimo synonymous, synonym
sinopsis synopsis
sintaxis syntax
síntesis synthesis
sintetizar (v) to synthesize
síntoma symptom
sintomático symptomatic
sinuoso sinuous
sinus sinus
sinusitis sinusitis
sirena siren
sirviente servant
sistema system
sistema de multiaccesos multiaccess system
sistema digestivo digestive system
sistema directo on-line system

sistema interactivo interactive system

sistema mixto hybrid system

sistema operativo operating system

sistema operativo de discos disk operating system

sistemas materiales hardware

sistemático systematic

sístole systole

sitiar (v) to besiege

sitio location, place, siege; Cuba: farm

situación location, situation

situar (v) to situate

snob snob

soberanía sovereignty

sobornador embracer

sobornar (v) to bribe

soborno bribery, bribe; Arg., Bol., Chile: overload

sobrante spare

sobrar (v) to remain

sobras remains

sobre concerning, upon

sobre (para cartas) envelope

sobrecarga overload

sobrecargar (v) to overcharge, surcharge

sobrecargo surcharge

sobrecrecido overgrown

sobredicho aforementioned

sobreestimar (v) to overestimate

sobreexcitado overwrought

sobreexponer (v) to overexpose

sobregirar (v) to overdraw

sobregiro real bank overdraft

sobrehumano superhuman

sobrenatural supernatural, unearthly

sobreponer (v) to superimpose

sobreponerse (v) to overlap

sobresaltar (v) to shock

sobresalto scare, shock

sobreseer (v) to supersede

sobretodo topcoat

sobreviviente survivor

sobrevivir (v) to survive

sobrina niece

sobrino nephew

sobrio sober

socavar (v) to undermine

sociable social, sociable

socialismo socialism

socialista socialist

socializar (v) to socialize

sociedad association, league, society, membership

sociedad bancaria banking company

sociedad de financiación finance company

sociedad propietaria close held corporation

socio member, partner

socio activo active partner

socio principal senior partner

sociología sociology

sodomía sodomy

sofá couch, sofa

sofisticado sophisticated

sofocación suffocation

sofocante sweltering, stifling, stuffy

sofocar (v) to stifle

sol sun

solapo overlap

solar solar

soldado soldier

soldador welder

soldadura welding

soldar (v) to weld

soleado sunny

soledad solitude

solemne   demure, dignified, solemn

solemnidad   solemnity

solicitante   applicant

solicitar (v)   to apply, woo

solicitud   application

sólidamente   soundly

solidaridad   solidarity, sympathy

solidificar (v)   to solidify

sólido   compact, solid, strong, stout

solitaria   tapeworm

solitario   lonely, recluse, solitary

solo   alone, but, only, single, solitary, solo; Arg., Uru.: boring conversation

soltar (v)   to loosen

soltero   bachelor, single person, single, unmarried

soluble   soluble

solución   solution

solvencia   solvency

solventar (v)   to settle

solvente   solvent

sollozar (v)   to sob

sollozo   sob

sombra   shadow, shade

sombreado   shady

sombrero   hat

sombrío   somber

someter (v)   to submit, subject

someterse (v)   to yield

sometimiento   subjection

somnífero   sleeping pill

sonámbulo   somnambulist

sonar (v)   to sound

sonda   probe

sondear (v)   to canvass, probe

sondeo   canvass

soneto   sonnet

sónico   sonic

sonido   sound, clang

sonoro   resounding

sonreír (v)   to grin, smile

sonrisa   smile, smirk

sonrojo   blush

soñador   dreamer

soñar despierto (v)   to daydream

soñoliento   drowsy, sleepy

sopa   soup

soplar (v)   to blow, huff

soplo   puff

soporte   bracket, backup, support

sordera   deafness

sordo   deaf

sordomudo   deaf and dumb

sorprender (v)   to astonish, stagger

sorpresa   surprise

sortear (v)   to raffle

sorteo, rifa   raffle

sosa   soda

sosegado   composed

soso   tasteless

sospecha   suspicion

sospechar (v)   to suspect

sospechoso   suspicious, suspect

sostén   bra

sostener (v)   to contend, sustain, uphold

sotana   cassock

sótano   basement, cellar

stock   inventory

su   his, her, your, their

suave   sleek, smooth

suavemente   smoothly

suavidad   mildness

subarriendo   sublease

subasta   auction

subastador   auctioneer

subconsciente   subconscious

subcontratista   subcontractor

subcontrato   subcontract

subdesarrollado   undeveloped, underdeveloped

súbdito subject
subdividir (v) to subdivide
subestimado underestimated
subestimar (v) to underestimate
subida raise, ascent, rise
subinquilino subtenant
subir (v) to ascend, climb, raise, rise, soar
subjetivo subjective
sublicencia sublicense
sublime sublime
submarino submarine, underwater
subordinado subordinate, underling
subproducto by-product
subrayar (v) to italicize, underline, underscore
subsidiario subsidiary
subsidiario dependiente subsidiary
subsiguiente subsequent, succeeding
subsistencia subsistence
subsistir (v) to subsist
substitución replacement
substracción subtraction
subterráneo underground
subtítulo subtitle
suburbano suburban
subvención grant, subsidy
subvencionar (v) to subsidize
subversión subversion
subversivo subversive
subvertir (v) to subvert
subyacente underlying
subzona subfield
sucesión offspring, sequence, series, succession
sucesivo consecutive, successive
suceso happening
sucesor successor
suciedad dirt, muck

sucinto succinct
sucio dirty, filthy, nasty, scruffy, unclean
sucumbir (v) to succumb
sucursal branch
sucursal bancaria bank branch
sudar (v) to perspire
sudor perspiration, sweat
Suecia Sweden
sueco Swedish
suegra mother-in-law
suegro father-in-law
sueldo salary, stipend
sueldo de despedida severance pay
suelo floor, ground, soil
suelto loose, odd, unattached
sueño dream, snooze, sleep, slumber
suero serum
suerte chance, luck
suéter sweater
suficiente adequate, smug, sufficient
sufijo suffix
sufrimiento ordeal, suffering
sufrir (v) to suffer, undergo
sugerencia indication, suggestion
sugerir (v) to suggest
sugestión suggestion
sugestivo suggestive
suicida suicidal
suicidio suicide
Suiza Switzerland
suizo Swiss
sujetador fastening
sujetapapeles paper clip
sujetar (v) to fasten
sujeto subject
sujeto a impuestos dutiable
suma addition, amount, sum
suma estimada estimated amount

sumador adder
sumamente extremely
sumario abstract, rundown, summary
sumergir (v) to plunge, sink, submerge
suministrar (v) to supply
sumisión submission
sumiso submissive
suntuoso sumptuous
superar (v) to excel, surmount, surpass
superávit surplus
superávit de capital surplus capital
superficial superficial
superficie area, surface
superfluo superfluous
superintendente superintendent
superior paramount, preeminent, superior, top, upper
superioridad mastery, superiority
superlativo superlative
supermercado supermarket
superordenador supercomputer
supersensible hypersensitive
supersónico supersonic
superstición superstition
supervisar (v) to supervise
supervisión supervision
supervisor supervisor
supervivencia survival
suplementario supplemental, supplementary
suplemento appendix, supplement
suplente deputy, understudy
suplicante precatory, suppliant
suponer (v) to assume, suppose
suposición assumption, supposition
supositorio suppository

supra supra
supremacía supremacy
supremo supreme
supresión abatement, omission, removal, suppression
suprimir (v) to cancel, delete, relieve, suppress
supuesto alleged, assumed, reputed, so-called, supposed
supuración suppuration
sur south
surco rut
sureste southeast
suroeste southwest
surrealismo surrealism
surrealista surrealist
surtido de productos range of goods
susceptible sensitive, squeamish, susceptible
suscribir (v) to subscribe
suscripción subscription
suscripción pública public warehouse, public offering
suscriptor subscriber
suspender (v) to cease, discontinue, fail, suspend
suspensión suspension, abeyance, stay
suspensión temporal reprieve
suspirar (v) to yearn
suspiro sigh; Arg., Chile: morning glory
sustancia matter, stuff, substance
sustancial substantial
sustitución substitution
sustituto substitute
susto fright, scare
sustracción subtraction
sustraer (v) to subtract
susurrar (v) to whisper
susurro sigh
sutil subtle

sutileza subtlety
sutura stitch, suture

suturar (v) to stitch
suyo his, theirs, hers, yours

T

tabaco tobacco; Mex.: bold, determined
taberna pub, saloon, tavern
tabla chart, schedule, slab, table
tabla de funciones function table
tabla de puntos scoreboard
tablero board, console, table
tableta tablet
tabletear (v) to rattle
tablilla splint
tabú taboo
tabular (v) to tabulate
taburete stool
tacaño tightfisted
tácito tacit
taciturno taciturn
taco cue; Mex.: tortilla (fried and stuffed)
táctica tactics
táctico tactical
táctil tactile
tachar (v) to fault
tachuela tack
tajada slice
tajar (v) to chop
tal such
tal como such as
tal vez perhaps
talar (v) to fell
talento talent
talón check, heel
talonario check book
talla size; C. Amer.: swindle
tallas únicas odd sizes
taller studio, workshop
tallo stalk, stem; Col.: cabbage

tamaño size
también too
tambor drum; Mex.: mattress (spring)
tamiz sieve
tamizar (v) to sift
tan as, so
tándem tandem
tangente tangent
tangible tangible
tanque tank
tantear (v) to score; Col., Chile: to estimate
tanteo score
tanto such
tapa lid, top
taparrabos trunks
tapicería tapestry, upholstery
tapón cap, stopper, tampon, swab, wad
taquigrafía shorthand
taquígrafo stenographer
taquilla box office, ticket window; C.R.: inn, bar
tardar (v) to tarry, delay
tarde afternoon, evening, late
tardío tardy
tarea chore, job, task, undertaking
tarifa fare, tariff
tarifa reducida cut-rate
tarjeta card
tarjeta de crédito credit card
tarjeta de memoria memory card
tarjeta magnética magnetic card
tarjeta postal postcard

tarro jar
tarso tarsus
tarta pie
tartamudeo stammer, stutter
tasa rate
tasa bancaria bank rate
tasa de interés interest rate, prime rate, rate of interest
tasa preferencial prime rate
tasa uniforme flat rate
tasación assessment, appraisal
tasador valuer
tatuaje tattoo
taxi cab, taxi
taxista taxi driver
taza cup, mug
taza de té teacup
té tea
teatral theatrical
teatro playhouse, theater
tecla key
tecla de entrada enter key, return key
teclado keyboard
teclado de membrana membrane keyboard
teclado numérico numeric keypad
técnica technique
técnico technical, technician
tecnología technology
techo ceiling, roof
tedioso tedious
teja tile
tejado roof
tejanos jeans
tejer (v) to weave
tejido texture, tissue, weave
tela cloth, web
telar loom
telaraña web
telecomunicaciones telecommunication

teledifusión telecast
teléfono telephone
teléfono celular cellular telephone
teléfono incorporado built-in telephone
teléfono portátil cordless phone
telégrafo telegraph
telegrama cable, telegram
teleimpresor teleprinter
telepatía telepathy
teleproceso teleprocessing
telescopio telescope
teletexto teletext
teletipo teletype
televisar (v) to televise
televisión television
televisor television set
télex telex
tema matter, theme, subject, topic
temblar (v) to quake, quiver, shiver, tremble
temblor quiver, quaver, tremor
temblores shivering
temer (v) to fear
temerario reckless
temeroso fearful
temible fearsome
temor awe, fear
témpano iceberg
temperamento temperament
temperatura temperature
tempestad storm, thunderstorm
tempestuoso stormy
templado mild; Amer.: tipsy; C. Amer., Mex.: clever; Col., Ven.: strict; S. Am.: enamored
templar (v) to tune
templo church, temple
temporada baja off peak
temporal temporary
temporización time out

temprano soon
tenacidad stubbornness
tenaz dogged, tenacious, stubborn
tenazas tongs
tendencia tendency, trend
tendencia de mercado market trend
tender (v) to tend
tendero grocer, shopkeeper
tendón sinew, tendon
tendón de Aquiles Achilles tendon
tenedor assignee, fork, holder, possessor
tenedor de bonos bondholder
tenedor de letra bill holder
tenedor de póliza policyholder
tenencia occupation, occupancy
tener (v) to hold, have
tener cuidado (v) to beware
tener éxito (v) to succeed
tener fugas (v) to leak
tener prisa (v) to hurry
tenia tapeworm
teniendo en cuenta considering
tenis tennis
tenor tenor
tensión tension, stress, strain
tentación temptation
tentador inviting, tantalizing
tentar (v) to tantalize, tempt
tentativa try
tenue tenuous
teñir (v) to dye
teología theology
teológico theological
teólogo theologian
teorema theorem
teoría theory
teoría de conjuntos set theory
teoría de juegos game theory

teoría de probabilidades probability theory
teóricamente theoretically
teorizar (v) to theorize
tequila tequila
terapeuta therapist
terapéutico therapeutic
terapia therapy
tercero third
terciopelo velvet
tergiversar (v) to misinterpret
térmico thermal
terminación completion, termination
terminal terminal
terminal inteligente intelligent terminal
terminar en (v) to result, terminate
término deadline, terminus, term
término límite deadline
término medio average
termita termite
termodinámico thermodynamic
termómetro thermometer
termonuclear thermonuclear
termostato thermostat
ternera veal
ternero calf
ternura tenderness
terraza terrace
terremoto earthquake
terreno terrain
terrenos land
terrestre terrestrial
terrible awful, terrible
territorial territorial
territorio territory
terror panic, terror
terrorismo terrorism
terrorista terrorist
terso satin

tertulia de té tea party
tesis thesis
tesorero bursar, treasurer
tesoro treasury, treasure
testador bequeather, devisor,
  legator
testamentario testamentary
testamento testament, will
testamento cerrado mystic will
testamentos mutuos mutual
  wills
testamentos recíprocos counter
  wills
testarudo stubborn
testículo testicle
testigo witness
testigo auricular earwitness
testigo esencial material witness
testigo ocular eyewitness
testigo presencial eyewitness
testimonio affidavit, attestation,
  testimony
teta teat
tétanos tetanus
tetera kettle, teakettle, teapot;
  Cuba, Mex., P.R.: nipple of a
  baby bottle
textil textile
texto text
textual textual
textura texture, weave
tez complexion
tía aunt
tibia tibia
tibio lukewarm, tepid
tic tic
tictac tick
tiempo time, tempo, weather
tiempo de acceso access time
tiempo compartido time sharing
tiempo de disponibilidad up
  time

tiempo de mantenimiento
  maintenance time
tiempo en reserva standby time
tiempo real real time
tiempo suplementario overtime
tiempos malos hard times
tienda shop, store
tienda de campaña tent
tierno tender; Chile, Ecuad.:
  green, unripe (vegetables)
tierra earth, land, soil
tierra baldía wasteland
tierra firme mainland
tierra natal homeland
tieso taut, tight
tifoidea typhoid
tifus typhus
tigre tiger
tijeras scissors
tijeretazo snip
timador con man
timbre bell, ring, stamp
timbre de llamada doorbell
timidez shyness, timidity
tímido bashful, self-conscious,
  shy, timid
timo swindle
timón rudder; Amer.: steering
  wheel (of a car)
tímpano tympanum
tinta ink
tinte stain, tinge, tint
tío guy, uncle
típico typical
tipo sort, type
tipo de cambio exchange rate
tipo de interés prevaleciente
  prevailing rates of interest
tipo de rendimiento yield rate
tipos flotantes floating rates
tipografía printing
tira slip, strip
tirador knob, trigger

tirano tyrant
tirante tense
tirar (v) to haul, pelt, pull, shoot, throw, toss, tug; Cuba, Chile: to carry; Peru, sl.: sexual intercourse
tirar el agua (v) to flush
tiro shot
tiro de arco archery
tiro de culata backfire
tiroides thyroid
tirón pull, tug
tisú tissue
títere puppet
titubear (v) to falter
titular headline, holder
título bond, caption, title, security
título de traspaso conveyance
título superior paramount title
títulos negociables marketable securities
títulos realizables marketable securities
tiza chalk
toalla towel
toalla de baño bath towel
tobillo ankle
tobogán toboggan
tocadiscos jukebox
tocador boudoir, toilet
tocar (v) to handle, pat, touch
tocar el timbre (v) to ring the bell
tocino ahumado bacon
tocología obstetrics
tocólogo obstetrician
todavía still, yet
todo everything, whole
todo el año yearlong
todo el día daylong
todo el mundo everyone
todo lo que whatever

todos all, everybody
tolerable tolerable
tolerancia allowance, tolerance
tolerante tolerant
tolerar (v) to stand, tolerate
tomador de crédito borrower
tomar (v) to take
tomar el pelo (v) to tease, twit
tomar juramento (v) to take an oath
tomar represalias (v) to retaliate
tomar sol (v) to sunbathe
tomate tomato
tonel barrel, drum
tonelada ton
tonelada neta net ton
tonelaje tonnage
tónico tonic
tono tone
tonterías baloney
tonto fool, silly; Col., C.R., Chile: card game (Old Maid)
tope deadline
tope límite deadline
topógrafo surveyor
toque touch
toque de queda curfew
torácico thoracic
tórax thorax
torbellino whirlpool
torcer (v) to bias, curve, distort, sprain, twist, wring
torcerse (v) to strain
torcido bent, crooked; Guat.: unlucky
tormenta storm
tormenta de nieve snowstorm
tornado tornado
torneo tournament
tornillo bolt, screw
torniquete tourniquet, turnstile
toro bull
torpe clumsy

torpedo torpedo
torre tower
torrencial torrential
torrente torrent
tórrido torrid
torsión twist
torta pancake
tortícolis torticollis
tortilla omelette; Mex.: pancake made of unleavened cornmeal
tortuga turtle
tortuoso tortuous
tortura torture
torturar (v) to torture
torunda swab
tos coughing, cough
toser (v) to cough
tostada toast; Arg., Uru.: bore
tostador toaster
tostar (v) to toast
tostarse (v) to bask
total total, utter
totalitario totalitarian
totalmente altogether, thoroughly
totalmente pagado paid in full
tourniquete tourniquet
toxicidad toxicity
tóxico toxic
toxicología toxicology
toxicómano drug addict
toxina toxin
trabajador worker
trabajar (v) to work, toil
trabajo work, employment, labor, job
trabajo a destajo piecework
trabajo excesivo overwork
trabajos forzados hard labor
tractor tractor
tradición tradition
tradicional traditional
traducción translation

traducir (v) to translate
traductor translator
traer (v) to bring, carry, fetch
tráfico traffic
tragar (v) to swallow
tragedia tragedy
trágico tragic
trago swallow
traición betrayal, treason, treachery
traicionar (v) to betray
traidor traitor, treacherous
traje attire, costume, suit
traje de baño bathing suit, swimsuit
traje de novia wedding dress
traje de smoking tuxedo
trama de página page frame
tramitar (v) to transact
trámite proceeding
trámite penal criminal procedure
trampa cheat, decoy, hoax, snare, trap
trampa explosiva booby trap
trampa mortal deathtrap
trampolín trampoline
tramposo tricky
tranquilidad unconcern, tranquility
tranquilizador reassuring, soothing, tranquilizer
tranquilizante tranquilizer
tranquilizar (v) to reassure, tranquilize
tranquilo cool, quiet, serene, tranquil
transacción deal, transaction
transacción financiera financial transaction
transacciones dealings
transacciones de mercancías merchandise transactions

transcribir (v) to transcribe
transductor transducer
transeúnte passerby, transient
transferencia transfer
transferencia bancaria bank transfer
transferencia cablegráfica cable transfer
transferible transferable
transferir (v) to transfer
transformación transformation
transformador transformer
transformar (v) to transform
transfundir (v) to transfuse
transfusión transfusion
transfusión de sangre blood transfusion
transición transition
transigente compromising
transigir (v) to compromise
transistor transistor
transitario freight forwarder, forwarder
transitivo transitive
tránsito transit
transitorio transitory
translúcido translucent
transmisión transmission
transmisión de alta velocidad high speed transmission
transmisión en paralelo parallel transmission
transmisión síncrona synchronous transmission
transmisor transmitter
transmisor-receptor transceiver
transmitir (v) to transmit
transparencia transparency
transparente transparent
transplante transplant
transponer (v) to transpose
transportador protractor

transportar (v) to ship, transport
transporte transport, conveyance, transportation
transporte aéreo transport by air
transporte marítimo maritime transport, transport by sea
transporte por ferrocarril railway transport
transporte terrestre haulage, transport by land
transposición transposition
transvestido transvestite
trapo rag
tráquea trachea, windpipe
traqueotomía tracheotomy
trascendental transcendental
trascender (v) to transcend
trasero backside, rear
traspasar (v) to transfer, transfix
traspaso cession, conveyance
trasplantar (v) to transplant
trasportar (v) to convey
trastornar (v) to overturn, upset
tratable amenable
tratado treaty, treatise
tratamiento treatment
tratamiento médico medication
tratar (v) to process
trato relationship
trato comercial business deal
trauma trauma
traumático traumatic
traumatología traumatology
travesura prank
travieso naughty
trayecto path
trayectoria trajectory
trazado layout
trazar (v) to draw
trece thirteen
trecho stretch

tregua cease fire, truce
treinta thirty
tremendo awful, terrific, tremendous
trementina turpentine
tren railroad, railway, train
trenza braid
tres three
tres cuartos three-quarter
triangular triangular
triángulo triangle
tribal tribal
tribu tribe
tribunal bench, court, court of law, forum, tribunal
tribunal civil civil court
tribunal de justicia law court
tribunal de ley law court
tribunal de presas prize court
tribunal de reclamaciones court of claims
tribunal superior superior court
tribunal supremo supreme court
tribunal testamentario prerogative court, surrogate's court
tributario tributary
tributo tax, tribute
triciclo tricycle
trigo wheat
trigonometría trigonometry
trillón trillion
trimestral quarterly
trinchar (v) to carve
trinchera trench coat
trino trill
trío trio
tripas gut, tripe
triple triple
tríplica surrejoinder
triplicar (v) to triple
trípode tripod
tripulación crew
triquinosis trichinosis

triste dismal, miserable, sad, wistful
tristeza sadness
triunfante triumphant
triunfar (v) to succeed, triumph
triunfo success, triumph
trivial trivial
trofeo trophy
trombosis thrombosis
trompa de Eustaquio Eustachian tube
trompa de Falopio Fallopian tube
tronada thunderstorm
tronar (v) to thunder; Mex.: to shoot dead
tronco log, stem, trunk
trono throne
tropa troop; Arg.: caravan
tropezar (v) to trip
tropical tropic
trópico tropic
tropiezo trip
trotar (v) to trot
trote trot
trozo hunk
truco gimmick, trick; Chile: punch, blow
trucha trout
trueno thunder
trueque barter, swap
trueques de venta trade-ins
truncar (v) to truncate
tú you
tuberculosis tuberculosis
tubería piping, pipeline
tubo pipe, tube
tubo capilar capillary tube
tulipán tulip
tumba tomb; Col., Cuba, Mex.: felling trees; Cuba: drum, folk dance
tumbar (v) to knock down

tumor   growth, node, tumor
tumor maligno   malignant tumor
tumulto   riot, tumult, uproar
tumultuoso   tumultuous
túnica   tunic
tupido   thick, deuse
turba   turf
turbante   turban
turbar (v)   to embarrass
turbina   turbine
turbulencia   turbulence
turbulento   turbulent
turco   Turkish

turismo   sightseeing, travel, tourism
turista   tourist
turno   shift, turn
turno de día   day shift
turno de noche   nightshift
turquesa   turquoise
Turquía   Turkey
tutela   tutorship, ward
tutelar   tutorial
tutor   guardian, tutor
tutoría   tutorship

U

ubicación   location
ubicuo   ubiquitous
ubre   udder
ujier   usher
úlcera   ulcer
úlcera gástrica   gastric ulcer
ulterior   ulterior
última instancia   last resort
ultimátum   ultimatum
último   final, last, latest, ultimate
ultramar   overseas
ultrasónico   ultrasonic
ultravioleta   ultraviolet
umbilical   umbilical
umbral   threshold
umbral de rentabilidad   break even
una vez   once
unánime   unanimous
unánimemente   unanimously
unanimidad   unanimity
undécimo   eleventh
ungüento   ointment, smear
únicamente   exclusively
único   unique, sole, single

unidad   unit, unity
unidad central de proceso   central processing unit
unidad de dispositivo de control   device control unit
unidad de visualización   visual display unit
unidad exploratoria   scanner
unidad principal de control   main control unit
unidireccional   unidirectional
unificación   unification
unificar (v)   to unify
uniforme   uniform, evenly
uniformidad   uniformity
unilateral   unilateral
unión   union, junction
unir (v)   to unite, unify, merge, link, join, couple, connect
unirse (v)   to copulate
universal   universal
universidad   university
universo   universe
uno, una   an, one
uno mismo   oneself
uña   nail

uña (de un dedo de la mano)
  fingernail
uña (del dedo del pie)   toenail
urbano urban
urea urea
urgencia urgency, pressure
urgente urgent, pressing
urinario urinary
urna ballot box
urología urology
urólogo urologist
urticaria urticaria
Uruguay Uruguay
uruguayo Uruguayan
usar (v) to wear, use
uso wear
usos contingentes executory
  uses

usted you
ustedes you
usual usual, customary
usuario user
usufructuario usufructuary
usura usury
usurpación usurpation, encroachment
usurpador squatter
usurpar (v) to usurp, encroach
utensilio utensil
útero uterus, womb, matrix
útil useful, helpful
utilidad utility
utilizable serviceable
utilizar (v) to utilize

V

vaca cow
vacación vacation, recess
vacante vacancy
vaciado dump
vaciar (v) to dump
vacilación hesitation, vacillation,
  faltering, indecision
vacío emptiness, empty, hiatus,
  vacuum
vacuna vaccine
vacunación vaccination
vacunar (v) to vaccinate
vadear (v) to wade
vagabundear (v) to loiter
vagabundeo roaming
vagabundo vagrant, tramp
vagancia vagrancy
vagar (v) to wander
vagina vagina
vago vague, loafer
vagón wagon, carriage

vaina pod; Col.: stroke of luck
vainilla vanilla
vale scrip; Col., Mex., Ven.: friend
valentía courage
validación validation
validar (v) to validate, probate
validez validity
válido valid
valiente brave, gallant, bold
valientemente bravely
valioso valuable
valor worth, value, courage
valor a la par par value
valor actual present value
valor añadido value added
valor de liquidación liquidation
  value
valor de mercado market
  value
valor declarado declared value
valor en cambio exchange rate

valor equitativo de venta   actual cash value

valor justo de mercado   fair market value

valor líquido   equity

valor nominal   face value

valor ordinario   equity

valor residual   salvage value

valor según libros   book value

valoración   assessment, appraisal

valoración de activos   valuation of assets

valoración de solvencia   credit rating

valorar (v)   to rate, assess, appreciate

valores   stock, valuables, securities

valores bancarios   bank papers

valores de primera   blue chips

valores extranjeros   foreign securities

valorización   valuation

vals   waltz

valuación   appraisal

válvula   valve

valla   hurdle

valle   valley

vampiro   vampire

vandalismo   vandalism

vanidad   vanity

vano   vain

vapor   vapor, steam

vaporizar (v)   to vaporize

vaquero   cowboy

vara   stick; Peru, coll.: pull, influence

variable   variable

variación   variation

variado   assorted

variante   variant

variar (v)   to vary

varicela   chickenpox, varicella

várices   varices

varicoso   varicose

variedad   variety

vario   various, diverse

varios   miscellaneous, several, sundry

vasco   Basque

vascular   vascular

vasectomía   vasectomy

vaso (sanguíneo)   blood vessel, vessel

vaso de vino   wineglass

vasto   vast

vatio   watt

vecindad   vicinity

vecindario   neighborhood

vecino   neighbor

vegetación   vegetation

vegetal   vegetable

vegetariano   vegetarian

vehemencia   vehemence

vehemente   vehement

vehículo   vehicle

veinte   twenty

vejiga   bladder

vela   wake, sail, candle

velar (v)   to veil

velo   veil

velocidad   speed, velocity

velocímetro   speedometer

veloz   swift

vena   vein

vencedor   winner, conqueror

vencer (v)   to overcome, master, defeat, expire, vanquish

vencido   overdue, due

vencimiento   maturity, expiration

venda   bandage

venda (en los ojos)   blindfold

vendaje   bandaging; Col., C.R., Ecuad., Peru: extra

vendaval   windstorm

vendedor   seller

vendedor a domicilio outdoor salesman
vendedor ambulante peddler
vendedor autorizado authorized dealer
vender (v) to sell, trade
vender (ambulante) (v) to peddle
vendible marketable
veneno poison, venom
venerable venerable
venéreo venereal
Venezuela Venezuela
vengador avenger
venganza revenge, vengeance
vengar (v) to avenge, revenge
vengativo vindictive
venir (v) to come
venta sale; Chile: booth or stall where food and drinks are sold
venta al detalle retail
venta al mayor wholesale
venta de mercancías sale of goods
venta de mercancías taradas fire sale
venta de usados rummage sale
venta en depósito consignment sale
venta en firme firm sale
venta exclusiva exclusive sale
venta por correo mail order
ventaja convenience, advantage
ventana window
ventanas de la nariz nostrils
ventanillas bank counters
ventilación ventilation
ventilador fan
ventilar (v) to ventilate
ventisca blizzard
ventisquero snowdrift
ventoso windy
ventrículo ventricle

ventrílocuo ventriloquist
ver (v) to see, watch
ver una causa (v) to hear a case
veracidad truthfulness
verano summer, dry season
verbal verbal, oral
verbo verb
verdad truth
verdaderamente truly
verdadero real, true
verde green
verdugo executioner, torturer
veredicto verdict
veredicto general general verdict
vergonzoso shameful
vergüenza shame, shyness, disgrace
verídico truthful
verificación verification
verificar (v) to verify
vernáculo vernacular
verosímil plausible
verosimilitud plausibility
verrugas warts
versátil versatile
versatilidad versatility
versión version, rendering
vértebra vertebra
vértebra cervical cervical vertebra
vertebrado vertebrate
verter (v) to spill, pour
vertical vertical, upright
vértigo vertigo
vesícula vesicle
vesícula biliar gallbladder
vestíbulo hall, lobby
vestido dress, attire
vestidor dressing room
vestidos wardrobe
vestir (v) to dress, attire
vestuario wardrobe
veterano veteran

veterinario veterinarian
veto veto
vez turn
vía track
Vía Láctea Milky Way
vía aérea airway
viabilidad feasibility, viability
viable viable
viaducto viaduct
viajar (v) to travel, commute, trek
viaje trip, voyage, tour, travel, ride, journey; C. Amer.: blow, push, shove
viaje de negocios business trip
viajero traveler
viajero diario commuter
vibrador buzzer
vibrar (v) to vibrate, shiver
vicepresidente vice-president
viceversa vice versa
vicioso vicious
víctima victim, prey
victoria victory, win
victorioso conquering
vida life
vida nocturna night life
vídeo video
vidrio glass
vidrio de color stained glass
viejo old, shabby
viento wind
vientre belly, tummy
viernes Friday
viga beam, cantilever
vigente vallid
vigésimo twentieth
vigilancia watch
vigilante vigilante, vigilant, lifeguard, caretaker
vigilar (v) to watch, police, overlook
vigilia wake

vigor vigor
vigoroso strenuous, dashing
vil vile
villancico carol
vinagre vinegar
vínculo bond, entail
vindicatorio vindicatory
vinilo vinyl
vino wine
vino de Jerez sherry
viña vineyard
viñedo vineyard
violación violation, rape, trespass
violador rapist
violar (v) to rape, ravish, violate
violencia violence
violentamente slapdash
violento violent, forcible
violoncelo cello
virar (v) to veer
virgen virgin
virginal maidenly
virginidad virginity
viril virile
virilidad manhood
virtualmente virtually
virtud virtue
viruela smallpox
virus virus
visado visa
visibilidad visibility
visible visible, conspicuous
visión vision
visionario visionary
visita visit
visitante visitor
visitar (v) to visit
vista view, sight, hearing; Peru, P.R.: enema
vista completa full hearing
vista fatigada eyestrain
vista imparcial fair hearing
vistazo glance

vistoso ornate
visual visual
visualizar (v) to visualize
vitalidad vitality
vitalizar (v) to vitalize
vitamina vitamin
viuda widow
víveres ration
viveza sharpness
vivienda dwelling, tenement
viviente living, alive
vivir (v) to live, reside, exist, dwell
vivo live, alive
vocabulario vocabulary
vocación vocation
vocacional vocational
vocal vocal, vowel
volante steering wheel
volar (v) to fly
volatería poultry
volátil volatile
volcánico volcanic
volcar (v) to capsize
voltaje voltage
voltio volt
volumen volume, bulk
volumen de negocio turnover
voluminoso voluminous, bulky
voluntad will
voluntario voluntary
voluntarioso willful

volver (v) to return, turn
volver a (v) to recur, do something again
volver a abrir (v) to reopen
volver a arreglar (v) to rearrange
volver a casarse (v) to remarry
volver a emitir (v) to reissue
volver a escribir (v) to rewrite
volver a jugar (v) to replay
volver a juzgar (v) to retry
volver a nombrar (v) to rename
volver a vivir (v) to relive
vomitar (v) to vomit, belch
vómito vomit
voraz voracious
vosotros you
votación voting, poll, polling, ballot
votante voter
votar (v) to vote
voto vote, vow
voto afirmativo yea
voz voice
voz baja undertone
vuelo flight
vuelta whirl, twirl, turn, stroll, return, bend
vulgar vulgar
vulnerable vulnerable
vulva vulva

X

xenofobia xenophobia

xilófono xylophone

Y

y and
yate yacht

yate de motor cabin cruiser
yema del dedo fingertip

161

yema de huevo yolk
yerno son-in-law
yeso plaster, chalk
yo I

yo mismo myself
yogur yogurt
yugular jugular
yuxtaposición juxtaposition

Z

zanahoria carrot; Arg., Uru.: fool
zancada stride
zanja ditch, trench
zapatero shoemaker
zapatilla slipper
zapato shoe
zar czar, tsar
zigoto zygote
zona zone

zona aduanera customs area
zona del dólar dollar area
zona franca free trade zone
zoológico zoo
zumbar (v) to buzz
zumbido buzz, hum
zumo juice
zurcir (v) to darn

English–Spanish
✧
Inglés–Español

A

abandonment abandono, dejación

abatement supresión, reducción, anulación

abdomen abdomen

abduction secuestro, rapto

abductor secuestrador, raptor

abetment instigación

abeyance espera, suspensión

abolition abolición, derogación

abort (v) abortar, terminar, cancelar

aborticide aborticidio

abortion aborto, aborción

abrasion abrasión, raspadura

abridgement abreviación, compendio

abscess absceso

absence ausencia, falta

absent ausente

absenteeism absentismo

absolute address dirección absoluta

absolute conveyance cesión libre

absolute instruction instrucción absoluta

absolute rights derechos singulares

absolution absolución

abstract resumen, sumario

abstract symbol símbolo abstracto

abstraction hurto, substracción

abuse abuso, injuria

abusive abusivo

abuttals lindes

abutter dueño colindante

abutting property propiedad lindante

accelerated depreciation depreciación acelerada

accelerator acelerador

acceptance aceptación

acceptance agreement contrato de aceptación

acceptor aceptante

access acceso

access method método de acceso

access mode modalidad de acceso

access time tiempo de acceso

accessory cómplice, encubridor

accident accidente, desgracia

accidental accidental, fortuito

accidental death muerte accidental

accidental jamming perturbación accidental

accomplice cómplice, correo; alicates (P.R.)

accomplish (v) lograr, acabar

accomplished realizado

accomplishment logro, realización

accord acuerdo, convenio

accordingly por consiguiente

account cuenta, informe

account book libro de cuentas

accountable responsable

accountant contable

accounting contabilidad

accounting cycle período contable

accounting department departamento de contabilidad

accounting entity entidad contable

accounting equation ecuación contable

accounting machine máquina contable

accounting note relación contable

accounting standards normas de contabilidad

accounts payable cuentas a pagar, cuentas pagaderas

accounts receivable cuentas a cobrar, cuentas deudoras

accreditation acreditación

accredited autorizado

accrual accounting contabilidad por acumulaciones

accrue (v) acumular, aumentar

accrued costs costes acumulados

accrued expenses gastos acumulados

accrued interest intereses acumulados

accrued liabilities deudas acumuladas

accumulated depreciation depreciación acumulada

accumulated earnings beneficios acumulados

accumulator acumulador

accuracy exactitud

accurate exacto, preciso

accusation acusación, cargo

accused acusado

ace as

acephalous acéfalo

acetone acetona

ache dolor

achieve (v) conseguir, lograr

achieveable factible

achievement logro, realización

Achilles tendon tendón de Aquiles

acid ácido

acidity acidez

acknowledge (v) reconocer, aceptar

acknowledgement confirmación, reconocimiento

acme cima, cumbre

acne acné

acoustic acústico

acquaint (v) conocer, informar

acquaintance conocimiento, trato

acquiesce (v) aceptar, consentir

acquiescent condescendiente

acquire (v) adquirir, obtener

acquisition adquisición

acquisitive ávido, codicioso

acquit (v) absolver

across a través de

acrylic acrílico

act hecho, acción

action acción, hecho
activation activación
activator activador, sensibilizador
active activo
active partner socio activo
activity actividad
activity ratio índice de actividad
actual efectivo, real
actual cash value valor equitativo de venta
actual cost costo efectivo
actually efectivamente
actuary actuario, actuario de seguros
acupuncture acupuntura
acute agudo (enfermedad)
Adam's apple nuez de la garganta; manzana (Amer.)
adamant firme, inexorable
adapt (v) adaptarse
adaptable adaptable
adaptation adaptación
adapter adaptador
add (v) añadir
addendum adición
adder sumador
addict adicto
addiction adición, suma
address dirección (postal), discurso
address (v) dirigir la palabra
addressee destinatario
adenoid adenoideo
adenoma adenoma
adept experto
adequate suficiente
adhere (v) adherir, pegarse
adipose adiposo
adjacent contiguo
adjective adjetivo
adjourn (v) aplazar, levantar
adjournment aplazamiento

adjudication decisión del tribunal
adjust (v) ajustar, conciliar
adjusted trial balance balance de comprobación ajustado
adjustment ajuste, arreglo
administer (v) administrar
administration administración
administration costs costes de administración
administrator administrador
admire (v) admirar
admission admisión, entrada
admit (v) admitir, dar entrada
adolescence adolescencia
adopt (v) adoptar
adoption adopción
adore (v) adorar
adorn (v) adornar
adrenalin adrenalina
adrift a la deriva
adsorption adsorción
adulate (v) adular
adult adulto
adulterate (v) adulterar
adultery adulterio
advance adelanto, anticipo, avance
advance (v) avanzar, adelantar
advance payment pago anticipado
advances from customers adelantos recibidos de clientes
advantage beneficio, ventaja
adventure aventura
adventurer aventurero
adverb adverbio
adversary adversario
adverse adverso, contrario
advertise (v) anunciar, avisar
advertisement anuncio, publicidad
advertising publicidad

advertising agencies agencias de publicidad
advice aviso, notificación, consejo
advisable aconsejable
advise (v) aconsejar
advisor asesor, consejero
advisory consultivo
advocate abogado, partidario
aerobe aerobio
aerobic aeróbico
aerosol aerosol
affair asunto, aventura
affect (v) afectar
affection afecto, cariño
affidavit acta, declaración jurada, testimonio
affiliated afiliado, filial
affiliated company compañía afiliada (filial)
affirm (v) afirmar, asegurar
affirmant afirmante
affirmation afirmación
affirmative relief reparación positiva
affix (v) pegar, añadir
afflict (v) afligir
affliction aflicción
affluent rico
afford (v) proporcionar, poder
affray refriega, riña
affront agravio, insulto
afloat a flote
afoot a pie
aforementioned sobredicho
afraid atemorizado
Africa África
after después
after sale service servicio post-venta
aftercare convalecencia
afternoon tarde
again otra vez

against contra
age edad
aged envejecido
ageless siempre joven
agency agencia
agenda orden del día
agent agente, representante
agglutination aglutinación
aggravate (v) agravar, irritar
aggravation agravante, irritación
aghast horrorizado
agile ágil
agility agilidad
aging cronología
aging of accounts análisis de cuentas cronológico
aging schedule method método de vencimiento programado
ago hace tiempo
agony dolor, angustia
agree (v) estar de acuerdo
agreeable conforme
agreement acuerdo, convenio, contrato
agricultural center asiento (Cuba)
agriculture agricultura
ahead adelante
aid ayuda
aide asistente, ayudante
AIDS SIDA
aim (v) apuntar, dirigir
aim meta, objetivo
air aire
airborne aerotransportado
aircraft avión
airlift puente aéreo
airmail correo aéreo
airplane avión
airport aeropuerto
airway vía respiratoria
airway bill conocimiento aéreo
airy aéreo, fresco

ajar entreabierto
alarm alarma
alarm clock despertador
alas ¡ay de mí!
albinism albinismo
albino albino
album álbum
albumin albúmina
alchemy alquimia
alcohol alcohol
alcoholic alcohólico
alcoholism alcoholismo
alert alerta
algebra álgebra
algid álgido, muy frío
algorithm algoritmo
alia otras cosas
alias alias, apodo, nombre supuesto
alibi coartada
alien ajeno, extraño, extranjero
alienable enajenable
alienate (v) apartar, ofender
align (v) alinear
alignment ajuste
alike idéntico, similar
alimentation alimentación
alimony alimentos, pensión
alive viviente, vivo
alkali álcali
alkaline alcalino
alkaloid alcaloide
alkalosis alcalosis
all todo, todos
all-inclusive income statement cuenta de ingresos totales
all right correcto, de acuerdo
all-star elenco de estrellas
all-time hasta el presente
allegation alegación
alleged supuesto
allegedly según parece
allergic alérgico

allergy alergia
alley callejuela
alliance alianza
allied aliado, relacionado
allocation asignación, cuota, cupo
allocation of costs asignación de costes
allotment asignación, reparto, ración, porción
allow (v) asignar, permitir
allowance bonificación; tolerancia, concesión
allowance for bad debts reservas para morosos
allowance for depreciation reservas para depreciación
allowance for sales returns reservas para devoluciones de ventas
allowance for uncollectibles reservas para impagados
ally (v) aliarse
almighty omnipotente
almond almendra
almost casi
aloft arriba, en alto
alone solo
along a lo largo de
alongside junto a, al lado de
aloof reservado, frío
aloud en voz alta
alphabet alfabeto
alphanumeric alfanumérico
alphanumeric data datos alfanuméricos
alter (v) alterar, cambiar
alteration modificación
alternate alternativo, alterno
alternate routing ruta alternativa
alternating current corriente alterna

alternation   alternancia
alternative   alternativo
alternator   alternador
although   aunque
altitude   altitud, altura
altogether   en total, totalmente
altruist   altruista
aluminum   aluminio
alveolus   alvéolo
always   siempre
amalgam   amalgama, mezcla
amalgamated   amalgamado, mez-
  clado
amass (v)   acumular
amateur   aficionado
amaze (v)   asombrar, pasmar
ambassador   embajador
ambidextrous   ambidextro
ambiguity   ambigüedad
ambiguous   ambiguo
ambitious   ambicioso
ambivalent   ambivalente
ambulance   ambulancia
ambulatory   ambulatorio
ambush   emboscada
ameliorate (v)   mejorar
amelioration   mejoría
amenable   tratable, sumiso
amendment   corrección, enmienda, rectificación
America   América
American   americano
amiable   afable, simpático
amicable   amistoso
amid   entre, en medio de
amino acids   aminoácidos
amonia   amoníaco
ammunition   munición
amnesia   amnesia
amnesty   amnistía, indulto
among   entre
amorphous   amorfo

amortizable loan   empréstito
  amortizable
amortization   amortización
amount   cantidad, suma, importe,
  monto
ampere   amperio
amphetamine   anfetamina
amphibian   anfibio
ample   amplio, extenso
amplifier   amplificador
amplify (v)   aumentar
amputation   amputación
amuse (v)   divertir, distraer
amusement   diversión
amusing   divertido; chispa (Mex.)
an   uno, una
anaerobe   anerobio
anaesthesia   anestesia
analgesic   analgésico
analog computer   ordenador analógico
analog data   datos analógicos
analogous   análogo
analogy   analogía
analysis   análisis
analyst   analista
anatomical   anatómico
anatomy   anatomía
ancestor   antepasado
ancestry   linaje, alcurnia
anchor   ancla
ancient   antiguo
ancillary   auxiliar
ancillary equipment   equipo auxiliar
ancillary letter of credit   carta
  de crédito auxiliar
ancillary suit   juicio secundario
and   y
androgen   andrógeno
android   androide, robot
anecdote   anécdota
anemia   anemia

anesthesia anestesia
anesthetic anestésico
anesthetist anestesista
aneurysm aneurisma
anew de nuevo, otra vez
angel ángel
anger cólera, enfado
angina angina
angioma angioma, tumor
angle ángulo
Anglo macho (C.R.)
angry enfadado, enojado
anguish angustia
aniline anilina
animal animal
animal bite mordedura de animal
animal's liver pana (Arg., Chile)
animation animación (dibujos)
animosity animosidad
ankle tobillo
annex (v) adjuntar, anexar
annexation anexión
annihilate (v) aniquilar
anniversary aniversario
annotation anotación
announce (v) anunciar, declarar
announcement anuncio, aviso
annoy (v) molestar, enojar; buscar (Arg., Uru., Chile, Mex.); calentar (Chile, Uru.); embromar (Amer.); fundir (Amer., coll.)
annoyance café (Mex.)
annoying molesto
annual anual
annual report informe anual
annuity anualidad
annuity due anualidad pagadera
annul (v) anular, invalidar
annulment anulación
anode ánodo
anomaly anomalía
anonymous anónimo

Anopheles Anófeles
anorexia anorexia
another otro
answer (v) contestar, replicar
answer réplica, respuesta
answering machine contestador automático
antacid antiácido
antagonism antagonismo
antagonist antagonista
antagonistic antagónico, contrario
antagonize (v) enemistar
antecedent antecedente
antenna antena
anthem himno
anthology antología
anthrax ántrax
anthropoid antropoide
anthropology antropología
anti-dumping duty impuesto de "antidumping"
anti-inflammatory antiinflamatorio
antiallergic antialérgico
antianemic antianémico
antibiotic antibiótico
antibody anticuerpo
anticipate (v) anticiparse
anticipated profit beneficio anticipado
anticipation prevención
anticlimax decepción
anticoagulant anticoagulante
anticonvulsant anticonvulsivo
antidote antídoto
antifebrile antifebril
antihistamines antihistaminas
antimigraine antimigraña
antioxidant antioxidante
antipathy antipatía
antique antigüedad
antiseptic antiséptico

antisocial antisocial
antispasmodic antiespasmódico
antitrust antimonopolio
antitrust laws leyes antimonopolistas
antonym antónimo
antrum seno, cavidad
anus ano
anvil huesecillo del oído
anxiety angustia, ansiedad, inquietud
anxious inquieto
any cualquier, cualquiera
anybody alguno, alguien
anyhow de todas maneras
anymore nunca más
anyone alguien
anything algo, alguna cosa
anytime a cualquier hora
anyway de todas formas
anywhere en todas partes
aorta aorta
apart aparte
apartheid separación social
apartment apartamento, piso
apathetic indiferente
apathy apatía, indiferencia
ape mono, simio
apex ápice, cima, cumbre, cúspide
aphagia afagia
aphasia afasia
aphonia afonía
aphrodisiac afrodisíaco
apiece cada uno
apology disculpa
apoplexy apoplejía
apostle apóstol
apostrophe apóstrofe
appall (v) asombrar, consternar
appalling pasmoso
apparent aparente
apparently por lo visto

appeal (v) presentar, aparecer
appeal apelación, alzada, interés, llamamiento
appearance apariencia
appease (v) apaciguar
appendectomy apendectomía
appendicitis apendicitis
appendix apéndice, suplemento
appetite apetito
applaud (v) aplaudir
applause aplauso
apple manzana
appliance aparato, instrumento
applicable aplicable
applicant solicitante
application solicitud, aplicación, blanco (P.R.)
application form hoja de solicitud
application program programa de aplicación
appoint (v) nombrar, citar
appointment cita, nombramiento
apportion (v) repartir
apportionment prorrateo
appraisal valoración, valuación, tasación
appreciate (v) valorar, apreciar
appreciation alza, apreciación
apprehend (v) percibir; abrochar (Mex.)
apprehension aprehensión, captura, recelo
apprehensive receloso
apprentice aprendiz
apprenticeship aprendizaje
approach (v) acercarse
appropriate adecuado, apropiado
appropriations of retained earnings asignación de beneficios no distribuidos

approval aprobación
approve (v) aprobar, sancionar
approximate aproximado
approximate (v) aproximarse
appurtenance anexo, adjunto
appurtenances pertenencias
April abril
apron delantal
apt apropiado
aptitude aptitud
aquatic acuático
aqueduct acueducto
Arab árabe
Arabia Arabia
arable cultivable
arbitrary arbitrario
arbitration arbitraje
arc arco
arcade galería
arch arco, bóveda
archaic arcaico
archbishop arzobispo
archer arquero
archery tiro de arco
archipelago archipiélago
architect arquitecto
architecture arquitectura
arctic ártico, glacial
ardent ardiente
ardor entusiasmo
arduous arduo, riguroso
area área, superficie
arena arena
areola aréola
Argentina Argentina
Argentinian argentino
argue (v) argumentar, razonar,
　discutir; averiguar (Mex., Hond.)
argument alegato y defensa, dis-
　cusión, disputa
arid árido
arise (v) levantar, plantear
aristocracy aristocracia

aristocrat aristócrata
arm arma, armamento, brazo,
　manga
armadillo peludo (Arg., Uru.)
armor armadura, coraza
army ejército
aroma fragancia
around alrededor
arouse (v) despertar, incitar
arrange (v) organizar, disponer
arrangement arreglo, disposi-
　ción, plan
array matriz, personal (del ju-
　rado), orden, serie
array processor procesador ma-
　triz
arrears atrasos, pagos atrasados
arrears of interest intereses
　atrasados
arrest arresto, detención
arrival llegada
arrive (v) llegar
arrogance arrogancia
arrogant enterado (Chile)
arrow flecha
arsenal arsenal
arsenic arsénico
arson incendio intencionado, de-
　lito
arsonist incendiario, pirómano
art arte, habilidad
arteriosclerosis arteriosclerosis
artery arteria
arthritis artritis
arthrosis artrosis
artichoke alcachofa
article artículo, cláusula, objeto
articles of incorporation regla-
　mentos de la sociedad
articulate articulado
articulation articulación
artifice ardid, artificio
artificial artificial

artificial insemination inseminación artificial

artificial intelligence inteligencia artificial

artificial language lenguaje artificial

artificially artificialmente

artillery artillería

artisan artesano

artist artista

artistic artístico

as tan, como

asbestos asbesto, amianto

asbestosis asbestosis

ascend (v) subir, elevar

ascendant predominante

ascension ascensión

ascent ascenso, subida

ascorbic acid ácido ascórbico

aseptic aséptico

ash ceniza

ashamed avergonzado

ashore en tierra

ashtray cenicero

Asia Asia

Asiatic asiático

aside aparte, a un lado

ask (v) preguntar, pedir

asleep estar dormido

asparagus espárrago

aspect aspecto, apariencia

asphalt asfalto

asphyxia asfixia

aspiration aspiración, anhelo

aspire (v) aspirar, ambicionar

aspirin aspirina

ass burro, imbécil

assail (v) atacar, acometer

assailant agresor, asaltante

assassin asesino

assault asalto, agresión, ataque

assemblage montaje

assemble (v) montar, reunir

assembler ensamblador

assembly asamblea, conjunto, montaje, reunión

assembly language lenguaje de ensamblaje

assembly line línea de montaje

assembly program programa de ensamblaje

assent consentimiento

assert (v) afirmar, declarar

assertion afirmación

assess (v) valorar, tasar

assessment tasación, valoración

asset activo, posesión

assets activos

assets and liabilities activo y pasivo

assets in hand bienes disponibles

asshole imbécil, ojo de ano

assiduous asiduo

assign (v) asignar, destinar

assignee beneficiario, tenedor

assignment asignación, cesión, tarea

assimilate (v) asimilar

assimilation asimilación

assist (v) asistir, ayudar

assistance ayuda

assistant auxiliar, adjunto

associate asociado

associate (v) asociarse, juntar

associated company compañía asociada

association asociación, sociedad

associative storage memoria asociativa

assort (v) concordar, convenir

assorted variado, surtido

assortment clasificación

assume (v) suponer, asumir

assumed fingido, supuesto

assuming arrogante**

assumption presunción, suposición

assurance garantía, promesa

assure (v) garantizar, prometer

asterisk asterisco

asthma asma

astigmatism astigmatismo

astonish (v) asombrar, sorprender

astringent astringente

astrology astrología

astronaut astronauta

astronomer astrónomo

astronomical astronómico

astronomy astronomía

astute astuto; condado (Chile)

astuteness astucia

asylum asilo

at en, a

atavism atavismo

atheism ateísmo

Athenian ateniense

Athens Atenas

athlete atleta

athletic atlético

Atlantic Ocean Océano Atlántico

atlas atlas

atmosphere atmósfera

atmospheric atmosférico

atom átomo

atomic atómico

atrium atrio, cavidad

atrocious atroz

atrocity atrocidad

atrophy atrofia

attach (v) adjuntar, atar

attaché agregado

attachment embargo, incautación

attachment bond fianza de embargo

attack ataque

attain (v) alcanzar, lograr

attainable realizable

attainment logro, consecución

attempt (v) intentar, probar

attempt atentado

attendance asistencia

attention atención, cuidado

attentive cortés, atento

attentiveness atención, cortesía

attestation testimonio

attic desván, ático

attire (v) vestir

attire traje, vestido

attitude actitud

attorney abogado, abogada

attorney general fiscal general

attract (v) atraer

attraction atracción

attractive agradable, atractivo

attribute atributo, cualidad

attribute (v) atribuir, achacar; acumular (Arg.)

attribution atribución

attrition desgaste

atypical atípico

auburn castaño rojizo

auction subasta, licitación

auctioneer subastador

audacious audaz, atrevido

audible audible, oíble

audience auditorio, público

audiogram audiograma

audiometer audiómetro

audit auditoría, revisión

auditing auditoría

audition audición

auditor auditor, censor, interventor

auditorium auditorio, sala

auditory auditivo

augment (v) aumentar

August agosto

aunt tía

aura aura

auricle aurícula

auscultation auscultación
auspicious favorable, propicio
austere austero, adusto
austerity austeridad
Australia Australia
Australian australiano
Austria Austria
Austrian austriaco
authentic auténtico
authentication reconocimiento
author autor
authoritarian autoritario
authority autoridad, mando
authorization autorización
authorize (v) autorizar
authorized dealer vendedor autorizado
authorized stock acciones autorizadas
autism autismo
autobiography autobiografía
autoclave autoclave
autocrat autócrata
autocratic autocrático
autogenous autógeno
autoinfection autoinfección
autointoxication autointoxicación
automatic automático
automatic coding codificación automática
automation automatización
automobile automóvil
autonomic autónomo
autonomous autónomo
autopsy autopsia
autosuggestion autosugestión

autumn otoño
auxiliary auxiliar
auxiliary memory memoria auxiliar
avail (v) aprovechar, valer
availability disponibilidad
available disponible
avalanche alud
avenge (v) vengar
avenger vengador
avenue avenida
average regular, promedio, término medio
average cost method método de coste medio
average price precio medio
aversion aversión
avert (v) apartar, desviar
aviation aviación
avid ansioso
avoid (v) evitar, guardarse
avoidance evitación, anulación
avowal reconocimiento
awake (v) despertar
awakening despertar (el)
award adjudicación, concesión, fallo, otorgamiento
award (v) premiar, adjudicar
aware enterado
away lejos, fuera
awe temor, pavor
awful tremendo, terrible
awkward desagradable
axiom axioma, postulado
axis axis, eje
axle eje

B

babble murmullo
baby pequeño, niño

babyhood infancia
babyish infantil

babysitter guardián de niños
bachelor soltero
bacillus bacilo
back to back credit crédito subsidiario
backache dolor de espalda
backbone espinazo, espina dorsal
backdate fecha atrasada
backer partidario
backfire tiro de culata
backgammon chaquete (juego)
backhanded ambiguo
backing ayuda, respaldo
backlash retroceso
backlog acumulación (de trabajo)
backside culo, trasero
backup apoyo, soporte
backward hacia atrás
bacon tocino ahumado
bacteria bacteria, microbios
bad malo, dañado
bad debt expense gastos de impagados
bad luck sal (Cuba, C. Am.)
bad-tempered mal genio
badge insignia, chapa
badger (v) acosar
baffle deflector
bail fianza
bail (v) afianzar
bailee depositario
bailiff alguacil
bait cebo, anzuelo
bake (v) cocer (al horno); cocinar (Arg., Uru., Col.)
baker panadero
bakery panadería
balance balance de cuentas, resto
balance sheet hoja de balance
balcony balcón, mirador

bald calvo
ball bola, pelota, baile (etiqueta)
ball bearing cojinete de bolas
ball-point pen bolígrafo
ballad balada, romance
ballast lastre
ballet ballet
ballistic balístico
balloon globo
ballot votación
ballot box urna
ballot paper papeleta de voto
baloney tonterías
balsam bálsamo
ban (v) prohibir, excluir
ban prohibición
banal insignificante
banana plátano
band banda, cinta, orquesta
bandage venda
bandaging vendajes
bandit bandido
bang (v) explotar, golpear
bang explosión, golpe
bangle ajorca
banishment deportación
banister pasamanos
banjo banjo
bank asiento, banca, banco, orilla
bank (v) amontonar, ladearse
bank acceptance aceptación bancaria
bank account cuenta de banco, cuenta bancaria
bank bill letra bancaria, efecto bancario
bank book libreta
bank branch sucursal bancaria
bank charges gastos bancarios
bank clerical staff empleados de banca
bank clerk empleado de banco
bank counters ventanillas

bank draft efecto bancario
bank note billete de banco
bank officials directivos del banco
bank operations operaciones bancarias
bank overdraft sobregiro real
bank papers valores bancarios
bank rate tasa bancaria
bank reconciliation conciliación bancaria
bank reserves reservas bancarias
bank statement extracto de cuenta
bank transfer transferencia bancaria
bankable descontable
banker banquero
banker in games banca (Arg., Uru.)
banker's check cheque de banco
banker's draft efecto bancario
banking banca
banking community comunidad bancaria
banking company sociedad bancaria
banking management gestión bancaria
banking policy política bancaria
banking regulations reglamentación de la banca
banking syndicate consorcio bancario
bankruptcy bancarrota, insolvencia, quiebra
banner bandera, pancarta
banquet banquete
bantam diminuto, gallinita
banter burlas
baptism bautizo
Baptist baptista

baptize (v) bautizar
bar abogacía, bar, barra; cantina (Amer.)
bar (v) excluir, obstruir
bar code código de barras
bar gold oro en barras
barbarian bárbaro
barbecue barbacoa; asado (Arg.)
barber peluquero, barbero
barbituric barbitúrico
bare desnudo, pelado
barefoot descalzo, sin zapatos
bareheaded cabeza descubierta
bargain ganga
bargain (v) regatear
barge barcaza
barge (v) empujar
baritone barítono
bark (v) escupir, ladrar
barley cebada
barn granero
barometer barómetro
baron barón, magnate
baroness baronesa
baroque barroco, grotesco
barrack caserón, cuartel
barrage presa, barrera
barrel barril, tonel
barren árido, estéril
barricade barricada
barrier barrera
barter comercio de trueque, trueque
base base
base (v) basar, fundar
base address dirección de base
basement sótano
bash golpe, intento
bashful tímido
bashfulness verguenza
basic básico, fundamental
basin cuenca, palangana
basis base, fundamento

bask (v) tostarse
basket cesta
basketball baloncesto
Basque vasco
Basque Country País Vasco
bass bajo, contrabajo
bass fish lubina, róbalo
bassoon bajón
bastard bastardo, ilegítimo
bastion baluarte
bat murciélago
bat (v) golpear
batch grupo, lote
batch processing procesamiento
  por lotes
bath baño, bañera
bath towel toalla de baño
bathe (v) bañarse
bathing suit traje de baño
bathroom aseo, lavabo
baton bastón, batuta
batter pasta, batido
battery batería, pila
battlefield campo de batalla
battleship acorazado
bawdy indecente, obsceno
bawl (v) cantar, gritar
bay bahía
bay leaf laurel
bayonet bayoneta
bazaar bazar
beach playa
beacon faro, almenara
bead cuenta, rosario
beak pico, nariz
beam (v) emitir
beam viga, rayo
bean judía, habichuela
bear oso
bear market mercado a la baja
beard barba
bearded barbudo
beardless imberbe, lampiño

bearer portador
bearer certificate resguardo al
  portador
bearer share certificate resguardo de acciones al portador
beast bestia, salvaje
beat golpe, latido
beat (v) golpear, latir; limpiar
  (Mex.)
beating salsa (Chile)
beauty belleza, hermosura
because porque, ya que
beckon (v) llamar, atraer
become (v) llegar a ser
become ashamed (v) chillar (C.
  Am.)
become expert at (v) jubilar
  (Cuba, Mex.)
becoming apropiado
bed cama
bedbug chinche
bedding ropa de cama
bedroom alcoba, dormitorio
bee abeja
beer cerveza
before antes
befriend (v) favorecer
beg (v) pedir, suplicar
beggar mendigo
begin (v) comenzar, empezar
begin to listen closely (v) parar
  (Amer.)
beginner principiante
beginning comienzo, principio
beginning inventory existencias
  iniciales
beguile (v) engañar
behalf beneficio, interés
behalf (on) a favor de
behave (v) comportarse
behavior comportamiento
behead (v) decapitar
behind detrás, atrás

behold (v)   mirar, contemplar
beige   beige
being   ser
belated   atrasado
belch   eructo
belch (v)   eructar, vomitar
Belgian   belga
Belgium   Bélgica
belief   creencia
believable   creíble
believe (v)   creer
believer   creyente
bell   campana, timbre
bell (v)   tocar el timbre
belligerent   beligerante
bellow   bramido, grito
bellow (v)   gritar, vociferar
belly   barriga, vientre
belong (v)   pertenecer
belongings   pertenencias
beloved   querido, amado
below   abajo, por debajo
belt   cinturón
bench   asiento, banco, tribunal
bend (v)   curvar, doblar
bend   curva, vuelta
beneath   abajo, por debajo
benefactor   bienhechor
beneficiary   beneficiario
benefit   beneficio, provecho
benefit of doubt   beneficio de la duda
benevolent   benévolo
benign   benigno
bent   doblado, torcido
benzene   benceno
bequeather   testador
bequest   manda, legado
bereaved   afligido
beret   boina
Berlin   Berlín
berserk   descontrolado
beside   al lado de, junto a

besiege (v)   asediar, sitiar
bespeak (v)   indicar, reservar
best   mejor, superior
bestseller   más vendido
bet   apuesta
bet (v)   apostar
Bethlehem   Belén
betray (v)   traicionar
betrayal   traición
better   mejor, preferible
better (v)   mejorar, superar
betterment   mejora, mejoría
between   entre, en medio de
beverage   bebida
beware (v)   tener cuidado
bewilder (v)   aturdir, desconcertar
beyond   más allá, más lejos
bias   diagonal, inclinación, parcialidad, prejuicio
bias (v)   influir en, torcer
bib   babero
Bible   Biblia
Biblical   bíblico
bibliographer   bibliógrafo
bibliography   bibliografía
biceps   bíceps
bicker (v)   altercar, disputar
bickering   riña, altercado
bicycle   bicicleta
bid   oferta
bid (v)   ofrecer
bid bond   garantía de licitación
bidder   postor
bidding   licitación
biennial   bienal
big   grande
bigamy   bigamía
bigot   fanático
bike   bicicleta
bikini   bikini
bilateral   bilateral
bile   bilis

biliary biliar
bilingual bilingüe
bilk (v) estafar
bill billete, factura, letra, giro, proyecto de ley
bill (v) facturar
bill holder tenedor de letra
bill holdings cartera de efectos
bill of exchange letra de cambio
bill of lading conocimiento de embarque
bill of sale escritura de venta
bill to order pagaré
billboard cartelera
billfold billetero
billing facturación
billion billón
bimonthly bimensual
binary binario
binary arithmetic aritmética binaria
binary numeral numeral binario
binary search búsqueda binaria
bind (v) atar, liar
binder resguardo provisional
binding encuadernación, obligatorio
binoculars gemelos
biochemistry bioquímica
biography biografía
biological biológico
biologist biólogo
biology biología
biopsy biopsia
bird pájaro
birth nacimiento, parto
birth certificate partida de nacimiento
birth control control de natalidad
birthday cumpleaños
birthplace lugar de nacimiento
bisexual bisexual

bishop obispo
bit bit
bit position posición de bit
bitch perra
bite mordedura
bite (v) morder, picar
bitter amargo
bizarre extraño, estrafalario
black negro
black and blue amoratado (Amer.)
black box registro de vuelo
black market mercado negro
black person moreno (Cuba)
Black Sea Mar Negro
blackboard pizarra
blacken (v) ennegrecer
blacklist lista negra
blackmail chantaje
blackness oscuridad
blackout apagón
bladder vejiga
blade cuchilla, hoja
blame culpa
blame (v) culpar
blameless inocente
blank en blanco
blank (v) tachar, borrar
blank acceptance aceptación en blanco
blank check cheque en blanco
blanket manta; abrigo (Arg.)
blare estrépito
blare (v) resonar
blasphemy blasfemia
blast estallido, chorro
blast (v) destruir, volar
blast-off lanzamiento
blatant flagrante, evidente
blaze llamarada, señal
blaze (v) arder, brillar
blazer chaqueta de deporte
bleach blanqueo

bleach (v) blanquear, descolorar

bleak nada prometedor, desierto, desolado

bleed (v) sangrar

bleeding sangría

blemish (v) manchar, mancillar

blend mezcla

blend (v) mezclar

bless (v) bendecir

blessing bendición

blind ciego

blindfold venda (en los ojos)

blindness ceguera

blink parpadeo

bliss felicidad

blister ampolla

blizzard ventisca

bloated hinchado

blob gota, mancha

block bloque

block (v) obstruir, cerrar

block of houses bloque (Arg., C. Am., Uru.)

blockade bloqueo

blocked account cuenta bloqueada

blond rubio, rubia

blood sangre

blood bath carnicería

blood donor donante de sangre

blood group grupo sanguíneo

blood pressure presión sanguínea

blood transfusion transfusión de sangre

bloodcurdling espeluznante

bloodstream corriente sanguínea

bloodthirsty sediento de sangre

bloody muy sangriento

bloom flor, floración

blot borrón

blouse blusa

blow golpe, soplo; truco (Arg.); viaje (C. Am.)

blow (v) golpear, soplar

blow-out pinchazo

blow-up explosión

blue azul

blue chip shares acciones de primera clase

blue chips valores de primera

blueprint anteproyecto

bluff engañar, brusco

blunder error grande

blur mancha, borroso

blur (v) empañar

blush rubor, sonrojo

board consejo, junta, mesa, tablero

board (v) entablar, abordar

board meeting junta de directiva

board of directors junta directiva, consejo directivo, consejo de administración

board room sala de juntas

boarding school internado (escuela)

boards abatido (Cuba, Col.)

boast (v) jactarse

boaster fanfarrón

boat barco, buque

body cuerpo

bodyguard guardaespaldas

bogus falso

boil (v) hervir

bold valiente, audaz; tabaco (Mex.)

boldface negrilla (letra)

boldness audacia

Bolivia Bolivia

Bolivian boliviano

bolt cerrojo, tornillo

bolt (v) atornillar

bomb bomba

bombard (v) bombardear

bona bienes

bona fide buena fe, genuino, auténtico

bond bono, fianza, título, vínculo

bond issue emisión de bonos

bondage esclavitud

bonded en garantía

bonded warehouse almacén de depósito aduanero, depósito

bondholder tenedor de bonos

bone hueso

bonfire hoguera, fogata

bonus paga extraordinaria, premio, prima

booby trap trampa explosiva

book libro

book (v) reservar

book value valor según libros, valor contable

bookkeeper contable

booklet folleto

bookseller librero

bookshop librería

boot bota

boot (v) dar un puntapié

booth puesto, cabina

booth or stall where food and drinks are sold venta (Chile)

booze bebida alcohólica

border frontera

borderline línea fronteriza

bore tostada (Arg.)

boredom aburrimiento

boring aburrido, perforación

boring conversation solo (Arg.)

born nacido

borrow (v) pedir prestado

borrower prestatario, tomador de crédito

bosom pecho, seno

boss director, jefe

botanic botánico

both ambos

both-way communication comunicación bidireccional

bother (v) molestar

bottle botella

bottleneck cuello de botella

bottom final, fondo

bottomless sin fondo

botulism botulismo

boudoir tocador

bounce (v) rebotar

bounced check cheque sin fondos

bound obligado

boundary linde, lindero, límite

bouquet ramo, aroma

bourgeois burgués

bow (v) inclinarse

bowel intestino

box caja, casilla

box office taquilla

boxer boxeador

boxing boxeo

boy chico, niño

boycott boicot

boyfriend amigo, novio

boyhood juvenil

bra sostén

brace abrazadera, tirante

brace (v) asegurar

bracelet pulsera; pulso (Cuba)

bracket soporte, puntal

braggart palangana (Amer.)

braid trenza

brain cerebro

brainwash lavado de cerebro

brainy inteligente

brake freno

brake pedal pedal de freno

branch bifurcación, sucursal

brand marca

brand loyalty lealtad a la marca

brand new nuevo, reciente
brandy coñac
brandy of inferior quality grapa (Arg.)
brash inculto, tosco
brass latón
brave valiente
brave (v) desafiar
brave man gallo (Amer.)
bravely valientemente
brawl alboroto, reyerta
brawn fuerza muscular
brawny fornido, musculoso
Brazil Brasil
Brazilian brasileño
breach abertura, brecha, rotura, violación
breach of contract incumplimiento de contrato
bread pan
bread crumb migaja de pan
breadth amplitud, anchura
break grieta, ruptura, rotura
break (v) romper, interrumpir
break even umbral de rentabilidad
breakage rotura
breakaway ruptura
breakdown análisis, avería, fracaso
breakfast desayuno
breaking point punto de interrupción
breakthrough avance, adelanto
breakup disolución
breast pecho, seno
breath aliento
breathe (v) respirar
breathing respiración
breed raza, casta
breed (v) criar
breeding cría
breeze brisa

brew brebaje
brewery fábrica de cerveza
bribe soborno
bribe (v) sobornar
bribery soborno
brick ladrillo
bride novia
bridge puente
brief breve, corte
brief (v) dar órdenes a
briefcase cartera; bulto (Col., Hond., Mex.)
briefing reunión, órdenes
briefly brevemente
bright claro, brillante
brighten (v) animarse
brightness claridad
brilliant brillante
bring (v) traer, conducir
bring legal action against (v) accionar (Amer.)
brink borde, al punto
Britain Gran Bretaña
British inglés
broad amplio, ancho
broadcast radiodifundido
broadcasting radiodifusión
broaden (v) ensanchar
broadly extensamente
brochure folleto
broil asado
broke desahuciado
broken roto
broken bone hueso roto
broker agente, corredor
brokerage corretaje
bronchitis bronquitis
broom escoba
broth caldo
brother hermano
brother-in-law cuñado
brotherhood fraternidad
brow ceja, frente

brown moreno, oscuro
browse (v) pacer, hojear
bruise contusión, morado
brunch desayuno-almuerzo
brunette moreno, morena
brush cepillo, escoba
brush (v) cepillar, barrer
Brussels Bruselas
brute brutal
bubble ampolla, burbuja
bubble gum chicle
buck dólar USA
buckle hebilla
buckle (v) abrochar, torcerse
bud brote, yema
bud (v) brotar
buddy compañero, amigo
budge (v) mover
budget presupuesto
budgetary presupuestario
buffer pool fondo estabilizador, reserva
bug bicho, defecto
build (v) construir, hacer
builder constructor
building edificio
built-in telephone teléfono incorporado
bulb bombilla, bulbo
bulge pandeo, comba
bulge (v) pandearse
bulk masa, volumen, carga
bulky voluminoso, grande
bull toro
bull market mercado alcista
bull's eye centro del blanco
bulldozer aplanadora
bullet bala
bullet-proof glass cristal a prueba de balas
bulletin anuncio, boletín
bullfight corrida de toros
bullion oro en barra

bullish mercado en alza
bullying abusivo (Amer.)
bumble (v) fallar, errar
bumper parachogues
bun bollo, panecillo
bunch manojo, ramo; mano (Amer.)
bundle bulto, fardo
bundle (v) agrupar, atar
bundle atado, bulto, fardo
bungalow casa simple
bunion juanete
bunk litera
buoy boya
buoyant boyante
burden carga, peso
bureau escritorio, oficina
bureaucracy burocracia
burglar ladrón
burglar alarm alarma de robo
burglary escalo, robo hurto
burial entierro
burn quemadura
burn (v) incendiar, quemar
burner quemador
burning ardiente
bursar tesorero
burst explosión, estallido
bury (v) enterrar
bus autobús
bus stop parada de autobús
bush arbusto
bushel busel (medida)
bushy espeso, tupido
business asunto, negocio
business data processing informática de gestión
business deal trato comercial
business letter carta comercial
business trip viaje de negocios
businesslike metódico, serio
businessman hombre de negocios

bust busto, pecho
bustle actividad, movimiento
busy atareado, ocupado
but menos, pero, solo
butcher carnicero
butler mayordomo
butter mantequilla
butterfly mariposa
butterfly jasmine (Cuban national flower) mariposa (la flor nacional de Cuba)
buttocks nalgas
button botón
buy-out compra de la parte de otro socio
buyer comprador

buzz zumbido
buzz (v) avisar, zumbar
buzzer avisador, vibrador
by airmail por correo aéreo
by land por tierra
by-product subproducto
by rail por ferrocarril
by sea por mar
by ship por vía marítima
bye-bye adiós
bygone pasado
bylaws estatutos, reglamentos
bypass desvío
bypass (v) evitar contacto
bystander espectador
byte octeto

C

cab taxi
cabaret cabaret
cabbage tallo (Col.)
cabin cabaña
cabin cruiser yate de motor
cabinet armario
cable cable, funicular, telegrama
cable transfer transferencia cablegráfica
cablecar funicular
cablegram cablegrama
cadaver cadáver
caddie ayudante (golf)
cadet cadete
caesarean cesárea
cafe café
caffeine cafeína
Cairo el Cairo
cake pastel, torta
calamity calamidad
calcium calcio
calculate (v) calcular, contar
calculated intencionado

calculating astuto
calculator calculadora
calendar calendario
calf ternero
caliber calibre, capacidad
call citación, convocatoria, llamada
call girl prostituta
call provision disposición de convocatoria
call waiting indicación de llamada en espera
callable bond bono amortizable anticipadamente, bono reembolsable
called up para abonar
calligraphy caligrafía
calling in of currency retiro de moneda
calm calma, tranquilidad
caloric calórico
calories calorías
calumniator calumniador

calumny calumnia
calves pantorrillas
camel camello
camera cámára, máquina fotográfica
camouflage camuflaje
camp campamento
campaign campaña
camper acampador
campground camping
campus recinto universitario
can lata
can (v) poder
can opener abrelatas
Canada Canadá
Canadian canadiense
canal canal
cancel (v) cancelar, suprimir
cancellation cancelación
cancer cáncer
candid franco, sincero
candidate aspirante, candidato
candidly francamente
candle vela
candor franqueza
candy dulce
cane bastón, caña
canine canino
cannibal caníbal
cannon cañón
canon canon, canónigo
canopy pabellón
canteen cantina
cantilever viga
canvas lona
canvass sondeo
canvass (v) discutir, sondear
cap gorra, tapón
cap (v) coronar, rematar
capability capacidad
capable capaz, competente
capacity capacidad
cape cabo, capa

capillary capilar
capillary tube tubo capilar
capital capital, capital social
capital account cuenta de capital, cuenta patrimonial
capital assets activo fijo, bienes de capital
capital dividends dividendos de capital
capital gains ganancias de capital
capital goods bienes de equipo
capital levy impuesto sobre capital
capital losses pérdidas de capital
capital markets mercados de capitales
capital stock capital social
capital tax impuesto sobre el capital
capitalization of interest capitalización de interés
capitalize capitalizar
Capitol capitolio
caprice capricho
capsize (v) tumbar, volcar
capsule cápsula
captain capitán
caption epígrafe, título
captivate (v) cautivar, encantar
captive cautivo
capture captura, presa
car coche, automóvil
car wash lavado de coche
caramel corn alboroto (Amer.)
carat quilate
caravan tropa (Arg.)
carbine carabina
carbohydrate hidrato de carbono
carbon carbón
carbon copy copia de carbón
carburetor carburador

carcass cadáver
carcinogen cancerígeno
carcinoma carcinoma, tumor maligno
card carta, ficha, fichero, naipe, tarjeta postal
card game (old maid) tonto (Col., C.R., Chile)
cardboard cartón, cartulina
cardiac cardíaco
cardinal cardenal
cardiograph cardiógrafo
cardiography cardiografía
cardiology cardiología
cardiopulmonary cardiopulmonar
cardiovascular cardiovascular
care cuidado
career carrera
carefully con cuidado
careless descuidado
caress caricia
caretaker vigilante
cargo carga
Caribbean Caribe
caricature caricatura
caries caries
carnage carnicería
carnal carnal, corporal
carnation clavel
carnival carnaval
carol villancico
carotid carótida
carpenter carpintero
carpet alfombra
carpus carpo
carriage vagón, coche
carrier portador
carrot zanahoria
carry (v) traer, transportar; tirar (Cuba, Chile)
cart carreta, carretilla

carte blanche carta blanca
cartel cartel, monopolio
cartilage cartílago
cartography cartografía
cartoon dibujo animado
cartridge cartucho
carve (v) trinchar, tallar
cascade cascada
case caja, causa, caso
cash efectivo
cash account cuenta de caja
cash against documents pago contra presentación de documentos, pago contra entrega de documentos
cash book libro de caja
cash disbursements gastos en efectivo
cash discount descuento por pronto pago
cash flow líquido circulante
cash holdings disponibilidades en efectivo
cash in bank efectivo en bancos
cash in hand efectivo
cash on delivery pago contra reembolso
cash on hand efectivo en caja
cash receipts comprobantes de caja
cash transaction operación al contado
cash voucher comprobante de caja
cashier caja
cashier's check cheque de caja
cashier's desk cajero
cashmere cachemira
casing envoltura
cask barril
casket ataúd, estuche
cassette cassette, cartucho

cassock sotana
cast enyesadura
cast-iron hierro fundido
castanets castañuelas
castigate (v) castigar
Castile Castilla (región)
Castilian castellano
castle castillo
castor oil aceite de ricino
castration castración
casual casual, fortuito
casually por casualidad
casualty accidente, pérdida, siniestro
casualty list lista de bajas
cat gato, felino
Catalan catalán (lengua)
catalepsy catalepsia
catalog catálogo
Catalonia Cataluña
Catalonian catalán
catalysis catálisis
catalyst catalizador
cataract catarata
catastrophe catástrofe
catch cerradura, pesca
catch (v) atrapar, coger; abrochar (Mex.)
catchy pegadizo
catechism catequismo
category categoría
cater (v) proveer, abastecer
caterer abastecedor
catering abastecimiento
caterpillar gusano
cathedral catedral
Catholic católico
catsup salsa de tomate
cattle ganado, vacuno; hacienda (Arg., Chile)
cattle breeding ranch cabaña (Arg., Uru.)

cattleman ganadero
cause causa, litigio
causeway calzada
cautery cauterización
caution precaución, prudencia, cautela
cautious prudente
cavalier arrogante
cavalry caballería
cave cueva, caverna
caveat advertencia
caviar caviar
cavity cavidad, hueco
cayenne pepper pimentón
CD ROM disco compacto ROM
cease (v) cesar, suspender
cease fire tregua
cedar cedro
ceiling techo
celebrate (v) celebrar
celebration celebración
celery apio
celestial celestial
celibacy celibato
cell célula, pila
cell flat battery pila plana
cellar bodega, sótano
cello violoncelo
cellophane celofán
cellular telephone teléfono celular
cellulitis celulitis
cement cemento
cemetery cementerio
censor censor
censorship censura
census censo
cent centavo, céntimo
center centro
center (v) centralizar
Central America América Central

Central American centroamericano

central bank banco nacional

central processing unit unidad central de proceso

central processor procesador central

centrifugal centrífugo

century siglo

cephalic cefálico

ceramic cerámico

cereal cereal

cerebellum cerebelo

cerebral cerebral

cerebrum cerebro

ceremony ceremonia

certain cierto, seguro

certainly certeza, ciertamente

certificate certificado

certificate of balance certificado de saldo de cuenta

certificate of damage certificado de averia

certificate of deposit certificado de depósito

certificate of incorporation escritura de constitución

certificate of indebtedness certificado de adeudo

certificate of origin certificado de origen

certificate of receipt certificado de recepción

certification certificación

certified certificado

certified bill of lading conocimiento de embarque certificado

certified check cheque certificado

Certified Public Accountant Censor jurado de cuentas

certify (v) declarar

cervical vertebra vértebra cervical

cession cesión, traspaso

chafe (v) frotar, raspar

chagrin disgusto

chain cadena

chain connection conexión en cadena

chain reaction reacción en cadena

chain store cadena de tiendas

chair silla, presidencia

chairman presidente del consejo de administración

chalet chalet

chalk tiza, yeso

challenge desafío, objeción, recusación, reto

challenge (v) desafiar, retar

challenger desafiador

chamber cámara, sala

Chamber of Commerce Cámara de Comercio

chameleon camaleón

champ campeón

champion campeón

championship campeonato

chance posibilidad, suerte

chance (v) probar

change cambio; feria (Mex.)

changeover alteración (sistema)

changing cambiante

channel canal

chaos desorden, caos

chaotic caótico

chapel capilla, iglesia

chaplain capellán

chapter capítulo

char (v) carbonizar

character naturaleza, carácter

character recognition reconocimiento de caracteres

characteristic característica

charcoal carbón vegetal
charge acusación, cargo, gasto, débito
charge (v) cargar, facturar
charging lien gravamen de abogado
charisma carisma
charity caridad
charm encanto
charm (v) encantar
charming encantador
charred quemado, carbonizado
chart esquema, tabla
charter carta, fuero
charter (v) alquilar, otorgar
chase caza, persecución
chase (v) cazar, perseguir
chasm sima, abismo
chassis chasis
chaste casto
chat charla
chatter (v) charlar; chasquear (dientes) (Amer.)
chauffeur conductor, chófer
chauvinist chauvinista
cheap barato
cheapen (v) abaratar
cheat fraude, trampa
cheat (v) engañar
cheating engaño, estafa
check cheque, talón; adición (in a restaurant, etc.) (Amer.)
check book talonario
check stub matriz de talonario
check to bearer cheque al portador
checkers juego de damas
checkpoint punto de control
checkup comprobación, reconocimiento (médico)
cheekbone pómulo
cheeks mofletes
cheer grito, aplauso

cheer (v) aplaudir, gritar
cheerful alegre
cheese queso
chef jefe de cocina
chemical químico
chemical burn quemadura química
chemistry química
chemotherapy quimoterapia
cherish (v) querer, apreciar
cherry cereza
chess ajedrez
chest pecho
chew (v) mascar
chewing gum chicle de mascar
chic elegante
chicken pollo
chickenpox varicela
chiefly principalmente
chilblain sabañón
child hijo, niño, niña
childhood infancia
childish pueril
Chile Chile
Chilean chileno
chill frío, resfriado
chill (v) congelar, enfriar
chimney chimenea
chin mentón
China China
Chinese chino
chink grieta
chip chip, pastilla
chiropodist pedicuro
chiropractor quiropráctico
chisel cincel
chivalry caballerosidad
chlorine cloro
chocolate chocolate
choice opción, selección
choir coro
choke (v) obstruir, atascar
choking atragantamiento

cholera cólera
cholesterol colesterol
choose (v) elegir, escoger
chop (v) cortar, tajar
chop corte, golpe
chopper cuchilla, helicóptero
chopping knife cuchillo de tajar
chopsticks palillos chinos
chore acorde, cuerda, faena, tarea
choreographer coreógrafo
chorus girl corista
Christ Cristo, Jesucristo
Christian cristiano
Christmas Navidades
Christmas card felicitación
Christmas party posada (Mex., Hond.)
chrome cromo
chronic constante, crónico
chronicle crónica
chronograph cronógrafo
chronological cronológico
chrysanthemum crisantemo
chubby gordinflón
chuckle risita, risa
chunk pedazo, trozo
church iglesia, templo
churchwarden fiscal (Bol., Perú)
churn (v) agitar, batir
chute conducto, tobogán
cider sidra
cigar cigarro puro
cigar or coal that dies out often apagón (Cuba, Mex.)
cigarette cigarrillo
cinema cine
cinnamon canela
cipher cifra
circle círculo
circuit circuito
circular circular
circulate (v) circular, divulgar

circulation circulación
circumcision circuncisión
circumference circunferencia
circumflex circunflejo
circumstantial circunstancial
circus circo
cirrhosis cirrosis
cistern cisterna
citation citación, cita
citizen ciudadano
citizenship ciudadanía
citric cítrico
city ciudad
civic cívico, municipal
civil code código civil
civil court tribunal civil
civil death muerte civil
civil law ley civil
civil status estado civil
civilian civil, paisano
civilization civilización
civilize (v) civilizar
claim reclamación
claimant demandante
clam almeja
clamp abrazadera
clandestine clandestino
clang sonido, estruendo
clap palmada
clap (v) hacer palmas
clarification esclarecimiento
clarify (v) aclarar
clarinet clarinete
clarity claridad
clash encuentro, choque
clasp broche, corchete
class clase
classic clásico
clatter ruido, estruendo
clause cláusula
claustrophobia claustrofobia
clavicle clavícula
claw garra, uña

clay arcilla, tierra
clean limpio
clean (v) limpiar
clean bill of lading conocimiento de embarque sin reservas
clean credit crédito simple
clean draft remesa simple
clear claro
clear (v) aclarar, despejar
clearance liquidación
clearance sale saldos
clearing compensación
clearing house cámara de compensación
clemency clemencia
clergy clero
clerical de oficina
clerk empleado
clever listo; templado (Mex., C. Am.)
cliché cliché
client cliente
cliff acantilado
climate clima
climax apogeo, colmo
climb (v) ascender, subir
cling (v) agarrarse, asirse
clinic clínica
clip grapa
clitoris clítoris
cloak capa
cloak and dagger asunto secreto
clock frequency cadencia
clock reloj
clock speed frecuencia
clog obstáculo
close cerca, junto
close (v) cerrar
close held corporation sociedad propietaria
close-up primer plano
closed cerrado

closed account cuenta saldada
closet armario
closing date fecha de cierre
clot coágulo, grumo
cloth ropa, tela
clothes rack árbol (Chile)
cloud nube
cloud (v) nublar, oscurecer
clown payaso
clue indicio, pista
clumsy chapucero, torpe
cluster mano (Amer.)
clutter desorden
co-drawer cogirador
co-op cooperativa
coach entrenador
coactive coactivo
coagulate (v) coagular
coalition coalición
coarse cloak manga (Hond.)
coarse wool litro (Chile)
coast litoral, costa
coat abrigo, chaqueta
coax (v) engatusar
coaxial cable cable coaxial
cobalt cobalto
cocaine cocaína
coccus coco
cock gallo, martillo
cock (v) amartillar
cocktail combinado; palo (P.R.)
cocoa cacao
cod bacalao
cod liver oil aceite de hígado de bacalao
code código
code converter convertidor de código
codefendant coacusado
codeine codeína
codify (v) codificar
coding codificación
coefficient coeficiente

coefficient of variation
  coeficiente de variación
coerce (v) coaccionar, forzar
coercion coacción
coffee café
coffin cajón (Amer.)
coheir coheredero
coherence coherencia
coil bobina, espiral, rollo
coin moneda
coin worth five centavos quinto
  (Mex., Chile)
coincide (v) coincidir
coitus coito
coke cocaína, coque
cold frío
cold cuts fiambre
coleslaw ensalada de col
colic cólico
colitigant colitigante
colitis colitis
collaborate (v) colaborar
collapse colapso
collapse (v) derrumbarse
collar collar, cuello
collateral aval, colateral, garantía, resguardo, seguridad
colleague colega
collect (v) cobrar, reunir
collect wages (v) rayar (Mex.)
collectibles cobraderos, por cobrar
collection acumulación, cobro,
  recaudación
collection remittance envío al
  cobro
collector coleccionador
college colegio mayor
collide (v) chocar, colisionar
colon colón
colonel coronel
color (v) colorear
colt potro

color color
color (v) colorear
Columbus Colón
column columna
coma coma
comatose comatoso
comb peine
combat combate
combination combinación
combine (v) combinar, coordinar
come (v) llegar, venir
comeback réplica, retorno
comedian cómico
comedy comedia
comfort alivio, comodidad
comfortable confortable, cómodo
command instrucción, orden
command (v) mandar, ordenar
command language lenguaje de
  mandatos
commemorate (v) conmemorar
commence (v) comenzar, empezar
comment comentario
commerce comercio
commercial comercial, mercantil
commercial bank banco de depósito
commercial draft efecto comercial
commercial invoice factura
  comercial
commercial letter of credit
  carta de crédito comercial
commission comisión, encargo
commit (v) declararse, obligar
commitment compromiso,
  promesa
commitments outstanding compromisos existentes
committee comité, comisión

commodities mercancías generales
commodity producto corriente
common común
common bail fianza ordinaria
common jury jurado ordinario
common law ley común
common stock acciones ordinarias
Commonwealth Mancomunidad
commorant residente
communicate (v) comunicar
communication comunicación
communism comunismo
community comunidad
commute (v) conmutar, viajar
commuter viajero diario
compact compacto, sólido
companion compañero
company compañía, empresa
company deeds actas de la sociedad
compare (v) comparar
comparison careo, comparación
compartment compartimiento
compass brújula
compassion compasión
compatibility compatibilidad
compatible compatible
compel (v) imponer, obligar
compensate (v) compensar, pagar
compensation compensación
compensatory duty impuesto compensatorio
compete (v) competir
competence aptitud, capacidad
competent apto, capaz, competente
competition competencia
competitor competidor
compile (v) recopilar
compiler compilador

complacent complaciente
complain (v) quejarse, reclamar
complaint demanda, queja, reclamación
complement complemento
complementary complementario
complete completo, entero
completion cumplimiento, terminación
complex complicado
complexion aspecto, tez
complexity complejidad
complicate (v) complicar
complicated complicado
complicity complicidad
compliment cumplido, saludo
complimentary complementario
comply (v) acorde a, obedecer
component componente, pieza
compose (v) componer, formar
composed sosegado
composition composición
compound compuesto, mezcla
compound interest interés compuesto
comprehend (v) comprender
comprehensive extenso, general
compress compresa
compress (v) comprimir, reducir
compromise arreglo, compromiso
compromise (v) ceder, transigir
compromising transigente
compulsory obligatorio
compulsory reserves reservas obligatorias
compute (v) computar, contar
computer ordenador, computadora
computer-aided design diseño por ordenador
computer graphics gráfica automatizada

193

er language lenguaje de
computadora

computer network red de ordenadores

computer science ciencia del
ordenador

computerize (v) preparar, programar

comrade amigo, camarada

con man timador

concavity concavidad

conceal (v) ocultar

concealed disimulado, oculto

concealment encubrimiento

concede (v) conceder

conceivable concebible

conceive (v) concebir

concentrate (v) concentrar, reunir

concept concepto

concern asunto, interés

concern (v) interesar, concernir

concerned preocupado

concerning acerca de, sobre

concert concierto

concession cesión, concesión,
privilegio

conciliate (v) conciliar

conciliation conciliación

concise conciso

conclude (v) concluir, terminar

conclusion conclusión

conclusive conclusivo, concluyente

concrete concreto, horimigón

concussion concusión, conmoción cerebral, golpe

condemn (v) condenar, censurar

condemnation enajenación

condensation condensación

condescend (v) dignarse

condition condición

conditional condicional

conditional endorsement endoso condicional

condom condón, preservativo

condone (v) condenar

conduct conducta

conduct (v) conducir, dirigir

conductor conductor

cone cono, barquillo

confectioner pastelero

confederation confederación

conference conferencia

conference table mesa de conferencias

confess (v) confesar, reconocer

confession confesión

confidant confidente

confide (v) confiar, fiarse de

confidence confianza

confidential confidencial

configuration configuración

confine (v) encerrar

confinement encierro

confirm (v) confirmar

confirmation confirmación

confirmed credit crédito confirmado

confiscate (v) confiscar, incautar

confiscation confiscación

conflict conflicto

conform (v) estar acorde a

conformist conformista

confound (v) confundir

confront (v) hacer frente

confrontation confrontación

confuse (v) confundir

confused confuso, perplejo

confusing desconcertante

confusion confusión, desorden

congenial compatible

congenital congénito

congestion congestión

conglomerate conglomerado

congratulate (v) felicitar

congratulations felicitaciones
congregate (v) congregarse
congress congreso
congressman diputado
conjectural conjetural
conjecture conjetura
conjunctivitis conjuntivitis
connect (v) conectar, unir
connected conectado
connection conexión
connector conector
connoisseur experto
connotation connotación
conquer (v) conquistar
conquering victorioso
conqueror vencedor
conscious consciente (estado), sabedor
conscription servicio militar
consecutive seguido, sucesivo
consensus consenso
consent aquiescencia
consent (v) estar de acuerdo
consequence consecuencia
consequent consiguiente
conservation conservación
conservative conservador
conserve (v) conservar
consider (v) considerar, pensar
considerable considerable
considering teniendo en cuenta
consign (v) consignar
consignee destinatario
consignment consigna, remesa
consignment sale venta en depósito
consist (v) consistir
console consola, tablero
consolidate (v) consolidar
consolidated consolidado
consolidated balance sheet cuenta de balance consolidada

consolidated financial statements estados financieros consolidados
consolidated shipment envío por grupaje
consolidation consolidación
consonant consonante
consortium consorcio
conspicuous visible
conspiracy conjuración, conspiración
constable guarda, policía
constant constante, continuo
constellation constelación
constipation estreñimiento
constituency distrito
constitute (v) componer, construir
constitution constitución
constitutional constitucional
constrain (v) obligar
constraint fuerza, reserva
constrict (v) apretar, estrechar
construct (v) construir
construction construcción
constructive constructivo
consul cónsul
consular invoice factura consular
consulate consulado
consult (v) consultar
consultant asesor, especialista
consultation consulta
consulting room consulta
consume (v) consumir
consumer consumidor
consumption consumo
contact contacto
contact (v) contactar, comunicar
contagious contagioso
contain (v) contener
container contenedor

contaminate contaminar
contemplate (v) contemplar
contemporary contemporáneo
contempt desprecio
contend (v) afirmar, sostener
contest concurso, disputa
contest (v) atacar, impugnar
context contexto
contingencies eventualidades,
　imprevistos
contingency contingencia
contingent condicional, contin-
　gente, eventual
contingent liabilities deudas
　imprevistas
continue (v) continuar, seguir
continuity continuidad
continuous continuo
contortion contorsión
contraband contrabando
contraceptive anticonceptivo,
　preservativo
contract contrato
contract (v) contraer, encoger
contract of sale contrato de
　compraventa
contracting contratante
contraction contracción
contractor contratista
contractual contractual
contradict (v) contradecir
contraindication contraindi-
　cación
contrary contrario
contrast contraste
contrast (v) contrastar
contribute (v) contribuir
contribution contribución
contributor contribuyente
control control, mando
control (v) controlar, mandar
control accounts control de
　cuentas

controlled exchange cambio
　controlado
controller controlador, inspector
controversial discutible
controversy controversia
controvert (v) contradecir
contumacy rebeldía
contusion contusión
convalesce (v) convalecer
convenience comodidad, ventaja
convent convento
convention asamblea, conven-
　ción
conversation conversación
converse contrario, inverso
conversion conversion
convert (v) convertirse
converter convertidor
convertible loan empréstito de
　obligaciones
convertible stock acciones con-
　vertibles
convey (v) llevar, transportar
conveyance título de traspaso,
　traspaso, transporte
convict presidiario
conviction condena
convulsions convulsiones
cook cocinero
cook (v) cocinar
cookbook libro de cocina
cooker cocina
cookie dulce, galleta
cookout asado (Arg.)
cool fresco, tranquilo
coop gallinero
cooperate (v) cooperar
coordinate (v) coordinar
coordination coordinación
cop policía
cope (v) arreglar, poder con
copier copiadora, multicopista
copulate (v) unirse

copy copia
copy (v) copiar, imitar
copy-protected protección de copia
copycat imitador
copyright derecho de autor
coral coral
cord cuerda (vocal)
cordial cordial, amable
cordless phone teléfono portátil
corduroy pana
core centro, núcleo
cork corcho
cork tree alcornoque
corkscrew sacacorchos
corn maíz, grano
cornea córnea
corner esquina
cornered acorralado
cornet corneta
corn (stewed) mote (Amer.)
corny gastado, viejo
coronary coronario
corporal cabo
corporation compañía, corporación, empresa
corporation certificates certificados de constitución
corps cuerpo
correct correcto
correlate (v) correlacionar
correspond (v) corresponder
correspondence correspondencia
correspondent bank banco corresponsal
corridor pasillo
corrosive corrosivo
corrugated ondulado
corrupt corrompido
corruption corrupción
cortisone cortisona
cosmetic cosmético

cosmetic surgery cirugía estética
cosmic cósmico
cost coste, costo
cost accounting contabilidad de costes
cost insurance and freight coste, seguro y flete
cost of capital coste de capital
cost of goods sold coste de bienes vendidos
cost of sales costes comerciales, costes de venta
cost price precio de coste
costs costes
costume traje
cotton algodón
cotton cloth manta (Mex.)
couch canapé, sofá
cough tos
cough (v) toser
coughing tos
counsel consejo
counselor asesor, consejero
count cálculo, cargo, cuenta, demanda
countdown cuenta atrás
counter contador, contrario, mostrador
counter (v) oponerse
counter-attack contraataque
counter wills testamentos recíprocos
counteract (v) contrarrestar
counteraffidavit contradeclaración
countercharge reconvención
counterclaim contrademanda
counterfeit falsificación, falsificado
counterfeit money dinero falso
counterfeiter falsificador
counterfoil matriz del talonario

counterpart contraparte, correspondiente
counterproof contraprueba
counterproposal contrapropuesta
counterseal contrasello
countervailing compensatorio
country país
country bank banco rural
country music música popular
countryside campo
county condado
county jail cárcel del condado
coup golpe
couple par, pareja
couple (v) juntar
coupling acoplamiento
coupon bono, cupón
coupon bond bonos al portador
courage valentía, valor; pan (Chile)
courier correo, portador
court juzgado, tribunal
court (v) afilar (Arg., Uru.)
court clerk secretario del juzgado
court of claims tribunal de reclamaciones
court of law juzgado, tribunal
court officer alguacil
courthouse palacio de justicia
courtroom sala del tribunal
covenant convenio, pacto
covenanter contratante
cover (v) cubrir, ocultar
cow vaca
cowardly morado (Arg.)
cowboy vaquero
cower (v) encogerse de miedo
crab cangrejo
crabbed complicado
crack cocaína, crujido, grieta

crack (v) crujir, romperse
cracker galleta crujiente
cradle cuna
craft artesanía, oficio
craftsman artesano
craftmanship artesanía
crafty astuto
cram (v) atestar, rellenar
cramp calambre, grapa
crane grúa
crank capricho, manivela
cranky caprichoso
crash accidente
crash (v) estrellar, chocar
crate caja de madera
crawl arrastramiento
crayon lápiz de pastel
craze locura, moda
crazy demente, loco
cream nata
credentials credenciales
credibility credibilidad
credible creíble
credit crédito, haber, mérito
credit (v) dar crédito, abonar
credit balance saldo acreedor
credit card tarjeta de crédito
credit line línea de crédito
credit note nota de crédito
credit rating valoración de solvencia, nivel de solvencia
credit report informe de solvencia
creditor acreedor
credits abonos, créditos
creed credo, creencia
creep (v) arrastrarse
cremate (v) incinerar
Creole criollo
crescent creciente
crest cresta
cretinism cretinismo

crew tripulación
crib pesebre
cricket grillo
crime crimen, delito
criminal criminal
criminal action acción criminal
criminal court juzgado criminal
criminal laywer abogado penalista
criminal offense delito penal
criminal procedure trámite penal
criminal process proceso criminal
criminal record antecedentes penales
criminalist criminalista
crinkle arruga
cripple inválido, lisiado
cripple (v) mutilar, invalidar
crisis crisis
crisp crujiente
criterion criterio
critic crítico
criticize (v) criticar
crocodile cocodrilo
crook estafador, defectuoso, ladrón
crooked deshonesto, torcido
crop cosecha, cultivo
croquette bigote (Mex.)
cross cruzado, oblicuo
cross (v) cruzar, atravesar
cross action contraquerella
cross-appeal contraapelación
crossed check cheque cruzado
cross-country campo a través
cross coupling acoplo cruzado
cross-eyed bizco
cross-reference referencia recíproca
cross talk diafonía, réplicas

crossfire fuego cruzado
crossing cruce, intersección
crossword crucigrama
crouch (v) agacharse
crow (v) cantar, jactarse
crowd manga (Amer.); punta (Amer.)
crucial decisivo
crucifix crucifijo
crucify (v) crucificar
crude crudo, bruto
cruel cruel; abusivo (Amer.)
cruelty crueldad
cruise crucero
cruise (v) navegar
crumb miga, migaja
crumble (v) desmenuzar
crumple (v) deshacerse
crunch (v) crujir
crusade crusada
crush apretón, presión
crust corteza, costra
crutch muleta
cry grito
cry (v) gritar, llorar
crystal cristal
cub cachorro
cube cubo
cubic cúbico
cucumber pepino
cuddle abrazo amoroso
cue cola, taco, entrada
cuff puño
cuff link broche (Ecuad.)
culinary culinario
culpa culpa, negligencia
culpable culpable
culprit culpable, delincuente, reo
cult culto
cultivate (v) cultivar
cultural cultural
cumbersome pesado, engorroso

cumulative acumulativo

cumulative penalty pena acumulativa

cumulative remedy recurdo adicional

cup copa, taza

curb freno, estorbo

curb (v) refrenar, estorbar

curettage raspado

curfew toque de queda

curiosity curiosidad

curious curioso

curl rizo

curl (v) rizar, arrollar

currency divisas, moneda extranjera; moneda

currency devaluation devaluación de moneda

current actual, corriente

current assets activo corriente

current liabilities pasivo corriente

current price precio actual

current price list lista de precios actual

current value valor actual

currently actualmente

curry curry

curse maldición

cursor cursor

curtain cortina

curve curva

curve (v) curvar, torcer

cushion cojín, colchón

custodial custodio

custodian custodio, guardián

custody custodia

custom aduana, costumbre

custom made hecho a medida

custom warehouse almacén de aduanas

customary acostumbrado, corriente, usual

customary law derecho usual

customer cliente

customhouse aduana

customize (v) fabricar a la medida

customs derechos de aduana

customs area zona aduanera

customs broker agente de aduanas

customs clearance despacho de aduana

customs court juzgado de aduanas

customs duties aranceles, derechos aduaneros, impuestos de aduanas

customs duty derechos de aduana

customs entry declaración de aduana

customs house aduanas

cut price precio rebajado

cut corte, seguro

cut (v) cortar, dividir

cut off corte, interrupción

cut-price precio reducido

cut-rate tarifa reducida

cut-throat competencia intensa

cutaneous cutáneo

cutback reducción

cute mono, lindo

cuts cortaduras, cortes

cybernetics cibernética

cycle ciclo

cyclic cíclico

cyclist ciclista

cylinder cilindro

cynical cínico, escéptico

cypress ciprés

cyst quiste

cystitis cistitis

cystostomy cistotomía

czar zar

D

dabbler aficionado
dactyloscopy dactiloscopia
dad papá
daddy papaíto
daffodil narciso
daft imbécil
dagger daga, puñal
daily diario
daily output producción diaria
dainty delicado, fino
daisy margarita
daisy wheel printer impresora de rueda de margarita
dam dique, presa
damage averia, daño, siniestro, perjuicio
damage (v) embromar (Arg., Chile, P.R.)
damages daños y perjuicios
damaging perjudicial
damn maldito, perdido
damn (v) condenar
damnification perjurio
damnify (v) damnificar
damp mojado, humedad
damp (v) mojar, humedecer
dance baile; manta (popular) (Col.); pasillo (folklórico) (S. Am.)
dance (v) bailar
dancer bailador, bailarín
dandruff caspa
danger peligro, riesgo
dangerous peligroso
dangerously peligrosamente
dark oscuro
dark room cuarto oscuro
darkness oscuridad
darling querido

darn (v) zurcir
dart dardo, saeta
dash guión, poquito
dashing brioso, vigoroso
data datos
data acquisition adquisición de datos
data base base de datos
data base management gestión de base de datos
data channel canal de datos
data code código de datos
data communication comunicación de datos
data conversion conversión de datos
data file fichero de datos
data line protector protector de línea
data multiplexer multiplexor de datos
data processing proceso de datos
data protection protección de datos
data security seguridad de los datos
data sheet especificaciones técnicas
date dátil, fecha
date (v) citar, datar
date of delivery fecha de entrega
date of issue fecha de emisión
date of maturity fecha de vencimiento
daughter hija
daughter-in-law nuera
dawn amanecer

day día
day shift turno de día
day-to-day cotidiano
daybook diario
daybreak amanecer
daydream (v) soñar despierto
daylight luz del día
daylong todo el día
daytime de día
daze aturdido
daze (v) aturdir
dazzling deslumbrante
de facto de hecho
deactivation desactivación
dead muerto; agotado (battery, etc.) (Amer.)
deadline fecha tope, límite, término límite, plazo o fecha límite
deadlock punto muerto
deaf sordo
deaf and dumb sordomudo
deafness sordera
deal transacción, pacto
dealer comerciante, detallista
dealings transacciones
dean decano
death muerte, defunción
death penalty pena de muerte
death rate mortalidad
death sentence sentencia de muerte
deathtrap trampa mortal
debate debate, discusión
debenture certificado, certificado de reintegro; obligación, orden de pago
debit adeudo, débito, cargo
debrief (v) interrogar
debris escombros
debt deuda
debtor deudor
debug (v) depurar
decadent decadente

decalcification descalcificación
decay decadencia
decay (v) deteriorarse
decease fallecimiento
deceased difunto
deceit engaño, fraude
deceiver impostor
December diciembre
decentralize (v) descentralizar
deceptive defraudante
decide (v) decidir, resolver
decimal decimal
decimal numeral número decimal
decipher (v) decifrar
decision decisión
decisory decisorio
deck cubierta, piso
declaration declaración
declare (v) declarar
declared value valor declarado
decline (v) declinar
decoder descifrador
decoding descifrado
decompose (v) descomponer
decorate (v) decorar
decoy señuelo, trampa
decrease (v) disminuir
decree decreto
decrepit decrépito
dedicate (v) dedicar
deduct (v) deducir, restar
deductible deducible
deduction deducción, descuento
deductive deductivo
deed escritura, hecho
deed of covenant escritura de garantía
deed of indenture escritura de traspaso
deed of sale escritura de compraventa
deer ciervo

deface (v) desfigurar, mutilar
defamation difamación
defamatory difamatorio
default bancarrota, bancarrota inicial, incumplimiento, incumplimiento inicial, parámetro
defeat (v) anular, derrotar, vencer
defecation defecación
defect defecto
defective defectuoso
defectiveness deficiencia
defend (v) defender
defendant acusado, demandado, procesado
defense defensa
defer (v) aplazar, diferir
deference deferencia, respeto
deferred annuities anualidades aplazadas
deferred charges cargos aplazados, cargos diferidos
deferred costs costes diferidos
deferred credits créditos diferidos
deferred revenue ingresos diferidos
defiant provocativo
deficiency deficiencia
deficient anormal, defectuoso
deficit déficit
define (v) definir, determinar
defined expenses gastos definidos
definite claro, categórico
definitely claramente
definitive definitivo
deflate (v) desinflar
deflation deflación
deform (v) deformar
defraud (v) defraudar, estafar
defrauder defraudador
defrost (v) descongelar

degenerate degenerado
degeneration degeneración
degrade (v) degradar
degraded degenerado
degree grado
dehydrate (v) deshidratar
dehydration deshidratación
delation acusación
delator acusador
delay dilación, retardo, retraso
delay distortion distorsión de retardo
delegate delegado
delegate (v) autorizar, delegar
delegation delegación
delete (v) borrar, suprimir
deliberate intencionado
deliberate (v) deliberar, meditar
deliberately deliberadamente
delicate delicado
delicious delicioso
delight deleite, placer
delinquency delincuencia
delinquent delincuente, moroso
delirious delirante
delirium delirio
deliver (v) entregar, repartir
delivery entrega, reparto
delivery date fecha de entrega
delivery of goods entrega de mercancías
delivery service servicio de reparto
delude (v) engañar
deluge diluvio, inundación
demagogic demagógico
demand demanda
demandable exigible
demandant demandante
dementia demencia, locura
demise arrendamiento
democracy democracia
democrat demócrata

demolish (v) demoler
demon demonio
demonstrate (v) demostrar
demonstration demostración
demoralize (v) desmoralizar
demoralized desmoralizado
demure grave, solemne
deniable negable
denial denegación, negativa
denim dril de algodón
denomination billete de banco, denominación
denote (v) denotar, indicar
denounce (v) censurar, denunciar
denouncer denunciante
dense denso, espeso
dense smoke húmero (Col.)
densely densamente
dent abolladura, inserción
dental dental
dental bridge puente
dentist dentista
dentistry odontología
dentition dentición
denture dentadura
denunciation denunciación
deny (v) denegar, negar
deodorant desodorante
depart (v) partir, salir
department departamento
departure salida
depend (v) depender
dependability confianza
dependent dependiente
dependent covenant convenio dependiente
depict (v) retratar
depletion disminución del capital
deplore (v) deplorar, lamentar
deponent declarante
deportation deportación

deposit depósito, ingreso
deposit account cuenta de depósito
deposit currency moneda de depósito
deposit passbook libreta bancaria
deposit slip resguardo de ingreso
deposition confesión, declaración
depositor depositante, imponente
depository depositario
depot almacén
depraved perverso
depreciate (v) depreciar, desvalorar
depreciation depreciación
depress (v) oprimir, presionar
depressed abatido, deprimido
depression depresión
deprive (v) privar, quitar
depth fondo, profundidad
deputy ayudante, delegado, suplente
derailment descarrilamiento
dereliction abandono
derive (v) derivar
dermatitis dermatitis
dermatologist dermatólogo
dermatone dermatoma
dermis dermis, cutis
derogation derogación
derogatory derogatorio, despectivo
descend (v) bajar, descender
describe (v) describir
description descripción
description of goods descripción de las mercancías
descriptive descriptivo
desert desierto

deserve (v) merecer, ser digno
deserved merecido
deserving merecido, de mérito
design diseño
design (v) diseñar, idear
designate (v) nombrar, señalar
designation denominación
desk despacho, escritorio, mesa
desktop computer ordenador personal de sobremesa
desktop publishing editor personal
desolate (v) arrasar, asolar
desolation arrasamiento
despair deseperación
desperate desesperado
despise (v) desdeñar, despreciar
despot déspota
dessert postre
destine (v) destinar
destroy (v) destruir
destruction destrucción
detach (v) separar
detail (v) detallar
detain (v) detener; embromar (Chile, Mex.)
detect (v) descubrir, detectar
detective detective
deter (v) disuadir, refrenar
detergent detergente
deteriorate (v) deteriorar
determine (v) determinar
determined tabaco (Mex.)
detest (v) detestar
detonate (v) detonar
detour desvío
detract (v) quitar valor
detriment detrimento, perjuicio
devaluation devaluación
devastate (v) devastar
develop (v) desarrollar
developer revelador, empresario

development desarrollo, progreso
deviate (v) desviar
device aparato, dispositivo, mecanismo
device control unit unidad de dispositivo de control
devil diablo, demonio
devisal legado
devise (v) inventar, legar
devisee legatario
devisor testador
devolution devolución
devote (v) dedicar
devour (v) devorar
dew rocío
dextrous diestro
diabetes diabetes
diabetic diabético
diagnose (v) diagnosticar
diagnosis diagnóstico
diagnostic diagnóstico
diagonal diagonal
diagram diagrama
dial (v) marcar, llamar
dialect dialéctico
dialogue diálogo
diameter diámetro
diamond diamante
diaper pañal
diaphragm diafragma
diarrhea diarrea
dice dados
dictate (v) dictar, mandar
dictating machine máquina de dictar
dictator dictador
dictionary diccionario
dictum fallo
die (v) morir
diesel diesel
diet dieta, régimen
diet (v) estar a dieta

differ (v) ser distinto
difference diferencia
different diferente
differential diferencial
differentiate (v) diferenciar
difficult difícil
difficulty dificultad
digest recopilación, resumen
digest (v) digerir
digestion digestión
digestive system sistema digestivo
digit dígito, cifra
digital digital
digital computer ordenador digital
digital gauge marcador digital
digital signal señal digital
dignified solemne, grave
dignity dignidad
dilapidate (v) dilapidar, arruinar
dilapidation dilapidación
dilate (v) dilatar
dilatory dilatorio
dilemma dilema
diligent diligente
dim débil, oscuro
dimension dimensión
diminish (v) disminuir
dimple hoyuelo
din estruendo
dine (v) cenar
dingy deslucido
dining room comedor
dinner cena
diode diodo
dioxide dióxido
dip baño
dip (v) bañar, mojar
diphthong diptongo
diploma diploma
diplomacy diplomacia
diplomat diplomático

dire horrendo
direct (v) administrar, dirigir, gobernar
direct access acceso directo
direct access storage memoria de acceso directo
direct damages daños directos
direct liability responsabilidad definida
direct loss pérdida directa
direct manufacturing costs costes directos de fabricación
direct memory access acceso directo a la memoria
direct tax impuesto directo
direct write-off method método de depreciación directa
directed dirigido
direction dirección
directly directamente
director director, gerente, vocal
directory anuario, directorio, guía, lista
dirt suciedad, basura
dirty sucio, manchado
disability incapacidad
disable (v) inutilizar
disabled incapacitado, inutilizado
disadvantage desventaja
disagree (v) discrepar, disentir
disagreeable desagradable
disagreement desacuerdo, discrepancia
disallow (v) desaprobar
disappear (v) desaparecer
disappoint (v) decepcionar
disappointment decepción
disapproval desaprobación
disapprove (v) desaprobar
disarm (v) desarmar
disarmament desarme
disaster desastre

disastrous desastroso
disavow (v) desautorizar
disbar (v) excluir de la abogacía
disbursements desembolsos, pagos
disc disco
discard (v) descartar
discern (v) percibir
discerning perspicaz
discharge (v) absolver, cumplir, descargar
disciple discípulo
discipline disciplina
disclaim (v) renunciar, rechazar, repudiar
disclaimer renuncia
disclose (v) revelar
disclosure revelación
discomfort incomodidad
disconnect (v) desconectar
discontinue (v) anular, interrumpir, suspender
discontinued anulado, producto que no se fabrica más
discord discordia
discount descuento, rebaja
discount (v) descontar, rebajar
discount and bills cartera
discount bank banco de descuento
discount market mercado de descuento de efectos
discourage (v) desalentar
discouragement disuasión
discouraging desalentador
discover (v) descubrir
discovery descubrimiento
discredit descrédito
discrepancy discrepancia
discrete discreto
discriminate (v) discriminar
discriminating perspicaz
discrimination discriminación

discriminatory discriminatorio
discuss (v) discutir, hablar
discussion discusión
disease enfermedad
diseased enfermo
disembark (v) desembarcar
disengage (v) retirar, separar
disgrace verguenza
disguise (v) disfrazar
disgust (v) dar asco, repugnar
dish plato
dishonest deshonesto, falso, tramposo
dishonesty deshonestidad
dishonor deshonor
dishonor (v) desatender
dishonored bill efecto impagado
dishonored draft efecto impagado
dishwasher lavaplatos
disillusion (v) desilusionar
disinfect (v) desinfectar
disinfectant desinfectante
disinherit (v) desheredar
disjointed descosido
disk disco
disk operating system sistema operativo de discos
disk storage memoria de discos
dislike (v) no gustar
dislocate (v) dislocar, interceptar
dislocation dislocación
dislodge (v) desalojar
disloyal desleal
dismal triste, fatal
dismantle (v) desmontar
dismay consternación
dismiss (v) dar por terminado, despedir, mandar a; bombear (Col.)
dismissal declaración sin lugar
disobedience desobediencia

disobedient desobediente
disobey (v) desobedecer
disorder confusión, desorden
disorderly conduct mala conducta
disorganize (v) desorganizar
disown (v) rechazar
disparage (v) acabar (S. Am., coll.)
disparity disparidad
dispatch (v) consignar, enviar, despachar
dispel (v) disipar
dispensatory farmacopea
dispense (v) dispensar, repartir
dispenser farmacéutico
disperse (v) dispersar
displace (v) desplazar
displacement dislocación, reemplazo
display exhibición, pantalla
display window aparador (Arg., Uru., Mex.)
displease (v) desagradar
disposable desechable
disposal disposición
dispose (v) disponer, colocar
disposition disposición
dispossession desahucio
dispute conflict, disputa, pleito
dispute (v) disputar, protestar
disqualified descalificado, inhabilitado
disqualify (v) incapacitar
disregard indiferencia
disrespect falta de respeto
disrupt (v) romper, interrumpir
disruptive destrozador
dissatisfaction insatisfacción
dissect (v) disecar
dissent disidencia
dissent (v) disentir
dissident disidente

dissimilar diferente
dissociate (v) disociar, separar
dissolute disoluto
dissolution disolución
dissolve (v) disolver
dissuade (v) disuadir
distaste aversión, distancia
distasteful repugnante
distil (v) destilar
distinct distinto, claro
distinguish (v) distinguir
distort (v) torcer, deformar
distortion distorsión
distract (v) distraer
distrain (v) embargar
distraint embargo
distress (v) doler, afligir
distribute (v) distribuir
distribution distribución
distributor distribuidor
district distrito, zona
district attorney fiscal público
district bank banco regional
distrophy distrofia muscular
disturb (v) alterar
disturbance perturbación
ditch zanja, cuneta
ditto lo mismo
diuretic diurético
dive salto, zambullida
diverge (v) apartarse de
divergence divergencia
diverse diverso, variado
diversification diversificación
diversify (v) diversificar
divest (v) deshacerse de una inversión, desposeer, despojar, retirar
divestiture desposeimiento
divide (v) dividir, partir
dividend dividendo, beneficio
divine divino
divorce divorcio

divorce suit juicio de divorcio
divorcee divorciada
divulge (v) divulgar
dizziness desvanecimiento
dizzy mareado
do (v) hacer
do-it-yourself hágalo Ud. mismo
dock muelle, dique
docket orden del día
doctor doctor, doctora, médico,
médica
doctor of law doctor en derecho
document documento
document feeder alimentador de
papel
documentary documental, documentario
documentary bill efecto documentario
documentary credit crédito documentario
documentary draft remesa documentaria
documentary letter of credit
carta de crédito documentario
documentation documentación
documents against payment
documentos contra pago
dodge (v) evadir, maniobrar
dog perro
dogged tenaz, obstinado
dogma dogma
dogmatic dogmático
doll muñeca
dollar dólar
dollar area zona del dólar
domain propiedad
domestic doméstico, nacional,
interior; criollo (Amer.)
domestic currency moneda del
país
domicile domicilio
domiciled bill letra domiciliada

domiciliary domiciliario
dominate (v) dominar
Dominican Republic República
Dominicana
domino dominó
donate (v) dar, regalar
donation donativo, regalo
donee donatario
donkey burro, asno
donor donante
doodle (v) hacer garabatos
doom fatalidad
doom (v) condenar
doomsday día del juicio final
door puerta
doorbell timbre de llamada
doorkeeper conserje, portero
dope (v) drogar
dormant dormido, inactivo
dot punto, mancha
dot matrix printer impresora de
matriz de puntos
double (v) doblar, duplicar
double-cross engaño, trampa
double density densidad doble
double-edged de dos filos
double entry partida doble
double-entry accounting method
método contable de doble entrada
doubt (v) dudar
doubtful dudoso
doughnut buñuelo
dove paloma
dowdy poco elegante
dower bienes dotales
down abajo, hacia abajo
down payment pago a cuenta,
primer pago
downcast cabizbajo
downhill cuesta abajo
download (v) introducir
datos

downstairs abajo, piso de abajo

downtime período de indisponibilidad

downtown centro de la ciudad

downturn recesión

dowry dote

dozen docena

draft letra, letra de cambio, giro

draft (v) girar, redactar

draft beer cerveza de barril

drag (v) arrastrar

dragonfly alguacil (Arg., Uru.)

drain (v) drenar, desaguar

drainage desague, drenaje

drama drama

dramatize (v) dramatizar

drape (v) cubrir, vestir

draw (v) trazar, dibujar

drawback desventaja, devolución

drawee librado

drawer cajonero (mueble), girador, librador

drawing dibujo

dream sueño

dreamer soñador

dress vestido

dress (v) vestir, formar

dress up (v) empaquetar (Amer.)

dresser aparador, cómoda

dressing room vestidor

drift (v) ir a la deriva

drill (v) perforar, entrenar

drilling perforación

drink (v) beber; chupar (Amer.)

drinker bebedor; músico (Col.)

drinking water agua potable

drip (v) gotear

drive (v) conducir, impulsar; manejar (Amer.)

driver conductor, programa de conexión

driveway calzada, avenida

driving license permiso de conducir

driving school escuela de conducir

drizzle llovizna

drop (v) caer, dejar caer

drop gota

dropout abandono

drought sequía

drown (v) ahogar, inundar

drowning ahogamiento

drowse (v) dormitar

drowsy soñoliento

drug droga, medicamento

drug addict toxicómano

drugstore droguería, farmacia

drum barril, tambor, tonel; tumba (Cuba)

drunk borracho

drunkard borracho

dry (v) secar

dry cell pila seca

dry season verano

dryer secador

dubbing doblaje

duck pato

due debido, merecido, pagadero, fecha de vencimiento, vencido

due payment pago vencido

dull apagado

duly sworn debidamente jurado

dumb mudo, estúpido

dump vaciado

dump (v) vaciar, abandonar

dumping dumping (venta bajo coste)

duodenum duodeno

dupe (v) engañar

duplex doble, dúplice

duplicate duplicado

duplicate (v) duplicar, doblar

durability durabilidad

durable duradero

durable goods bienes duraderos
duration duración
during durante
dust polvo
Dutch holandés
dutiable gravable, sujeto a impuestos
duty deber, derechos, impuesto
duty-free libre de impuestos
dwarfism enanismo

dwell (v) vivir
dwelling vivienda
dye (v) teñir
dying moribundo
dynamic dinámico
dynamic memory memoria dinámica
dynamite dinamita
dysentery disentería
dyspepsia dispepsia

E

each cada
eager impaciente
eagle águila
ear oído, oreja
earache dolor de oído
earned surplus beneficios acumulados
earnest money arras, señal
earnings ganancias, ingresos
earphones auriculares
earring pendiente
earth tierra
earthquake terremoto
earwitness testigo auricular
ease facilidad
easement servidumbre
easy fácil, sencillo
easy chair butaca, sillón
easy-going acomodativo
eat (v) comer
eccentric excéntrico
echo eco
ecological ecológico
ecology ecología
economic sanctions sanciones económicas
economics economía
economist economista
economize (v) ajustar (Col.)

economy economía
ecstasy éxtasis
Ecuador Ecuador
Ecuadorian ecuatoriano
eczema eczema
edema edema
edge filo, corte
edible comestible
edict edicto
edit (v) editar, corregir
edition edición
editor editor, director
educate (v) educar
educated educado
education educación
effect (v) efectuar
effective efectivo, logrado
efficient eficiente
effort esfuerzo
egg huevo
ego el yo
egocentric egocéntrico
egoist egoísta
Egypt Egipto
Egyptian egipcio
eight ocho
eighteen dieciocho
eighth octavo
eighty ochenta

either cualquier, tampoco
either-way communication comunicación bidireccional alterna
ejaculate (v) exclamar, eyacular
eject (v) expulsar
ejection expulsión
ejectment desahucio
ejector desahuciador
elaborate complicado, detallado
elaborate (v) elaborar, explicar
elastic elástico
elbow codo
elderly de avanzada edad
eldest el más viejo
elect (v) elegir
election elección
electric eléctrico
electric light bulb bomba (Perú)
electric typewriter máquina de escribir eléctrica
electrical shock descarga eléctrica
electrician electricista
electricity electricidad
electrify (v) electrificar
electrocardiograph electrocardiógrafo
electrode electrodo
electrodialysis electrodiálisis
electroencephalograph electroencefalógrafo
electronic data processing proceso de datos
electronic mail correo electrónico
electronics electrónica
elegance elegancia
elegant elegante
element elemento
elemental elemental
elementary school escuela primaria

elephant elefante
elevate (v) elevar, alzar
elevated elevado
elevator ascensor
eleven once
eleventh undécimo
eligibility elegibilidad
eligible elegible
eliminate (v) eliminar
elimination eliminación
elite élite
eloquence elocuencia
eloquent elocuente
elsewhere en otra parte
elude (v) eludir, evitar
elusive esquivo, evasivo
emancipated emancipado
emancipation emancipación
embargo embargo, prohibición
embarrass (v) turbar, desconcertar
embarrassing embarazoso
embarrassment desconcierto
embassador embajador
embassy embajada
embezzle (v) desfalcar
embezzlement desfalco, estafa
embezzler desfalcador, malversador
emblem emblema
embody (v) encarnar
embolism embolia
emboss (v) realzar, resaltar
embrace abrazo
embracer sobornador
embracery soborno
embryo embrión
emergency emergencia
emigrant emigrante
emigrate (v) emigrar
emigration emigración
emission emisión
emitter emisor

emolument dotación, emolumento
emotion emoción
emotional emocional
empathy empatía
empire imperio
empirical empírico
employ (v) emplear, ocupar
employee empleado
employer empleador, patrón
employment trabajo, empleo
empower (v) dar poder
emptiness vacío
empty vacío
enable (v) habilitar, permitir
enact (v) decretar, legislar
enamel esmalte
encase (v) encerrar
encephalitis encefalitis
encircle (v) rodear
enclose (v) incluir, cercar
enclosure adjunto, cerco
encode (v) codificar
encourage (v) animar
encouragement ánimo, estímulo
encouraging alentador
encroach (v) usurpar
encroachment usurpación
encumbrance gravamen
encylopedia enciclopedia
end fin
end (v) acabar, finalizar
endanger (v) poner en peligro
endeavor esfuerzo
endeavor (v) esforzarse
endless interminable
endocardium endocardio
endocrine endocrina
endorse (v) endosar, aprobar
endorsee endosado
endorsement endoso, aprobación
endorser endosador, endosante

endow (v) dotar
endowment dote, dotación
endurance resistencia
enema enema, lavativa; vista (Perú, P.R.)
enemy enemigo
energetic enérgico
energize (v) activar, dar energía
enforcement obligación
engage (v) ocupar, dedicarse
engaged ocupado, dedicado
engagement compromiso
engine motor
engineer ingeniero
England Inglaterra
English inglés
engrave (v) grabar
engraving grabado
enhance (v) realzar, mejorar
enjoin (v) prohibir
enjoy (v) disfrutar, gozar
enjoyment disfrute
enlarge (v) aumentar, ampliar
enlighten (v) informar, instruir
enlightened ilustrado, instruido
enlist (v) alistar
enough bastante, suficiente
enrage (v) enfurecer
enrich (v) enriquecer
enrichment enriquecimiento
enroll (v) inscribir, inscribirse
enrollment inscripción
ensure (v) asegurar
entail vínculo
enter (v) entrar, penetrar
enter key tecla de entrada
enteritis enteritis
enterprise compañía, empresa
enterprising emprendedor
entertain (v) divertir, entretener
enthusiasm entusiasmo
enthusiastic entusiasta
enticing atractivo

entirely enteramente
entitle (v) dar derecho
entity entidad
entrance entrada
entrance (v) fascinar, encantar
entrepreneur emprendedor
entrust (v) encargar, recomendar
entry asiento, entrada
entry credit asiento de abono
entry debit asiento de cargo
enumerate (v) enumerar
enunciate (v) pronunciar
envelope sobre (para cartas)
enviable envidiable
envious envidioso
environment medio ambiente
environmental ambiental
envision (v) imaginar, prever
envoy enviado
enzymes enzimas
epidermis epidermis, piel
epilepsy epilepsia
epileptic epiléptico
episode episodio
epitomize (v) compendiar
equal igual
equal (v) ser igual a
equalize (v) igualar, compensar
equation ecuación
equator ecuador
equatorial ecuatorial
equip (v) equipar
equipment equipos, equipos productivos, material
equitable equitativo
equity acción, acción ordinaria, equidad, valor líquido
equity capital acciones, capital propio
equivalence equivalencia
equivalent equivalente
erasable borrable

erase (v) borrar
eraser goma de borrar
erasion extirpación por raspadura
erect parado (Amer.)
erection erección
ergonomics del trabajo y cuerpo
erosion erosión, desgaste
erotic erótico
err (v) equivocarse, errar
erratic irregular
erroneous erróneo
error equivocación, error; mote (Chile)
error control control de error
erudite erudito
erupt (v) hacer erupción
erythema eritema
escalation intensificación
escalator clause cláusula de revisión de precios
escape (v) escapar, fugar
escheat reversión al estado
escort acompañante
escort (v) acompañar
escrow custodia, en depósito, plica
escrow account cuenta en depósito
escrow funds fondos en plica
Eskimo esquimal
esophagus esófago
esoteric esotérico, privado
especial especial
espionage espionaje
esprit espíritu
esplanade paseo
espouse (v) casarse, adherirse
espy (v) divisar
essential esencial
essentially esencialmente
establish (v) establecer, fundar
established conocido, sólido

establishment establecimiento
estate bienes, finca, hacienda, propiedad
estimate oferta, presupuesto
estimate (v) calcular, estimar; tantear (Col., Chile)
estimated amount suma estimada
estrogen estrógeno
etcetera etcétera
eternal eterno
eternity eternidad
ethical ética, ético
ethics moralidad
ethnic étnico
etiquette etiqueta
etymology etimología
eulogize (v) elogiar
euphemism eufemismo
euphoric eufórico
eurodollar eurodólar
Europe Europa
European europeo
Eustachian tube trompa de Eustaquio
euthanasia eutanasia
evacuate (v) evacuar, desocupar
evacuation evacuación
evade (v) evadir, eludir
evader evasor
evaluate (v) evaluar
evaluation evaluación
evangelist evangelista
evaporate (v) evaporar, desaparecer
evaporation evaporación
evasion evasión
even igual, liso, par
evening noche, tarde
evenly uniforme, liso
event evento, hecho, acontecimiento
eventual final, decisivo

eventually finalmente
ever siempre
everlasting eterno
every cada
everybody todos, todo el mundo
everyday cada día
everyone todo el mundo
everything todo
everywhere en todas partes
evict (v) desahuciar
eviction desahucio
evidence evidencia, prueba
evil malo, maldad
evolution evolución
evolve (v) desarrollar
ex factory franco fábrica
ex mill franco fábrica
ex works franco fábrica
exacerbate (v) exacerbar
exact exacto
exactitude exactitud
exactly exactamente
exaggerate (v) exagerar
exaggerated exagerado
exaggeration (v) exageración
examination examen, registro, reconocimiento
examine (v) examinar
examiner examinador
example ejemplo
exasperate (v) exasperar
excavate (v) excavar
exceed (v) exceder, sobrepasar
exceeding excesivo
excel (v) superar
excellence excelencia
excellent excelente; almendra (Cuba)
except excepto
exception excepción
exceptional excepcional
excerpt extracto
excess exceso

excessive excesivo

exchange bolsa, cambio, cambio de divisas

exchange broker agente de cambio

exchange control control de cambios

exchange devaluation pérdida por devaluación de moneda

exchange office oficina de cambio

exchange rate tipo de cambio; valor en cambio

excise (v) cortar, quitar

excise tax impuesto sobre consumo

excite (v) excitar, emocionar

excitement emoción, excitación

exclaim (v) exclamar

exclamation exclamación

exclude (v) excluir

exclusion exclusión

exclusions exclusiones

exclusive exclusivo

exclusive remedy recurso exclusivo

exclusive sale venta exclusiva

exclusively únicamente

excoriation desolladura

excrement excremento

excretion excreción

excruciating dolorosísimo

excuse disculpa, perdón, excusa

excuse (v) disculpar, perdonar

execute (v) ejecutar, realizar

executed efectuado, legalizado

execution ejecución

execution of an order ejecución de un pedido

executioner verdugo

executive administrador, ejecutivo, director

executor albacea

executory ejecutorio

executory contracts contratos de cumplimiento obligado

executory process proceso ejecutivo

executory uses usos contingentes

exemplary damages daños punitivos

exemplification copia certificada

exemplify (v) ilustrar

exempt exento, franco, libre

exemption exención

exercise ejercicio

exercise (v) ejercer, emplear

exercises ejercicios

exhale (v) espirar

exhaust (v) agotar

exhausted agotado

exhausting agotador

exhibit exposición

exhibit (v) exhibir, mostrar

exhibition exposición

exhibitionism exhibicionismo

exhibitor expositor

exhort (v) aconsejar, exhortar

exhortation exhortación

exigent exigente

exigible exigible

exile (v) exiliar, desterrar

exist (v) vivir, existir

existing right derecho existente

exit salida

exit (v) finalizar

exodus éxodo

exonerate (v) exculpar, exonerar

exorbitant price disparate (Arg., coll.)

expand (v) ampliar, dilatar

expandable expansible, dilatable

expanding extensible

expansion ampliación

expansionist expansionista

expatriate expatriado
expect (v) esperar
expectation expectación
expedite (v) acelerar
expend (v) gastar
expenditure desembolso, gasto
expense gasto
expense budget presupuesto de gastos
expenses gastos
expensive caro
experience experiencia
experienced con experiencia
experiment experimento
experimental de prueba
expert experto, hábil
expertise habilidad
expiration espiración, vencimiento
expiration date plazo de validez
expire (v) acabar, expirar, vencer
explain (v) explicar
explanation explicación
explanatory explicativo
explicit explícito
explode (v) explotar
exploit hazaña, proeza
exploration exploración
explore (v) explorar
explosion explosión
exponent exponente
export exportación
export credit crédito de exportación
export licence licencia de exportación
export promotion promoción de exportaciones
export quota contingente de exportación
export trade comercio de exportación

exporter exportador
exporting exportación
expose (v) exponer, mostrar
exposed expuesto
exposition exposición
exposure riesgo
express expreso, rápido
expression expresión
expressive expresivo
expropriate (v) expropiar, enajenar
expropriation expropiación
expulsion expulsión
extend (v) extender, alargar
extended extendido
extended area service servicio de zona ampliada
extension ampliación, extensión, prolongación, prórroga
extensive extenso, ancho
extent alcance, extensión
exterminate (v) exterminar
external exterior
external debt deuda externa
external memory memoria externa
extinction extinción
extinguish (v) extinguir
extort (v) extorsionar
extortion extorsión
extra adicional, además; vendaje (Col., C.R., Ecuad., Perú)
extra gratuity ajuste (C. Amer.)
extra payment pago complementario
extract extracto
extracts of account extractos de cuenta
extradition extradición
extralegal extrajurídico
extraordinary extraordinario
extravagance dispilfarro
extravaganza extravagante

extreme extremo
extremely sumamente
extremist extremista
extremities extremidades
extremity extremidad, punta
extrovert extrovertido
exuberance euforia
exude (v) destilar
exult (v) regocijarse
exultant jubiloso

eye ojo
eye-catching llamativo
eye infection infección en el ojo
eyeball globo del ojo
eyebrow ceja
eyelash pestaña
eyelid párpado
eyewitness testigo ocular, testigo presencial
eyestrain vista fatigada

F

fabricate (v) inventar
fabulous fabuloso
face cara
face-saving guarda-apariencia
face value valor nominal
facial facial
facility planta, facilidad
facsimile facsímil
fact hecho
faction facción
factor agente, elemento, factor
factoring factoring
factory fábrica
factory overhead costs costes de fabricación generales
factual objetivo
faculty facultad
fad manía, novedad
fade (v) desvanecerse
faded descolorido
Fahrenheit Fahrenheit
fail (v) fracasar, fallar, suspender; derrumbarse (Amer.)
fail an exam (v) aplazar (Arg., Uru.)
fail safe prevención contra fallos
failing defecto, falta
failure fracaso, fallo, malogro, quiebra

failure rate proporción de fallos
faint pálido, tenue; fallo (Chile)
faint (v) desmayarse
fainting desmayo
fair exhibición, feria, hermoso, justo
fair hearing vista imparcial
fair market value valor justo de mercado
fair price prácticas comerciales legítimas
fair trade feria de muestras
fair trial juicio imparcial
fairly justamente
fait accompli hecho consumado
faith fe, confianza
fake falso, impostor
fall (v) caer, bajar
fall guy cabeza de turco
fallacious engañoso
fallacy mentira
falling descenso
falling price precio a la baja
Fallopian tube trompa de Falopio
false falso
false arrest arresto ilegal
false claim reclamación fraudulenta

false oath perjurio
false teeth dentadura postiza
falsehood falsedad
falsification falsificación
falsify (v) falsificar
falter (v) titubear, vacilar
faltering vacilante
fame fama, reputación
famed famoso
familiar familiar, conocido
family familia
famine hambre
famous famoso
fan admirador, ventilador
fanatic fanático
fancy fantasía, capricho
fancy (v) desear, imaginar
fanfare fanfarria
fantastic fantástico
fantasy fantasía
far lejos
Far East Lejano Oriente
far-reaching de largo alcance
faraway alejado, lejano
fare tarifa, billete
fare (v) prosperar, viajar
farewell despedida, adiós
farm granja; sitio (Cuba)
farm (v) cultivar
farmer granjero
farming cultivo, agricultura
fart pedo
farther más allá, además
F.A.S. price precio F.A.S.
fascinating fascinante
fashion moda
fashionable de moda
fasten (v) sujetar, abrochar
fastener cierre, grapa
fastening sujetador
fat gordo, grasa
fatal fatal, funesto
fatal injury lesión mortal

fatality fatalidad
fate destino, sino
father padre
father-in-law suegro
fatherhood paternidad
fatigue cansancio, fatiga
fatten (v) engordar
faucet grifo; pila (Cuba); pluma
  (Col., Cuba, P.R.)
fault avería, defecto, falta
fault (v) fallar, tachar
faulty defectuoso
favor favor, servicio
favor (v) favorecer
favorable faborable, propicio
favored favorecido
favorite favorito
fax machine facsímil
fear miedo, temor
fear (v) temer
fearful temeroso
fearless intrépido, sin temor
fearsome temible
feasibility viabilidad
feasibility study estudio de viabilidad
feasible factible
feather pluma
feature característica
February febrero
feces excrementos, heces
fecundity fecundidad
fed up harto, hastiado
federal federal
fee derecho, honorario
feed comida
feed (v) alimentar
feedback realimentación
feeder alimentador
feel (v) sentir
feeling sensación, sentido, tacto
feet pies
feign (v) aparentar**

feline felino
fell (v) talar, cortar
felling trees tumba (Cuba, Col., Mex.)
fellow compañero, amigo
fellowship compañerismo
felon criminal, delincuente
felony crimen, delito
female hembra
feminine femenino
feminism feminismo
feminist feminista
femur fémur
fence cerca
fender guardabarros
ferment fermento
ferment (v) fermentar
ferocious feroz
fertile fértil
fertility fertilidad
fertilizer fertilizante
fervor fervor
festival festival
fetch (v) traer, buscar
fetus feto
feud enemistad
feud (v) reñir
feudal feudal
fever fiebre
feverish febril
few pocos, algunos
fewer menos
fiasco fiasco, decepción
fiber fibra
fiber optics fibras ópticas
fiberglass fibra de vidrio
fibrosis fibrosis
fibula fíbula
fiction ficción
fictitious ficticio
fideicommissary fideicomisario
fidelity fidelidad
fiduciary fiduciario

fiduciary money papel moneda
field campo, especialidad
fierce feroz, salvaje
fiery ardiente
fifteen quince
fifth quinto
fifty cincuenta
fight lucha, combate
fight (v) pelear, luchar
figure cifra, figura
figure (v) figurar, imaginar
figure out (v) deducir, explicarse
filament filamento
file archivo, expediente, fichero, lima
file cabinet archivador
file control control de ficheros
file conversion conversión de ficheros
file maintenance mantenimiento de ficheros
file organization organización de ficheros
file recovery recuperación de datos
filling empaste
film película, carrete
film (v) filmar
filth basura
filthy sucio, obsceno
final decisivo, final, último
final payment pago final
finalize (v) completar, ultimar
finally finalmente
finance finanzas
finance (v) financiar
finance company sociedad de financiación
financial analysis análisis financiero
financial statement balance financiero; estado financiero

financial transaction
transacción financiera

financier financiero

financing financiación

find encuentro

find (v) encontrar, hallar

finding decisión, fallo, hallazgo

fine bueno, fino, multa

fine gold oro fino

fineness contraste

finesse finura, sutileza

finger dedo

fingernail uña (de un dedo de la mano)

fingerprint huella digital

fingers dedos

fingertip yema del dedo

finish final, llegada

finish (v) acabar, terminar

fire fuego

fire (v) quemar

fire a person from a job (v)
correr (Amer.)

fire engine coche de bomberos

fire extinguisher extintor

fire insurance seguro contra incendio

fire sale venta de mercancías taradas

firearm arma de fuego

fireman bombero

fireworks fuegos artificiales

firm empresa, firma

firm offer oferta en firme

firm sale venta en firme

firmness firmeza

firmware programas fijos

first primero

first aid cura de urgencia, primeros auxilios

first-aid clinic asistencia (Perú, Uru.)

first-class primera clase

first-in, first-out (FIFO) FIFO (primero-dentro/primero-fuera)

firsthand directamente

fiscal fiscal, monetario

fiscal year año fiscal, ejercicio

fish pez, pscado

fishbone espina de pez

fishbowl pecera

fisherman pescador

fishing pesca

fishing rod caña de pescar

fishy de pez, sospechoso

fissure fisura

fist puño

fistful puñado

fit adecuado, apto, ataque

fit (v) ajustar, adaptar

fitness buena salud

fitting adecuado

five cinco

fix (v) arreglar, asegurar, fijar

fixed fijo, permanente

fixed assets activos fijos

fixed charges gastos fijos

fixed costs costes fijos

fixed period deposit depósito a plazo fijo

fixed rate cambio fijo

fixture instalación fija

flag bandera

flagrant escandaloso, flagrante

flair instinto, aptitud

flamboyant rimbombante

flame llama

flannel franela

flap faldilla, solapa

flare llamarada, bengala

flare (v) brillar, fulgurar

flash destello, ráfaga

flash (v) destellar, brillar

flashlight linterna

flat plano, llano

flat commission comisión fija

flat rate   tasa uniforme
flatten (v)   allanar, aplanar
flatter (v)   adular, halagar
flatterer   barbero (Mex.)
flattering   halagüeño
flattery   adulación
flatulence   flatulencia
flavor   gusto, sabor
flaw   imperfección
flawless   impecable
flea   pulga
flee (v)   huir, abandonar
flesh   carne
flexibility   flexibilidad
flexible   flexible
flicker   parpadeo
flight   vuelo
flip-flop   báscula biestable, flip-flop
flirt   flirt, coqueteo
flirt (v)   flirtear, coquetear
flirtation   flirteo
float   corcho, flotador, fluctuación
float (v)   flotar
floating rates   tipos flotantes
flood   inundación
flood (v)   inundar, desbordar
floor   suelo, fondo
floppy disk   disco flexible
florist   florista
flour   harina
flourish (v)   florecer, prosperar
flourishing   próspero
flow   corriente, flujo
flow (v)   fluir, correr
flow control   control de flujo
flow line   línea de flujo
flowchart   diagrama de flujo, organigrama
flower   flor
flower shop   floristería, florería
flowing   fluido, corriente
flu   gripe

fluctuation   fluctuación
fluctuation margins   banda de fluctuación
fluency   fluidez, elocuencia
fluent   fluido, elocuente
fluffy   lanudo, peludo
fluid   líquido
flunk an exam (v)   aplazar (Arg., Uru.)
fluorescent   fluorescente
fluoride   fluoruro
flush (v)   tirar el agua
fly   mosca
fly (v)   volar
foam   espuma
focus   foco, centro
foe   enemigo
fog   niebla
foggy   nebuloso, brumoso
foil   hoja, lámina
foil (v)   frustrar
fold (v)   doblar, plegar
folder   carpeta
folding   plegado
foliage   follaje
folk   pueblo
folk dance   baile popular; marinero (Chile, Ecuad., Perú); tumba (Cuba)
follow (v)   seguir
follower   seguidor, partidario
following   siguiente
follow-up   continuación
fond   afectuoso
fondly   afectuosamente
fondness   afecto, cariño
food   comida, alimento
food poisoning   envenenamiento, intoxicación de comida
fool   tonto, imbécil; zanahoria (Arg.)
fool (v)   engañar, bromear
foolish   estúpido, necio

foot pie
football fútbol
footprint huella
footstep pisada, paso
for por, para
forbid (v) prohibir
forbidden prohibido
force eficacia, fuerza
force (v) forzar
forced forzado
forcible violento
forearm antebrazo
forebrain cerebro anterior
forecast previsión
foreclosure ejecución de hipoteca, exclusión, juicio hipotecario
foregoing precedente
forehead frente
foreign extranjero
foreign credit crédito extranjero
foreign currency divisas; moneda extranjera
foreign exchange cambio de divisas; moneda extranjera
foreign exchange counter mostrador de cambio de moneda
foreign markets mercados extranjeros
foreign notes billetes extranjeros
foreign securities valores extranjeros
foreigner extranjero; macho (C.R.)
foreman capataz; mayordomo (Chile)
foreman of the jury presidente del jurado
foremost primero
forensic forense
forensic medicine medicina forense

foresee (v) prever
foreseeable previsible
foresight previsión
foreskin prepucio
forest bosque
forever para siempre
forewoman presidenta del jurado
foreword prefacio
forfeit decomiso, multa, pérdida
forfeiture pérdida
forge (v) falsificar, forjar, fundir
forgery falsificación
forget (v) olvidar
forgive (v) perdonar
forgo (v) renunciar
fork tenedor
form forma, formulario, hoja
formal formal, protocolario, serio, solemne
formalities formalidades
formality seriedad
format formato, modelo
format (v) modelar, ordenar sectores
former anterior
formerly anteriormente
formula fórmula
formulate (v) formular
fornication fornicación
forsake (v) abandonar, dejar
forthcoming próximo
forthright directo
forthwith en seguida
fortuitous fortuito
fortunate afortunado
fortunately afortunadamente
fortune fortuna, suerte
forty cuarenta
forum tribunal, foro
forward delantero, adelante
forward transaction operación a plazo

forwarder agente de transportes, transitario

forwarding charges gastos de envío

foundation fundación, cimiento

founder fundador

foundling expósito

fountain fuente, manantial; pila (Amer.)

four cuatro

fourteen catorce

fourth cuarto

fraction fracción

fractions fracciones

fracture fractura

fracture (v) fracturar

fradulence fraude

fradulent fradulento

fragile frágil

fragment fragmento

fragrance fragancia

fragrant fragante

frail frágil, delicado

frame marco, armazón

frame-up paquete (Cuba, coll.)

framed evidence prueba falsificada

France Francia

franchise concesión, franquicia, licencia

franchiser concesionario

frank franco, sincero

frantic frenético

fraternal fraternal

fraternity hermandad

fraternize (v) confraternizar

fratricide fratricidio

fraud fraude

fraudulence fraudulencia

freckles pecas

free libre, gratis

free (v) poner en libertad

free alongside vessel franco al costado del buque

free on board libre a bordo

free trade libre cambio

free trade zone zona franca

freedom libertad

freedom on bail libertad provisional

freehold dominio absoluto

freelance independiente

freeloader agregado (Arg., Par., Uru.)

freeze (v) congelarse

freezer nevera, frigorífico

freezing helado

freight flete, carga

freight forwarder transitario

freight prepaid portes pagados

French francés

fresh nuevo, fresco

friction fricción

Friday viernes

fried frito

friend amigo; vale (Mex., Col., Ven.)

friendly amistoso, amable

friendship amistad

fright susto, sobresalto

frighten (v) asustar, espantar

frightening espantoso, aterrador

fringe benefits beneficios remunerativos adicionales; busca (Cuba, Mex.)

fritter bollo (Sp.)

frivolous frívolo

from de, desde

front frente, delantero

frostbite congelación

fruit fruta

fruit salad macedonia

fruitful fructuoso

frustrate (v) frustrar

fry (v) freír

frying pan sartén
fuel combustible
fugitive fugitivo
fugue amnesia temporal
fulfil (v) cumplir, realizar
fulfillment cumplimiento
full completo, lleno, válido
full authority autoridad completa
full brother hermano carnal
full convertibility convertibilidad total
full court pleno del tribunal
full covenant garantía de título
full hearing vista completa
full time plena dedicación
fun diversión
function función, uso
function table table de funciones
functional design diseño funcional
fund fondo

funding operación de consolidación
funeral funeral, entierro
fungus infection infección fungosa
funny divertido, gracioso
fur piel
furious furioso
furnace horno
furnish (v) proveer, suministrar
furniture mueble
further más lejos, más allá
further (v) promover, adelantar
furthermore además
furuncle furúnculo
fury furia, violencia
fuse fusible, plomo
fuss bulla, lío
futile inútil, vano
future futuro
futures market mercado de futuros

G

gain aumento, ganancia
gains ganancias, beneficios
galaxy galaxia
gall bilis
gallant valiente
gallbladder vesícula biliar
gallery galería
gallstone cálculo biliar
gamble juego, jugada
gamble (v) jugar
gambler jugador
gambling juego
game juego, deporte
game theory teoría de juegos
gang banda, pandilla, barra (Arg., Col., Uru.)
ganglia ganglios

ganglion ganglio
gangrene gangrena
gangster gángster, pistolero
gap intervalo, hueco
garage garaje
garbage basura
garden jardín
gardener jardinero
gardening jardinería
gargle gárgaras
garlic ajo
garment prenda, vestido
gas gas, gasolina
gastric juice jugo gástrico
gastric ulcer úlcera gástrica
gastritis gastritis
gastroenteritis gastroenteritis

gastrointestinal gastrointestinal
gather (v) reunir, recoger
gathering reunión, asamblea
gauge medida, calibre
gear mecanismo, equipo
gem joya
gender género
gene gen
general corriente, general
general acceptance aceptación sin reservas
general covenant garantía general
general damages daños generales
general executor albacea universal
general ledger libro mayor
general lien gravamen general
general purpose computer ordenador de uso general
general verdict veredicto general
generally generalmente
generation generación
generator generador
generous generoso
genes genes
genital organs órganos genitales
genius genio
genocide genocidio
genteel fino, elegante
gentle amable, cuidadoso
gentleman caballero
gently con cuidado
genuine auténtico, genuino
geography geografía
geology geología
geometry geometría
geriatrics geriatría
German alemán
German measles rubéola
germane impertinente

Germany Alemania
germination germinación
germs microbios
gesture gesto, ademán
get (v) coger, obtener
get-together reunión
getaway fuga
ghost fantasma
giant gigante
gift regalo, obsequio
gigantic gigantesco
gigantism gigantismo
giggle risilla
gimmick truco
gin ginebra
girl chica, muchacha
give (v) dar, entregar
give blows (v) afirmar (Chile, Mex.)
giveaway precio de ruina
given dado, otorgado
glad alegre, contento
glamorous atractivo
glamour encanto, atractivo
glance vistazo, mirada
glance (v) mirar, divisar
gland glándula
glanders muermo
glandular glandular
glare brillo, luminosidad
glaring deslumbrador
glass vidrio, cristal
glassware artículos de cristal
glaucoma glaucoma
global mundial, global
globe globo, esfera
glorify (v) glorificar, alabar
glory gloria
gloss lustre, brillo
glove guante
glow luz, brillo
glucose glucosa
glue adhesivo, pega

glue (v) pegar, encolar
go (v) ir, marchar
go bankrupt (v) fundir (Amer., coll.)
go-getter ambicioso
goal gol, objetivo
goalkeeper portero
God Dios
godfather padrino
godmother madrina
goggles gafas de nadar
gold oro
gold bullion lingote de oro
gold nugget pepita de oro
gold reserve reserva de oro
golden dorado, de oro
goldsmith joyero (Amer.)
golf golf
gonorrhea gonorrea
good bueno, bien
good behavior buena conducta
good faith buena fe
good luck leche (Amer.)
goodbye adiós
goodlooking chulo (Amer.); mango (Mex.)
goodness bondad
goods mercancías, bienes
goods in transit mercancías en tránsito
goods quota contingente de mercancías
goodwill fondo de comercio, plusvalía
gospel evangelio
gossip chisme, murmuración
gossip (v) murmurar, chismear
gossip column notas de sociedad
Gothic gótico
gourmet gastrónomo, gourmet
govern (v) gobernar
government gobierno

governor gobernador
grab (v) arrebatar, agarrar
grace gracia, finura
grace period período de gracia
graceful gracioso, agraciado
gracious clemente, cortés
grade grade, clase
grade (v) clasificar
grade of service grado de servicio
gradual gradual
graduate graduado
grain grano, cereal
gram gramo
grammar gramática
grand magnífico, estupendo
grandchild nieto
granddaughter nieta
grandfather abuelo
grandmother abuela
grandparents abuelos
grandson nieto
grant concesión, subvención
grapefruit pomelo (Sp.); naranja (Mex.)
graph gráfica
graphic characters caracteres gráficos
graphical display representación gráfica
graphics gráficos
grass hierba
grateful agredecido
gratify (v) complacer
gratitude agradecimiento
gratuity propina
grave sepultura
gravel grava
gravity gravedad
grease grasa
greasy grasiento
Great Britain Gran Bretaña
great grande, estupendo

greater mayor
greatest el mayor
greatgrandchild biznieto
greatgrandfather bisabuelo
greatgrandmother bisabuela
Greece Grecia
greed codicia, avaricia
greedy codicioso, avaro
Greek griego
green verde
green, unripe vegetables tierno
(Chile, Ecuad.)
greet (v) saludar, recibir
greeting saludo, bienvenida
grief dolor, aflicción
grievance agravio
grieve (v) dar pena
grill parrilla
grin (v) sonreír
grip asa, mango
groan (v) gemir, quejarse
grocer tendero
grocery comestibles, bodega
(Amer.)
grocery store cajón (Mex., Perú)
gross margin margen bruto
gross national product producto nacional bruto
gross profit beneficio bruto
gross weight peso bruto
ground suelo, tierra
ground floor planta baja
group grupo, conjunto
group (v) agrupar
group of friends barra (Arg.,
Col., Uru.)
grow (v) crecer, desarrollar

grower cultivador
growth crecimiento, aumento,
tumor
guaranteed bills letras avaladas
guarantor avalador, fiador
guaranty garantía
guard (v) guardar, proteger
guardian tutor, guardián
guess adivinanza
guess (v) adivinar, suponer
guest invitado
guidance guía, consejo
guide guía
guide (v) guiar, dirigir
guidelines líneas generales (de
actuación)
guilt culpa, culpabilidad
guilty culpable
guitar guitarra
gulf golfo
gullet esófago
gum encía, goma, cola
gun arma
gunman pistolero
gunpowder pólvora
gunshot wound herida de arma
de fuego
gut tripas, intestinos
gutter canalón, gotera
guy tío, individuo
gym gimnasio
gymnasium gimnasio
gymnast gimnasta
gynecologist ginecólogo
gynecology ginecología
gypsy gitano

H

habit costumbre, hábito
habitat habitat

habitual habitual, usual
hack (v) cortar

Hague, The La Haya
hail pedrisco, granizo
hail (v) llamar a, saludar
hailstone granizo
hair cabello, pelo
hairbrush cepillo
haircut corte de pelo
hairdresser peluquero
hairy peludo
Haiti Haití
Haitian haitiano
half medio, mitad
half-and-half a mitades
half dozen media docena
half hour media hora
half price mitad de precio
half-time descanso, mitad
halfway mitad de camino
hall vestíbulo, sala
hallmark contraseña de acuña-
    ción, sello de
hallucinations alucinaciones
halt alto, parada, barajar (Chile,
    Mex., Arg.)
halve (v) partir por el medio
ham jamón
hamburger hamburguesa
hammer martillo
hammock hamaca
hand mano; manojo (de tabaco)
    (Amer.)
hand (v) dar la mano, entregar;
    alcanzar (Amer.)
hand and seal firma y sello
handbag bolso
handbook manual
handcuffs esposas
handicap desventaja
handicapped disminuido
handicraft artesanía
handiwork obra hecha a mano
handkerchief pañuelo
handle (v) tocar, tratar

handle stolen goods (v) reducir
    (Amer.)
handling manipulación
handling charges gastos de
    manipulación, cargos por
    operación
handmade hecho a mano
handout distribución
handrail pasamano
handshake apretón de manos
handsome hermoso, guapo
handwriting escritura a mano,
    letra manuscrita
handy cercano, a mano
hang (v) colgar, suspender,
    ahorcar
hang-up obsesión
hangar hangar
hanger percha, colgador
hangover resaca; crudo (Mex.);
    perseguidor (Perú)
hankering añoranza
haphazard fortuito
happen (v) pasar, suceder
happening suceso
happiness felicidad
happy feliz, contento
harass (v) acosar, hostigar
harassment acosamiento
harbor puerto
hard duro, sólido
hard copy documentación im-
    presa
hard currency moneda en efec-
    tivo
hard drive disco duro
hard labor trabajos forzados
hard times tiempos malos
hard worker muy trabajador
harden (v) endurecer
hardness dureza
hardship apuro, infortunio, opre-
    sión

hardware sistemas materiales, hardware
hardware store ferretería
hardy fuerte, robusto
harm daño, mal
harm (v) embromar (Arg., Chile, P.R.)
harmful perjudicial
harmless inofensivo
harmonic armónico
harmony armonía
harp arpa
harsh severo, duro
harvest cosecha, recolección
haste prisa, precipitación
hasten (v) acelerar
hasty apresurado
hat sombrero
hatch (v) criar, incubar
hate odio
hate (v) odiar
hatred odio, aborrecimiento
haughty arrogante
haul (v) tirar, transportar
haulage transporte terrestre
have (v) tener, poseer
have an orgasm (v) acabar (Arg., Uru., vulg.)
have sex with coger (Arg., Uru., Mex.)
haven refugio
havoc estrago, destrucción
hay heno
hay fever fiebre del heno
hazard riesgo, peligro
hazardous peligroso
hazy nebuloso
he él
head cabeza
head (v) encabezar
head of family cabeza de familia
head office oficina central
headache dolor de cabeza

header encabezamiento
heading encabezamiento
headlight faro delantero
headline titular
headphones auriculares
headquarters oficina central
headway progreso, avance
heal (v) curar, sanar
healing curativo
health salud
healthy sano, saludable
heap montón, pila
hear (v) oir
hear a case (v) ver una causa
hearing audiencia, vista, oído
hearing aid audiófono
hearsay rumores
hearsay evidence evidencia por referencia
hearse coche fúnebre
heart corazón
heart attack ataque cardíaco, ataque de corazón
heartbeat latido del corazón
heartbreaking angustioso
heartburn acidez, amargura
hearth hogar, casa
hearty sincero, cordial
heat calor
heat exhaustion agotamiento por calor
heat stroke insolación
heater calentador
heaven cielo
heavy pesado
heavy sentence condena grave
heavyweight peso pesado
Hebrew hebreo
hectare hectárea
hectic febril
hedging operación de cobertura
heedless desatento
heel talón, tacón

hefty   pesado, fornido
height   altura, alto
heighten (v)   aumentar
heir   heredero
heir at law   heredero legal
heiress   heredera
heirloom   reliquia familiar
heist   robo
helicopter   helicóptero
hell   infierno
hellish   infernal
hello   hola
helmet   casco
help   ayuda, auxilio
help (v)   ayudar, auxiliar
helper   alicates (P.R.)
helpful   útil, atento
helpless   inútil, incapaz
hemiplegy   hemiplejia
hemisphere   hemisferio
hemoglobin   hemoglobina
hemophilia   hemofilia
hemophiliac   hemofílico
hemorrhage   hemorragia
hemorrhoids   hemorroides
hen   gallina
hence   de aqui a, desde aquí
henceforth   de aquí en adelante
hepatitis   hepatitis
her   ella, le, la
herb   hierba
herbal   herbáceo
herd   rebaño
here   aquí
hereafter   en el futuro
hereby   por la presente
hereditary   hereditario
heredity   herencia
herein   en esto
hereupon   en seguida
heritage   herencia
heritance   herencia
hermetic   hermético

hernia   hernia
hero   héroe
heroic   heroico
heroin   heroína
herpes   herpes
hers   suyo, de ella
herself   ella misma
hesitant   dudoso, indeciso
hesitate (v)   dudar, vacilar
hesitation   vacilación
hexadecimal   hexadecimal
heyday   apogeo
hi-fi   alta fidelidad
hiatus   vacío, interrupción
hibernate (v)   invernar
hide (v)   esconder, ocultar
hideaway   posada (Cuba)
high   alto
high-class   clase alta
high finance   altas finanzas
high frequency   alta frecuencia
high-level   alto nivel
high-level language   lenguaje de
   alto nivel
high resolution   alta resolución
high speed transmission   transmisión de alta velocidad
higher court   juzgado mayor
highlight   aspecto notable
highlight (v)   destacar
highway   autopista
hike   caminata, excursión
hike (v)   ir de excursión
hilarious   divertido
hill   colina
hillside   ladera
hilly   montañoso
him   él, le, lo
himself   él mismo
hinder (v)   estorbar, impedir
hindrance   estorbo, obstáculo
hinge   bisagra
hint   insinuación

hint (v) insinuar
hip cadera
hire (v) emplear
hire purchase compra a plazos
his suyo, de él
Hispanic hispánico, latino
hiss silbido
histamine histamina
historic histórico
historical histórico
historical costs costes históricos
history historia
hit (v) golpear, pegar; afirmar
  (Chile, Mex.); mandar (Amer.)
hitchhiker autoestopista
hitherto hasta ahora
hive colmena
hoard acumulación
hoax trampa; caña (Col., Ecuad.,
  Ven.); pluma (C. Am.)
hobby pasatiempo, afición
Hodgkin's disease enfermedad
  de Hodgkin
hog cerdo, puerco
hold (v) tener, poseer, asir, agarrar
hold a hearing (v) efectuar una
  audiencia
hold up (v) embromar (Chile,
  Mex.)
holder tenedor, poseedor, titular
holding propiedad, cartera
holding company compañía de
  valores
holdings haberes, disponibilidades
holdup atraco
hole agujero
holiday fiesta, festivo
Holland Holanda
hollow hueco
holograph ológrafo
holy sagrado, bendito

homage homenaje
home casa, hogar
home town pueblo natal
homecoming regreso a casa
homeland tierra natal
homeless sin casa
homemade casero
homesick nostálgico
homework deberes, ejercicios
homicide homicidio
homogenous homogéneo
homonym homónimo
homosexual homosexual; pato
  (Amer.)
homosexuality homosexualidad
honest honrado, honesto
honestly honradamente
honesty honestidad, honradez
honey miel
honeymoon luna de miel
honor honor, honra
honorary honorario
hood caperuza, capucha
hook anzuelo
hook (v) engancharse
hooker ramera, prostituta
hookup acomplamiento
hookworm lombriz intestinal
hoop aro, argolla
hop salto, brinco
hope esperanza
hope (v) esperar, confiar
hopeful esperanzado
hopeless desesperado
horde horda, multitud
horizon horizonte
hormone hormona
horn cuerno, bocina
hornet sting picadura de avispa
horoscope horóscopo
horrible horrible
horrid inaguantable
horrify (v) horrorizar

horror horror
horse caballo
horsepower caballo (potencia)
horseshoe herradura; casquillo (Perú, Ven.)
horticulture horticultura
hose medias, manguera
hosiery medias, calcetines
hospice hospicio
hospital hospital
hospitality hospitalidad
host huésped, multitud
host computer ordenador central
hostage rehén
hostess anfitriona
hostile hostil
hostility hostilidad
hot caliente
hot money capital flotante
hotel hotel
hound perro, podenco
hour hora, tiempo
hourly a horas, cada hora
house casa
house (v) hospedar, alojar
house arrest arresto domiciliario
housebreaker ladrón (de casas)
housebreaking escalo, allanamiento
housecleaning limpieza de la casa
householder cabeza de la casa
housekeeper ama de llaves
housewares artículos domésticos
housewife ama de casa
housing alojamiento
hover (v) estar inmóvil
how cómo
however sin embargo
howl (v) aullar

hub centro; maza (de una rueda) (Chile)
hue color, matiz
huff (v) soplar
hug abrazo
huge enorme, vasto
hulk barco
hull casco
hum zumbido
human humano
humanitarian humanitario
humanity humanidad
humankind género humano
humble humilde
humdrum monótono
humerus húmero
humid húmedo
humidifier humedecedor
humiliate (v) humillar
humiliating humillante
humiliation humillación
hummingbird colibrí rumbo (Col.)
humor humor, gracia
hump joroba
humpbacked jorobado
hunch presentimiento
hunchback jorobado
hundred cien
hundredth centésimo
Hungarian húngaro
Hungary Hungría
hunger hambre
hunger pain dolor de hambre
hungry hambriento
hunt caza, cacería
hunter cazador
hurdle obstáculo, valla
hurricane huracán
hurry prisa
hurry (v) tener prisa; abreviarse (C. Amer.)
hurt (v) herir, dañar

hurt herida, daño
husband marido
husbandry agricultura
hush silencio
husk cáscara, vaina
husky ronco, fornido
hustle actividad febril
hustle (v) empujar, codear
hut cabaña, barraca; chabola
  (Sp.)
hybrid híbrido
hybrid computer ordenador
  híbrido
hybrid system sistema mixto
hydrant hidrante
hydraulic hidráulico
hydrocarbon hidrocarburo
hydrogen hidrógeno
hydroplane hidroplano
hygiene higiene
hygienic higiénico

hymn himno
hyperactivity hiperactividad
hyperbole hipérbole
hypersensitive supersensible
hypertension hipertensión
hyphen guión
hyphenate (v) escribir con guión
hyphenation separación con
  guión
hypnosis hipnosis
hypnotic hipnótico
hypochondria hipocondría
hypochondriac hipocondríaco
hypocrite hipócrita; músico
  (Mex.)
hypothesis hipótesis
hypothetical hipotético
hysterectomy histerectomía
hysteria histeria, histerismo
hysterical histérico

I

I Yo
I/O devices dispositivos de entrada y salida
Iberia Iberia
ice hielo
ice cube cubito de hielo
ice cream helado
ice skating patinaje sobre hielo
iceberg témpano
icebreaker rompehielos
iced helado
Iceland Islandia
icicle carámbano, canclón
icon icono, estatua
iconoclast iconoclasta
icy helado, glacial
idea idea, noción
ideal ideal

idealize (v) idealizar
identical idéntico
identification identificación
identify (v) identificar
identity identidad
identity card cédula de identificación
idiocy idiotez
idiom idioma
idiot idiota
idle ocioso, desocupado
idol ídolo
idolatry idolatría
idyllic idílico
if si
ignite (v) encender, incendiar
ignition key llave de contacto
ignition ignición, encendido

ignore (v) ignorar
ignorance ignorancia
ignorant ignorante
ill enfermo
ill-advised mal aconsejado
ill-humored malhumorado
ill-suited no conveniente
ill-timed inoportuno
illegal ilegal
illegality ilegalidad
illegible ilegible
illegitimate ilegítimo
illicit ilícito
illiterate analfabeto
illness enfermedad
illogical ilógico
illuminate (v) iluminar
illumination iluminación
illusion ilusión, apariencia
illustrate (v) ilustrar, aclarar
illustration ilustración, ejemplo
image imagen
image processing procesa-
    miento de imagen
imagination imaginación
imaginative imaginativo
imagine (v) imaginar
imbalance desequilibrio
imbecile imbécil
imitate (v) imitar
imitation imitación
immaculate inmaculado
immaterial inmaterial, sin impor-
    tancia
immature inmaduro
immediate inmediato
immediately inmediatamente
immense inmenso
immersion inmersión
immigrant inmigrante
immigration inmigración
immobilize (v) inmovilizar
immoral inmoral

immortal inmortal
immovable inmóvil
immune inmune
immunity inmunidad
immunization inmunización
impact impacto
impair (v) debilitar, dañar
impaired disminuido, dañado
impart (v) comunicar
impartial imparcial
impasse sin salida
impassive impasivo
impatient impaciente
impeach (v) impugnar
impeachment impugnación,
    acusación
impediment obstáculo, estorbo
impel (v) impulsar
impending inminente
impenetrable impenetrable
imperative imprescindible
imperfect imperfecto
imperfection imperfección
imperial imperial
imperialism imperialismo
imperil (v) arriesgar
impersonal impersonal
impersonate (v) imitar
impertinence impertinencia
impertinent impertinente
impetuous impetuoso
impetus ímpetu
implant (v) implantar
implead (v) entablar pleito
implement herramienta
implement (v) realizar,
    ejecutar
implicate (v) comprometer, im-
    plicar
implication insinuación, compli-
    cidad
implicit implícito
implied implícito

implied admission admisión implícita

implied allegiance lealtad natural

implied consent consentimiento implícito

implied covenant convenio implícito

implied rescission rescisión tácita

implied waiver renuncia implícita

implore (v) implorar

imply (v) implicar

import importación

import (v) importar, implicar

import duties aranceles de importación

importance importancia

important importante

impose (v) imponer

imposition imposición

impossible imposible

impost impuesto, contribución

impostor impostor

impotence impotencia

impound (v) encerrar, embargar, incautar

impoverish (v) empobrecer

impractical poco práctico

imprecise inexacto

impregnate (v) impregnar

impress (v) confiscar

impression impresión, sello

impressive impresionante

imprint (v) imprimir

imprison (v) encarcelar

imprisonment encarcelación, encarcelamiento

improbable improbable

impromptu improvisado

improper impropio

improperly indebidamente

improve (v) mejorar, reformar

improvement mejora, reforma

improvisation improvisación

improvise (v) improvisar

imprudent imprudente

impugn (v) impugnar

impulse impulso

impulsive irreflexivo

impunity impunidad

in en, dentro

in between en medio

inability incapacidad

inaccessible inaccesible

inaccurate incorrecto, inexacto

inactive inactivo

inadequacy insuficiencia

inadequate inadecuado

inadmissible inadmisible, inaceptable

inalienable inalienable

inappropriate inoportuno

inasmuch puesto que

inaugurate (v) inaugurar

inauguration estreno, inauguración

incalculable incalculable

incandescent incandescente

incapable incapaz

incapacity incapacidad

incarceration encarcelamiento

incendiary incendiario

incense incienso

incentive estímulo, incentivo

inception comienzo, principio

incessant incesante

incest incesto

incestuous incestuoso

inch pulgada

incidence incidencia

incident incidente

incidental incidental, fortuito

incidentally a propósito

incinerate (v) incinerar

incineration cremación
incision corte
incite (v) incitar
inclination inclinación
incline (v) inclinar, tender
include (v) incluir
including incluso
incoherent incoherente
income ingresos, renta
income statement declaración de ingresos
income tax impuesto sobre ingresos personales, impuesto personal
incommunicado incomunicado
incomparable incomparable
incompatible incompatible
incompetence incompetencia
incompetent incompetente
incompetent person paquete (Amer.)
incomplete incompleto
incomprehensive incomprensivo
inconclusive cuestionable, inconcluyente
incongruent incongruente
inconsequent inconsecuente
inconsistent inconsistente
inconspicuous poco aparente
incontinence incontinencia
inconveniente inconveniente
incorporate (v) incorporar
incorporated constituido en ley
incorporation incorporación
incorrect incorrecto
increase (v) aumentar
increasing creciente
incredible increíble
increment aumento, incremento
incremental cost coste incremental
incriminate (v) incriminar
incumbency incumbencia

incumbrance gravamen
incur (v) incurrir
indebted obligado, que está en deuda
indecent indecente
indecision vacilación
indecisive indeciso, vacilante
indeed de verdad
indefensible indefendible
indefinite indefinido
indemnify (v) indemnizar
indemnity indemnización
indenture contrato, escritura
independent independiente
index índice
indexing hacer índices, indexación
India India
Indian indio
indicatable procesable
indicate (v) indicar
indication sugerencia
indicative indicativo
indicator indicador
indict (v) procesar, acusar
indictee procesado
indictment procesamiento, acusación
indifference indiferencia
indifferent indiferente
indigestion indigestión; insulto (Mex., Nic.)
indignant indignante
indirect indirecto
indirect cost coste indirecto
indiscretion indiscreción
indispensable imprescindible
individual individual, personal
indivisible indivisible
indolence pereza, desidia
indoor interior, en casa
indorsement endoso
indorser endosante

induce (v) inducir
inducement incentivo
inductor inductor
indulge (v) satisfacer, complacer
indulgence satisfacción, capricho
industrial industrial
industrial computer ordenador industrial
industrial process control control de proceso industrial
industrious industrioso
industry industria
inefficient incapaz
inept inepto, incapaz
inequality desigualdad
inequity injusticia
inert inerte
inertia inercia
inevitable inevitable
inexact incorrecto
inexcusable injustificable
inexpensive económico, barato
infallible infalible
infamous infame, vil
infamy infamia
infancy infancia
infant niño, menor
infanticide infanticida
infantil infantil
infantry infantería
infatuate (v) enamorar locamente, infatuar, abobar
infect (v) infectar
infected infectado
infection infección
infectious contagioso
infer (v) inferir
inference inferencia
inferior inferior
inferiority inferioridad
infernal infernal
infertile estéril

infertility esterilidad
infidelity infidelidad
infiltrate (v) infiltrarse
infinite infinito
infirm débil
infirmary hospital, enfermería
inflame (v) inflamar
inflammable inflamable
inflammation inflamación
inflate (v) inflar, hinchar
inflation inflación
inflection inflexión
inflict (v) infligir
influence influencia; vara (Perú)
influential influencial
influenza gripe
influx entrada
inform (v) informar
informal desenvuelto, afable
informality afabilidad
informant informante
information información, informática
information counter mostrador de información
information processing procesamiento de información
information retrieval recuperación de información
informative informativo
informer delator
infraction infracción
infrastructure infraestructura
infrequent poco frecuente
infringe (v) infringir
infringement infracción
infringer infractor
infuriate (v) enfurecer
infuriating exasperante
infusion infusión
ingenious ingenioso

ingenuity inventiva
ingenuous ingenuo, inocente
ingot barra, lingote
ingot of gold lingote de oro
ingredient ingrediente
inhabit (v) habitar, vivir
inhale (v) aspirar
inhaler inhalador
inherent inherente
inherit (v) heredar
inheritable hereditable
inheritance herencia
inheritor heredero
inhibit (v) inhibir
inhibition inhibición
inhuman inhumano
inhumanity inhumanidad
iniquitous injusto
iniquity injusticia
initial inicial
initially primeramente
initials iniciales
initiate (v) iniciar
initiation iniciación
inject (v) inyectar
injection inyección
injunction interdicto
injure (v) herir, lastimar
injury herida, lesión
injustice injusticia
ink tinta
ink pad almohadilla
  (Arg., Uru.)
inland interior
inlet cala, entrada
inmate ocupante, preso
inn posada, mesón; taquilla
  (C.R.)
inner interior
innermost más adentro
innocence inocencia
innocent inocente

innovative novedoso
inoculate (v) inocular
inopportune inoportuno
inorganic inorgánico
inpatient enfermo interno
input entrada
input-output device dispositivo
  de entrada y salida
inquest juicio de indagación, investigación
inquire (v) preguntar
inquiry investigación, pregunta,
  petición
inquisition inquisición, investigación
inquisitive curioso
insane loco, demente
insanity locura
insatiable insaciable
inscription inscripción
insect insecto
insect bites picaduras de insec-
  tos
insecure inseguro
insecurity inseguridad
insensitive indiferente
insert adición, inserto
insertion inserción
inside dentro, interior
insight intuición
insinuate (v) insinuar
insist (v) insistir
insistence insistencia
insistent insistente
insolence insolencia
insolvency insolvencia
insolvent insolvente
insomnia insomnio
inspect (v) inspeccionar
inspection inspección
inspector inspector
inspiration inspiración

inspire (v) inspirar
install (v) instalar
installation instalación
installment plazo, pago
installment plan plan de pagos aplazados
installment purchase compra a plazos
instance instancia, ejemplo
instant inmediato, instante
instant earnings ganancias inmediatas
instantaneous instantáneo
instantly instantáneamente
instead en vez, en cambio
instigate (v) provocar, incitar
instigator instigador, incitador, provocador
instinct instinto
instinctive instintivo
institute instituto, escuela
institute (v) establecer
institution institución
instruct (v) instruir
instruction instrucción
instruction format formato de instrucción
instructive educativo
instructor instructor, profesor
instrument instrumento
insubordinate insubordinado
insufficient insuficiente
insulate (v) aislar
insulation aislamiento
insulin insulina
insult insulto
insulting ofensivo
insurance seguros
insurance of goods seguro de mercancías
insurance policy póliza de seguro

insure (v) asegurar
insured asegurado
insurer asegurador
intact intacto
intake admisión
intangible assets activos nominales, aparentes
integrate (v) integrar
integrated circuit circuito integrado
integrity integridad, honradez
intellect intelecto
intellectual intelectual
intelligence inteligencia
intelligent inteligente
intelligent terminal terminal inteligente
intelligible comprensible
intend (v) proponerse, intentar
intense intenso
intensify (v) intensificar
intensity intensidad
intensive intensivo
intensive care cuidados intensivos
intent intento, propósito
intention intención
intentional intencional
intentionally intencionadamente
interaction acción recíproca
interactive system sistema interactivo
intercede (v) interceder
intercept (v) interceptar, barajar (Arg., Uru.)
interchange intercambio
interchangeable intercambiable
interdict (v) prohibir
interdiction prohibición
interest interés
interest (v) interesar

interest calculation cálculo de intereses

interest coupon cupón de intereses

interest in arrears intereses en retrasos

interest payable intereses a pagar

interest rate tasa de interés

interest to date intereses hasta la fecha

interest-free notes pagarés libres de intereses

interesting interesante

interface acoplamiento, interface

interfere (v) intervenir

interference interferencia

interim intermedio

interior interior

interjection interjección

interlace entrelazado

interlocutory interlocutorio

interlude intervalo

intermediary intermediario

intermediate intermedio

interminable inacabable

intermission descanso

intermittent intermitente

internal interno

internal injuries heridas internas

internal storage memoria interna

international internacional

international loan empréstito internacional

internist internista

interpellation interpelación

interplea instancia del demandado

interpret (v) interpretar

interpreter intérprete

interrogate (v) interrogar

interrupt (v) interrumpir

interruption interrupción

intersection intersección

interstate interestatal

interval intervalo, pausa

intervene (v) intervenir

intervening cause causa interpuesta

intervention intervención

interview entrevista

intestinal intestinal

intestine intestino

intimacy intimidad

intimate íntimo

into a, dentro de

intolerant intolerante

intoxicated borracho, embriagado

intoxication intoxicación, embriaguez

intrepid intrépido

intricate confuso, enredado

intrigue intriga

intrinsic intrínseco

introduce (v) presentar

introduction presentación

introductory introductorio

introverted introvertido

intrude (v) imponer, introducir

intruder intruso

intrusion intrusión

intuition intuición

inundate (v) inundar

invade (v) invadir

invader invasor

invalid nulo, inválido

invaluable inestimable

invariable invariable, constante

invasion invasión

invention invención

inventor inventor

inventory stock, existencias
inventory turnover rotación de stock
inversion inversión
inverter inversor
invest (v) invertir
investigation investigación
investigator investigador
investment tax credit devolución de impuestos
investment inversión
investor inversionista, inversor
invincible invencible
inviolable inviolable
invisible invisible
invitation invitación
invite (v) invitar
invited error decisión errónea
inviting tentador
invoice factura
invoke (v) invocar, rogar
involuntary involuntario
involve (v) implicar, meter
involved envuelto, afectado, complicado
inward interior, interno
Iran Irán
Iraq Irak
irate colérico
Ireland Irlanda
iris iris
Irish irlandés
irk (v) fastidiar
iron hierro, plancha
iron (v) planchar
iron holder almohadilla (Chile, Perú)
irksome molesto
ironic irónico
irony ironía
irrational irracional
irreconcilable irreconciliable
irrefutable irrefutable

irregular irregular, anómalo
irrelevant sin importancia, improcedente
irremissible imperdonable
irresistible irresistible
irresponsibility irresponsabilidad
irresponsible irresponsable
irrevocable irrevocable
irrevocable letter of credit carta de crédito irrevocable
irrigate (v) irrigar, regar
irrigation riego, irrigación
irritate (v) calentar (Chile, Uru.)
irritation café (Mex.)
island isla
isolate (v) aislar
isolation aislamiento
issuance of common stock emisión de acciones ordinarias
issuance of preferred stock emisión de acciones preferentes
issue emisión, publicación, cuestión, resultado
issue (v) emitir, editar
issuing house banco de inversión
it él, ella, ello, lo, la
Italian italiano
italic en bastardilla
italicize (v) subrayar
Italy Italia
itch picazón
itch (v) picar
item artículo, ítem
itemize (v) detallar
itinerary itinerario, ruta
itself ello mismo
ivory marfil
ivy hiedra

J

jab pinchazo, golpe
jack enchufe
jacket chaqueta, envoltura
jackpot premio gordo
jagged dentado, desigual
jail cárcel
jam mermelada, atasco
jam (v) atascar, obstruir
jammer emisor perturbador
janitor conserje, portero
jar tarro, jarra
jargon jerga
jaunt excursión
jaw mandíbula
jazz jazz
jealous celoso, envidioso
jeans tejanos, vaqueros
jeep jeep
jelly gelatina
jeopardize (v) poner en peligro
jeopardy peligro
jerk (v) sacudir
Jesus Jesús
jettison alijo forzoso
Jew judío
jewel joya
jeweller joyero
Jewish judío
jigsaw rompecabezas
job trabajo, empleo, puesto, tarea
jobber intermediario, agente
jog (v) empujar, correr
join (v) unir, juntar
joint común, combinado
joint account cuenta conjunta
joint cost coste de producción común
joint venture negocio conjunto

jointly conjuntamente
joke chiste
joker chistoso
jolly alegre
jolt sacudida
journal periódico, diario
journalism periodismo
journalist periodista
journey viaje
jovial jovial
joy alegría; alboroto (Mex.)
joyous alegre
joystick palanca de control
jubilant jubiloso
jubilee aniversario
judge juez
judge (v) juzgar, arbitrar
judgment juicio, opinión
judicatory tribunal
judicial judicial
judicial admission admisión judicial
judicial decision resolución judicial
judicial notice aviso judicial
judicial remedy recurso legal
judiciary poder judicial
judo judo
jug jarro
juggle (v) hacer malabarismos
jugular yugular
juice zumo, jugo
juicy jugoso, zumoso
jukebox tocadiscos
jumble confusión
jump salto
jump (v) saltar
junction cruce, unión

juncture coyuntura
June junio (mes)
jungle jungla, selva
junior joven, menor
junk junco (bote chino), basura
junk mail propaganda postal
junkie drogadicto
jural jurídico
juration juramento
juratory juratorio
juridical jurídico
jurisdiction jurisdicción
jurisdictional jurisdiccional

jurisprudence jurisprudencia
jurist jurista
juristic jurídico
juristiction jurisdicción
juror jurado (persona)
jury panel panel de jurados
just justo, solamente
justice justicia
justifiable justificable
justify (v) justificar
juvenile juvenil
juxtaposition yuxtaposición

K

kaleidoscope caleidoscopio
keen afilado, perspicaz
keep (v) guardar, cumplir
keeper guardián, portero
kennel perrera
ketchup salsa de tomate
kettle tetera
key llave, tecla
keyboard teclado
keyhole ojo de cerradura
keypunch perforadora
kick patada, puntapié
kick (v) dar patadas, chutar
kickback pago bajo mano, pago
  ilegal, comisión oculta
kickoff inicio de juego
kid chico, niño
kid (v) bromear
kidnap secuestro
kidnap (v) secuestrar
kidnapper secuestrador
kidnapping secuestro
kidney riñón
kill (v) matar, asesinar; estirar
  (Arg., Perú)
killer asesino

killing matanza
kilo kilo (medida)
kilogram kilograma
kilometer kilómetro
kin familiar, allegado
kind amable, clase
kindergarten jardín de infancia
kindle (v) encender
kindness bondad, amabilidad
king rey
kingdom reino
kiosk quiosco
kiss beso
kit conjunto, equipo
kitchen cocina
kite águila (Chile)
kitten gatito
knack maña, destreza
knapsack maleta (Arg., Uru.)
knee rodilla
knife cuchillo
knight caballero
knit (v) hacer punto (textil)
knob tirador, botón
knock golpe
knock (v) golpear, llamar

knock down (v)   rodar (Hond.)
knock someone unconscious (v)
  dormir (Arg., Uru., coll.)
knockout   golpe aplastante
knot   nudo
knowhow   experiencia, saber
knowing   astuto

knowingly   a sabiendas
knowledge   conocimiento
knowledgeable   entendido, erudito
knuckle   nudillo
Korea   Corea
Korean   coreano

L

label (v)   calificar
label   etiqueta, marca
labor   labor, trabajo
labor cost   costes de mano de obra
labor laws   leyes laborales
laboratory   laboratorio
lack   ausencia, carencia
lack of evidence   falta de evidencia
lactation   lactancia
ladder   escalera
ladies' man   guapo (Sp.)
lady   señora, dama
lag   retraso
lagoon   laguna
lake   lago
lame   cojo, inválido
lamentable   lamentable
lamp   lámpara
lamp post   farol
lampshade   pantalla
lance   lanza
land (v)   desembarcar
land   terrenos, tierra, propiedad
landed price   precio puesto en destino
landing   desembarco, aterrizaje
landing certificate   certificado de descarga
landlord   dueño, patrón
landmark   punto destacado

lane   camino, vereda
language   lenguaje
languish (v)   languidecer
lantern   linterna, farol
lap   falda, vuelta
lapse   error, falta, lapso
laptop computer   ordenador de bolsillo
larceny   hurto, latrocinio, robo
large   grande, extenso
large intestine   intestino grueso
large scale integration   integración a gran escala
larynx   laringe
laser printer   impresora láser
last (v)   durar, resistir
last   final, último
last-in, first-out (LIFO)   LIFO (último-dentro/primero-fuera)
last resort   última instancia
lasting   duradero
late   tarde, retrasado
lately   recientemente
later   más tarde, después
lateral   lateral
latest   último, más reciente
Latin   latino, latín
Latin America   América Latina
Latin-American   latinoamericano
latitude   latitud
latter   posterior
laugh   risa, carcajada

laugh (v)   reír, reírse
laughable   cómico, ridículo
laughter   risa
launder (v)   lavar
launderette   lavandería
laundry   lavadero, lavado
lavatory   lavabo, servicio
law   derecho, ley
law court   tribunal de justicia, tribunal de ley
law office   bufete de abogados, oficina de abogados
law school   escuela de derecho
lawbreaker   infractor de la ley
lawbreaking   infracción de la ley
lawful   legal
lawless   ilegal
lawmaker   legislador
lawmaking   legislación
lawn   césped
lawn mower   cortacésped
lawsuit   litigio, pleito
lawyer   abogado, abogada
lax   flojo, negligente
laxative   laxante
lay (v)   colocar, poner
layer   capa, estrato
layman   lego, seglar
layout   trazado, disposición
laziness   pereza, indolencia
lazy   perezoso, vago
lead   delantera, plomo
lead (v)   dirigir, guiar
leader   jefe, líder; mandatario (Amer.)
leadership   liderazgo
leading   delantero
leading case   causa determinante
leaf   hoja
leaflet   folleto
league   liga, sociedad
leak   agujero, gotera
leak (v)   gotear, tener fugas

lean (v)   reclinarse
leaning   inclinado
leap (v)   brincar, saltar
leap   brinco, salto
leap year   año bisiesto
leapfrog   pídola, salto mortal; burro (Col., P.R.)
learn (v)   aprender, estudiar
learner   estudiante
learning   estudio, aprendizaje
lease   alquiler, arrendamiento, arriendo
lease (v)   alquilar, arrendar
leaseholder   arrendatario
leasing   alquiler, leasing
least   menor, más pequeño
leather   cuero, piel
leather bag   garra (Col.)
leave   permiso
leave (v)   dejar, marchar
lecture   clase, lección
lecture (v)   dar una conferencia
lecturer   conferenciante
ledge   reborde
ledger   libro mayor
left   izquierda
leftist   izquierdista
leg   pierna
legacy   legado
legal   legal
legal adviser   asesor legal
legal capital   capital legal
legal evidence   evidencia legal
legal fees   honorarios de abogados
legal heir   heredero legal
legal liability   responsabilidad legal
legal notice   notificación legal
legal obligation   obligación legal
legal principle   principio legal
legal proceeding   acto legal
legal remedies   recursos legales

legal rights   derechos legales
legal services   servicios legales
legal status   estado legal
legal year   año civil
legalistic   legalista, legalístico
legality   legalidad
legalize (v)   legalizar
legally   legalmente
legally liable   responsable legalmente
legator   testador
legend   leyenda
legendary   legendario
legible   legible
legion   legión
legislate (v)   legislar
legislation   legislación
legislative   legislativo
legislator   legislador
legislature   legislatura
legitimacy   legitimidad
legitimate   legítimo
legitimate (v)   legitimar
legs   piernas
leisure   descanso, ocio
lemon   limón
lemonade   limonada
lend (v)   prestar
lend money at usury rates (v)
   ahorcar (Arg., Uru., Mex.)
lender   prestador
lending limit   límite de crédito
lending rate   índice de crédito
length   largo, longitud
lengthy   largo, extenso
leniency   indulgencia
lenient   poco severo, blando
lens   lente, lupa
Lent   Cuaresma
lentil   lenteja
leprosy   lepra
lesbian   mujer homosexual
lesion   lesión

less   menos
lessee   arrendatario
lessen (v)   disminuir, reducir
lesson   lección
lessor   arrendador
let (v)   permitir
lethal   letal, mortal
lethargic   letárgico
letter   carta, letra
letter of attorney   poder
letter of authority   carta de autorización
letter of complaint   carta de reclamación
letter of credit   carta de crédito
letter of confirmation   carta de
   confirmación
letter of guarantee   carta de garantía
letter quality   calidad tipográfica
lettuce   lechuga
leukemia   leucemia
level (v)   allanar, nivelar
level   llano, nivel, raso
lever   palanca
leverage   influencia, medios, ventaja
leviable   exigible
levy   ejecución, exacción, impuesto
levy (v)   exigir, imponer
liabilities   obligaciones, pasivo
liability   pasivo, responsabilidad
liable   responsable
liaison   enlace, conexión
libel   calumnia, libelo
libelant   demandante
libelee   demandado
libeler   difamador
libelous   difamante
liberal   liberal, generoso
liberate (v)   libertar
liberty   libertad

librarian bibliotecario
library biblioteca
lice piojos
licence (v) autorizar, licenciar
licence licencia, permiso
licencee concesionario
licensee autorizado
licensor concedente
licentiate licenciado
licitation licitación
lick (v) lamer
lid párpado, tapa
lie mentira
lie (v) mentir
likely probable
lien embargo preventivo, gravamen
lienee embargado
lienor embargador
lieutenant lugarteniente
life vida
life imprisonment cadena perpetua
life jacket chaleco salvavidas
life sentence cadena perpetua
lifeboat bote salvavidas
lifeguard vigilante, salvavidas
lift levantamiento, ascensor,
transporte
lift (v) levantar, llevar
ligament ligamento
light (v) alumbrar, encender
light fácil, lámpara, leve, ligero
light sentence condena leve
lighten (v) aligerar, iluminar
lighter encendedor
lighthouse faro
lighting alumbrado
lightning rayo, relámpago
like (v) gustar, querer
like parecido, tal como
likeable simpático
likelihood probabilidad

likely probable
liking preferencia
limb miembro
lime lima, cal
limit límite
limit (v) limitar, restringir
limitation limitación
limited limitado
limited appeal apelación limitada
limited liability pasivo limitado
limited oath juramento condicional
limousine limusina (coche)
limp cojera, flojo
line (v) alinear
line cola, cuerda, línea
line of credit línea de crédito
line printer impresora rápida
lineage linaje
linear lineal
linear modulation modulación
lineal
linear programming programación lineal
linen lino
linger (v) permanecer
lingerie ropa íntima
linguist linguista
lining forro
link conexión, enlace, relación
link (v) enlazar, unir
lion león
lip labio
lipstick barra de labios
liquidate (v) liquidar
liquidation liquidación
liquidation value valor de liquidación
liquidity liquidez
liquor licor
Lisbon Lisboa
list lista

list (v) listar, relacionar
listen (v) escuchar, oír
listener oyente
listless indiferente
liter litro
literature catálogos, literatura
litigant litigante
litigate (v) litigar
litigation litigio
litigator litigante
litigious litigioso
litter (v) dar cama, ensuciar
litter basura, cama, camilla, litera
little poco
liturgy liturgia
live (v) vivir
live vivo, viviente
livelihood medio de vida
liver hígado
livery entrega
livestock hacienda (Arg., Chile)
livid amoratado
living viviente, vida
living room sala de estar; asistencia (Mex.)
load carga, peso
load (v) cargar peso, entrar datos
loaded cargado
loading platform manga (Arg., Chile, Mex.)
loaf pan
loafer vago, gandul
loan crédito, préstamo
loan (v) prestar
loan account cuenta de créditos
loan department departamento de créditos
loathe (v) aborrecer, detestar
lobby (v) presionar en grupo
lobby vestíbulo, grupo, camarilla
lobster langosta
local local, vecinal

local area network red de ordenadores locales
local mode modo local
local taxes impuestos locales
locality localidad
localize (v) localizar
locally localmente
locate (v) colocar, localizar
location sitio, situación, ubicación
lock (v) cerrar, trabar
lock cerradura, traba
locker armario, cerrador
lockout cierre patronal
locomotive locomotor
lodge hostal, hotel
lodge (v) hospedar, alojar
lodger huésped
lodging hospedaje, pensión
loft desván
lofty alto, elevado
log (v) conectar, registrar
log leño, tronco
logarithm logaritmo
logic lógico
logistics logística
loiter (v) vagabundear
London Londres
lonely aislado, solitario
long largo, mucho
long-distance larga distancia
long-lived assets activos duraderos
long-range largo alcance
long-term largo plazo
long-term debt deuda a largo plazo
long-term investments inversiones a largo plazo
long-term liabilities deudas a largo plazo
longevity longevidad
longhand manuscrito

longing anhelo, ansia
longitude longitud
longitudinal longitudinal
look mirada, parecido
look (v) mirar, parecer
look-out observatorio; campana (Amer.)
loom telar
loom (v) aparecer, surgir
loop (v) hacer lazo
loop lazo, vuelta
loophole escapatoria
loose (v) aflojar, desatar
loose flojo, suelto
loose-leaf hojas sueltas
loosen (v) soltar, aflojar
loot botín, presa
looting saqueo
lord señor, el Señor
lose (v) perder
loser perdedor
loss pérdida
loss in weight pérdida de peso
losses pérdidas
lost perdido
lot cantidad, lote de mercancías, porción
lotion loción
lottery lotería
loud fuerte, ruidoso
loudly en voz alta
loudspeaker altavoz
lounge (v) haraganear
lounge salón
louse piojo
lousy piojoso, malísimo
lovable amable, simpático
love (v) amar, querer
love amor, cariño
love affair aventura amorosa
lovely hermoso, precioso
low bajo, malo

low-interest loan préstamo a bajo interés
low-priced barato
lower (v) bajar, reducir
lower más bajo
lower court juzgado menor
loyal leal, fiel
loyalty lealtad
lubricant lubricante
lubricate (v) lubricar
lucid claro, lúcido
luck suerte, fortuna; leche (Amer.)
lucrative lucrativo
ludicrous absurdo, ridículo
lug (v) arrastrar, tirar de
luggage equipaje
lukewarm tibio, templado
lull calma pasajera
lull (v) calmar, arrullar
lumbago lumbago
lumbar lumbar
lumber madera
lumberyard almacén de madera
luminous luminoso
lump (v) amontonar, mezclar
lump masa, bulto
lump sum cantidad total
lump-sum payment pago global
lumpy desigual, amontonado
lunatic demente, loco
lunch (v) almorzar, comer
lunch almuerzo, comida
lunchtime hora de comer
lungs pulmones
lurch (v) dar tumbos, sacudir
lurch sacudida
lure (v) atraer, tentar
lure cebo, encanto
lurid sensacional
lurking oculto
luscious delicioso, exquisito

lush frondoso, pródigo
lust lujuria
luster brillo, lustre
luxury lujo

luxury goods bienes de lujo
lymph linfa
lynch (v) linchar
lyric lírico, letra

M

macabre macabro
macaroni macarrones
mace maza, porra
machine máquina
machine gun ametralladora
machine instruction instrucción de máquina
machine language lenguaje de máquina
machinery maquinaria
macroprogramming macroprogramación
mad loco, demente
madam señora
madden (v) enfurecer
made hecho
made without sugar amargo (Arg., Uru.)
madness locura
magazine revista
magic magia
magical mágico
magician mago
magisterial magistral
magistrate magistrado
magnanimous magnánimo
magnate potentado
magnet imán
magnetic magnético
magnetic card tarjeta magnética
magnetic disk disco magnético
magnetic disk storage memoria a discos magnéticos

magnetic storage memoria magnética
magnetic tape cinta magnética
magnetic tape file fichero de cintas
magnetism magnetismo
magnificent magnífico
magnify (v) aumentar
magnifying glass lente, lupa
magnitude magnitud
maid criada, doncella
maiden virginal, intacto
mail correo
mail (v) enviar por correo
mail box buzón
mail order venta por correo
mailing list lista de clientes
mailman cartero
main principal, mayor
main control unit unidad principal de control
main hall sala principal
main line línea principal
main storage memoria central
mainframe procesador central
mainland tierra firme
mainstay pilar, principal
maintain (v) mantener, guardar
maintenance mantenimiento
maintenance costs costes de mantenimiento
maintenance time tiempo de mantenimiento
major (v) especializarse

major mayor, principal
majority mayoría
make (v) hacer, producir
make-believe simulación
make-up maquillaje
maker constructor
makeshift provisional
malaise indisposición
malaria paludismo
male macho, varón
malefactor malhechor
malfeasance malversación
malice malicia
malicious malicioso
malign (v) calumniar
malignant grave, maligno
mall alameda, galería
malpractice conducta ilegal, conducta no profesional, incompetencia, negligencia, negligencia ilegal, negligencia profesional
Malta fever fiebre de Malta
malversation malversación
mammoth gigantesco
man hombre
manageable manejable
management dirección, gerencia
management advisory services servicios asesores de dirección
manager director, jefe
managerial directivo
mandate mandato
maneuver (v) maniobrar, manejar
maneuver maniobra
mandatory mandatario, obligatorio
mandible mandíbula
manhood virilidad
mania manía
maniac maniático
manicure manicura
manifest manifiesto, patente

manifest (v) mostrar, revelar
manifold múltiple
manipulate (v) manipular
manner manera, modo
manor feudo, finca
manpower mano de obra
mansion palacio, mansión
manslaughter homicidio no premeditado
mantel repisa de chimenea
mantle capa, manto
manual manual
manually manualmente
manufacture fabricación
manufacture (v) fabricar
manufactured goods productos manufacturados
manufacturer fabricante
manufacturing costs costes de producción
manuscript manuscrito
many muchos
map mapa
marathon maratón
march marcha, caminata
March marzo (mes)
margarine margarina
margin margen, reserva
marginal marginal
marginal cost coste marginal
marina embarcadero
marine marino, marítimo
marital matrimonial
maritime marítimo
maritime transport transporte marítimo
mark marca, señal
mark (v) marcar, señalar
mark-up beneficio bruto (aumento sobre coste)
marked marcado
market bolsa, mercado; parada (Perú)

market price precio de mercado
market research estudio de mercado
market survey estudio de mercado
market trend tendencia de mercado
market value valor de mercado
marketable vendible
marketable securities títulos, títulos negociables, títulos realizables
marketing comercialización, comercio
maroon (v) abandonar
marriage matrimonio
married casado
marrow médula
marry (v) casarse
marsh pantano, marisma
marshal alguacil, guarda, mariscal
marshaling ordenamiento
mart mercado
martial marcial, militar
martial law ley marcial
martyr mártir
martyrdom martirio
marvel maravilla
marvelous maravilloso
Marxism marxismo
mascara rimel (pestañas)
masculine masculino
mask careta, máscara
masochism masoquismo
masochist masoquista
mason albañil
masonry albañilería
masquerade mascarada, farsa
mass (v) amasar, concentrar
mass masa, magnitud, misa
mass production fabricación en serie

massacre masacre
massage masaje
massive masivo, grande
mast palo, torre, bellota
master amo, dueño
master (v) vencer, dominar
masterpiece obra maestra
mastery superioridad
mastitis mastitis
masturbate (v) masturbarse
match cerilla, partido
match (v) igualar, ser igual
matchbox caja de cerillas
mate compañero
material importante, material
material witness testigo esencial
materialist materialista
materialize (v) realizar
maternal maternal
maternity maternidad
mathematical model modelo matemático
mathematics matemáticas
matinée función de la tarde
matricide matricidio
matrimonial matrimonial
matrimony matrimonio
matter asunto, materia, sustancia, tema
matter (v) importar
matter of fact cuestión de hecho
matter of law cuestión de derecho
mattress colchón
mature maduro
maturity vencimiento
maturity date fecha de vencimiento
maul (v) destrozar
maxilla mandíbula
maximum máximo
maximum penalty pena máxima
May mayo (mes)

may (v)   poder, ser posible
maybe   quizás, tal vez
mayday   auxilio, socorro
mayhem   mutilación criminal
mayonnaise   mayonesa
mayor   alcalde
maze   laberinto
me   me, mí
meal   comida
mean   medio, mediano
mean (v)   significar, intentar
meaning   intención
meaningful   significativo
meaningless   sin sentido
measles   sarampión
measure (v)   medir, estimar
meat   carne
mechanic   mecánico
mechanism   mecanismo
medal   medalla
medallion   medallón
meddle (v)   entrometerse
media   medios informativos
mediate (v)   intervenir
mediation   mediación
mediator   mediador
medical   médico
medical help   ayuda médica
medicaments   medicamentos
medication   tratamiento médico
medicine   medicina
medieval   medieval
mediocre   mediocre
meditate (v)   meditar
Mediterranean   Mediterráneo
medium   medio, mediano
medium term   a medio plazo
meet (v)   encontrar, conocer
meeting   cita, encuentro, reunión
megaphone   megáfono
melancholic   melancólico
melanoma   melanoma, tumor maligno

mellow   dulce, suave
melodrama   melodrama
melody   melodía
melon   melón
melt (v)   fundir, derretir
melting   fundente
member   miembro, socio
membership   sociedad
membrane   membrana
membrane keyboard   teclado de membrana
memo   nota
memorable   memorable
memorandum   apunte, memorándum, nota
memorize (v)   aprender de memoria
memory   memoria, recuerdo
memory card   tarjeta de memoria
men   hombres
menace   amenaza
menace (v)   amenazar
mend   remiendo
mend (v)   mejorar, reponerse
menial   criado, bajo
meningitis   meningitis
meniscus   menisco
menopause   menopausia
menstrual   menstrual
menstruation   menstruación
mental   mental
mental cruelty   crueldad mental
mental health   salud mental
mental incapacity   incapacidad mental
mention   mención, alusión
menu   lista, menú
mercantile   mercantil
mercantile agency   agencia mercantil
mercenary   mercenario
merchandise   mercancía

merchandise transactions transacciones de mercancías

merchandising comercialización

merchant comerciante, mercader

merchant fleet flota mercante

merciful misericordioso

mercury mercurio

mercy clemencia, misericordia

mere mero, simple

merge (v) fusionar, unir

merger fusión, fusión de empresas

meridian meridiano

merit (v) merecer

merit mérito

merry alegre, feliz

mess confusión, lío

mess (v) desordenar, liar

mess up enredo, fracaso

message mensaje

messenger mensajero

metabolic metabólico

metabolism metabolismo

metacarpus metacarpo

metal metal

metallic metálico

metallurgic metalúrgico

metamorphosis metamorfosis

metaphor metáfora

metatarsus metatarso

meteor meteoro

meteorologist meteorólogo

meteorology meteorología

meter contador, metro

method método, sistema

Methodist metodista

meticulous meticuloso

metric métrico

metropolis metrópoli

metropolitan metropolitano

Mexican mexicano

Mexico México

mice ratones

microcircuit microcircuito

microbe microbio

microcomputer microordenador

microfloppy disk microdisco flexible

microorganism microorganismo

microprocessor microprocesador

microscope microscopio

microsurgery microcirugía

microwave microonda

mid medio

midday mediodía

middle medio, central

middle-class clase media

middleman intermediario

midget enano

midnight medianoche

midst entre, en medio

midsummer pleno verano

midway a medio camino

midweek entre semana

Midwest mediooeste

might fuerza, poder

mighty fuerte, poderoso

migraine migraña, jaqueca

migrant migratorio

mild templado, manso

mildew moho, mildiu

mildness suavidad

mile milla

mileage distancia

milestone piedra miliaria

militant militante

military militar, bélico

military law ley militar

milk leche

Milky Way Vía Láctea

mill fábrica, molino

millennium milenio, milenario

milligram miligramo

million millón

millionaire millonario

mime pantomima
mimic (v) imitar
mince (v) picar, trinchar
mincer máquina de picar
mind mente, entendimiento
mind (v) cuidarse, fijarse en
mine mina, mío, mía
mineral mineral
minesweeper dragaminas
mingle (v) mezclar
miniature miniatura
minicomputer miniordenador
minimize (v) minimizar
minimum mínimo
minister ministro
ministry ministerio
minor menor
minority minoría
minority interest interés minoritario
minority stockholders accionistas minoritarios
minstrel juglar
mint acuñación de moneda,
casa de moneda, menta
(hierba)
mint (v) acuñar
minus menos
minute minuto, acta
miracle milagro
miraculous milagroso
mirage espejismo
mirror espejo
misadventure desgracia
misallege (v) alegar falsamente
misappropriation malversación
misbehavior mala conducta
miscalculation cálculo errónea
miscarriage malparto, aborto
miscellaneous varios, diversos
mischief mal, daño
misconduct mala conducta
misdeed malhecho

misdemeanor delito, delito
menor, ofensa menor
miserable triste, desgraciado
misery miseria
misfit mal ajustado
misfortune desgracia
misguided equivocado
mishap despiste
misinterpret (v) tergiversar
mislay (v) extraviar, perder
mislead (v) engañar, despistar
misleading engañoso
misplace (v) colocar mal
miss (v) errar, perder
miss error, pérdida, señorita
missile proyectil
missing perdido, ausente
mission misión
missionary misionero
misspell deletrear mal
mist niebla
mistake equivocación, error,
barro (Arg., Uru.)
mistaken equivocado
mistrial juicio nulo
mistrust desconfianza
misunderstanding malentendido
misunderstood mal entendido
misuse abuso
mitigate (v) mitigar, calmar
mix mezcla
mix (v) mezclar, combinar
mix-up confusión, enredo
mixture mezcla
mnemonic code código mnemónico
moan gemido
mob multitud
mobile móvil
mobility movilidad
mock (v) ridiculizar
mocking burlón
mode modo

model modelo
modem módem
moderate moderado
moderately moderadamente
modern moderno
modernize (v) modernizar
modest modesto
modesty modestia
modifier modificador
modify (v) modificar
modulate (v) modular
modulation modulación
module módulo
moist húmedo, mojado
moisten (v) mojar, humedecer
molar teeth molares, muelas
mold (v) amoldarse
mold moho, molde
moles lunares de la piel
moment momento
momentarily momentáneamente
momentum ímpetu
monarch monarca
monarchy monarquía
Monday lunes
monetary items artículos monetarios
monetary policy política monetaria
monetary supply disponibilidad monetaria
money dinero
money market mercado financiero
money order giro bancario
mongolism mongolismo
monitor monitor, pantalla
monk monje
monkey mono
monochrome monitor pantalla monocroma
monopolize (v) monopolizar
monopoly monopolio

monotonous monótono
monsoon monzón
monster monstruo
month mes
monthly mensual
monument monumento
monumental monumental
mood humor, disposición
moon luna
moonlight luz de la luna
moor (v) amarrar
mop fregasuelos
moral moral, ética
moral law ley moral
morale estado de ánimo
moratorium moratoria
morbid insano, mórbido
more más
moreover además
morgue depósito (cadáveres)
morning mañana
morning glory suspiro (Arg., Chile)
moron imbécil, retrasado mental
morphine morfina
morphology morfología
morphone morfina
mortal mortal
mortality mortalidad
mortar mortero
mortgage hipoteca
mortgage bank banco hipotecario
mortgage credits créditos hipotecarios
mortgage law derecho hipotecario
mortify (v) mortificar, humillar
mortuary mortuorio
mosaico mosaico
Moscow Moscú
mosquito mosquito
moss musgo

most más, mayoría
mostly en su mayor parte
motel motel
mother madre
mother-in-law suegra
motherhood maternidad
motion moción, movimiento
motion granted petición admitida
motivation motivación
motive motivo, motor
motor motor
motorbike motocicleta
motorboat lancha motora
motorcycle motocicleta
motorist motorista
mottled multicolor
mountain montaña
mourn (v) llorar, afligirse
mourning lamentación, luto
mouse apuntador, ratón
mousetrap ratonera
mouth boca
mouth-to-mouth boca a boca
move (v) mover, mudar, peticionar
move movimiento, jugada
moveable móvil
movement movimiento
movie película
much mucho
muck suciedad
mucous mucosa
mud barro
muddle desorden
muddy fangoso
muffle (v) amortiguar
muffler silenciador
mug taza
mule mulo
multi-access system sistema de multiaccesos
multicolored multicolor

multiple múltiple
multiple sclerosis esclerosis múltiple
multiplexing multiplexación
multiply (v) multiplicar
multitasking multitarea
multitude multitud
mumps paperas
munch (v) mascar
mundane mundano
municipal municipal
municipal bonds bonos municipales
municipal court juzgado municipal
municipal ordinance ordenanza municipal
muniments documentos de título
mural mural
murder (v) asesinar
murder asesinato, homicidio
murderer asesino
murky oscuro, lóbrego
murmur murmullo
muscle fuerza, músculo
muscular dystrophy distrofia muscular
musculature musculatura
muse (v) meditar, reflexionar
museum museo
mushroom champiñón, seta
music música
musical musical
musician músico
Muslim musulmán
muslin muselina
mussel mejillón
must obligación
mustache bigote
mustard mostaza
mutant mutante
mutation mutación
mute mudo, silencioso

mutilate (v) mutilar
mutilation mutilación
mutiny motín
mutter murmullo
mutual mutuo, común
mutual consent consentimiento mutuo, mutuo acuerdo
mutual covenant pacto de obligación mutua
mutual wills testamentos mutuos

mutuality mutualidad
my mi, mío, de mí
mycosis micosis
myopia miopía
myself yo mismo
mystery misterio
mystic místico
mystic will testamento cerrado
mystify (v) hacer misterio
mystique misterio, pericia

N

nag (v) regañar, criticar
nail clavo, garra, uña
nails uñas
naïve ingenuo
naïvety ingenuidad
naked desnudo
naked confession confesión sin confirmación
naked promise promesa sin causa
name nombre
nameless anónimo
namely a saber
nap siesta, sueño corto
napkin servilleta
narcissism narcisista
narcotic narcótico
narrate (v) narrar
narration relato
narrative narrativo
narrator narrador
narrow estrecho, reducido
narrowly estrechamente
nasal nasal
nasty sucio, obsceno
nation nación
national nacional
nationality nacionalidad

native de orígen, nativo, natural; criollo (Amer.)
natural natural
natural allegiance lealtad natural
natural heir heredero natural
natural resources recursos naturales
naturalist naturalista
naturalize (v) establecerse
nature esencia, naturaleza
naughty pícaro, travieso
nausea náusea
nautical náutico, marítimo
naval naval, de marina
navel ombligo
navigable navegable
navigate (v) navegar
navigation navegación
navigator navegante
navy marina de guerra
navy blue azul marino
nay no (voto negativo)
near cerca
Near East Próximo Oriente
nearly casi
neat limpio, pulcro
necessary necesario

necessitate (v) necesitar, exigir
necessity necesidad
neck cuello
necklace collar
need apuro, necesidad
need (v) necesitar
needle aguja
needless innecesario
needlework costura
needy necesitado, pobre
negative negativo
negative evidence evidencia
  negativa
negative proof prueba negativa
neglect (v) descuidar
neglected descuidado
negligence negligencia
negligent descuidado, negligente
negotiable negociable
negotiable bonds bonos negociables
negotiate (v) negociar, gestionar
negotiation negociación
negotiator negociador
neighbor vecino
neighborhood vecindario
neither ninguno, tampoco
nephew sobrino
nephritis nefritis
nepotism nepotismo
nerve nervio
nervous nervioso
nest nido
nestle (v) acomodarse
net red, neto
net amount importe neto
net assets activos netos
net earnings ganancias netas
net income ingresos netos
net price precio neto
net profits beneficios netos
net ton tonelada neta
net weight peso neto

net worth activo neto
Netherlands Países Bajos
network red
network architecture arquitectura de red
neuralgia neuralgia
neurasthenia neurastenia
neurologist neurólogo
neurology neurología
neurone neurona
neurosis neurosis
neurosurgery neurocirugía
neurotic neurótico
neuter neutro
neutral neutral
neutrality neutralidad
neutralize (v) neutralizar
never nunca
nevermore nunca más
nevertheless sin embargo
new nuevo
new trial nuevo juicio
New York Nueva York
New Yorker neoyorquino
newborn recién nacido
newcomer recién llegado
news noticias
newsletter hoja informativa
newspaper periódico
newsstand quiosco
next próximo, siguiente
next door de al lado
nibble mordisco
nice simpático, fino
nicety finura, refinamiento
niche nicho
nick muesca, corte
nickname apodo, mote
nicotine nicotina
niece sobrina
night noche
night club club nocturno
night court juzgado de noche

night life vida nocturna
nightmare pesadilla
night safe caja de seguridad nocturna
nightshift turno de noche
nil cero
nimble ágil, ligero
nine nueve
nineteen diecinueve
ninety noventa
ninth noveno
nip (v) pellizcar
nipple pezón; tetera (del biberón) (Cuba, Mex., P.R.)
nitrogen nitrógeno
no no
noble noble, ilustre
nobody nadie
nod inclinación (cabeza)
nod (v) asentir, cabecear
node bulto, tumor
noise ruido
noisy ruidoso
nomad nómada
nominal nominal
nominate (v) nombrar, proponer
nomination nombramiento
nominative nominativo
non-amortizable loan empréstito no amortizable
non-current assets activos no corrientes
non-current liabilities pasivos no corrientes
non-monetary items artículos no monetarios
non-profit organization empresa no lucrativa
non-recurring items artículos ocasionales
non-stop sin parada, directo
nonacceptance no aceptación

nonamortizable loan empréstito no amortizable
nonappearance incomparecencia
nonattendance inasistencia
nonbailable no caucionable
noncollectable incobrable
noncompliance incumplimiento
nonconformist rebelde, disidente
none nadie, ninguno
nonetheless no obstante
nonfeasance omisión
nonfulfillment incumplimiento
nonlegal no jurídico
nonleviable no gravable
nonliable no responsable
nonlinear programming programación no lineal
nonresident no residente
nonsense disparate, tontería
noon mediodía
nor ni, tampoco
norm norma, tipo
normal normal, regular
north norte
northbound hacia el norte
northeast nordeste, noreste
northern del norte
northwest noroeste
nose nariz
nosebleed hemorragia nasal
nostalgia nostalgia
nostalgic nostálgico
nostril ventana (de la nariz)
not no
not guilty no culpable
notable notable, señalado
notably notablemente
notarial notarial
notary notario
notary public notario público
notation notación

notch   muesca, mella
note   billete, documento, pagaré
   nota
note printing press   prensa de
   billetes
notebook   libro de apuntes
noted   célebre, conocido
notes payable   documentos por
   pagar, letras a pagar
notes receivable   letras a cobrar
nothing   nada
notice   anuncio, aviso
notice (v)   notar, observar
noticeable   evidente
notification   notificación
notify (v)   comunicar, notificar
notion   noción, concepto
notoriety   notoriedad
notorious   muy conocido
notwithstanding   no obstante
noun   nombre
nourish (v)   alimentar, nutrir
nourishing   alimenticio, rico
nourishment   alimento
novel   nuevo, original
November   noviembre
novice   principiante
now   ahora
nowhere   en ninguna parte
nuclear   nuclear

nucleus   núcleo
nude   desnudo
nude contract   pacto sin causa
nudge   codazo ligero
nudist   nudista
nuisance   molestia, perjuicio
null   nulo, inválido
null and void   nulo y sin valor
null modem   módem anulador
nullify (v)   anular
nullity   nulidad
numb   insensible
number   número, cifra
numeral   numeral
numeric keypad   teclado numérico
numerical   numérico
numerical control   control numérico
numerical data   datos numéricos
numerous   numeroso
nun   monja
nurse   enfermero, enfermera
nursery   guardería infantil
nursery school   jardín de infancia
nursing home   hospital geriátrico
nurture (v)   nutrir
nutrition   nutrición
nylon   nilón

O

oar   remo, remero
oath   juramento
obedience   obediencia
obedient   obediente
obese   obeso
obesity   obesidad
obey (v)   obedecer
obituary   necrológicas
object (v)   objetar, oponerse

object   objeto
object language   lenguaje resultante
object program   programa resultante
objection   objeción, oposición
objective   objetivo
obligation   obligación, título
obligatory   obligatorio

oblique oblicuo
obliterate (v) borrar, eliminar
oblivion olvido
oblivious inconsciente
oblong apaisado, rectangular
obnoxious detestable, odioso
obscene obsceno
obscenity obscenidad
obscure oscuro
obscure (v) oscurecer
observant observador
observation observación
observatory observatorio
observe (v) observar, cumplir
obsess (v) obsesionar
obsession obsesión
obsolescence caída en desuso
obsolete obsoleto, desusado
obstacle obstáculo
obstetrician obstétrico, tocólogo
obstetrics obstetricia, tocología
obstinacy obstinación
obstinate obstinado
obstruct (v) obstruir, bloquear
obstruction obstrucción
obstructive obstructivo
obtain (v) obtener, adquirir
obtuse obtuso, estúpido
obvious evidente, obvio
obvious risk riesgo evidente
occasion oportunidad, ocasión
occasional circunstancial
occasionally a veces
occipital bone hueso occipital
occult oculto, misterioso
occupancy tenencia
occupant inquilino
occupation ocupación, tenencia
occur (v) ocurrir, suceder
occurrence acontecimiento
ocean océano
ocean freight flete marítimo
octagon octágano

octagonal octagonal
October octubre
octoroon albino (Mex.)
ocular ocular
oculist oculista
odd impar, raro, suelto
odd sizes tallas únicas
oddity manía, rareza
odds probabilidad
odious odioso
odontology odontología
odor olor, fragancia
of de, desde
off fuera, a la altura
off-peak temporada baja
offend (v) ofender
offender delincuente, ofensor
offense delito, ofensa
offensive ofensiva
offer oferta, ofrecimiento
offer (v) ofrecer
offerer oferente
offering ofrecimiento
offhand brusco, informal
office despacho, oficina
office boy cadete (Arg., Bol., Uru.)
officer director, ejecutivo, oficial; jefe (when speaking to a policeman) (Perú, Uru.)
official ejecutivo, funcionario, oficial
offset (v) compensar
offset compensación
offset accounts cuenta de compensación
offset dollar dólar de compensación
offshore de mar adentro
offspring descendencia, sucesión
often a menudo
oil aceite, petróleo
oil well pozo de petróleo

oil field   campo petrolífero
oily   aceitoso
ointment   pomada, ungüento
old   viejo, usado
old-fashioned   anticuado
olive   aceituna, oliva
olive oil   aceite de oliva
olograph   ológrafo
omelette   tortilla
omen   presagio
ominous   siniestro
omission   omisión, supresión
omit (v)   omitir, olvidar; mandar
(Amer.)
omnipotent   omnipotente
on   en, sobre
on account   a cuenta
on behalf of   a favor de
on consignment   en depósito
on demand   a la vista
on-line equipment   control en
línea
on-line storage   memoria directa
on-line system   sistema directo
on sight   a la vista
once   una vez
oncology   oncología
oncoming   que se acerca
one   uno, una
one hundred   cien
one thousand   mil
one-way   dirección única
one-way communication   comunicación unidireccional
onerous   oneroso
oneself   uno mismo
onion   cebolla
onlooker   espectador
only   solo
onset   ataque
onshore   hacia la tierra
onslaught   ataque violento
onus   carga

onward   progresivo
opaque   opaco
open   abierto, público
open account   cuenta abierta
open air   aire libre
open check   cheque abierto
open market   mercado libre
open-minded   liberal
open wound   herida abierta
opening   abertura, principio
opening balance   saldo inicial
opera   ópera
operable   operable
operate (v)   manejar, impulsar
operation   funcionamiento
operating costs   costos de explotación
operating leases   arrendamientos
en vigor
operating system   sistema operativo
operating theater   quirófano
operational   en buen estado
operative   en vigor
operator   agente, operador
ophthalmologist   oftalmólogo
ophthalmology   oftalmología
opinion   opinión, parecer
opium   opio
opponent   adversario
opportune   oportuno
opportunist   oportunista
opportunity   oportunidad
oppose (v)   oponerse a
opposed   opuesto
opposer   oponente
opposite   en frente
opposition   oposición
oppress (v)   oprimir
oppression   opresión
oppressor   opresor
opt (v)   optar por
optic   óptico

optician óptico
optimism optimismo
optimist optimista
optimistic optimista
optimization optimización
optimum óptimo
option opción
optional opcional, optativo
optometry optometría
opulence opulencia
or o, ni
oral bucal, oral, verbal
oral evidence evidencia verbal
orange naranja
orbit órbita
orchard huerto
orchestra orquesta
orchestrate (v) orquestar
ordain (v) ordenar, decretar
ordeal sufrimiento
order decreto, método, orden
order (v) ordenar
order acceptance aceptación de pedido
order check cheque a la orden
order confirmation confirmación de pedido
order form hoja de pedido
orderly ordenado
ordinal ordinal (número)
ordinance ordenanza
ordinary ordinario
ordinary annuity anualidad ordinaria
organ órgano
organic orgánico
organic law ley orgánica
organism organismo
organization organización
organize (v) organizar
organizer organizador
orgasm orgasmo
orgy orgía

oriental oriental
orientate (v) orientar
orientation orientación
orifice orificio
origin origen
original original
original cost coste original
original process proceso inicial
originate (v) producir
ornament ornamento
ornamental decorativo
ornate vistoso
orphan huérfano
orthodox ortodoxo
orthodoxy ortodoxia
orthopedic ortopédico
orthopedics ortopedia
oscillate (v) oscilar
osmosis ósmosis
ostensible aparente, ostensible
ostracism ostracismo
other otro
otherwise de otra manera
otitis otitis
ought (v) deber, tener que
our nuestro
ourselves nosotros mismos
oust (v) desalojar, expulsar
ouster desahucio
out fuera
out-of-date anticuado
outboard fuera borda
outbreak erupción
outburst explosión
outcast paria, proscrito
outcome resultado
outcry grito, protesta
outdo (v) exceder
outdoor al aire libre
outdoor salesman vendedor a domicilio
outdoors al aire libre
outer exterior, externo

outfit equipo, herramientas
outgoing saliente
outgrow (v) crecer más que
outing paseo
outlaw (v) proscribir
outlaw proscrito
outlawed proscrito
outlay desembolso
outlays gastos operativos
outlet almacén de ventas, salida
outline contorno, perfil
outlook perspectiva
outnumber (v) exceder
outpatient paciente externo
output producción, salida, volumen
outrage atrocidad
outrageous atroz, escandaloso
outright completo, entero
outset principio
outside fuera, exterior
outsider forastero, ajeno
outsize enorme
outskirts alrededores
outspoken franco, abierto
outstanding excepcional
outstanding debt deuda existente
outstanding interest intereses vencidos
outstanding stock capital suscrito
outward exterior
outweigh (v) pesar más
oval ovalado
ovary ovario
ovation ovación
oven horno
over encima, sobre
overall en conjunto
overalls guardapolvo
overcast (v) obscurecer
overcharge (v) sobrecargar

overcharge cargo en exceso
overcoat abrigo
overcome (v) vencer, superar
overcrowded atestado, muy lleno
overdo (v) hacer demasiado
overdraft descubierto, giro en descubierto
overdraw (v) sobregirar
overdue atrasado, vencido
overdue account cuenta al descubierto
overdue bills efectos pendientes de pago
overestimate (v) sobrestimar
overexpose (v) sobreexponer
overflow (v) rebosar, desbordarse
overflow exceso de capacidad
overgrown sobrecrecido
overhang (v) colgar
overhaul (v) repasar, revisar
overhead por lo alto
overhead costs costes operacionales
overland por tierra
overlap (v) sobreponerse
overlap solape
overlay recubrimiento
overlay (v) cubrir, sobreponer
overload sobrecarga; soborno (Arg., Bol, Chile)
overlook (v) vigilar, olvidar
overnight al día siguiente, por la noche
override (v) invalidar
overripe fruit borracho (Chile)
overrule (v) anular
overseas extranjero, ultramar
oversight descuido
oversleep (v) quedarse dormido
overt público, patente

overtake (v) alcanzar, sorprender

overthrow (v) derribar

overtime horas suplementarias de trabajo, tiempo suplementario; faena (Guat.)

overturn (v) trastornar, derribar

overweight demasiado pesado

overwhelm (v) aplastar, arrollar

overwhelming aplastante

overwork trabajo excesivo

overwrought sobreexcitado

ovulation ovulación

owe (v) deber

owing adeudado, debido

own propio, lo suyo

owner dueño, propietario

ownership propiedad, posesión

oxygen oxígeno

P

pace paso, marcha

pacemaker marcador de pasos

pacific pacífico

Pacific Ocean Océano Pacífico

pacifist pacifista

pacify (v) pacificar

pack (v) cargar, empaquetar

pack carga, paquete

package embalaje, bulto, paquete

packaging embalaje, envase

packet paquete

packing embalaje

packing list lista de contenido

pact acuerdo, pacto

pad almohadilla

pad (v) acolchar

padding relleno, acolchado

paddle canalete, paleta

paddle (v) chapotear, remar

padlock candado

page (v) buscar, llamar

page botones, página, paje

page frame trama de página

pageant desfile

pageantry espectacular

pagination paginación

paid pagado

paid in full totalmente pagado

pain (v) doler

pain dolor, pena

pain killer calmante

painful doloroso

painless sin dolor

painstaking laborioso

paint pintura

paint (v) pintar

pair par, pareja

pajamas pijama

pal compinche, amigo

palace palacio

palatable sabroso

palate paladar

pale pálido

Palestinian palestino

palm palma (de mano), palmera

palpitation palipitación

palpitations palpitaciones

palsy parálisis

paltry miserable

pamper (v) mimar

pamphlet folleto, octavilla

pan cazuela, sartén

Panama Panamá

pancake torta, tortita

pancreas páncreas

panel panel

paneling paneles

panic pánico, terror

panic (v) perder la calma
panorama panorama
pantomine pantomina
pantry despensa
pants pantalones
paper papel
paperback libro de bolsillo
paper clip sujetapapeles; broche (Chile)
paper work administración
par equivalencia
par value valor a la par
parachute paracaídas
parade desfile
paradise paraíso
paradox paradoja
paragraph párrafo
parallel paralelo
parallel processing procesamiento en paralelo
parallel to serial converter convertidor de paralelo a serie
parallel transmission transmisión en paralelo
paralysis parálisis
paralytic paralítico
paralyze (v) paralizar
paramedics practicantes
parameter parámetro
paramount superior
paramount title título superior
paranoia paranoia
paranoid paranoico
paraph rúbrica
paraphernalia bienes parafernales, mobiliario
parasite parásito
parcel paquete
parcel post paquete postal
parcenary herencia conjunta
parcener coheredero
pardon indulto, perdón
pare (v) cortar, reducir

parent padre, madre
parent company empresa matriz
parental paternal
parenthesis paréntesis
parenthood paternidad
parish parroquia
parishioner feligrés
parity igualdad, paridad
park parque, aparcamiento
parking estacionamiento
parking meter parquímetro
Parkinson's disease enfermedad de Parkinson
parliament parlamento
parlor sala, salón
parochial parroquial
parody parodia
parol verbal
parol contract contrato verbal
parole libertad condicional
paroxysm paroxismo
parricide parricida
part (v) dividir, separar
part parte, trozo
part-time a horas
partial parcial
participant partícipe, participante
participate (v) participar
participation participación
participle participio
particle partícula, átomo
particular especial, concreto
particular lien gravamen específico
particulars detalles
partisan partidario
partition partición, segmento
partner socio
partnership asociación
party fiesta, parte, partido
pass (v) aprobar, pasar; alcanzar (Amer.)

pass paso, pase, permiso, tránsito

pass a law (v) aprobar una ley

passenger pasajero

passerby transeúnte

passion pasión; pelota (Cuba, Mex.)

passionate apasionado

passive pasivo

passport pasaporte

password contraseña

past pasado, por delante

past due bills efectos pendientes de pago

pasta pasta de harina

paste (v) engomar, pegar

pastel pastel, pintura

pasteurize (v) pasteurizar

pastime pasatiempo

pastry pasta

pasture pasto

pasture in winter (v) invernar (Arg., Uru.)

pasturing fee piso (Cuba)

pat (v) tocar, acariciar

patch (v) componer, parchar

patch pedazo, remiendo

patchy desigual

patent patente

patent law derecho patentario

patent lawyer abogado de patentes

paternal paternal

paternity paternidad

path paso, trayecto, senda

pathetic patético

pathologist patólogo

patience paciencia

patient paciente

patio patio

patricide parricida

patrimonial patrimonial

patrimony patrimonio

patriot patriota

patriotic patriótico

patriotism patriotismo

patrol patrulla

patrol (v) patrullar

patrol car perseguidor (Cuba)

patron cliente

patronage protección

patronize (v) patrocinar, favorecer

patronizing protector

patter golpeteo, jerga

patter (v) golpetear

pattern modelo, diseño

paunch panza, barriga

pauper mendigo, pobre

pause pausa, intervalo

pavement pavimento

pavilion pabellón, caseta

paw garra, pata

pawn empeño, garantía, instrumento, peón, prenda

pawn (v) empeñar, aventurar

pawn shop agencia (Chile); empeño (Mex., Arg., Uru.)

pawned bills efectos pignorados

pay paga, retribución

pay (v) pagar

pay back (v) restituir

pay by check pagadero con cheque

pay damages (v) pagar daños

pay up (v) aflojar (Amer., coll.)

pay workers (v) rayar (Mex.)

payable pagadero

payable to bearer pagadero al portador

payable on demand pagadero a la vista

payable at sight pagadero a la vista

payday día de paga

payee beneficiario, beneficiario

del pago, portador, portador del pago, tenedor

payer pagador, remitente

payment pago

payment by transfer pago por transferencia

payment in advance pago por anticipado

payment in cash pago al contado

payment order orden de pago

payment terms forma de pago

payoff resultado final

payroll nómina, nómina de personal

payroll expenses gastos de personal

peace paz, calma

peaceful pacífico

peacemaker conciliador

peak punta, cumbre

peal repique

pearl perla

peasant campesino

pebble guija, piedra

peck (v) picar

peck picotazo

peculation desfalco

peculiar peculiar, especial

pecuniary monetario

pedal pedal

peddle (v) vender (ambulante)

peddler vendedor ambulante

pedestal pedestal

pedestrian peatón

pediatrics pediatría

pedigree genealogía, linaje

peel (v) pelar

peel piel

peep (v) mirar furtivamente

peep mirada, ojeada

peer igual, par

peerless incomparable

peg pinza, clavija

Peking Pekín

pelt (v) arrojar, tirar

pelt pellejo, piel

pelvis pelvis

pen bolígrafo, corral

penal penal

penal action acción penal

penal clause cláusula penal

penal laws leyes penales

penal suit juicio penal

penalize (v) penalizar

penalties multas, sanciones

penalty multa, castigo

penance penitencia

pencil lápiz

pencil sharpener sacapuntas

pendant medallón, pendiente

pendency pendencia

pending pendiente

pendulum péndulo

penetrate (v) penetrar

penetration penetración

penicillin penicilina

peninsula península

penis pene, bicho (Amer.)

penitent penitente

penitentiary penitenciaria

pennant banderola

pension pensión, retiro

pension fund fondo de pensiones

pensioner pensionista

pensions pensiones

pensive pensativo

pentagon pentágono

penthouse ático

people gente, pueblo

pepper pimienta

per por, a

per cent por ciento

per diem por día

perceivable perceptible

perceive (v) percibir, notar
percent porcentaje
percentage porcentaje
perceptible perceptible
perception percepción
perceptive perspicaz
perch (v) posarse, sentarse
percolate (v) filtrar, colar
percolator cafetera
percussion percusión
peremptory perentorio
peremptory plea instancia perentoria
peremptory rule fallo definitivo
perennial perenne
perfect perfecto
perfect (v) perfeccionar
perfection perfección
perfectionist perfeccionista
perfidy perfidia
perforation perforación
perform (v) realizar, cumplir
performance acción, cumplimiento, ejecución
performance bond garantía de ejecución
perfume perfume
perhaps tal vez, quizás
pericardium pericardio
peril peligro, riesgo
perilous peligroso
perimeter perímetro
period período
period of grace período de gracia
periodic periódico
periodical periódico, revista
peripheral periférico
periphery periferia
periscope periscopio
perish (v) deteriorar
perishable perecedero
peritonitis peritonitis

perjure (v) perjurar
perjurer perjuro
perjury perjurio
perk (v) reanimar
perky alegre
permanent permanente
permanent capital capital permanente
permanent storage memoria permanente
permeable permeable
permeate (v) penetrar, saturar
permissible permisible, lícito
permission permiso
permissive permisivo
permit licencia, permiso
permit (v) permitir, autorizar
pernicious pernicioso
perpendicular perpendicular
perpetrate (v) cometer
perpetration comisión
perpetrator autor, perpetrador, responsable
perpetual perpetuo
perpetual inventory method método de inventario perpetuo
perpetual statute ley permanente
perpetuity perpetuidad
perplex (v) confundir
perplexed perplejo, confuso
perplexing confuso
perquisites emolumentos
persecute (v) perseguir
perseverance perseverancia
persevere (v) perseverar
persist (v) continuar, persistir
persistence persistencia
persistent persistente
person persona
personal personal, privado
personal computer ordenador personal

personal contract contrato personal

personal exemption exención personal

personal liability responsabilidad personal

personal tort agravio personal

personality personalidad

personally personalmente

personification personificación

personify (v) personificar

personnel personal

perspective perspectiva

perspiration sudor

perspire (v) sudar, transpirar

persuade (v) persuadir

persuasion persuasión

persuasive persuasivo

pert impertinente

pertain (v) pertenecer a

pertinent pertinente

perturb (v) perturbar

perturbation perturbación

Peru Perú

perusal lectura cuidadosa

peruse (v) leer con atención

perverse perverso

pervert pervertido

pervert (v) pervertir

pessimism pesimismo

pessimist pesimista

pessimistic pesimista

pest plaga, insecto

pester (v) molestar, acosar

pesticide pesticida

pet animal doméstico

pet (v) acariciar

petal pétalo

petition petición

petitioner peticionario

petrify (v) petrificar

petrol gasolina

petroleum petróleo

pettifogger picapleitos

petty insignificante

petty cash caja pequeña, gastos menores

petty jury jurado de juicio

petty larceny hurto menor

petulant malhumorado

pew asiento, banco

phalanges falanges

phantom fantasma

pharmaceutical farmacéutico

pharmacist farmacéutico

pharmacy farmacia

pharynx faringe

phase fase, etapa

phenomenal fenomenal

phenomenon fenómeno

philanthropic filantrópico

philatelic filatélico

philosopher filósofo

philosophy filosofía

phimosis fimosis

phlebitis flebitis

phobia fobia

phonetic fonético

phonetics fonética

phony falso, postizo

photo foto

photocopier fotocopiadora

photocopy fotocopia

photograph fotografía

photograph (v) fotografiar

photographer fotógrafo

photographic fotográfico

photography fotografía

phrase frase, expresión

physical físico

physical inventory inventario físico

physical obsolescence obsolescencia física

physician médico, médica

physiological fisiológico

physiotherapy fisioterapia
physique físico
pianist pianista
piano piano
pick lo mejor, pico
pick (v) picar, romper
pickpocket carterista
pickup recolección
picnic comida campestre
pictorial gráfico, ilustrado
picture cuadro, película
picture frame marco de cuadro
picture gallery sala de arte
pie tarta
piece pedazo, trozo
piecemeal poco a poco
piecework trabajo a destajo
pier muelle, embarcadero
pierce (v) penetrar, atravesar
piercing cortante, penetrante
piety piedad, devoción
pig cerdo, puerco
pigment pigmento
pignoration pignoración
pigskin piel de cerdo
pile masa, montón, pila; alto
  (Amer.)
pile (v) amontonar
**pile of fruit or vegetables (in a
  market)** mono (Chile)
piles hemorroides
pileup accidente múltiple
pilfer (v) hurtar
pilferage hurto, robo de mercancías
pilferer ratero
pilgrim peregrino
pilgrimage peregrinación
pill píldora
pillage saqueo
pillar columna, pilar; estanque
  (Amer.)
pillow almohada

pilot piloto
pilot (v) pilotar, guiar
pimp alcahuete, chulo
pimple grano
pin alfiler, clavija
pin (v) prender el alfiler
pinch apuro, pellizco
pinch (v) apretar
pioneer pionero
pioneer patent patente básica
pipe tubo, pipa
pipeline tubería
piping tubería
pique piquete
pique (v) picar, herir
piracy piratería
pirate pirata
pirate (v) plagiar
piss orina
pistol pistola
piston pistón, émbolo
pitch campo, lanzamiento
pitch (v) lanzar, tirar
pitfall escollo, trampa
pithy jugoso, expresivo
pittance miseria
pity piedad, compasión
pivot pivote
placard cartel, letrero
placate (v) aplacar, apaciguar
place lugar, sitio
place (v) colocar, poner
place of payment lugar de pago
placemat piso (Chile, Perú)
placenta placenta
plagiarist plagiario
plagiarize (v) plagiar
plague plaga, peste
plain sencillo, franco, banco
  (Col.); plan (Arg., Chile, Guat.,
  Mex., Ven.)
plain-clothes con traje de calle
plaint querella

plaintiff demandante, querellante
plan plan, programa
plane avión, plano
planet planeta
plant equipo, planta
plant (v) plantar, sembrar
plant assets activos de producción
plantation plantación
plaque placa
plasma plasma
plaster enlucido, enyesado, yeso
plastic plástico
plate (v) chapear, platear
plate plato, lámina
plateau banco (Arg., Col., Uru.); plan (Arg., Chile, Guat., Mex., Ven.)
platform plataforma
platter palangana (C. Am., Col.)
plausibility verosimilitud
plausible verosímil
play juego, diversión
play (v) jugar, representar
player jugador, actor
playground patio de recreo
playhouse teatro
plea alegato, defensa, pretexto
plead (v) alegar, defender
plead guilty (v) declararse culpable, declaración de culpabilidad
pleader abogado
pleading alegación
pleasant agradable
please por favor
please (v) agradar, contentar
pleased alegre, contento
pleasing agradable, grato
pleasure placer, gusto
plebiscite plebiscito
pledge (v) ayudar, empeñar, prendar, prometer

pledge empeño, caución
plenary plenario
plenipotentiary plenipotenciario
plenty abundancia
pleura pleura
plevin garantía
pliable flexible, plegable
pliers alicates
plight condición, situación
plod (v) caminar despacio
plot complot, parcela; placer (Cuba)
plow arado
plow (v) arar, surcar
plug enchufe, tapón
plug (v) enchufar, taponar
plummet (v) caer a plomo
plump rechoncho, rollizo
plunder pillaje, saqueo
plunderer saqueador
plunge inmersión, zambullida
plunge (v) sumergir, hundir
plural plural
plus más, además de
plush felpa
plushy lujoso, elegante
ply capa, pliegue
ply (v) manejar
plywood contrachapada
pneumonia neumonía
poach (v) escalfar, robar
poached escalfado
poacher cazador furtivo
pocket bolsillo
pocket calculator calculadora de bolsillo
pod vaina
podiatry podiatría
poetic poético
poetry poesía
poignant conmovedor
point aspecto, punto
point (v) indicar, señalar

point of sale punto de venta
pointed puntiagudo
pointing device apuntador
pointless inútil, sin motivo
poise (v) equilibrar
poise equilibrio
poison veneno, tóxico
poisoning envenenamiento
poke (v) empujar, remover
poker atizador, póquer
Poland Polonia
polar polar
pole palo, polo
police policía
police (v) vigilar
police car bola (Col.)
police court juzgado de guardia
policeman policía, guardia
policy póliza, política
policyholder tenedor de póliza
poligamy poligamia
polio polio
poliomyelitis poliomielitis
polish brillo, betún
polite atento, cortés
politeness cortesía
political político
political law derecho político
politician político
politics política
poll encuesta, votación
pollen polen
polling votación
pollute (v) contaminar
pollution contaminación
polo polo
polyester poliéster
polyp pólipo
polytechnic politécnico
pomp pompa
pompous pomposo
poncho manta (Arg.); manga
  (Mex.)

pond estanque, charco
ponder (v) ponderar
pool consorcio, piscina
poor pobre
poor horserider músico (C.
  Am.)
pop (v) estallar, reventar
pope Papa
popular popular
popularity popularidad
popularize (v) popularizar
populate (v) poblar
population población
porch pórtico, portal
pore poro
pork carne de cerdo
pornographic pornográfico
pornography pornografía
porous poroso
port puerto
port of destination puerto de
  destino
portable portátil
portable computer ordenador
  portátil
portent presagio, augurio
porter portero, mozo
portfolio cartera
portion porción, parte
portrait retrato
portray (v) retratar
portrayal retrato
Portugal Portugal
Portuguese portugués
pose postura
pose (v) colocarse, posar
posh elegante
position posición
positive positivo
positive defense defensa positiva
positive fraud fraude flagrante
possess (v) poseer
possession posesión

possessive dominante, posesivo
possessor tenedor
possessory posesorio
possessory lien gravamen posesorio
possibility posibilidad
possible posible
post correo, poste
post office oficina de correos
postage franqueo, gastos de correo
postal postal
postcard tarjeta postal
postdate postdata, posdata
postdated posfechado
poster cartel
posterior posterior
posteriority posterioridad
posterity posteridad, posterioridad
posting entrada (en los libros)
postmark matasellos
postmaster administrador
postpartum postnatal
postpone (v) aplazar, retrasar
postponement aplazamiento, retraso
postprocessor postcompilador
postscript postdata, posdata
posture actitud, postura
pot olla, pote
potato patata
potato dessert bocadillo (Cuba, Hond.)
potent potente
potential posible, potencial
pothole bache
pottery cerámica
poultry aves, volatería
pounce ataque, salto
pounce (v) atacar de repente
pound libra
pound (v) machacar, golpear

pour (v) derramar, verter
poverty pobreza
powder polvo, pólvora
powder (v) pulverizar
power poder, potencia
power (v) accionar, impulsar
power of attorney carta de poderes, poder legal, poderes
power supply fuente de alimentación
powerful poderoso
powerless impotente
pox erupción dérmica
practicable factible
practical joke broma pesada
practice (v) ejercer, practicar
practice costumbre, ejercicio, práctica
practitioner especialista médico, profesional
pragmatic pragmático
prairie pradera
praise alabanza, elogio
praise (v) alabar, elogiar
prance (v) bailar, saltar
prank travesura
pray (v) rogar, suplicar
prayer oración, petición, rezo
pre-emption prioridad
preach (v) predicar
preacher predicador
preamble preámbulo
precarious precario
precatory suplicante
precaution precaución
precede (v) preceder
precedence prioridad
precedent precedente
precept precepto
precinct distrito, recinto
precious precioso
precipice precipicio
precipitate apresurado

precipitation precipitación
precise exacto, preciso
preclude (v) excluir, impedir
precocious precoz
preconceived malice malicia premeditada
precondition condición precedente
precontractual precontractual
precursor precursor
predator predator, rapaz
predecessor predecesor
predestine (v) predestinar
predicament apuro
predicate (v) predicar, proclamar
predicate predicado
predict (v) predecir
predictable pronosticable
prediction predicción
predominance predominio
predominant predominante
preeminent superior
preemptive rights derechos de prioridad
preface prólogo
prefer (v) preferir
preference preferencia
preferential preferente
preferred preferido
preferred stock acciones preferentes
prefix prefijo
pregnancy embarazo
pregnant embarazada
prehistoric prehistórico
prejudge (v) prejuzgar
prejudgment prejuicio
prejudice parcialidad
prejudice (v) predisponer
prejudiced interesado, parcial
preliminary preliminar
prelude preludio
premature prematuro

premeditate (v) premeditar
premeditated premeditado
premeditation premeditación
premenstrual premenstrual
premier primero
premiere estreno
premise premisa, local
premises establecimiento
premium premio, prima
premonition presentimiento
preoccupation preocupación
preoccupied preocupado
prepaid pagado con antelación
prepaid expenses gastos anticipados
preparation preparación
preparatory preparatorio
prepare (v) preparar
prepayment pago anticipado
preposition preposición
preprocessor precompilador
prerogative prerrogativa
prerogative court tribunal testamentario
prescribe (v) prescribir
prescription prescripción, receta
prescriptive prescriptivo
presence presencia
present (v) presentar, ofrecer
present actual, presente, regalo
present value valor actual
presentable presentable
presentation presentación
presently actualmente
preservation conservación
preservative preservativo
preserve confitura, conserva
preserved en conserva
preside (v) presidir
presidency presidencia
president presidente
presidential presidencial
press (v) apretar, presionar

press prensa, presión
pressing urgente
pressure presión, urgencia
pressure gauge manómetro
pressure points puntos de compresión
pressurized a presión
prestige prestigio
presume (v) presumir, suponer
presumption atrevimiento, presunción
presumptive presuntivo
presumptuous presuntuoso
pretax earnings beneficios antes de impuestos
pretence (v) pretensión
pretend (v) fingir, aparentar
pretext pretexto
pretty guapo, precioso
prevail (v) prevalecer
prevailing predominante
prevailing rates of interest tipo de interés prevaleciente
prevalent predominante
prevent (v) impedir, evitar
prevention prevención
preventive preventivo
preventive arrest detención preventiva
preventive medicine medicina preventiva
preview anticipo, preestreno
previous anterior, previo
previously previamente
prey (v) atacar, devorar
prey presa, víctima
price (v) evaluar, valorar
price precio
price ceiling precio límite
price-level adjustments ajustes en el nivel de precio
price list lista de precios
price range gama de precios

pride orgullo, soberbia
priest cura, sacerdote
priesthood sacerdocio
primary primario, principal
primary liability responsabilidad directa
primary rights derechos primarios
prime primero, principal
prime rate tasa de interés, tasa preferencial
primitive primitivo
prince príncipe
princess princesa
principal jefe, principal, principal (del préstamo)
principle principio
principles of consolidation principios de consolidación
print (v) grabar, imprimir
print marca, impresión
printed impreso
printer impresora
printing imprenta, tipografía
printout impresión
prior anterior, previo
prior negligence negligencia indirecta
priority prioridad
prison cárcel, prisión
prisoner prisionero
privacy confidencial, intimidad, reserva, reservado
private privado
private bank banca privada
private law derecho privado
private rights derechos particulares
private seal sello particular
privative privativo
privies copartícipes
privilege privilegio
privileged privilegiado

prize (v) apreciar, estimar
prize premio
prize court tribunaL de presas
pro-forma invoice factura pro-
forma
probability probabilidad
probability theory teoría de
probabilidades
probable probable
probably probablemente
probate (v) validar
probate jurisdiction derecho de
sucesiones
probation libertad condicional
probe (v) investigar, sondear
probe sonda
problem problema
problematic problemático
procedural procesal
procedure procedimiento
proceed (v) continuar, proceder
proceeding procedimiento, proceso, trámite
process proceso
process (v) preparar, procesar,
tratar
processal procesal
procession desfile
processor procesador
proclaim (v) proclamar
proclamation edicto, proclamación
procreation procreación
proctor procurador
procuration fee comisión sobre
un préstamo
procurator procurador
procure (v) obtener
prod (v) empujar
prodigious prodigioso
prodigy prodigio
produce (v) presentar, producir
produce producto de granja

producer productor
product producto
product cost coste del producto
production producción
productive productivo
productivity productividad
profane profano
profanity profanidad
profess (v) declarar, profesar
profession profesión
professional profesional
professional ethics ética profesional
professor profesor
proficiency habilidad, pericia
proficient hábil, perito
profile perfil
profit beneficio, provecho
profit (v) beneficiarse
profit-loss statement cuenta de
pérdidas y ganancias
profit margin margen de beneficio
profitable provechoso
profound profundo
profoundly profundamente
profuse pródigo, profuso
profusion profusión, abundancia
program programa
program flowchart lógica del
programa
program module módulo de
programa
programmable logic array matriz lógica programable
programmer programador
programming programación
programming flowchart organigrama de programación
programming language lenguaje
de programación
programming module módulo
de programación
progress (v) progresar

progress progreso
progression progresión
progressive progresivo
prohibit (v) prohibir
prohibition prohibición
project (v) proyectar, resaltar
project proyecto
projectile proyectil
projection proyección
projector proyector
proletarian proletario
proliferate (v) multiplicar
proliferation proliferación
prolific prolífico
prologue prólogo
prolong (v) prolongar
prolongation prolongación
promenade paseo
prominence importancia
prominent destacado, eminente
promiscuity libertinaje
promiscuous inmoral, libertino
promise promesa
promise (v) asegurar, prometer
promising prometedor
promisor prometedor
promissory promisorio
promissory note nota, nota de deuda, pagaré, reconocimiento de deuda, reconocimiento de pago
promissory oath juramento promisorio
promote (v) fomentar, promover
promotion promoción
prompt inmediato, pronto
prompt (v) apuntar
prompt payment pronto pago
prompter apuntador
prone dispuesto a
pronoun pronombre
pronounce (v) pronunciar
pronouncement declaración, pronunciamiento

pronunciation pronunciación
proof (v) demostrar, probar
proof prueba
prop (v) apoyar, sostener
prop apoyo
propaganda propaganda
propagate (v) propagar
propel (v) impulsar, propulsar
propeller hélice
proper apropiado, propio
proper evidence prueba admisible
properly correctamente
property propiedad
property taxes impuesto sobre la propiedad
property tort agravio a la propiedad
prophecy profecía
proponent proponente
proportion proporción
proportional proporcional
proposal propuesta
propose (v) ofrecer, proponer
proposition proposición
proprietary propietario
proprietor propietario
proprietorship patrimonio, propiedad
propriety corrección, decencia
propulsion propulsión
prorogue (v) prorrogar
proscribe (v) proscribir
proscription proscripción
prose prosa
prosecute (v) demandar, procesar
prosecution causa, proceso, procesamiento
prosecutor fiscal
prospect perspectiva, posible cliente, vista
prospect (v) explorar

prospective anticipado, esperado
prospectus programa
prosper (v) favorecer, prosperar
prosperity prosperidad
prosperous próspero
prostate próstata
prostitute prostituta
prostitution prostitución
prostrate (v) postrar
prostration postración
protagonist protagonista
protect (v) proteger
protection protección
protective protector, protectivo
protege protegido
protein proteína
protest protesta
protest (v) protestar
Protestant protestante
protestee protestado
protester protestador
protocol protocolo
prototype prototipo
protractor transportador
protrude (v) sacar afuera
protruding saliente
proud orgulloso
prove (v) demostrar, probar
proverb proverbio
proverbial proverbial
provide (v) proporcionar, dar
provided siempre que
providence providencia
provident previsor
providential providencial
province provincia
provincial provincial
provision provisión
provisional provisional
provocation provocación
provocative provocativo
provoke (v) causar, producir; buscar (Arg., Uru., Chile, Mex.)

prow proa
prowess destreza, habilidad
prowl ronda
prowl (v) rondar
prowler rondador
proximity proximidad
proxy apoderado, poder(es)
prudence prudencia
prudent prudente
prune (v) podar
psalm salmo
pseudonym seudónimo
psoriasis psoriasis
psychiatry psiquiatría
psychoanalyst psicoanalista
psychologist psicólogo
psychology psicología
psychopath psicópata
psychopathy psicopatía
psychosis psicosis
pub bar, taberna
puberty pubertad
pubic púbico
pubis pubis
public público
public attorney abogado
public clerk evangelista (Mex.)
public law derecho público
public notice aviso público
public offering suscripción pública
public service servicio público
public warehouse suscripción pública
publication publicación
publicity publicidad
publicize (v) anunciar, publicar
publish (v) publicar
publisher editor
publishing publicación
pudding pudín
puddle pozo (Chile, Col.)
puerile pueril

puff racha, soplo
pull estirón, tirón; vara (Perú)
pull (v) sacar, tirar
pulley polea
pullout retirada
pullover jersey
pulmonary pulmonar
pulp pulpa, pasta
pulpit púlpito
pulsate (v) pulsar
pulsation pulsación
pulse pulso
pulverize (v) pulverizar
puma león (Amer.)
pump bomba
pump (v) bombear, elevar
punch golpe, puñetazo; truco (Chile)
punch (v) golpear, perforar
punched card carta perforada
punctual puntual
punctuality puntualidad
punctuate (v) puntuar
punctuation puntuación
puncture perforación, pinchazo
pungent picante
punish (v) castigar; limpiar (Mex.)
punishable castigable
punishment castigo
punitive punitivo
punitive damages daños punitivos
punter jugador
puny débil
pupil alumno, pupila (del ojo)
puppet marioneta, títere

puppy cachorro
purchase compra
purchase (v) comprar
purchase discount descuento de compra
purchase method método de compra
purchase order pedido
purchase price precio de compra
purchaser comprador
pure puro
purgatory purgatorio
purge (v) depurar, disculpar, purgar
purge purga
purify (v) purificar
purity pureza
purloin (v) hurtar
purple morado
purport significado
purpose intención, propósito
purr (v) ronronear
purse bolsa, premio
pursuant to según
pursue (v) acosar, seguir
pursuer perseguidor
pursuit perseguimiento
pus pus, humor
push (v) empujar, presionar
push empuje, ofensiva; viaje (C. Am.)
put (v) colocar, poner
putrid podrido
puzzle rompecabezas
puzzling enigmático
pyramid pirámide

Q

quadrangle cuadrángulo
quadrant cuadrante

quadriplegia cuadriplegia
quadruped cuadrúpedo

quadruple cuádruple
quagmire atolladero, cenagal
quaint curioso
quake (v) estremecerse, temblar
qualification aptitud, reserva
qualified apto, calificado, competente
qualify (v) calificar, estudiar,
habilitar
quality calidad, categoría
quality control control de calidad
quandary apuro, dilema
quantity cantidad
quarantine cuarentena
quarrel (v) disputar, reñir
quarrel disputa, pelea; bola
(Mex.)
quarrelsome pendenciero
quarter cuarto, cuarta parte
quarterly trimestral
quartermaster comisario, furriel
quartet cuarteto
quash (v) invalidar
quaver temblor
queen reina
quell (v) calmar, reprimir
quench (v) apagar
query (v) preguntar
query pregunta
quest busca, búsqueda

question (v) dudar de, preguntar
question pregunta
questionable discutible, dudoso
questionar interrogador
questionnaire cuestionario
quick rápido, pronto
quick assets activo disponible
quick charger cargador rápido
quicken (v) acelerar, apresurar
quicklime óxido de calcio
quickly rápidamente
quicksilver mercurio
quiet (v) calmar
quiet quieto, tranquilo
quietness silencio
quilt abrigo (Arg.)
quilt (v) acolchar
quinine quinina
quintet quinteto
quirk peculiaridad
quit (v) abandonar, dimitir
quite completamente
quittance finiquito
quiver (v) temblar
quiver temblor
quiz examen
quorum quórum
quota cuota, cupo
quotation cita, cotización, oferta
quotation marks comillas
quote (v) citar, cotizar

R

rabbi rabino
rabbit conejo
rabble canalla, chusma; lana (C.
Am.)
rabid rabioso
rabies rabia
race carrera, raza
race (v) competir, correr

racehorse caballo de carreras
racket alboroto, extorsión, raqueta, ruido
racketeer extorsionador
racketeering extorsión
radar radar
radial radial
radiance radiación

radiant radiante, brillante
radiate (v) difundir, radiar
radiate radiado
radiation radiación
radiator radiador
radical radical
radio (v) radiar, transmitir
radio radio
radio control control remoto
radioactive radioactivo
radioactivity radioactividad
radiography radiografía
radiologist radiólogo
radiology radiología
radius radio
raffle (v) rifar, sortear
raffle rifa, sorteo
raffle ticket acción (Perú)
raft almadía, balsa
rag (v) bromear, burlar
rag trapo
rage (v) estar furioso
rage furor, rabia
ragged harapiento, roto
raging furioso, rabioso
raid ataque, incursión
raider incursos, invasor
rail barandilla, carril
railroad ferrocarril, tren
railway ferrocarril, tren
railway transport transporte por ferrocarril
rain (v) llover
rain lluvia
rainbow arco iris
raincoat impermeable
raindrop gota de agua
rainfall precipitación
rainwater agua de lluvia
rainy lluvioso
raise (v) aumentar, subir
raise aumento, subida
ramble (v) divagar, pasear

ramble excursión, paseo
ramp rampa
rampage desboque, desmán
ranch hacienda, rancho
rancor rencor
random aleatorio, fortuito
random access memory acceso aleatorio, memoria de acceso aleatorio
random access storage memoria de acceso directo
random processing proceso aleatorio
range alcance, extensión
range of goods surtido de productos
rank categoría, fila
ransack (v) registrar
ransom rescate
rap (v) golpear, tocar
rap golpecito
rape (v) forzar, violar
rape rapto, violación
rapid rápido
rapidity rapidez
rapids rápidos
rapist violador
rapport armonía, concordia
rapture éxtasis, rapto
rare poco común, raro
rascal pícaro, pillo
rash erupción
rat canalla, rata
rate (v) estimar, valorar
rate proporción, tasa, tipo
rate of interest tasa de interés
rather más bien, bastante
ratify (v) ratificar
rating clasificación
ratio coeficiente, índice, proporción, relación
ration ración, víveres
rational lógico, racional

rational doubt duda razonable
rationale razón fundamental
rationalize (v) hacer racional
rattle sonajero
rattle (v) agitar, tabletear
raucous estridente
ravage destrozo, estrago
rave (v) delirar, desvariar
ravine barranca
ravish (v) encantar, violar
ravish rapto, violar
ravishing encantador
raw crudo, bruto
raw materials materia prima
rawness crudeza
ray rayo
rayon rayón
razor navaja
razor blade hoja de afeitar
re-examination reexaminación
reach (v) alcanzar, llegar a
reach alcance, extensión
react (v) reaccionar
reaction reacción
reactionary reaccionario
reactor reactor
read (v) interpretar, leer
read only memory memoria
  inalterable
reading lectura
readjust (v) reajustar
readjustment reajuste
ready listo, preparado
ready-made confeccionado, hecho
ready money fondos disponibles
reaffirm (v) reafirmar
real real, verdadero
real estate bienes raíces, inmue-
  bles
real estate investment trust
  fondo de inversión en bienes
  raíces

real evidence evidencia real
real law ley real
real right derecho real
real time tiempo real
real time processing procesamiento a tiempo real
real time simulation simulación
  en tiempo real
realist realista
reality realidad
realizable realizable
realize (v) darse cuenta
realization comprensión
realm esfera, reino
realty bienes raíces
reap (v) cosechar
reaping siega
reappear (v) reaparecer
reappraisal reevalúo
rear detrás, trasero
rear (v) erigir, levantar; reparar
  (un caballo) (Mex., Guat.)
rear admiral contraalmirante
rear-view retrovisor
rearguard retaguardia
rearrange (v) volver a arreglar
rearrangement nueva adaptación
rearrest (v) arrestar de nuevo
reason (v) razonar que
reason motivo, razón
reasonable razonable
reasonable doubt duda razonable
reasoning racional, argumento
reassurance noticia
reassure (v) tranquilizar
reassuring tranquilizador
rebate descuento, rebaja
rebate (v) descontar, rebajar
rebellion rebelión
rebellious rebelde
rebound rebote

rebound (v) rebotar
rebuff repulsa
rebuff (v) rechazar
rebuild (v) reconstruir
rebuke reprimenda
rebuttal refutación
recall aviso, llamada
recall (v) llamar, retirar
recant (v) retractar
recap (v) recubrir
recap recapitulación
recapture (v) recobrar
recapture recobro, reconquista
recede (v) retroceder
receipt recibo
receivables cuentas a cobrar
receive (v) cobrar, recibir
receiver administrador judicial, liquidador, receptor
receivership administración judicial
recent nuevo, reciente
receptacle receptáculo
reception recepción
receptionist recepcionista
receptive receptivo
recess descanso, receso, vacación
recession recesión, retroceso
recharge (v) recargar
recharger recargador
recipe receta
recipient destinatario
reciprocal recíproco
reciprocate (v) intercambiar
reciprocity reciprocidad
recital recital, concierto
recite (v) narrar, referir
reckless imprudente, temerario
recklessness imprudencia
reckon (v) contar, calcular
reckoning cálculo, cuenta
reclaim (v) reclamar, rescatar

reclamation reclamación
recline (v) apoyar, descansar
recluse solitario
recognition reconocimiento
recognizable reconocible
recognize (v) reconocer
recoil retroceso
recoil (v) retroceder
recollect (v) recordar
recollection recuerdo
recommend (v) recomendar
recommendation recomendación
recompense recompensa
recompense (v) recompensar
reconcile (v) ajustar, reconciliar
reconsider (v) reconsiderar
reconstruct (v) reconstruir
reconstruction reconstrucción
reconvene (v) convocar de nuevo
record (v) apuntar, registrar
record documento, registro, disco, acta, expediente, informe, record
recorded grabado
recorder contador, registro
recording grabación, registro
records archivos, registros
recount (v) contar, referir
recoup (v) recobrar, recuperar
recourse recurso
recover (v) recuperar
recoverable recuperable
recovery recuperación
recovery procedure proceso de restablecimiento
recreation recreación
recriminate (v) recriminar
recrimination recriminación
recruit (v) reclutar
recruit recluta
recruitment reclutamiento

rectangle rectángulo
rectangular rectangular
rectify (v) rectificar
rectum recto
recuperate (v) recuperar
recuperation recuperación
recur (v) repetirse, volver
recurrence repetición
recurrent constante, repetido
recusable recusable
recusation recusación
recuse (v) recusar
red rojo
Red Cross Cruz Roja
red handed in fraganti
red tape papeleo
redeem (v) amortizar, redimir
redeemable rescatable
redeemable loan empréstito amortizable
redemption reembolso, rescate, redención
redemption gains beneficios de reembolsos
redemption of bonds rescate de bonos
redhaired pelirrojo
redirect (v) reexpedir
rediscount redescuento
redress compensación, remedio, reparación
redress (v) rectificar
reduce (v) rebajar, reducir
reduction rebaja, reducción
redundancy exceso
redundant escesivo
reel (v) devanar, tambalear
refer (v) atribuir, referir, remitir
referee árbitro
reference referencia, relación
referendum referéndum
refill (v) recambiar, rellenar
refill recambio, repuesto

refine (v) purificar, refinar
refinement refinamiento
refinery refinería
reflect (v) reflejar, pensar
reflection reflexión, reproche
reflex reflejo
reflexive reflexivo
reform reforma
reform (v) reformar
reformation reformación
reformed reformado
refract (v) refractar
refrain (v) abstenerse
refresh (v) refrescar
refresher refresco
refreshing refrescante
refreshment refresco
refrigerator frigorífico, nevera
refuel (v) reabastecer
refuge asilo, refugiado
refund (v) devolver, reembolsar
refund abono, devolución, reembolso
refunding reintegro
refusable rechazable
refusal denegación, rechazo
refuse basura, desperdicios
refuse (v) denegar, rechazar, rehusar
refutable refutable
refutation refutación
refute (v) rebatir
regain (v) cobrar, recobrar
regal regio
regard respecto, respeto
regarding en cuanto a
regardless a pesar de
regeneration regeneración
regenerator regenerador
regent regente
regime régimen
regiment regimiento
regiment (v) organizar

regimental   de regimiento
region   comarca, región
regional   regional
register   lista, registro
register (v)   inscribir, registrar
register of deeds   registro de títulos
registered   registrado
registered bonds   bonos registrados
registered shares   acciones nominativas
registered trademark   marca registrada
registrar   registrador
registration   inscripción, registro
regression   regresión
regret (v)   lamentar, sentir
regret   remordimiento
regrettable   lamentable
regular   corriente, ordinario, regular
regularity   regularidad
regulate (v)   ajustar, regular
regulation   reglamento (s)
regulatory   regulador
rehabilitation   rehabilitación, restablecimiento
rehearing   nueva audiencia
rehearsal   ensayo, repetición
rehearse (v)   ensayar
reign (v)   imperar, reinar
reign   reinado, dominio
reimburse (v)   reembolsar
reimbursement   reembolso
rein (v)   detenerse
rein   rienda
reincarnate (v)   reencarnar
reinforce (v)   reforzar
reinforcement   refuerzo
reinstate (v)   reintegrar, restablecer
reinstatement   reintegro

reinvest (v)   reinvertir
reissue (v)   volver a emitir
reject (v)   rechazar
rejection   devolución, rechazo
rejoice (v)   alegrar, regocijar
rejoin (v)   replicar, contestar
rejoinder   réplica
relapse   recaída
relapse (v)   recaer
relate (v)   contar, relacionar
related   afín, relacionado
relation   narración, relación
relational data base   base de datos relacionada
relationship   relación, trato
relative   familiar, relativo
relative fact   hecho relativo
relative rights   hechos relativos
relax (v)   descansar, descansar
relaxant   relajante
relaxation   descanso, relajación
relay (v)   retransmitir
release   descargo, emisión, liberación
release (v)   emitir, libertar
relentless   implacable
relet (v)   readjudicar
relevance   conexión, relación
relevancy   aplicabilidad
relevant   conexo, pertinente
relevant cost   coste pertinente
reliability   confiabilidad, exactitud, fiabilidad, seriedad
reliable   exacto, serio, cumplidor, digno de confianza, veraz; cumplido (Perú)
reliance   confianza
relief   alivio, ayuda, consuelo
relieve (v)   aliviar, suprimir
religion   religión
religious   religioso
relinquish (v)   abandonar, ceder, dimitir, renunciar

relish gusto, sabor
relish (v) paladear, saborear
relive (v) volver a vivir
reluctance desgana, renuncia
reluctant poco dispuesto
rely (v) confiar en
remain (v) sobrar, quedar
remainder residuo, resto
remains restos, sobras
remand (v) reencarcelar
remark observación
remark (v) hacer observaciones
remarkable notable, singular
remarriage segundas nupcias
remarry (v) volver a casarse
remedial curativo, reparador
remedy recurso, remedio
remember (v) recordar
remembrance recuerdo, memoria
remind (v) recordar
reminder recordatorio
reminiscence recuerdo
reminiscent que recuerda
remiss descuidado
remission remisión
remit (v) enviar, remitir
remittance envío, giro de fondos, remesa
remittee beneficiario
remittent fever fiebre remitente
remnant remanente, resto
remorse remordimiento
remote distante, remoto
remote cause causa indirecta
remote control control a distancia
remote damages daños indirectos
removal expulsión, separación, supresión
remove (v) eliminar, quitar
remunerate (v) remunerar

remuneration remuneración
renal renal
rename (v) volver a nombrar
render (v) ceder, entregar
rendering reproducción, versión
rendezvous cita
renegade renegado
renegotiation renegociación
renew (v) renovar
renewal renovación
renounce (v) renunciar
renovate (v) renovar
renown fama, renombre
renowned conocido, famoso
rent (v) alquilar
rent alquiler, rotura
rent space local por alquilar
rental alquiler, arriendo
renunciation renuncia
reopen (v) volver a abrir
reopen a case (v) reabrir una causa
reopening reapertura
reorganization reorganización
reorganize (v) reorganizar
rep representante
repair (v) componer, reparar
repair reparación
repair cost costes de reparación
reparation reparación
repatriate repatriado
repay (v) devolver, reembolsar
repayment reembolso
repeal revocación
repeal (v) abrogar, revocar
repealing clause cláusula derogatoria
repeat (v) repetir
repeater repetidor
repel (v) rechazar
repellent repugnante
repercussion repercusión
repertoire repertorio

repetition demanda de reembolso, repetición
repetitive reiterativo
replace (v) reemplazar
replacement substitución
replay (v) volver a jugar
repledge (v) rehipotecar
replenish (v) rellenar
replenishment relleno
replevy reivindicación
repliant replicante
replica copia, reproducción
reply (v) contestar, responder
reply contestación
report (v) informar, relatar
report informe, relato
reporter periodista
repose (v) descansar
repose reposo
repossess (v) recobrar
represent (v) representar
representation representación
representative agente, representante
repress (v) reprimir
repression represión
repressive represivo
reprieve alivio, respiro, suspensión temporal
reprieve (v) indultar
reprimand reprimenda, represión; café (Amer.)
reprint reimpresión
reprint (v) reimprimir
reprisal represalia
reproach censura, reproche
reproduce (v) reproducir
reproduction reproducción
reproof reproche
reptile reptil
republic república
republican republicano

repudiate (v) rechazar
repudiation rechazo
repugnant repugnante
repulsion repulsión
reputable acreditado
reputation fama, reputación
repute (v) reputar
reputed supuesto
request ruego, petición
request (v) rogar, pedir
requiem requiem
require (v) necesitar, requerir
requirement requisito
requisite imprescindible
requisitory requisitorio
reroute (v) desviar
rerun reposición
resale reventa
resale price precio de reventa
rescind (v) rescindir
rescission rescisión
rescissory rescisorio
rescue rescate, salvamento
rescue (v) rescatar, salvar
rescuer salvador
research investigación
research (v) investigar
research and development investigación y desarrollo
researcher investigador
resell (v) revender; rescatar (Mex.)
resemblance semejanza
resemble (v) parecerse
resent (v) ofenderse por
resentful ofendido, resentido
resentment resentimiento
reservation reserva
reserve reserva
reserve (v) reservar
reserved reservado
reserves reservas

reservoir depósito, presa
reset salida, puesta a cero
reside (v) residir, vivir
residence residencia
resident residente
residential residencial
residual residual
residual income ingresos residuales
residuary remanente
residuary legacy legado remanente
residue residuo, resto
resign (v) dimitir, renunciar
resignation dimisión, renuncia
resilience resistencia
resilient elástico, resistente
resist (v) resistir
resistance resistencia
resistant resistente
resistor resistencia
resolute resuelto
resolution resolución
resolutive resolutivo
resolve resolución
resolve (v) acordar
resonance resonancia
resonant resonante
resort punto de reunión
resort (v) concurrir
resound (v) resonar, retumbar
resounding sonoro
resource medio, recurso
resources medios
respect respecto, respeto (sentimiento)
respect (v) respetar
respectable respetable
respectful respetuoso
respective respectivo
respiration respiración
respirator respirador

respite espera, respiro, prórroga
respond (v) reaccionar, responder
response reacción, respuesta
responsibility responsabilidad
responsible responsable
responsive que coopera
rest (v) descansar, pararse
rest descanso, resto
restaurant restaurante
restful descansado
restitution restitución
restive inquieto
restless inquieto, intranquilo
restoration restauración
restore (v) restaurar
restrain (v) contener, prohibir, reprimir
restraint control, freno
restrict (v) limitar, restringir
restricted limitado, restringido
restriction restricción, limitación
restrictive restrictivo
restrictive practice práctica restrictiva
result resultado
result (v) terminar en
resultant consiguiente
résumé curriculum vitae
resume (v) reanudar, continuar
resumption reanudación
resurgence resurgimiento
resurrect (v) resucitar
resurrection resurrección
resuscitation resucitación
retail detalle (venta), venta al detalle
retail inventory method método de inventario al detalle
retail price list lista de precios al detalle
retailer detallista al menor

retain (v) retener

retained earnings beneficios no distribuidos

retainer anticipo, pago adelantado, partidario

retaliate (v) tomar represalias

retaliation represalias

retard (v) retardar

retarded atrasado

retention retención

reticence reticencia

reticent reticente

retina retina

retire (v) jubilar, retirarse

retired jubilado, retirado

retirement retiro

retirement gains ganancias por retiro

retort réplica

retract (v) retractar

retreat refugio, retiro

retrial revisión

retrial (v) volver a juzgar

retrieval recuperación

retrieve (v) cobrar, recuperar

retriever cobrador, perdiguero

retroactive retroactivo

retroactivity retroactividad

retrograde retrógrado

retrospect retrospección

retrospective retrospectivo

retry (v) volver a juzgar, volver a procesar

return (v) regresar, volver

return devolución, regreso, vuelta

return key tecla de entrada

return on investment rendimiento de la inversión

return ticket billete de vuelta

reunion reunión

reunite (v) reconciliar, reunir

rev revolución

revaluation revaluación, revalorización

reveal (v) revelar

revealing revelador

revelation revelación

revelry diversión, jolgorio

revenge venganza

revenge (v) vengar

revenue ingresos, renta

reverberate (v) resonar, retumbar

reverberation retumbo, resonancia

revere (v) reverenciar

reverence reverencia

reversal inversión, revocación

reverse invertido, inverso

reverse (v) invertir

reversible reversible

reversion reversión

revert (v) revertir

review (v) examinar, repasar

reviewer crítico

revise (v) revisar

revision revisión

revival restablecimiento

revive (v) revivir, resucitar

revocable revocable

revocable credit crédito revocable

revoke renuncia

revoke (v) renunciar, revocar

revolt rebelión

revolting asqueroso

revolution revolución

revolutionary revolucionario

revolutionize (v) revolucionar

revolve (v) girar, dar vueltas

revolver revólver

revolving credit crédito renovable

revue revista

revulsion asco, repugnancia

reward recompensa
reward (v) recompensar
rewind (v) dar cuerda, rebobinar
rewinding rebobinado
rewrite (v) volver a escribir
RGB monitor pantalla de color
rheumatic reumático
rheumatism reumatismo
rhinitis rinitis
rhyme rima
rhythm ritmo
rhythmic rítmico
rib costilla
ribbon cinta
rice arroz
rich rico, sabroso
riches riqueza
richness riqueza
rid (v) librase, liberarse
riddle acertijo, criba
ride (v) pasear, montar
ride paseo, viaje
rider jinete
ridge lomo, cerro
ridicule burlas, ridículo
ridiculous ridículo, absurdo
riding equitación
rife común, abundante
rifle (v) robar, saquear
rifle rifle, fusil
rift grieta, abertura
rig aparejo, atuendo
rig (v) aparejar, arreglar
right derecha, correcto, bien
right angle ángulo recto
right of appeal derecho de recurso
right of lien derecho prendario
right of redemption derecho de
 retracto
right-of-way prioridad de paso
rightful legítimo
rights derechos

rigid rígido, severo
rigidity rigidez
rigor rigor, severidad
rigorous riguroso
rim borde, canto
rind corteza, cáscara
ring anillo, timbre, campana, aro,
 camarilla
rinse (v) aclarar, enjuagar,
rinse clothes (v) batir (Chile,
 Guat., Perú)
riot disturbio, tumulto, perturbación del orden
rioter manifestante, perturbador
ripe maduro
ripen (v) madurar
rise (v) subir, salir
rise subida, salida
rising creciente, saliente
risk (v) arriesgar
risk riesgo, peligro
risky arriesgado
rite rito
ritual ritual
rival opuesto, rival
rivalry rivalidad
river río
riverside ribera
rivet remache
road calle, carretera
roadblock barricada
roadside borde
roadway calzada
roaming vagabundeo
roar (v) rugir, bramar
roar rugido, bramido
roast (v) asar, tostar
roast asado, tostado
rob (v) robar
robber ladrón
robbery robo
robe manto, albornoz
robot robot, autómata

robust robusto
rock roca, piedra
rock (v) sacudir
rock (a child) (v) arrullar (Amer.)
rocket cohete
rocking chair balance (Cuba, Col.)
rodent roedor
rogatory rogatorio
rogue pícaro, pillo
role papel (personaje)
roll rollo, lista
roll (v) empujar, rodar
roll in (v) reincorporar
roll out (v) descargar
roller (in a sugar mill) maza (Cuba)
roller coaster montaña rusa
roller skate patín de ruedas
Roman romano
romance novela, cuento
romantic romántico
Rome Roma
roof techo, tejado
room habitación, sala
roommate compañero de cuarto
roost percha
rooster gallo
root raíz, idea esencial
root (v) echar raíces, apoyar
rope cable
rope (v) atar con una cuerda
rosary rosario
rose rosa, rosado
rose garden rosaleda
roseola roseola
rosy prometedor, rosado
rot (v) pudrir, corromper
rotate (v) dar vueltas
rouge colorete, carmín
rough áspero, rudo, tosco
roughly más o menos

roughness aspereza, desigualdad
roulette ruleta
round redondo, alrededor
round up cattle (v) reclutar (Arg.)
roundup redada, detención
rouse (v) despertar, excitar
rout derrota
route ruta, rumbo, camino
routine rutina
row fila, disputa
row (v) remar, bogar
rowboat bote de remos
rowdy ruidoso, pendenciero
royal real, regio
royally magníficamente
royalties derechos industriales
royalty realeza, derechos
rub frotamiento, roce
rub (v) frotar, rozar
rubber goma
rubber band liga elástica
rubber stamp sello de goma
rubbish basura
rubble escombros
rubella rubéola
rubeola rubéola, sarampión
rudder timón
rude rudo, grosero
rudeness grosería
rudiment rudimento
rudimentary rudimentario
rue (v) arrepentirse
ruffian matón, canalla
ruffle (v) arrugar
rug alfombra
rugged áspero, accidentado
ruin ruina, perdición
ruinous ruinoso
rule (v) gobernar, mandar
rule norma, regla, reglamento
ruler regla, gobernante
ruling resolución, decisión

rum ron
rumble ruido, rumor
rummage (v) buscar revolviendo
rummage sale venta de usados
rumor rumor; caña (Col., Ecuad., Ven.)
run carrera, corrida, serie, período
run (v) correr, dirigir
runaway fugitivo, desertor
rundown resumen, sumario
runner corredor, atleta
runway pista de aterrizaje

rupture ruptura
rural rural
rush (v) lanzarse, apresurar
rush prisa, ímpetu
rush hour hora punta
Russia Rusia
Russian ruso
rust corrosión, óxido
rustic rústico
rusty oxidado
rut rodada, surco
ruthless despiadado
rye centeno

S

Sabbath dia de descanso
saber sable
sabotage sabotaje
saboteur saboteador
saccharin sacarina
saccharose sacarosa
sack saco; botín (Chile)
sacrament sacramento
sacred sagrado
sacrifice sacrificio
sacrilege sacrilegio
sacrum sacro
sad triste, lamentable
sadden (v) entristecer
sadism sadismo
sadistic sádico
sadness tristeza
safe seguro, caja fuerte, caja de seguridad
safe deposit box caja de seguridad
safeguard protección
safety seguridad
safety pin imperdible
safety vault cámara acorazada
sagacious sagaz

sage salvia, sabio
said dicho
sail (v) navegar
sail vela, aspa
sailboat barco de vela
sailing navegación
sailor marino, marinero
saint santo
sake en atención a
salad ensalada
salary salario, sueldo
sale venta, liquidación
sale invoice factura de venta
sale of goods venta de mercancías
sales discount descuento comercial por pronto pago
sales journal libro de ventas
sales price precio de venta
sales promotion promoción de ventas
sales tax impuesto de venta, impuesto de consumo
salesmanship arte de vender
saline salino
saliva saliva

salmonella salmonela
salon salón
saloon salón, taberna
salt sal
salty salado, salobre
salute saludo
salute (v) saludar
salvage (v) salvar, recuperar
salvage salvamento, recuperación
salvage value valor residual
salvation salvación
same igual, lo mismo
sample muestra
sample order pedido de prueba
sampling muestreo
sanatorium sanatorio
sanctify (v) santificar
sanction sanción
sanctuary santuario
sand arena
sandal sandalia
sandbag saco de arena
sandpaper papel de lija
sandwich bocadillo, sandwich
sandwich (v) insertar, intercalar
sandy arenoso
sane sano, cuerdo
sanitary sanitario
sanitation sanidad, higiene
sanity cordura, sensatez
sarcasm sarcasmo
sarcoma sarcoma
sartorius sartorio
sash faja, marco (ventana)
Satan Satanás
satanic satánico
satellite satélite
satin raso, terso
satire sátira
satisfaction satisfacción
satisfactory satisfactorio

satisfy (v) liquidar, pagar, satisfacer
saturate (v) saturar, empapar
Saturday sábado
sauce salsa
saucepan cacerola
saucer platillo
saucy fresco, descarado
sauna sauna
sausage salchicha
savage salvaje, feroz
save (v) salvar, ahorrar
save salvo, excepto
saving económico
savings ahorros
savings bank caja de ahorros
savings pass book libreta de ahorros
savior salvador
savor sabor, gusto
savory sabroso
saw sierra, refrán
sawdust serrín
sawmill aserradero
saxophone saxofón
say dicho, voz
say (v) decir, manifestar
saying dicho, refrán
scab costra, roña
scaffold andamio, estructura
scaffolding andamiaje
scald escaldadura
scalding abrasador
scale balanza, escala
scale-down reducción progresiva
scalp cuero cabelludo
scalpel escalpelo
scan (v) examinar
scandal escándalo
scandalize (v) escandalizar
scandalous escandaloso
scanner explorador, unidad exploratoria

scant   escaso
scanty   escaso
scapegoat   cabeza de turco
scar   cicatriz
scarce   escaso
scarcity   escasez
scare   susto, sobresalto
scarecrow   espantapájaros
scarf   bufanda
scarlatina   escarlatina
scathing   mordaz, duro
scatter   dispersión
scatter (v)   esparcir, dispersar
scatterbrain   cabeza de chorlito
scavenge (v)   limpiar, barrer
scene   escena, escándalo
scenery   paisaje
scenic   pintoresco
scent   olor, aroma
schedule (v)   catalogar, proyectar
schedule   lista, horario, programa, tabla
scheme   disposición, plan
schizophrenia   esquizofrenia
schizophrenic   esquizofrénico
scholar   escolar
scholarship   erudición, beca
scholastic   escolástico
school   escuela, colegio
schooling   enseñanza
sciatic   ciático
sciatica   ciática
science   ciencia
science fiction   ciencia ficción
scientific   científico
scientist   científico
scissors   tijeras
sclerosis   esclerosis
scoff (v)   mofarse
scoop   cuchara, pala
scooter   patinete
scope   alcance, envergadura

scorch (v)   chamuscar, abrasar
score (v)   marcar, tantear
score   tanteo, cuenta
scoreboard   tabla de puntos
scorer   marcador
scorn   desprecio
scoundrel   sapo (Chile, Mex.)
scour (v)   fregar, recorrer
scout   explorador
scout (v)   bombear (Arg.)
scowl   ceño
scramble (v)   revolver, cifrar
scrambler   desmodulador
scrap (v)   desechar, descartar
scrap   pedazo, chatarra
scrape (v)   raspar, raer
scrape   raspadura, rasguño
scratch (v)   rayar, rasgar
scratch   raya, rasguño
scrawl   garabatos
scream (v)   gritar, chillar
scream   grito, chillido
screen (v)   ocultar, proteger
screen   pantalla
screw (v)   atornillar, roscar
screw   tornillo, rosca
screwdriver   destornillador
scribble   garabatos
scrip   póliza, vale
script   escritura, guión
scripture   escrito (religioso)
scroll   rollo de escritura
scrotum   escroto
scrub (v)   fregar, restregar
scruff   nuca, cogote
scruffy   sucio, piojoso
scruple   escrúpulo
scrupulous   escrupuloso
scrutinize (v)   escuadriñar
scrutiny   escrutinio
scuffle   pelea, refriega
sculptor   escultor
sculpture   escultura

scum espuma, escoria
scurf caspa
scurry (v) correr, ir de prisa
sea mar
sea gull gaviota
seafood pescado (de mar)
seal (v) sellar, cerrar
seal sello, foca, timbre
sealed sellado
sealing wax lacre
seam costura
seaman marinero
search (v) buscar, examinar
search búsqueda, busca
search and replace búsqueda y reemplazo
search cycle ciclo de búsqueda
search warrant orden de registro
seashore costa, litoral
seasick mareado (del mar)
season estación, época
seasonal estacional
seasoning condimento, salsa
seat asiento
seat (v) sentarse
seat belt cinturón de seguridad
sebaceous sebáceo
seborrhea seborrea
secluded retirado, apartado
seclusion retiro, apartamiento
second segundo
second class segunda clase
second-hand goods mercancías usadas
secondary secundario
secrecy secreto, reserva
secret secreto, oculto
secretarial de secretario
secretary secretario
secrete (v) esconder
secretion secreción
secretive reservado, callado

sectarian sectario
section sección, segmento
sector sector
secular secular
secure (v) asegurar
secure seguro, estable
secured loan empréstito con garantía
securities títulos, valores
security seguridad
sedative calmante, sedante
sediment sedimento
sedition sedición
seduce (v) seducir
seduction seducción
seductive seductor
see (v) ver, comprender
seed semilla, simiente
seed (v) sembrar
seek búsqueda
seem (v) parecer
seeming aparente
seemingly aparentemente
seepage filtración
seethe (v) hervir
segment segmento
segregate (v) segregar
segregation segregación
seize (v) incautar, coger
seizin in deed posesión efectiva
seizure confiscación, embargo
seldom rara vez
select (v) escoger, seleccionar
selection selección
selective selectivo
self mismo
self-assurance confianza en sí mismo
self-centered egocéntrico
self-confident seguro de sí mismo
self-conscious tímido
self-contained independiente

self-control   autodominio
self-defense   autodefensa, defensa propia
self-discipline   autodisciplina
self-educated   autodidacta
self-employed   independiente
self-interest   en propio interés
self-made   hecho por sí mismo
self-pity   lástima de sí mismo
self-respect   amor propio
self-sacrifice   abnegación
self-service   autoservicio
self-sufficient   auto-suficiente
selfish   egoísta
selfishness   egoísmo
sell (v)   vender
sell meat (v)   pesar (Col.)
sell-off   baja de valores
seller   vendedor
selling price   precio de venta
semantic   semántico
semblance   apariencia
semen   semen
semicircle   semicírculo
semicircular   semicircular
semicolon   punto y coma
semiconductor   semiconductor
semifinal   semifinal
seminar   seminario
senate   senado
senator   senador
send (v)   enviar, remitir
sender   emisor
senile   senil
senior   mayor
senior partner   socio principal
seniority   antigüedad
sensation   sensación
sensational   sensacional
sense   juicio, sentido
sense of humor   sentido de humor
senseless   sin sentido

sensible   sensato, lógico
sensitive   sensible, susceptible
sensor   sensor
sensual   sensual
sentence   oración, sentencia
sentiment   sentimiento
sentimental   sentimental
sentry   centinela, guardia
separate (v)   separar, desunir
separate   separado, distinto
separation   separación
separator   separador
September   septiembre
septic   séptico
septicemia   septicemia
sequel   consecuencia
sequence   sucesión, orden
sequential access   acceso secuencial
sequential processing   procesamiento secuencial
sequester (v)   secuestrar
sequestration   secuestro
serenade   serenata
serene   sereno, tranquilo
serenity   serenidad
sergeant   sargento
serial   consecutivo, serie
serial access   acceso secuencial
serial number   número de fabricación
serial processing   proceso en serie
serial storage   memoria secuencial
series   serie, sucesión
serious   serio, grave
sermon   sermón
serous   seroso
serpent   serpiente
serum   suero
servant   criado, sirviente
serve (v)   servir

serve a sentence (v) cumplir una sentencia
service servicio
service charge comisión por operación
service circuit circuito de servicio
service counter mostrador de servicios
serviceable utilizable
serviceman militar
session sesión
set (v) poner, fijar
set aparato, conjunto, juego (en tenis)
set aside (v) anular
set for trial (v) fijar fecha de juicio
set theory teoría de conjuntos
setoff compensación
settle (v) colocar, establecer
settlement arreglo
seven siete
seventeen diecisiete
seventh séptimo
seventy setenta
sever (v) cortar, dividir
several varios, algunos
severance pay sueldo de despedida
severity gravedad
sew (v) coser
sewage aguas residuales
sewer alcantarilla, cloaca
sewing costura
sex sexo
sexual sexual
sexual intercourse tiro (Perú, sl.)
sexuality sexualidad
shabby viejo, gastado
shack choza, chabola
shade (v) dar sombra, proteger

shade sombra, pantalla
shadow sombra
shadowy oscuro
shady sombreado
shake sacudida, temblor
shake (v) sacudir, inquietar
shaky inestable, débil
shallow poco profundo
sham falso, simulado
sham defense defensa ficticia
shame vergüenza
shameful vergonzoso
shameless desvergonzado
shampoo champú
shape (v) formar
shape forma, corte
shapeless deforme
shapely bien formado
share (v) compartir, dividir
share parte, contribución, acción (capital), participación
shareholder accionista
sharer partícipe
sharp afilado, listo
sharpen (v) afilar
sharpness viveza, agudeza
shatter (v) romper, destrozar
shattered destrozado
shave (v) afeitar, rasurar
shaving cream crema de afeitar
shawl chal
she ella
shear (v) esquilar
shed (v) despojarse, quitarse
sheen lustre, brillo
sheep oveja
sheer (v) desviarse
sheer puro, completo
sheet sábana, lámina
shelf estante
shelter (v) refugiarse
shelter refugio
shelve (v) aplazar

shelving estanterías
sheriff alguacil (policía)
sherry vino de Jerez
shield escudo, blindaje
shield (v) proteger
shift (v) cambiar, moverse
shift turno, cambio
shift register registro de desplazamiento
shimmer reflejo
shin espinilla
shin bone espinilla
shine (v) brillar, relucir
shine brillo, lustre
shingles herpes
ship (v) transportar, enviar
ship barco, buque
shipment envío, embarque
shipper expedidor
shipping embarque, envío
shipping documents documentos de envío
shipwreck naufragio
shirk (v) eludir, esquivar
shirt camisa
shirt sleeves mangas de camisa
shiver (v) temblar, vibrar
shivering temblores
shock (v) sobresaltar, disgustar
shock choque, descarga, sobresalto
shocking horrible, escandaloso
shockproof a prueba de golpes
shoddiness mala calidad
shoddy de baja calidad
shoe zapato
shoelace cordón de zapato
shoemaker zapatero
shoot (v) disparar, tirar
shoot dead (v) tronar (Mex.)
shop tienda; negocio (Arg., Chile, Uru.)
shop (v) comprar

shopkeeper tendero; cajonero (Mex.)
shoplifter ladrón de tiendas
shoplifting robo de tiendas
shopper comprador
shopping compras, de tiendas
shopping bag bolsa de compras
shopping center centro comercial
shore orilla, playa
short corto, breve
short-circuit cortocircuito
short-lived efímero
short notice aviso rápido
short-sighted miope, corto de vista
short-term corto plazo
short-term bill letra a plazo corto
shortage escasez, insuficiencia, penuria
shortcoming defecto
shorten (v) acortar, abreviar
shorthand taquigrafía
shortly en breve
shot bala, inyección, proyectil, tiro
shoulder hombro, espaldas
shoulder blade omoplato
shout (v) gritar
shout grito
shove empujón; viaje (C. Am.)
shovel pala
show demostración, espectáculo
show (v) mostrar, aparecer
shower ducha
shower (v) duchar, llover
showroom salón de ventas
shrink (v) encoger, contraer
shrinkage merma
shrub arbusto
shudder estremecimiento
shuffle (v) mezclar, barajar

shun (v) esquivar
shut (v) cerrar, encerrar
shutter contraventana
shuttle lanzadera
shy tímido, avergonzado
shyness timidez, vergüenza
sick enfermo
sicken (v) dar asco, repugnar
sickening repugnante, asqueroso
sickly enfermizo
sickness enfermedad
sickroom enfermería
side parte, lado, aspecto
side effect efecto secundario
sideline línea secundaria
sidelong lateralmente
sidestep esquivar
siege sitio, cerco
sieve tamiz, cedazo
sift (v) tamizar, cribar
sigh susurro, suspiro
sight (v) mirar, divisar
sight vista, mirada
sight draft efecto a la vista
sightseeing excursión, turismo
sigmoidoscope sigmoidoscopio
sign (v) firmar, marcar
sign señal, indicador
signal (v) hacer señales
signal señal
signature firma
signer firmante
significance significación
significant significante
signify (v) significar
signpost poste indicador
silence silencio
silence (v) acallar, silenciar
silencer silenciador
silent silencioso, callado
silhouette silueta
silicon sílice
silicosis silicosis

silk seda
silky sedoso
silliness estupidez
silly estúpido, tonto
silver plata
similar similar, parecido
simmer (v) cocer lentamente
simple sencillo, simple
simplicity sencillez
simplify (v) simplificar
simply sencillamente
simulate (v) simular
simulation simulación
simulator simulador
simultaneous simultáneo
sin pecado
since desde, entonces
sincere sincero
sincerity sinceridad
sine die sin día fijo
sinew tendón
sinful pecador
sing (v) cantar
singer cantante
single único, solo, soltero
single-minded resuelto, firme
single person soltero
single-sided disk disco de una cara
singular singular, raro
sinister siniestro
sink (v) hundir, sumergir
sink fregadero
sinking fund fondo de amortización
sinner pecador
sinuous sinuoso
sinus seno, sinus
sinusitis sinusitis
sir señor
siren sirena
sister hermana
sister-in-law cuñada

sit (v)   sentar, sentarse
sitting   reunión
sitting room   sala de estar
situate (v)   situar
situation   situación
six   seis
sixteen   dieciséis
sixteenth   decimosexto
sixth   sexto
sixty   sesenta
size   tamaño, talla
sizeable   considerable
skate   patín
skate (v)   patinar
skating   patinaje
skeleton   esqueleto
sketch (v)   esbozar, bosquejar
sketchy   incompleto
ski (v)   esquiar
skid   patinazo, derrape
skier   esquiador
skill   habilidad, destreza
skilled   hábil, especializado
skin   piel, corteza
skip (v)   omitir, saltar
skipper   capitán, patrón
skirmish   escaramuza
skirt (v)   ceñir, rodear
skirt   falda
skull   calavera, cráneo
sky   cielo
skylight   claraboya
skyline   horizonte
skyscraper   rascacielos
slab   bloque, tabla
slack   flojo, inerte
slacken (v)   aflojar
slacks   pantalones
slam (v)   golpear, cerrar
slam   golpe, portazo
slander   calumnia
slander (v)   acabar (S. Am., coll.); pelar (Amer.)

slanderer   calumniador
slang   argot
slant   inclinación
slap (v)   abofetear, pegar
slap   bofetada, manotada
slapdash   violentamente
slapstick   payasada
slash (v)   acuchillar, rasgar
slats   abatido (Cuba, Col.)
slaughter   matanza
slaughter (v)   matar, sacrificar
slaughterhouse   matadero, carnicería (Ecuad.)
slave   esclavo
slavery   esclavitud
sledge hammer   golpe (Mex.)
sleek   suave, pulcro
sleep (v)   dormir
sleep   sueño
sleeping bag   saco de dormir
sleeping pill   somnífero
sleepy   soñoliento
sleet   aguanieve
sleeve   manga
sleight of hand   pruebas (Amer.)
slender   delgado, limitado
slice   tajada, rodaja
slick   hábil, diestro
slide (v)   deslizar, resbalar
slide projector   proyector de diapositivas
slide ruler   regla de cálculo
slight   delgado, leve
slightly   ligeramente
slim   delgado, esbelto
slime   cieno
sling   eslinga, cabestrillo
slip   resbalón, caída, resguardo, tira
slip (v)   resbalar, caer
slipper   zapatilla
slippery   resbaladizo
slit   resquicio, raja

slit (v) cortar, dividir
slope pendiente, declive
slope (v) inclinar
sloppy descuidado
slot ranura
slot machine máquina tragaperras
slovenly desgarbado
slow lento, despacio
slow (v) reducir, retardar
slowdown retraso
slug (v) pegar
sluggish lento, inactivo
slum barrio bajo
slumber sueño
slump depresión, retroceso
slur borrón, mancha
sly astuto
small pequeño
small change calderilla, cambio, moneda de metal
small print letra menuda
small talk banalidades, charla superficial
small tube bombilla (Arg., Uru.)
smallpox viruela
smart elegante, inteligente
smash choque, colisión
smash (v) destruir, aplastar
smear mancha, ungüento
smear (v) manchar
smell olor, olfato
smell (v) oler, olfatear
smelly que huele mal
smile sonrisa
smile (v) sonreír
smirk sonrisa
smoke humo
smoke (v) fumar, ahumar
smoke screen pantalla de humo
smoky humeante
smooth suave, afable
smoothly suavemente

smother (v) ahogar
smoulder (v) arder sin llama
smudge mancha
smug suficiente, presumido
smuggle (v) hacer contrabando
smuggler contrabandista
smuggling contrabando
snack bocadillo
snack bar cafetería
snag nudo, obstáculo
snap chasquido, estallido
snap (v) castañear, chasquear
snapshot foto instantánea
snare lazo, trampa
snare (v) coger con trampas
snarl gruñido
snarl (v) enredar
snatch (v) asir, coger
sneak (v) robar, birlar
sneer desprecio
sneering burlador
sneeze estornudo
sneeze (v) estornudar
sniff (v) husmear, olfatear
snip tijeretazo
sniper francotirador
snivel (v) lloriquear
snob snob
snoop fisgón, curioso
snoop (v) curiosear
snooze siesta, sueño
snore ronquido
snore (v) roncar
snoring ronquidos
snort bufido
snow nieve
snow (v) nevar
snowball bola de nieve
snowdrift ventisquero
snowfall nevada
snowflake copo de nieve
snowman muñeco de nieve
snowstorm tormenta de nieve

snub desaire, repulsa
snuffles resuellos
snug cómodo, abrigado
so tan, así
so-called llamado, supuesto
so-so regular, así así
soak (v) empapar, mojar
soap jabón
soap powder jabón en polvo
soapdish jabonera
soapy jabonoso
soar (v) remontarse, subir
sob sollozo
sob (v) sollozar
sober serio, sobrio
soccer fútbol
sociable sociable, afable
social social, sociable
social security seguridad social
socialism socialismo
socialist socialista
socialize (v) socializar
society sociedad, asociación
sociology sociología
sock calcetín
socket enchufe, casquillo
soda refresco, sosa
sodium chloride cloruro de sodio
sodomy sodomía
sofa sofá
soft blando, flexible
soft job botella (Cuba)
soften (v) ablandar
softness blandura
software equipo lógico, programas
soggy empapado
soil suelo, tierra
soil (v) ensuciar
solar solar, del sol
sold out agotado
soldier soldado

sole exclusivo, único
sole heir heredero único
sole proprietorship propiedad
de una sola persona
sole trader agente exclusivo
solemn solemne
solemnity solemnidad
solicitor abogado
solid sólido, macizo
solidarity solidaridad
solidify (v) solidificar
solitary solitario, solo
solitude soledad
solo solo
soluble soluble
solution solución
solve (v) resolver
solvency solvencia
solvent solvente
somber sombrío
some algún, alguno
somebody alguien
someday algún día
somehow de algún modo
someone alguien
someplace en alguna parte
something algo, alguna cosa
sometime algún día, alguna vez
sometimes a veces
somewhat algo
somewhere en alguna parte
somnambulism sonámbulo
son hijo
son-in-law yerno
song canción
sonic sónico
sonnet soneto
soon pronto, temprano
soothing tranquilizador
sophisticated sofisticado
sordid asqueroso
sore inflamado, dolorido
soreness inflamación

sorrow pesar, dolor
sorry perdón, apenado
sort clase, tipo
sort (v) clasificar
sound sano, firme, sonido, ruido
sound (v) sonar
sound barrier barrera del sonido
sound effects efectos sonoros
sound track banda sonora
soundly sólidamente
soundproof insonorizado
soup sopa, caldo
soup plate plato sopero
soupspoon cuchara sopera
sour agrio
sour (v) agriar
source fuente, origen
source documents documentos
  originarios
source language lenguaje fuente
source program programa de
  base
sourness acidez
south sur
South America América del Sur
South Africa Africa del Sur
southeast sureste
southern meridional
southwest suroeste
souvenir recuerdo
sovereignty soberanía
spa balneario
space espacio
spacious espacioso
Spain España
span (v) medir, cruzar
Spaniard español
Spanish español
spare sobrante, repuesto
spare parts recambios, repuestos
spark chispa
spark plug bujía
spasm espasmo

spastic espasmódico
spatula espátula
speak (v) decir, hablar
speaker conferenciante, altavoz,
  orador
special especial
special bail fianza especial
special case causa especial
special consideration consideración especial
special defense defensa especial
special delivery envío urgente
special issue cuestión especial
special jury jurado especial
special lien gravamen específico
special offer oferta especial
special plea alegación especial
special rule regla especia
specialist especialista
speciality especialidad
specialize (v) especializarse
specific específico
specific denial negación específica
specification especificación
specifications especificaciones
specify (v) especificar
specimen muestra
specimen signature firma de
  registro
speck mancha pequeña
spectacles gafas
spectacular espectacular
spectator espectador
spectroscope espectroscopio
spectrum espectro
speculate (v) especular
speculation especulación
speculative especulativo
speech discurso
speechless mudo, estupefacto
speed rapidez, velocidad
speed limit límite de velocidad

speeding exceso de velocidad
speedometer velocímetro
speedup aceleración
spell encanto, hechizo
spell (v) deletrear
spellbound embelesado
spelling ortografía
spend (v) gastar, dedicar
spending gasto
sperm esperma
spermatozoid espermatozoide
sphere esfera
spherical esférico
spice especia
spicy picante, sabroso
spider araña
spill (v) derramar, verter
spin (v) girar, dar vueltas
spinach espinaca
spinal espinal
spine espina, espinazo
spinster mujer soltera
spiral espiral
spire aguja, cima
spirit espíritu, ánimo
spirited animoso
spiritual espiritual
spit saliva, escupida
spit (v) escupir
spite rencor
spite (v) mortificar, herir
splash salpicadura
splash (v) salpicar, rociar
spleen malicia, capricho
splendor esplendor
splice (v) empalmar, juntar
splint tablilla
splinter astilla
split dividido, división, ruptura
split (v) dividir, partir
spoil (v) estropear, deteriorar
spoke rayo, radio
spokesman portavoz

sponge esponja
sponsor patrocinador
sponsor (v) patrocinar
sponsorship patrocinio
spontaneous espontáneo
spoon cuchara
sporadic esporádico
spore espora
sport deporte
sporting deportivo
sports car coche deportivo
sports coat saco (Amer.)
sportsman deportista
sportsmanship ética deportiva
spot lugar, punto, grano
spot (v) observar, manchar
spot contract contrato, contrato
   al contado, contrato de cambio
   al contado
spotless sin manchas
spotlight foco, proyector
spotty manchado
spouse esposa, cónyuge
sprain dislocación, esguince
sprain (v) torcer
spray (v) rociar, pulverizar
spread extensión, difusión
spread (v) extender, propagar
spreadsheet hoja de cálculo
spree juerga, excursión; rumbo
   (Guat.)
spring pozo (Ecuad.)
spring mattress tambor (Mex.)
sprint (v) correr rápido
sputum esputo
spy (v) espiar, divisar
spy espía
spying espionaje
squabble riña, pelea
squabble (v) reñir, pelear
squad pelotón, brigada
squadron escuadrón
squalid escuálido

squalor miseria
squander (v) malgastar, derrochar
square cuadrado, plaza
square (v) cuadrar, ajustar
squash (v) aplastar
squat (v) agacharse
squatter usurpador, intruso
squawk graznido
squeak chirrido
squeal chillido, grito
squeal (v) chillar, gritar
squeamish delicado, susceptible
squeeze (v) estrujar, apretar
squint bizquera, estrabismo
squint (v) bizquear, ser bizco
squinter bizco
squirm (v) retorcerse
squirrel ardilla
squirt (v) salir a chorros
stab (v) apuñalar
stability estabilidad
stabilize (v) estabilizar
stabilizer estabilizador
stable estable, firme
stack montón, pila
stack (v) apilar, amontonar
stadium estadio
staff personal
stage estrado, escenario
stage (v) representar, organizar
stagger (v) asombrar, sorprender
staggering asombroso
stagnant estancado, paralizado
stagnate (v) estancarse
stagnation estancamiento, paralización
staid serio, formal
stain mancha, tinte
stain (v) manchar
stain remover quitamanchas
stained glass vidrio de color

stainless steel acero inoxidable
stair escalón, peldaño
stairway escalera
stake aguja (Amer.)
stale pasado, rancio
stale check cheque caducado
stalk tallo, caña
stalk (v) atascarse, cazar al acecho
stall establo, puesto
stamina resistencia, nervio
stammer tartamudeo
stamp sello, marca, timbre, sello de correos
stamp (v) estampar, imprimir
stamp collector filatelista
stamped estampado, sellado
stampede (v) causar terror
stampede estampida
stand posición, parada
stand (v) tolerar, estar situado
standard norma, modelo, nivel
standard of living nivel de vida
standard program programa standard
standby time tiempo en reserva
standing de pie, posición
standpoint punto de vista
standstill parada, alto
stanza estrofa, estancia
staple grapa
stapler grapadora
star estrella
starch almidón
stare mirada
stare (v) mirar fijamente
start principio, comienzo
start (v) empezar, comenzar
start a race (v) mandar (Chile)
start an engine (v) arrancar (Amer.)
start element elemento de arranque

start signal señal de comienzo
starter motor de arranque
startle (v) asustar, alarmar
startling asombroso
starvation hambre, privación
starve (v) morir de hambre
state condición, estado
state (v) declarar, afirmar
stated capital capital declarado
stately majestuoso
statement declaración, estado de cuenta
statement of account estado de cuenta
statement of income
  declaración de ingresos
static estático, inactivo
station estación, puesto
stationary estacionario
stationery papelería
statistic estadística
statistics estadísticas
statue figurilla
stature estatura
status condición, categoría, estado, estado legal
statute estatuto, ley
statutory estatuario, legal
stay estancia, permanencia
stay (v) quedar, permanecer
steadfast firme, resuelto
steadily firmemente, fijamente
steadiness firmeza, estabilidad
steady firme, fijo, constante
steak filete, bistec
steal (v) robar
stealing robo
steam vapor, humo
steam (v) cocer al vapor
steel acero
steep escarpado, abrupto
steer (v) conducir, dirigir
steering dirección

steering wheel volante; timón (Amer.)
stem tallo, tronco
stem (v) detener, refrenar
stench hedor
stencil plantilla
stenographer taquígrafo
step (v) dar un paso
step paso, medida
stepbrother hermanastro
stepdaughter hijastra
stepfather padrastro
stepladder burro (Mex.)
stepmother madrastra
stepson hijastro
stereo estereofónico
stereotype estereotipo
sterile estéril
sterile gauze gasa esterilizada
sterility esterilidad
sterilization esterilización
sterilize (v) esterilizar
sterilizer esterilizador
stern severo, duro, popa
sternum esternón
steroids esteroides
stertor estertor
stew (v) cocer, guisar; ahogar (Perú)
stew cocido
stewardess azafata
stick palo, vara
stick (v) resistir, pararse
sticker price precio de etiqueta
sticky pegajoso
sties orzuelos
stiff rígido, inflexible
stiffen (v) endurecer
stiffness rigidez
stifle (v) ahogar, sofocar
stifling sofocante
still todavía, aún, inmóvil, quieto
stillborn nacido muerto

stimulant estimulante
stimulate (v) estimular
stimulating estimulante
stimulus estímulo
sting (v) picar, escocer
stings picaduras
stink hedor, mal olor
stipend sueldo
stipulate (v) estipular, especificar
stipulation estipulación
stir agitación, conmoción
stir (v) remover, conmover
stitch (v) coser, suturar
stitch puntada, sutura
stitch or sharp pain in one's side puntada (Amer.)
stock (v) abastecer, proveer
stock acciones, existencias, capital, valores, ganado, caldo
stock certificates certificado de acciones
stock dividends dividendo en acciones
stock exchange bolsa de valores
stock exchange broker agente de cambio y bolsa
stockbroker agente de cambio y bolsa
stockholder accionista
stocking media, calceta
stockpile reserva
stockpile (v) acumular
stockroom almacén
stockyard corral de ganado
stolen robado
stomach estómago
stomachache dolor de estómago
stone cálculo, piedra
stool taburete
stoop inclinación
stoop (v) inclinar, bajar

stop (v) parar, detener, barajar (Chile, Mex., Arg.)
stop alto, parada
stoppage parada, interrupción
stopper tapón
stopwatch cronómetro
storage almacenaje, memoria
store (v) almacenar, guardar
store tienda, almacén
storm tormenta, tempestad
storm (v) asaltar, rabiar
stormy tempestuoso
story historia, piso
stout sólido, robusto
stove estufa
stow (v) meter, poner
stowaway pavo (Chile, Pan., Perú)
strabismus estrabismo
straight derecho, directo
straight loan empréstito reembolsable al vencimiento
straightaway en seguida
straighten (v) enderezar
straightforward honrado, franco
strain (v) estirar, torcerse
strain tensión, esfuerzo, distensión
strainer colador, filtro
strait estrecho
strange desconocido, raro
stranger forastero
strangle (v) estrangular
strangler estrangulador
strangulation estrangulación
strapping robusto, fornido
strategic estratégico
strategy estrategia
stratum estrato
straw paja
straw bail fianza sin valor
strawberry fresa
stray extraviado, perdido

stray (v) extraviarse

streak raya

stream corriente, río; pozo (Ecuad.)

stream (v) correr, fluir

streamline (v) perfeccionar

street calle

strength resistencia

strengthen (v) reforzar, consolidar

strenuous enérgico, vigoroso

stress tensión, presión

stretch extensión, trecho

stretch (v) extender, estirar

stretcher camilla

stricken eliminado

strict estricto, preciso; templado (Col., Ven.)

strict foreclosure ejecución forzosa

stride (v) dar zancadas

stride zancada, paso largo

strident estridente

strife lucha, contienda

strike (v) golpear, chocar

strike huelga, ataque

striker huelguista

striking notable

string cadena

strip (v) desnudar, desmontar

strip tira, banda

stripe raya

strive (v) esforzarse

stroke golpe, ataque, apoplejía, caricia

stroke of luck vaina (Col.)

stroll paseo, vuelta

strong fuerte, sólido

strong-minded resuelto de carácter

stronghold fortaleza

structural estructural

structure estructura

struggle (v) luchar, esforzarse

struggle lucha, contienda

stub matriz del talonario

stubborn tenaz, testarudo

stubbornness tenacidad

student estudiante

studio estudio, taller

studious estudioso

study (v) estudiar

study estudio, despacho

stuff (v) rellenar, llenar

stuff materia, sustancia

stuffy sofocante

stun (v) aturdir

stunning pasmoso, maravilloso

stunt ejercicio acrobático

stupid estúpido

sturdiness robustez

sturdy robusto, fuerte

stutter tartamudeo

sty orzuelo

style estilo

stylish elegante

suave afable

subconscious subconsciente

subcontract subcontrato

subcontractor subcontratista

subdivide (v) subdividir

subdue (v) dominar, avasallar

subfield subzona

subject to (v) estar sujeto a

subject (v) someter, dominar

subject sujeto, tema, súbdito

subjection sometimiento

subjective subjetivo

sublease subarriendo

sublet (v) realquilar

sublicense sublicencia

sublime sublime

submarine submarino

submerge (v) sumergir, inundar

submission sumisión

submissive sumiso

submit (v) someter, proponer
subordinate subordinado
subpoena citación
subscribe (v) suscribir
subscriber suscriptor
subscription suscripción
subsequent subsiguiente
subsequently después de
subside (v) bajar, hundirse
subsidiary dependiente, empresa filial, subsidiaria
subsidiary companies empresas filiales
subsidize (v) subvencionar
subsidy subvención
subsist (v) subsistir
subsistence subsistencia
substance sustancia
substandard inferior al normal
substantial sustancial, cuantioso
substitute sustituto
substitution sustitución
subtenant subinquilino
subtitle subtítulo
subtle sutil, fino
subtlety sutileza
subtract (v) sustraer, restar
subtraction sustracción, resta
suburb barrio
suburban suburbano
subversion subversión
subversive subversivo
subvert (v) subvertir
subway metro subterráneo
succeed (v) triunfar, tener éxito
succeeding futuro, subsiguiente
success éxito, triunfo
successful que tiene éxito
successfully con éxito
succession sucesión, serie
successive sucesivo
successor sucesor
succinct sucinto

succumb (v) sucumbir
such tal, tanto, tal como
suck (v) chupar, sorber
sudden repentino
sue (v) demandar
suffer (v) sufrir, aguantar
suffering sufrimiento
suffice (v) satisfacer
sufficient suficiente
suffix sufijo
suffocate (v) asfixiar
suffocation sofocación, asfixia
sugar azúcar
sugar cane caña (Amer.)
suggest (v) sugerir
suggestion sugerencia, sugestión
suggestive sugestivo
suicidal suicida
suicide suicidio
suit (v) ajustar, adaptar
suit litigio, pleito, traje
suitable conveniente, apto
suitcase maleta
suitor demandante
sulk (v) estar malhumorado
sum suma, cantidad
summarize (v) resumir
summary sumario, resumen
summer verano
summit cima, cumbre
summon citación, convocatoria
summon (v) convocar, llamar
summons citación, llamada
sumptuous suntuoso
sun sol
sunbathe (v) tomar sol
sunbeam rayo de sol
sunburn quemadura de sol
sunburned quemado de sol
Sunday domingo
sundry creditors acreedores diversos
sunflower girasol

sunglasses gafas de sol
sunlight luz de sol
sunny soleado
sunrise salida de sol
sunset puesta de sol
sunshine luz de sol
sunstroke insolación
super estupendo, super
superannuation jubilación
superb magnífico
supercilious arrogante
supercomputer superordenador
superficial superficial
superfluous superfluo
superhuman sobrehumano
superimpose (v) sobreponer
superintendent superintendente
superior superior
superior court tribunal superior
superiority superioridad
superlative superlativo
supermarket supermercado
supernatural sobrenatural
supersede (v) invalidar, sobreseer
supersonic supersónico
superstition superstición
supervise (v) supervisar
supervisor supervisor
supper cena
supple flexible
supplement suplemento
supplemental suplementario
supplementary suplementario
suppliant suplicante
supplier proveedor
supplies aprovisionamientos
supply (v) suministrar
supply oferta, existencias
supply and demand oferta y demanda
support (v) apoyar
support apoyo, soporte

supporter partidario
suppose (v) suponer, imaginarse
supposed supuesto
supposedly según cabe suponer
supposing en el caso de que
supposition suposición
suppository supositorio
suppress (v) suprimir
suppression supresión
suppuration supuración
supra supra
supremacy supremacía
supreme supremo
supreme court tribunal supremo
surcharge sobrecargo,
recargo
surcharge (v) sobrecargar
sure seguro, cierto
surely seguramente
surety garantía, fianza
surf espuma, olas
surface superficie
surge oleaje, aumento
surge protector protector de
línea
surgeon cirujano
surgery cirugía
surgical quirúrgico
surly malhumorado
surmount (v) superar
surname apellido
surpass (v) superar, exceder
surplus excedente, superávit
surplus capital superávit de capital
surprise sorpresa, asombro
surrealism surrealismo
surrealist surrealista
surrejoinder tríplica
surrender (v) rendirse, renunciar
surrender rendición, renuncia
surreptitious clandestino

surrogate's court tribunal testamentario

surround (v) rodear, cercar

surroundings alrededores

surtax impuesto adicional

surveillance observación

survey estudio, inspección

surveying agrimensura

surveyor inspector, topógrafo

survival supervivencia

survive (v) sobrevivir

survivor sobreviviente

susceptible susceptible

suspect (v) sospechar, recelar

suspect sospechoso

suspend (v) interrumpir, suspender

suspense incertidumbre

suspension suspensión

suspicion sospecha

suspicious sospechoso

sustain (v) sostener, continuar

suture sutura

swab tapón, torunda

swallow trago, golondrina

swallow (v) tragar, engullir

swamp pantano, ciénaga; balsa (Mex.)

swampy pantanoso

swanky ostentoso

swap intercambio de divisas, trueque

swarm enjambre

swarthy moreno

swat (v) aplastar, matar

sway (v) balancear, inclinar

swear (v) jurar

sweat sudor

sweater suéter

Sweden Suecia

Swedish sueco

sweep (v) barrer

sweet dulce

sweeten (v) endulzar

sweetheart amado

sweetness dulzura

sweetshop bombonería

swell (v) hinchar, inflar

swelling hinchazón, bulto

swelter (v) abrasarse

sweltering sofocante

swerve (v) desviar bruscamente

swift rápido, veloz

swiftness rapidez

swim (v) nadar

swimmer nadador

swimming natación

swimming pool piscina, alberca

swimsuit traje de baño

swindle estafa, timo; talla (C. Am.)

swindler estafador

swing (v) balancearse

swirl remolino

swirl (v) arremolinarse

Swiss suizo

switch interruptor, cambio, conmutación

switch box caja de conmutación

switchboard cuadro de mandos

switched line línea conmutada

switching center centro de conmutación

switching network red de conexión

switching station estación de conmutación

Switzerland Suiza

sword espada; latón (Bol., Col.)

sworn declaration declaración jurada

syllable sílaba

symbiosis simbiosis

symbol símbolo

symbolic simbólico

symbolize (v) simbolizar

symmetrical simétrico
symmetry simetría
sympathetic compasivo
sympathize (v) compadecer
sympathy solidaridad
symphonic sinfónico
symphony sinfonía
symptom síntoma
symptomatic sintomático
synagogue sinagoga
synchronization sincronización
synchronous transmission
  transmisión síncrona
syncopate (v) sincopar
syncope síncope

syndicate sindicato
syndrome síndrome
synonym sinónimo
synonymous sinónimo
synopsis sinopsis
syntax sintaxis
synthesis síntesis
synthesize (v) sintetizar
syphilis sífilis
syringe jeringa
syrup jarabe
system sistema
systematic sistemático
systole sístole

T

table mesa, tablero
tablecloth mantel
tablemat salvaplatos
tablespoon cucharón
tablet pastilla, tableta
taboo tabú
tabulate (v) tabular
tacit tácito
tacit dedication dedicación implícita
taciturn taciturno
tack tachuela
tack (v) clavar
tackle (v) atacar, blocar
tact discreción
tactical táctico
tactics tácticas, métodos
tactile táctil
tag etiqueta
tail limitación de propiedad, cola, rabo
tail light calavera (Mex.)
tailor sastre
taint infección

take (v) tomar, coger, recibir
take an oath (v) tomar juramento
take back (v) revocar
takeoff despegue
takeover absorción, adquisición
taker adquirente
talc powder polvos de talco
tale cuento, historia
talent talento
talented con talento
tales jurados adicionales
talesman jurado suplente
talk (v) hablar, conversar
talk conversación
talkative hablador
tall alto, grande
tally cuenta, lote
tally (v) corresponder
talon garra
tamale bollo (Col.)
tambourine pandereta
tame (v) domesticar, domar
tame domesticado

tamper (v) forzar, falsificar
tampon tapón
tan bronceado
tandem tándem
tangent tangente
tangerine mandarina
tangible tangible
tangible assets activos tangibles
tangle nudo, enredo
tangle (v) enredar, enmarañar
tank tanque
tanker buque petrolero
tantalize (v) tentar, provocar
tantalizing tentador
tantamount equivalente
tantrum rabieta
tantrums enfados
tap grifo, golpecito
tap (v) agujerear, derivar
tape (v) grabar en cinta
tape cinta
tape recorder cinta magnetofónica
tapestry tapicería
tapeworm solitaria, tenia
tar alquitrán
tardy tardío
target objetivo
target language lenguaje resultante
target program programa resultante
tariff arancel, tarifa
tarnish (v) deslustrar
tarpaulin alquitranado
tarry (v) quedarse, tardar
tarsus tarso
tartar sarro dental
task tarea, deber
task force grupo de acción
taste (v) saborear, probar
taste sabor
tasteful elegante

tasteless insípido, soso
tasty sabroso
tattered andrajoso
tattoo tatuaje
taunt (v) mofarse
taunting insultante
taut tieso
tavern taberna; cantina (Amer.)
tax impuesto, tributo
tax free libre de impuestos
tax payer contribuyente
tax refund devolución de impuestos
tax return declaración
tax services impuestos de servicios
taxable gravable de impuestos
taxation impuestos
taxes impuestos
taxi taxi
taxi driver taxista
tea té
tea bag bolsa de té
tea tray bandeja de té
tea party tertulia de té
teach (v) enseñar
teacher maestro, profesor
teaching enseñanza
teacup taza de té
teakettle tetera
team equipo
teamster camionero
teamwork labor de equipo
teapot tetera
tear lágrima
tear (v) desgarrar, rasgar
tear gas gas lacrimógeno
tearful lloroso
tears lágrimas
tease (v) embromar, molestar
teasing burlas, guasas
teaspoon cucharita
teat teta

technical técnico
technician técnico
technique técnica
technology tecnología
teddy bear oso de felpa
tedious tedioso
teenager joven diezañero
teens en los dieces
teeth dientes
teething dentición
telecast teledifusión
telecommunications telecomunicaciones
telegram telegrama
telegraph telégrafo
telepathy telepatía
telephone teléfono
telephone book guía telefónica
telephone booth cabina de teléfonos
telephone call llamada telefónica
teleprinter teleimpresor
teleprocessing teleproceso
telescope telescopio
teletext teletexto
teletype teletipo
televise (v) televisar
television televisión
television set televisor
telex telex
tell (v) decir, informar
teller cajero, narrador
telltale revelador
temper genio, humor
temperament temperamento
temperamental excitable
temperature temperatura
template plantilla
temple templo, sien
tempo tiempo
temporal bone hueso temporal
temporary temporal, provisional

temporary import importación temporal
temporary investments inversiones temporales
temporary offer oferta temporal
tempt (v) tentar, seducir
temptation tentación
ten diez
tenacious tenaz
tenancy inquilino
tenant inquilino
tend (v) tender, inclinarse a
tendency tendencia
tender oferta, tierno
tenderness ternura
tendon tendón
tenement vivienda
tenet principio
tennis tenis
tenor tenor
tense tirante, estirado
tension tensión
tent tienda de campaña
tentative provisional
tenth décimo
tenuous tenue
tenure posesión
tepid tibio
tequila tequila
term término
terminal final, terminal
terminal emulation emulación de terminal
terminate (v) terminar, acabar
terminus término
termite termita
terms condiciones
terms of delivery condiciones de entrega
terms of payment forma de pago
terrace terraza
terrain terreno
terrestrial terrestre

terrible terrible
terrific tremendo
terrify (v) aterrorizar
terrifying aterrador
territorial territorial
territory territorio
terror terror, horror
terrorism terrorismo
terrorist terrorista
terrorize (v) aterrorizar
terse breve, conciso
test análisis, ensayo, prueba
test (v) probar, ensayar
test program programa de
  prueba
testament testamento
testamentary testamentario
testicle testículo
testify (v) declarar, atestiguar
testimonial certificado
testimony testimonio
tetanus tétanos
text texto
text editor editor de textos
textbook libro de texto
textile textil
textual textual
texture textura, tejido
than que, de
thank (v) dar las gracias
thankful agradecido
thankfulness gratitud
thanks gracias
that ese, aquel
thaw (v) deshelar, derretir
the el, la, los, las
theater teatro
theatrical teatral
theft hurto, robo
their su
theirs suyo, suya
them los, las, ellos, ellas
theme tema

themselves ellos mismos
then entonces
theologian teólogo
theological teológico
theology teología
theorem teorema
theoretically teóricamente
theorize (v) teorizar
theory teoría
therapeutic terapéutico
therapist terapeuta
therapy terapia
there allí, allá
thereabouts por ahí
thereafter después
therefore por consiguiente
therein en este respecto
thereof de eso, de esto
thermal térmico
thermodynamic termodinámico
thermometer termómetro
thermonuclear termonuclear
thermostat termostato
these estos, estas
thesis tesis
they ellos, ellas
thick espeso, grueso
thicken (v) engrosar
thickness espesor
thief ladrón
thigh muslo
thimble dedal
thin delgado, ligero
thing cosa, objeto
think (v) pensar
thinness delgadez
third tercero
thirst sed
thirsty sediento
thirteen trece
thirteenth decimotercero
thirty treinta
this este, esta

thoracic torácico
thorax tórax
thorny espinoso
thorough completo, acabado
thoroughly totalmente
thoroughness minuciosidad
those esos, aquellos
though aunque, si bien
thought pensamiento, idea
thoughtful pensativo
thoughtfulness seriedad
thoughtless descuidado
thousand mil
thread hilo, fibra
threat amenaza
threaten (v) amenazar
threatening amenazante
three tres
three-quarter tres cuartos
three-way conference conferencia tripartita
threshold umbral
threshold decoding descifrado de umbral
thrift economía, frugalidad
thrifty económico, frugal
thrill (v) emocionar
thrill emoción, sensación
thriller novela, misterio
thrilling emocionante
thrive (v) prosperar, florecer
thriving próspero
throat garganta
throb latido
thrombosis trombosis
throne trono
throng multitud
throttle (v) estrangular
through a través de
throughout por todas partes
throw (v) tirar, echar
throw someone out (v) correr (Mex.)

throwaway desechable
thrush afta
thrust empuje, avance
thrust (v) empujar, impulsar
thud ruido sordo
thumb pulgar
thump golpazo
thunder (v) tronar
thunder trueno
thunderbolt rayo
thunderstorm tronada, tempestad
thunderstruck pasmado
Thursday jueves
thus de este modo, así
thwart (v) impedir, desbaratar
thyroid tiroides
tiara diadema
tibia tibia
tic tic
tick ácaro, garrapata, tictac, instante
ticket billete
ticket office despacho de billetes
ticket window taquilla
tickle (v) hacer cosquillas
tide marea
tidiness limpieza
tidy ordenado, limpio
tie lazo, atadura, corbata, empate
tie (v) atar, enlazar, empatar
tie-up enlace
tier grada, fila
tiger tigre
tight tieso, apretado
tighten (v) apretar, estirar
tightfisted tacaño
tightrope cuerda floja (circo)
tightrope walker funámbulo
tile baldosa, teja
till caja, cajón
tiller labrador
tilt inclinación

tilt (v)   inclinar, caer
timber   madera, árboles
time   tiempo, época
time frame   base de tiempo
time limit   plazo limitado
time loan   préstamo a plazo fijo
time out   temporización
time payments   pagos a plazos
time-saving   que ahorra tiempo
time sharing   tiempo compartido
timeless   eterno
timely   oportuno
timer   cronómetro, reloj de arena
timetable   horario
timid   tímido
timidity   timidez
timing   medida del tiempo
tin   estaño
tin can   lata
tinfoil   papel de estaño
tinge   tinte
tinsel   oropel
tint   tinte
tiny   pequeñito
tip   punta, extremidad, propina,
   aviso; feria (C.R., Salv.)
tip (v)   inclinar, dar propina
tipsy   alumbrado (Chile, coll.);
   templado (Amer.)
tire   neumático
tire (v)   cansar, fatigar; aplastar
   (Arg., Uru.)
tired   cansado
tiredness   cansancio
tireless   infatigable
tiresome   molesto, pesado
tissue   gasa, tejido, tisú
tissue paper   papel de seda
title   título
to   a, hacia, hasta
toad   sapo
toast   brindis, tostada
toast (v)   tostar, brindar

toaster   tostador
tobacco   tabaco
toboggan   tobogán
today   hoy
toddler   pequeñito
toe   dedo del pie
toenail   uña del dedo del pie
toes   dedos de los pies
together   junto, juntamente
toil (v)   trabajar
toil   labor, trabajo
toilet   tocador; lugar (Chile)
toiletries   artículos de tocador
token   señal, muestra, ficha
tolerable   tolerable
tolerance   tolerancia
tolerant   tolerante
tolerate (v)   tolerar
toll   peaje
toll free   llamada revertida
tollway   autopista de peaje
tomato   tomate
tomb   tumba
tomorrow   mañana
ton   tonelada
tone   tono, matiz
tongs   tenazas
tongue   lengua
tonic   tónico
tonight   esta noche
tonnage   tonelaje
too   también, muy
tool   herramienta
tooth   diente
toothache   dolor de dientes
toothbrush   cepillo de dientes
toothpaste   pasta de dientes
toothpick   palillo
top   tapa, superior, cumbre, parte
   alta
top (v)   rematar, coronar
top-secret   secreto absoluto
topcoat   sobretodo

topic tema
topical actual, de interés
topple (v) derribar, derrocar
torch antorcha, linterna
torment (v) atormentar
tornado tornado
torpedo torpedo
torrent torrente
torrential torrencial
torrid tórrido
tort agravio
torticollis tortícolis
tortilla tortilla
tortuous tortuoso
torture tortura
torture (v) torturar
torturer verdugo
toss sacudida, sorteo
toss (v) sacudir, tirar
total total, completo
totalitarian totalitario
touch toque, contacto
touch (v) tocar, contactar
touch-screen pantalla sensorizada
tough duro, fuerte
toughen (v) endurecer
toughness dureza
tour viaje, excursión
tourism turismo
tourist turista
tournament torneo, concurso
tourniquet torniquete
tow (v) remolcar
toward hacia, cerca de
towel toalla
tower torre
towering elevado, muy alto
town ciudad, población
toxic tóxico
toxicity toxicidad
toxicology toxicología
toxin toxina

toy juguete
toy shop juguetería
trace rastro, huella
trace (v) seguir, averiguar
trachea tráquea
tracheotomy traqueotomía
tracing paper papel de calco
track (v) rastrear, encontrar
track pista, vía
tract región, folleto
tractor tractor
trade comercio, industria
trade (v) comerciar, vender
trade discount descuento comercial
trade in intercambio
trade-ins trueques de venta
trade union sindicato
trademark marca registrada
trader comerciante
tradesman comerciante
tradition tradición
traditional tradicional
traffic tráfico, circulación
traffic jam embotellamiento
traffic lights semáforos
traffic sign señal de tráfico
tragedy tragedia
tragic trágico
trail rastro, estela, camino, sendero
trail (v) arrastrar
trailer remolque
train tren; carril (Chile, P.R.)
train (v) entrenar, adiestrar
trainee aprendiz profesional
trainer entrenador
traitor traidor
trajectory trayectoria
tramp vagabundo
tramper barco discrecional
trample (v) pisar
trampoline trampolín

trance rapto, catalepsia
tranquil tranquilo
tranquility tranquilidad
tranquilize (v) tranquilizar
tranquilizer tranquilizante
transact (v) tramitar
transaction transacción
transceiver transmisor-receptor
transcend (v) trascender
transcendental trascendental
transcribe (v) transcribir
transcription copia
transducer transductor
transfer transferencia
transfer (v) transferir, traspasar
transferable transferible
transferable share acción transferible
transfix (v) traspasar
transform (v) transformar
transformation transformación
transformer transformador
transfuse (v) transfundir
transfusion transfusión
transgression ofensa
transgressor infractor
transient pasajero, transeúnte
transistor transistor
transit tránsito
transition transición
transitional de transición
transitive transitivo
transitory transitorio
translate (v) traducir
translation traducción
translator traductor
translucent translúcido
transmission transmisión
transmit (v) transmitir
transmitter transmisor
transparency transparencia
transparent transparente
transplant transplante

transplant (v) trasplantar
transport transporte
transport (v) transportar
transport by air transporte aéreo
transport by land transporte terrestre
transport by sea transporte marítimo
transportation transporte
transportation costs costes de transporte
transpose (v) transponer
transposition transposición
transvestite travestí
trap (v) atrapar
trap trampa
trash basura
trauma trauma, lesión
traumatic traumático
traumatology traumatología
travel viaje, turismo
travel (v) viajar
traveler viajero
traveler's checks cheques de viajeros
travesty parodia
tray bandeja
treacherous traidor, falso
treachery traición, falsedad
tread (v) pisar, pisotear
tread paso, pisada
treason traición
treasure tesoro
treasurer tesorero
treasury tesoro, tesorería
treat regalo, convite
treat (v) invitar, convidar
treatise tratado
treatment tratamiento
treaty trato, tratado
tree árbol
trek (v) emigrar, viajar

tremble temblor
tremble (v) temblar
tremendous tremendo, inmenso
tremor temblor
trench zanja, foso
trench coat trinchera
trend tendencia
trend (v) tender
trendy a la moda
trespass (v) entrar sin derecho
trespass intrusión, violación
trespasser intruso
trial proceso, juicio, prueba, concurso
trial balance balance de comprobación
trial court juzgado de instrucción
trial jury jurado procesal
triangle triángulo
triangular triangular
tribal tribal
tribe tribu
tribunal tribunal
tributary tributario
tribute tributo
trichinosis triquinosis
trick truco, engaño
trick (v) engañar, hacer trucos
trickery astucia
trickle (v) gotear
tricky astuto, tramposo
tricycle triciclo
trier juez
trifle (v) bromear, frivolizar
trifling insignificante
trigger gatillo, tirador
trigger (v) provocar, desencadenar
trigonometry trigonometría
trill trino
trillion trillón
trinket chuchería

trio trío
trip viaje, excursión, tropiezo
trip (v) tropezar, hacer caer
tripe callos, tripas
triple (v) triplicar
tripod trípode
triumph triunfo, éxito
triumph (v) triunfar
triumphant triunfante
trivial trivial
troop tropa, banda
trophy trofeo
tropic trópico, tropical
trot trote
trot (v) trotar
trouble apuro, aprieto
trouble (v) inquietar, preocupar
troubled preocupado
troublemaker alborotador
troublesome molesto, fastidioso
trousers pantalones
trout trucha
trowel paleta, llana
truancy ausencia
truant gandul, haragán
truce tregua
truck camión
truckdriver camionero
true verdadero
truly verdaderamente
truncate (v) truncar
trunk baúl, tronco, circuito
trunk group haz de circuitos
trunks taparrabos
trust confianza, consorcio, monopolio
trust (v) confiar, creer
trust bank banco de depósito
trustee despositario
trustworthy formal, honrado
trusty fiel, leal
truth verdad, realidad
truthful verídico

truthfulness veracidad
try (v) intentar, probar
try tentativa
tryout prueba
tsar zar
tub bañera, cubo
tube tubo
tuberculosis tuberculosis
tuck (v) plegar
Tuesday martes
tug (v) tirar, estirar
tug tirón, estirón
tuition enseñanza
tulip tulipán
tumble (v) caer, tropezar
tummy vientre
tumor tumor
tumult tumulto
tumultuous tumultuoso
tuna atún
tune melodía
tune (v) afinar, templar
tuner afinador
tunic túnica
turban turbante
turbine turbina
turbulence turbulencia
turbulent turbulento
turf césped, turba
turkey pavo
Turkey Turquía
Turkish turco
turmoil confusión, desorden
turn (v) girar, volver
turn vuelta, revolución, turno, vez
turn key contract contrato llaves en mano
turnout concurrencia
turnover volumen de negocio
turnstile torniquete
turntable giradiscos
turpentine trementina

turquoise turquesa
turtle tortuga
tusk colmillo
tussle lucha
tutor preceptor, profesor
tutorial tutelar
tutorship tutela, tutoría
tuxedo traje de smoking
tweed mezcla de lana
tweezers pinzas
twelfth duodécimo
twelve doce
twentieth vigésimo
twenty veinte
twice dos veces
twig ramita
twilight crepúsculo
twin gemelo
twine hilo, guita
twinge punzada
twinkle centelleo
twinkle (v) centellear
twirl vuelta, giro
twist torsión, giro
twist (v) torcer, estafar
twit (v) tomar el pelo
two dos
two-faced falso
two-way communication comunicación en doble sentido
tycoon magnate
tympanum tímpano
type tipo
type (v) escribir a máquina
typesetting composición gráfica
typewriter máquina de escribir
typhoid tifoidea
typhoid fever fiebre tifoidea
typhus tifus
typical típico
typist mecanógrafo
tyrant tirano

U

ubiquitous ubicuo, omnipresente
udder ubre
ugliness fealdad
ugly feo
ulcer úlcera, llaga
ulterior ulterior
ultimate último, final
ultimately por último
ultimatum ultimátum
ultrasonic ultrasónico
ultraviolet ultravioleta
umbilical umbilical
umbrella paraguas
umpire árbitro
umpteen muchísimos
umpteenth enésimo
unable incapaz
unabridged íntegro
unacceptable inaceptable
unaccompanied sin acompañamiento
unaided sin ayuda
unanimity unanimidad
unanimous unánime
unanimously unánimemente
unappealable inapelable
unarmed desarmado
unattached suelto, separable
unattractive sin atractivo
unauthorized desautorizado, no autorizado
unavoidable inevitable
unaware sin información
unbalanced desequilibrado
unbearable inaguantable
unbelievable increíble
unbend (v) enderezar
unbending inflexible

unbiased imparcial
unbreakable irrompible
unbutton (v) desabrochar
uncanny misterioso
uncertain incierto
unchallenged incontestado
unchanged sin alterar
uncharted inexplorado
uncivil descortés
uncivilized incivilizado
unclaimed sin dueño
uncle tío
unclean sucio
unclog (v) desatrancar
uncollectible incobrable
uncomfortable incómodo
uncommon poco común
uncomplaining resignado
uncompromising intransigente
unconcern calma, tranquilidad
unconditional incondicional
unconfined ilimitado
unconscious inconsciente, desmayado
unconstrained libre
uncontested no disputado
unconventional original
uncooked sin cocer
uncover (v) descubrir
uncovered check cheque sin fondos
uncut sin cortar
undamaged indemne, intacto
undaunted impávido
undecided indeciso
undefeated imbatido
undefended sin defensa
undefiled puro, inmaculado

325

undemonstrative reservado
undeniable innegable
under abajo, debajo
under bond bajo fianza
under oath bajo juramento
underbid (v) cotizar más bajo
underclothes ropa interior
undercover secreto, clandestino
undercut (v) rebajar precios
underdevelopment subdesarrollado
underdog desvalido
underestimate (v) subestimar
underestimate subestimación
underfoot debajo del pie
undergo (v) sufrir, experimentar
underground subterráneo
underhand poco limpio
underline (v) subrayar
underling subordinado
underlying subyacente
undermine (v) socavar, minar
underneath debajo
underpaid mal pagado
underpants calzoncillos
underprivileged desamparado
underrate (v) menospreciar
underscore (v) subrayar
undershirt camiseta
undershorts calzoncillos
undersigned el abajo firmante
understaffed con poco personal
understand (v) comprender, entender
understandable comprensible
understanding comprensivo
understudy suplente
undertake (v) emprender, acometer
undertaking empresa, tarea
undertone voz baja
underwater submarino
underwear ropa interior

underwrite (v) asegurar
underwriter compañía aseguradora
undesirable indeseable
undetected inadvertido
undeveloped subdesarrollado
undo (v) anular, deshacer
undoing ruina, perdición
undoubtedly indudablemente
undress (v) desnudar
undue indebido
undulate (v) ondular
unduly indebidamente
undying imperecedero
unearth (v) desenterrar
unearthly sobrenatural
uneasiness inquietud
uneasy inseguro
uneducated ineducado, ignorante
unemotional impasible
unemployed parado, sin empleo
unemployment desempleo, paro
unendurable inaguantable
unenthusiastic poco entusiasta
unequal desigual
unequivocal inequívoco
uneven desigual
unexpected inesperado
unexpired costs costes vigentes
unfailing indefectible
unfair injusto
unfairness injusticia
unfaithful infiel
unfamiliar desconocido
unfashionable pasado de moda
unfasten (v) desatar
unfavorable desfavorable
unfeeling insensible
unfinished inacabado
unfit incapaz, inservible
unfold (v) desplegar, desdoblar
unforeseen imprevisto
unforgivable imperdonable**

unfortunate desgraciado
unfounded infundado
unfriendly poco amistoso
unfulfilled incumplido
unfurnished sin muebles
ungrateful desagradecido
unguarded indefenso
unhappy molesto, infeliz
unharmed ileso, indemne
unhealthy enfermo, malsano
unheard inaudito
unhurt ileso, indemne
unidirectional unidireccional
unification unificación
uniform uniforme
uniformity uniformidad
unify (v) unificar, unir
unilateral unilateral
unimaginative sin imaginación
unimpeachable intachable
unimportant sin importancia
uninhibited nada cohibido
unintentionally sin querer
uninterested desinteresado
uninteresting sin interés
union unión, enlace, sindicato
unique único
unison armonía
unit unidad
unit cost coste unitario
unit price precio unitario
unite (v) unir
United Kingdom Reino Unido
United Nations Naciones Unidas
United States Estados Unidos
unity unidad
universal universal
universe universo
university university
unjust injusto
unjustified injustificado
unkempt desaseado
unkind poco amable

unknown desconocido
unlawful ilegal, ilícito
unleavened cornmeal pancake
tortilla (Mex.)
unless a menos que
unlike a diferencia de
unlikely improbable
unlimited ilimitado
unload (v) descargar
unlucky desgraciado, nefasto;
torcido (Guat.)
unmarketable invendible
unmarried soltero
unnecessary innecesario
unnoticed inadvertido
unobtainable agotado
unobtrusive discretamente
unoccupied deshabitado
unofficial extraoficial
unorthodox heterodoxo
unpack (v) desembalar
unpaid impagado, no pagado
unpleasant desagradable
unpopular impopular
unpredictable imprevisible
unqualified incompetente
unquestionable indiscutible
unravel (v) desenmarañar
unreal irreal, ilusorio
unrealistic ilusorio
unrealized gains beneficios no
convertidos
unreasonable irrazonable
unreliable informal
unrest malestar, inquietud
unsafe inseguro, peligroso
unscrew (v) destornillar
unscrupulous sin escrúpulos
unsecured bonds bonos no garantizados
unsecured debtor deudor sin
garantía
unselfish desinteresado

unsettled inquieto
unskilled no cualificado
unsound defectuoso
unspeakable indecible
unspecified no especificado
unsteady inestable, inseguro
unsuccessful fracasado
unsuitable inapropiado
unsure poco seguro
untangle (v) desenmarañar
untenable insostenible
untested no probado
until hasta, hasta que
untrue falso
unused nuevo, sin usar
unusual insólito, poco común
unwanted no deseado
unwilling reacio, contrario
unwind (v) desenvolver
unwise imprudente
unworthy indigno
unwrap (v) desenvolver
up arriba, hacia arriba
up time tiempo de disponibilidad
up-to-date actualizado
update (v) actualizar
upheaval cataclismo
uphill cuesta arriba
uphold (v) sostener, apoyar
upholstery tapicería
upkeep conservación
upon en, sobre, encima
upper superior, más alto
upper class clase alta
uppermost el más alto
upright vertical, derecho
uprising alzamiento
uproar tumulto, alboroto; bola (Mex.)
uproot (v) desarraigar

upset (v) enfadar, trastornar
upshot resultado
upside down estar al revés
upstairs arriba
upstream aguas arriba
upward ascendente
urban urbano
urea urea
urge impulso, deseo
urgency urgencia
urgent urgente
urinary urinario
urinate (v) orinar
urine orina
urologist urólogo
urology urología
urticaria urticaria
Uruguay Uruguay
Uruguayan uruguayo
use (v) usar, emplear
useful útil, provechoso
useless inútil, inservible
user usuario
user-friendly fácil de usar
usher ujier, portero
usual usual, habitual
usually por lo general
usufructuary usufructuario
usurp (v) usurpar
usurpation usurpación
usury usura
utensil utensilio
uterus útero
utility utilidad, servicio público
utility program programa auxiliar
utilize (v) utilizar
utmost mayor, supremo
utter completo, total

V

vacancy vacante, disponible
vacant libre, desocupado
vacate (v) desocupar
vacation vacación
vacation pay expenses gastos de pagas de vacaciones
vaccinate (v) vacunar
vaccination vacunación
vaccine vacuna
vacillate (v) oscilar
vacillation vacilación
vacuum vacío
vacuum cleaner aspirador
vagina vagina
vagrancy vagancia
vagrant vagabundo
vague vago, indistinto
vain vano, inútil
valid válido, vigente
validate (v) validar
validation validación
validity validez
valley valle
valuable valioso
valuables valores
valuation valorización
valuation of assets valoración de activos
value valor, coste, importancia
value added valor añadido
value added tax impuesto sobre el valor añadido
valuer tasador
valve válvula
vampire vampiro
vandalism vandalismo
vandalize (v) destruir
vanilla vainilla
vanish (v) desaparecer

vanity vanidad
vanquish (v) vencer, derrotar
vapor vapor
vaporize (v) vaporizar
variable variable
variable costs costes variables
variant variante
variation variación
varicella varicela
varices varices
varicose varicoso
variety variedad
various vario, diverso
varnish barniz
vary (v) variar, cambiar
vascular vascular
vase florero
vasectomy vasectomía
vast vasto, inmenso
vault bóveda, cámara
veal ternera
veer (v) virar, girar
vegetable vegetal
vegetarian vegetariano
vegetation vegetación
vehemence vehemencia
vehement vehemente
vehicle vehículo
veil (v) velar
veil velo
vein vena
velocity velocidad
velvet terciopelo
vending machine máquina automática
vendor's lien gravamen de vendedor
veneer chapa
venerable venerable

venereal venéreo
Venezuela Venezuela
vengeance venganza
venom veneno
vent (v) purgar
ventilate (v) ventilar
ventilation ventilación
ventricle ventrículo
ventriloquist ventrílocuo
venture aventura, empresa
venture (v) arriesgarse
verb verbo
verbal verbal
verbatim al pie de la letra
verdict veredicto, fallo
verge margen, borde
verification comprobación, verificación
verify (v) verificar, comprobar
vermin bichos, sabandijas
vernacular vernáculo
versatile versátil
versatility versatilidad
verse estrofa
version versión
versus contra
vertebra vértebra
vertebral column columna vertebral
vertebrate vertebrado
vertical vertical
vertigo vértigo
very muy
vesicle vesícula
vessel vaso (sanguíneo)
vest camiseta
vested fijado, efectivo
veteran veterano
veterinarian veterinario
veto veto
via por, por vía de
viability viabilidad
viable viable

viaduct viaducto
vibrate (v) vibrar
vice versa viceversa
vice-president vicepresidente
vicinity vecindad, región
vicious vicioso, cruel
victim víctima
victimize (v) castigar
victory victoria
video vídeo
view vista, perspectiva
view (v) mirar, contemplar
viewer espectador
viewpoint punto de vista
vigilant vigilante
vigilante vigilante
vigor vigor
vile vil, infame
village pueblo, pueblecito
villain malvado, malo
vindicatory vindicatorio
vindictive vengativo, rencoroso
vine parra
vinegar vinagre
vineyard viña, viñedo
vinyl vinilo
violate (v) violar
violation violación
violence violencia
violent violento
virgin virgen
virginity virginidad
virile viril
virtually virtualmente
virtue virtud
virus virus
visa visado
visibility visibilidad
visible visible
vision visión
visionary visionario
visit visita
visit (v) visitar

visitor visitante
visual visual
visual display unit unidad de visualización
visualize (v) visualizar
vital esencial
vitality vitalidad
vitalize (v) vitalizar
vitamin vitamina
vivacious animado
vivid intenso
vocabulary vocabulario
vocal vocal
vocal cords cuerdas vocales
vocalist cantante
vocation vocación
vocational vocacional
vociferous ruidoso
voice voz
void (v) anular, invalidar
void nulo, inválido
void contract contrato nulo
void marriage matrimonio inválido
voidable anulable
volatile volátil

volcanic volcánico
volt voltio
voltage voltaje
volume volumen
voluminous voluminoso
voluntary voluntario
volunteer (v) ofrecerse voluntario
vomit vómito
vomit (v) vomitar
voracious voraz
vote voto
vote (v) votar
voter votante
voting votación
vouch (v) garantizar
voucher comprobante, justificante
vow (v) jurar, hacer voto
vow voto, promesa
vowel vocal
voyage viaje
vulgar vulgar, ordinario
vulnerable vulnerable
vulva vulva

W

wad fajo de billetes, tapón
wade (v) vadear
wafer oblea, pastilla
wage salario, paga
wage increase aumento de salario
wager apuesta
wages salarios
wagon carro, vagón
wail lamento
waist cintura
wait espera, pausa
wait (v) esperar, aplazar

waiter camarero
waiting list lista de espera
waiting room sala de espera
waitress camarera
waive (v) renunciar
waiver renuncia
waiver of rights renuncia de derechos
wake vela, vigilia
wake (v) despertar
walk (v) pasear
wall pared
wall charger cargador mural

wall mount montaje mural
wall socket enchufe de pared
wallet cartera, billetero
wallop golpe, bofetada
wallow (v) revolcarse
wallpaper papel pintado
walnut nogal, nuez
waltz vals
wan pálido
wander (v) vagar, divagar
wane (v) menguar, decaer
want (v) querer, exigir
want falta, ausencia
wanton injury perjuicio intencional
war guerra
ward tutela, custodia
warden guardián, director
wardrobe vestidos, vestuario
warehouse almacén
warehouse receipt recibo de almacén
wares mercancías
warfare guerra
warhead cabeza atómica
warm caliente
warm (v) calentar
warm-up precalentamiento
warmly efusivamente
warmth calor, afecto
warn (v) avisar, advertir
warning aviso, advertencia
warp deformación
warrant certificado, póliza, garantía
warranted garantizado
warrants pólizas de depósito
warranty garantía
warrior guerrero
warts verrugas
wary cauteloso
wash (v) lavar
washable lavable

washbasin palangana
washing machine máquina de lavar
washroom aseo público
waste desecho, derroche, merma
waste (v) derrochar, malgastar
waste money (v) disparar (Mex.)
wasteful derrochador
wasteland tierra baldía
watch reloj, vigilancia
watch (v) ver, mirar, vigilar
watchdog perro guardián
watchmaker relojero
watchman guardián
water agua
water (v) regar
water ski esquí acuático
waterlogged anegado
watermelon sandía
waterproof impermeable
watertight hermético
waterworks central depuradora
watt vatio
wave ola
wave (v) agitar, hacer señas
wavelength longitud de onda
waver (v) oscilar
wavering irresoluto
wax cera
way camino, manera
we nosotros
weak débil, flojo; fallo (Chile)
weaken (v) debilitar
weakling delicado
weakness debilidad
wealth riqueza, abundancia
wealthy rico, acaudalado
weapon arma
wear uso
wear (v) usar, llevar
wearily cansadamente
weariness cansancio

weather tiempo

weather bureau oficina meteorológica

weather forecast pronóstico del
tiempo

weave tejido, textura

weave (v) tejer

web tela, telaraña

wed (v) casarse

wedding boda, casamiento

wedding dress traje de novia

wedding ring anillo de boda;
alianza, aro (Amer.)

wedge pedazo, cuña

wedge (v) acuñar, calzar

wedlock matrimonio

Wednesday miércoles

weed mala hierba

weed (v) limpiar (Chile)

weedkiller herbicida

week semana

weekday día laborable

weekend fin de semana

weekly semanal

weep (v) llorar

weigh (v) pesar, ponderar

weighing platform báscula

weight peso, carga

weighted average method
método de promedio ponderado

weird raro, extraño

welcome bienvenido

welcome (v) dar la bienvenida

weld (v) soldar

welder soldador

welding soldadura

welfare bienestar, asistencia

well bien, pozo, fuente

well-built bien construido

well-dressed bien vestido

well-educated instruido, culto

well-informed bien informado

well-kept bien guardado

well-known bien conocido

well-made bien hecho

well-off acomodado

well-timed oportuno

well-to-do acomodado

wellbeing bienestar

west oeste

western del oeste

wet mojado, húmedo

wet (v) mojar, humedecer

wharf muelle

what qué, que

whatever lo que, todo lo que

wheat trigo

wheel rueda

wheelchair silla de ruedas

wheeler dealer negociante poco
escrupuloso

when cuando

whenever siempre que

where donde

whereas mientras que, considerando

wherever dondequiera que

whether si

which quien, cual, que

whichever cualquier

while mientras, rato

whim capricho

whimper quejido

whip látigo

whiplash látigo (Ecuad., Hond.)

whipping azotamiento

whirl giro, vuelta

whirlpool torbellino

whiskers bigotes

whisper (v) susurrar, hablar
bajo

whistle (v) silbar

white blanco

White House Casa Blanca

whiten (v) blanquear

whiteness blancura

whiz kid   niño listo
who   quien
whoever   quienquiera
whole   todo, entero
wholehearted   enthusiasta
wholesale   venta al mayor
wholesaler   mayorista
wholesome   sano, saludable
whore   puta
whose   de quién, cuyo
why   por qué, para qué
wicked   mal, perverso
wide   ancho, extenso
wide band   banda ancha
widespread   extendido
widow   viuda
width   anchura, ancho
wield (v)   manejar
wife   esposa, mujer
wig   peluca
wild   salvaje, silvestre
wildlife   fauna
wildly   furiosamente
will   voluntad, testamento
will (v)   querer, hacer
willful   voluntarioso, premeditado
willing   complaciente
willingness   buena voluntad
wilt (v)   marchitar
wily   astuto
win   victoria, triunfo
wince   mueca de dolor
wind   viento
wind (v)   enrolar, envolver
window   ventana
window cleaner   limpiaventanas
windpipe   tráquea
windstorm   vendaval
windy   ventoso
wine   vino
wine bottle   botella de vino
wine list   lista de vino

wineglass   vaso de vino
wing   ala
winner   vencedor, ganador
winter   invierno
wintry   frío, glacial
wipe (v)   limpiar, enjugar
wipe out (v)   aniquilar, destruir
wire   alambre, cable
wireless   radio
wisdom   sabiduría
wise   sabio, prudente
wish (v)   desear
wish   deseo
wistful   triste
wit   inteligencia, gracia, ingenio
witch   bruja
witch hunt   caza de brujas
witchcraft   brujería
with   con
withdraw (v)   retirar, sacar
withdrawal   retiro (de fondos)
withdrawn   reservado
wither (v)   marchitar, secar
withhold (v)   retener
withholding   retención
within   dentro, dentro de
without   sin, a falta de
withstand (v)   resistir
witness   testigo
witness (v)   presenciar
witty   ingenioso
wizard   genio, hechicero
wobbly   inseguro
woman   mujer
womanly   femenino
womb   matriz, útero
wonder   maravilla
wonderful   maravilloso
woo (v)   cortejar, solicitar
wood   madera
wooden   de madera
wool   lana

woolly lanudo, lanoso
word (v) expresar, redactar
word palabra
word of mouth por referencias
word processor procesador de textos
word wrap envoltura de texto
wording fraseología
wordy prolijo
work (v) trabajar, funcionar
work trabajo
workable práctico
workday día laboral
worker trabajador
working assets activos circulantes
working class de clase obrera
working capital activo circulante
working days días laborales
working man obrero
workshop taller
workstation ordenador comercial
world mundo
world-wide mundial
worn out gastado
worried inquieto, preocupado
worry inquietud
worse peor
worsen (v) empeorar, agravar
worship adoración
worst peor, lo peor
worth equivalente, valor
worthless sin valor, inútil
would (v) querer

wound (v) herir
wounds heridas
woven hilado
wrap (v) envolver
wrapping envoltura, envase
wrapping paper papel de envolver
wreath corona, guirnalda
wreathe (v) rodear, coronar
wreck (v) naufragar, destruir
wreck naufragio, destruido
wreckage naufragio
wrench (v) arrancar
wrestle (v) luchar
wring (v) torcer
wrinkle (v) arrugar
wrist muñeca
writ auto, mandato, escritura, orden
write (v) grabar información, escribir
write-off pérdida total
write protect protección de grabado
writer escritor
writhe (v) retorcerse
writing escritura, letra
writing desk escritorio
writing paper papel de escribir
written escrito
wrong equivocado, malo, impropio
wrongful injusto
wryly irónicamente

X

X-ray rayos X
X-ray apparatus aparato de rayos X

xenophobia xenofobia
Xmas Navidad
xylophone xilófono

Y

yacht yate
yap ladrido
yarn hilo, historia
yawn (v) bostezar
yea voto afirmativo
year año
year-end adjustments ajustes a final del ejercicio
yearbook anuario
yearlong todo el año
yearly anual
yearn (v) suspirar
yearning ansioso
yeast levadura
yell alarido
yellow amarillo

yellow fever fiebre amarilla
yellowish amarillento
yes sí
yesterday ayer
yesteryear antaño
yet todavía, aún, con todo, a pesar de
yield (v) producir, someterse
yield cosecha, producción, rédito, rendimiento
yield rate tipo de rendimiento
yogurt yogur
yolk yema de huevo
you tú, usted, ustedes, vosotros
young joven
youth juventud

Z

zeal entusiasmo
zero cero
zest gusto
zip code distrito postal

zone zona
zoo zoológico
zygote zigoto

Numbers
◇
Números

CARDINAL NUMBERS—NUMEROS CARDINALES

zero, nought	0	cero
one	1	uno, una
two	2	dos
three	3	tres
four	4	cuatro
five	5	cinco
six	6	seis
seven	7	siete
eight	8	ocho
nine	9	nueve
ten	10	diez
eleven	11	once
twelve	12	doce
thirteen	13	trece
fourteen	14	catorce
fifteen	15	quince
sixteen	16	dieciséis
seventeen	17	diecisiete
eighteen	18	dieciocho
nineteen	19	diecinueve
twenty	20	veinte
twenty-one	21	veintiuno
twenty-two	22	veintidós
twenty-three	23	veintitrés

twenty-four	24	veinticuatro
twenty-five	25	veinticinco
thirty	30	treinta
forty	40	cuarenta
fifty	50	cincuenta
sixty	60	sesenta
seventy	70	setenta
eighty	80	ochenta
ninety	90	noventa
one hundred	100	cien, ciento
two hundred	200	doscientos
three hundred	300	trescientos
three hundred and fifty	350	trescientos cincuenta
four hundred	400	cuatrocientos
five hundred	500	quinientos
six hundred	600	seiscientos
seven hundred	700	setecientos
eight hundred	800	ochocientos
nine hundred	900	novecientos
one thousand	1,000	mil
five thousand	5,000	cinco mil
one hundred thousand	100,000	cien mil
two hundred thousand	200,000	doscientos mil
five hundred thousand	500,000	quinientos mil, medio millón
one million	1,000,000	un millón
two million	2,000,000	dos millones

ORDINAL NUMBERS—NUMEROS ORDINALES

first	1	primer, primero, primera
second	2	segundo, segunda
third	3	tercer, tercero, tercera
fourth	4	cuarto, cuarta
fifth	5	quinto, quinta
sixth	6	sexto, sexta
seventh	7	séptimo, séptima
eighth	8	octavo, octava
ninth	9	noveno, novena
tenth	10	décimo, décima
eleventh	11	undécimo, undécima
twelfth	12	duodécimo, duodécima

thirteenth	**13**	decimotercero(a)
fourteenth	**14**	decimocuarto(a)
fifteenth	**15**	decimoquinto
sixteenth	**16**	decimosexto
seventeenth	**17**	decimoséptimo
eighteenth	**18**	decimooctavo
nineteenth	**19**	decimonoveno
twentieth	**20**	vigésimo

After the twelfth, Spanish ordinals are rarely used and cumbersome. Cardinal numbers are used instead:

24th page	página veinticuatro
32nd chapter	capítulo treinta y dos
50th position	posición (lugar) cincuenta

FRACTIONAL NUMBERS—NUMEROS FRACCIONARIOS

one-half, a half	**1/2**	medio, media
one-third, a third	**1/3**	un tercio
one-quarter, a quarter	**1/4**	un cuarto
one-eighth	**1/8**	un octavo
one-tenth	**1/10**	un décimo
two-thirds	**2/3**	dos tercios
two-fifths	**2/5**	dos quintos
three-quarters	**3/4**	tres cuartos

PERCENTAGES—PORCENTAJES

five percent	**5%**	cinco por ciento
ten percent	**10%**	diez por ciento
eighteen percent	**18%**	dieciocho por ciento
twenty-five percent	**25%**	veinticinco por ciento
fifty percent	**50%**	cincuenta por ciento
hundred percent	**100%**	cien por ciento
two hundred percent	**200%**	doscientos por ciento

Weights and Measures
◇
Pesos y Medidas

WEIGHTS—PESOS

1 ounce (onza) = 28.350 grams (gramos)
1 pound (libra) = 453.59 grams (gramos)
1 stone = 6.350 kilograms (kilogramos)
1 quarter (cuarto) = 12,701 kilograms (kilogramos)
1 British ton (tonelada) = 1,016 kilograms (kilogramos)
1 US ton (tonelada americana) = 907.18 kilograms (kilogramos)

Remarks

In Spain and Latin America, a comma represents the fraction (one inch = 2,54 cms). In the U.S., a period represents the fraction (one inch = 2.54 cms).

Time and the Calendar
✧
La Hora y el Calendario

TIMETABLE—HORARIO

one o'clock	la una (hora)
two o'clock	las dos (horas)
three o'clock	las tres (horas)
nine o'clock	las nueve (horas)
ten o'clock	las diez (horas)
eleven o'clock	las once (horas)
It's a quarter to two	son las dos menos cuarto
It's a quarter past two	son las dos y cuarto
It's half past two	son las dos y media
It's five past two	son las dos y cinco
It's half past six	son las seis y media
It's noon	son las doce (del mediodía)
It's midnight	son las doce (de la noche)

MONTHS—MESES

January	enero
February	febrero
March	marzo

April	abril
May	mayo
June	junio
July	julio
August	agosto
September	septiembre
October	octubre
November	noviembre
December	diciembre

DAYS OF THE WEEK—DIAS DE LA SEMANA

Monday	lunes
Tuesday	martes
Wenesday	miércoles
Thursday	jueves
Friday	viernes
Saturday	sábado
Sunday	domingo

SEASONS—ESTACIONES

spring	primavera
summer	verano
autumn,	
fall	otoño
winter	invierno

TIME EXPRESSIONS—TERMINOS DE TIEMPO

afternoon	tarde (primeras horas)
annual	anual
biennial	bianual

bimonthly	bimensual, bimestral
biweekly	quincenal, bisemanal
calendar	calendario
centennial	centenario
century	siglo, centuria
evening	tarde (últimas horas)
fortnight	quincena
holiday	fiesta, vacaciones
hour	hora
in two weeks	dentro de dos semanas
last evening	ayer por la tarde
last month	el mes pasado
last night	anoche
last week	la semana pasada
last year	el año pasado
lustrum	lustro, quinquenio
midday	mediodía
midnight	medianoche
millennium	milenio
minute	minuto
next month	el mes entrante
next Wednesday	el próximo miércoles
next week	la semana próxima
night	noche
on the following day	al día siguiente
quarter	trimestre
second	segundo
semester	semestre
the day after tomorrow	pasado mañana
this evening	esta tarde
this month	este mes
this morning	esta mañana
this week	esta semana
this year	este año
today	hoy
tomorrow	mañana
tomorrow evening	mañana por la tarde
tomorrow morning	mañana por la mañana

tomorrow night	mañana por la noche
tonight	esta noche
week	semana
year	año
yesterday	ayer
yesterday morning	ayer por la mañana

Spanish Verbs
✧
Verbos Españoles

SER (TO BE)

Singular	Plural	Singular	Plural
Present Indicative		**Present Perfect Indicative**	
soy	somos	he sido	hemos sido
eres	sois	has sido	habéis sido
es	son	ha sido	han sido
Imperfect Indicative		**Past Perfect**	
era	éramos	había sido	habíamos sido
eras	erais	habías sido	habíais sido
era	eran	había sido	habían sido
Preterite		**Past Anterior**	
fui	fuimos	hube sido	hubimos sido
fuiste	fuisteis	hubiste sido	hubisteis sido
fue	fueron	hubo sido	hubieron sido
Future		**Future Perfect**	
seré	seremos	habré sido	habremos sido
serás	seréis	habrás sido	habréis sido
será	serán	habrá sido	habrán sido

Conditional

sería	seríamos
serías	seríais
sería	serían

Conditional Perfect

habría sido	habríamos sido
habrías sido	habríais sido
habría sido	habrían sido

Present Subjunctive

sea	seamos
seas	seáis
sea	sean

Past Subjunctive

haya sido	hayamos sido
hayas sido	hayáis sido
haya sido	hayan sido

Imperfect Subjunctive

fuera	fuéramos
fueras	fuerais
fuera	fueran
or	
fuese	fuésemos
fueses	fueseis
fuese	fuesen

Past Perfect Subjunctive

hubiera sido	hubiéramos sido
hubieras sido	hubierais sido
hubiera sido	hubieran sido
or	
hubiese sido	hubiésemos sido
hubieses sido	hubieseis sido
hubieses sido	hubieses sido

Future Imperfect

fuere	fuéremos
fueres	fuereis
fuere	fueren

Imperative

sé (tú)
sea (él)
seamos (nosotros, nosotras)
sed (vosotros, vosotras)
sean (ellos, ellas)

ESTAR (TO BE)

Singular	Plural	Singular	Plural

Present Indicative

estoy	estamos
estás	estáis
está	están

Present Perfect Indicative

he estado	hemos estado
has estado	habéis estado
ha estado	han estado

Imperfect Indicative

estaba	estábamos
estabas	estabais
estaba	estaban

Past Perfect

había estado	habíamos estado
habías estado	habíais estado
había estado	habían estado

Preterite		*Past Anterior*	
estuve	estuvimos	hube estado	hubimos estado
estuviste	estuvisteis	hubiste estado	hubisteis estado
estuvo	estuvieron	hubo estado	hubíeron estado

Future		*Future Perfect*	
estaré	estaremos	habré estado	habremos estado
estarás	estaréis	habrás estado	habréis estado
estará	estarán	habrá estado	habrán estado

Present Subjunctive		*Past Subjunctive*	
esté	estemos	haya estado	hayamos estado
estés	estéis	hayas estado	hayáis estado
esté	estén	haya estado	hayan estado

Imperfect Subjunctive		*Past Perfect Subjunctive*	
estuviera	estuviéramos	hubiera estado	hubiéramos estado
estuvieras	estuvierais	hubieras estado	hubierais estado
estuviera	estuvieran	hubiera estado	hubieran estado
or		or	
estuviese	estuviésemos	hubiese estado	hubiésemos estado
estuvieses	estuvieseis	hubieses estado	hubieseis estado
estuviese	estuviesen	hubieses estado	hubiesen estado

Future Imperfect	
estuviere	estuviéremos
estuvieres	estuviereis
estuviere	estuvieren

Imperative
está (tu)
esté (él)
estemos (nosotros, nosotras)
estad (vosotros, vosotras)
estén (ellos, ellas)